THE FUTURE FOR THE CITY CENTRE

Special Publications of the Institute of British Geographers

For a complete list of titles in this series, see end of book.

THE FUTURE FOR THE CITY CENTRE

INSTITUTE OF BRITISH GEOGRAPHERS
SPECIAL PUBLICATION, NO. 14

Edited by

R. L. DAVIES

and

A. G. CHAMPION

Department of Geography,
University of Newcastle upon Tyne

1983

ACADEMIC PRESS

A Subsidiary of Harcourt Brace Jovanovich, Publishers

London · New York · Paris · San Diego · San Francisco
São Paulo · Sydney · Tokyo · Toronto

ACADEMIC PRESS INC. (LONDON) LTD.
24/28 Oval Road,
London NW1

United States Edition published by
ACADEMIC PRESS INC.
111 Fifth Avenue
New York, New York 10003

British Library Cataloguing in Publication Data

The Future for the city centre. — (Special publication/
Institute of British Geographers ISSN 0073-9006;
v. 14)
1. Cities and towns — Planning — Congresses
I. Davies, R. L. II. Champion, A. G.
711'.4 HT166

ISBN 0-12-206240-X

Text set in 11/13 Plantin
by Dobbie Typesetting Service, Plymouth
Printed in Great Britain by
Galliard (Printers) Ltd, Great Yarmouth

CONTRIBUTORS

R. M. ANGELL, City Planning Officer, City of Newcastle, Civic Centre, Newcastle upon Tyne NE1 8PH

M. BATEMAN, Department of Geography, Portsmouth Polytechnic, Lion Terrace, Portsmouth PO1 3HE

SIR W. BURNS, *Formerly* Deputy Secretary and Chief Planner, Department of the Environment, 2 Marsham Street, London SW1P 3EB

D. BURTENSHAW, Department of Geography, Portsmouth Polytechnic, Lion Terrace, Portsmouth PO1 3HE

M. FOULKES, Assistant Chief Planner, Department of Transport and Development, Greater London Council, County Hall, London SE1 7PB

J. B. GODDARD, Centre for Urban and Regional Development Studies, University of Newcastle upon Tyne, Newcastle upon Tyne NE1 7RU

C. HAMNETT, Social Science Faculty, The Open University, Walton Hall, Milton Keynes MK7 6AA

P. J. HILLS, Transport Operations Research Group, Claremont Tower, University of Newcastle upon Tyne, Newcastle upon Tyne NE1 7RU

J. C. HOLLIDAY, Planning and Landscape Consultant, 9 Clarendon Crescent, Leamington Spa, Warwickshire CV32 5NR

O. KERNDAL-HANSEN, Director, Institut for Center Planlaegning, Carolinevej 5, DK-2900 Hellerup, Copenhagen, Denmark

M. LEE, Consultant Economist, Donaldson and Sons, 70 Jermyn Street, London SW1Y 6PE

B. S. MAITLAND, Department of Architecture, The Arts Tower, University of Sheffield, Sheffield S10 2TN

J. N. MARSHALL, Department of Geography, University of Birmingham, P.O. Box 363, Birmingham B15 2TT

A. D. MAY, Institute for Transport Studies, University of Leeds, Leeds LS2 9JT

W. PACE, Department of Town and Country Planning, University of Newcastle upon Tyne, Newcastle upon Tyne NE1 7RU

B. D. ROBSON, School of Architecture, University of Newcastle upon Tyne, Newcastle upon Tyne NE1 7RU

D. THORPE, Head of Research, John Lewis Partnership, 4 Old Cavendish Street, London W1A 1EX

J. W. R. WHITEHAND, Department of Geography, University of Birmingham, Birmingham B15 2TT

PREFACE

In successive decades since the Second World War, planning and academic studies of the urban environment seem to have focused on particular issues that have been prominent in one part of the city or another. During the 1950s, the question of housing and the eradication of slum conditions commanded most attention, with much excitement generated over the potential contributions that New Towns would make to the alleviation of these problems. In the 1960s, the suburbs as a whole came under increasing discussion with much debate ensuing about the consequences of changes in travel behaviour for transport, shopping and educational provisions. In the 1970s, the economic decline of the inner city and the social impoverishment that had become exacerbated there brought an immense response in public scrutiny that was often coloured by extreme political views. At various points within and around the pursuit of these themes, the city centre has drawn special interest, not least in terms of the commercial pressures it has had to absorb over the last two decades and the ambitious plans that were prepared to accommodate them, but at no time has it been the dominant focus of academic or planning concern in the way that other areas have.

Looking to the 1980s and beyond, however, we may well be at the dawn of an age when the central area, traditionally the most important part of the entire city, becomes the main spatial context within which most of our fears and expectations about contemporary processes at work will be manifest. There are several reasons for suggesting this. First, the demographic changes which have emerged in recent years and the different life-styles that have accompanied these, will present in the short- and medium-term a requirement for a set of housing and living conditions, especially for small households, that are quite unlike those aspired to in the past. Secondly, the decline in living standards for large sections of the population, coupled with the high cost of energy, may lead to new forms of travel behaviour which, if not reflected in the use of public transport services, may be seen in shorter distances being travelled and a greater concentration of these within particular localities. Thirdly, the increase in unemployment and the possibility that this will remain at a high level in the longer term through the impact of technological change, can mean that there will be both a further erosion of the economic base of our cities and more leisure or free time that people will seek to devote to particular places. The city centre will not necessarily be that part of the city where any one of these trends will ultimately be seen to have its greatest effects; but the city centre is the "natural" area where new housing initiatives could be made, where potential changes in travel behaviour could best be accommodated, and where there could be most social compensation in the occupation of people's time if unemployment remains high.

There are also two particular considerations to take into account with respect to the environmental character of the city centre itself. Having witnessed an era of massive redevelopment in most central areas, the public seems less willing to accept further substantial physical change in the future and is likely, as has already been indicated in some recent Local Plans, to prefer more conservation of older buildings and streets and a scaling down of new centres of activity. This might be seen as fortuitous, given the depths of the current recession and its curtailment of much speculative investment as well as the government's cut-back on local authority expenditure, although it could be argued that the shift in public attitudes is a contributory factor. Whether these cautious, conservative views will last through to the 1990s, however, is difficult to perceive, especially if and when some of the more dramatic forecasts regarding the effect of the new "chip" technology on office and retailing functions come through. How will people reconcile their desire for modest change within the city centre with the need perhaps to take bold steps either to arrest the proliferation of vacant floorspace or to convert vast structures to some other, as yet unidentified, land uses? The second point is related to this in the sense that it concerns the longer term changes in the role of the city centre from being essentially a hub of commercial activity to one that fulfils a greater cultural expression and symbolizes the values and tastes of future society. It would not be an exaggeration to say that each of the past periods of urban change that we have referred to has been accompanied by new cultural and societal demands, particularly reflected in the fashions and behaviour of the young. The late 1950s saw the emergence of the "New Towns' blues", the late 1960s the development of "flower-power" and beatniks which, for all their association with the Vietnam War, were also a reaction to suburban living conditions; and the late 1970s witnessed the arrival of the punk and, in Britain for the first time in the post-war years, extreme forms of antisocial behaviour that culminated in riots in several inner city areas. If the city centre is to become the new urban focus in the 1980s or beyond, how will the functional and physical changes that take place there contribute to the attitudes and aspirations of future generations and have we the ability to help shape the reactions of the young by the particular emphasis that is given to planning the city centre?

These are profound questions and the city centre may not assume such overriding importance in future city affairs. But the changing outlook of people towards the city centre, in terms both of its physical form and functional role, suggests that a new approach to its planning and development is desirable in the next few years. This seems to be all the more propitious in the light of the changing complexion of planning itself, as it moves from a position of being concerned in a general sense with the accommodation of growth to being increasingly tuned to arresting decline.

It was these considerations that prompted the convening of a special conference on the subject of "The Future for the City Centre" to cast some light on what might emerge during the next decade and beyond. The conference was organized on behalf of the Urban Geography Study Group and the Geography and Planning Study Group of the Institute of British Geographers and was held at Newcastle University in July, 1981. It differed from the conventional type of geographical meeting, however, in two fundamental respects. First, the contributors who gave papers on the various selected topics and which are reproduced in this book, were all invited to do so as acknowledged experts in their fields. Secondly, the contributors were mostly drawn from outside geography itself and comprised a mixture of academics from different disciplines and professional practitioners, from both the public and private sectors, who are concerned with day-to-day decision-making within the city centre. The papers reflect to a large extent the rather cosmopolitan nature of the authors. Some are strongly research based, others conceptual and detached, others again report on recent experiences regarding the processes of change. The editors have not altered the essential style and content of the papers that were first prepared, preferring instead to let them stand as testimonials to the various ways in which the subject can be addressed and the different types of interests that need to be represented. The papers constitute a set of individual views about the future of the city centre, seen from widely varying perspectives.

The authors, however, were given some initial guidelines regarding the structure and scope in coverage of their papers. First, they were asked to restrict their reviews to the city centres of London and the major provincial cities. Arguably, London is a special case and could warrant a collection of essays all to itself but because the main emphasis of the conference and hence this book was on the process of change, London needed to be included because it reflects so well on certain kinds of processes at work and exaggerates, by virtue of its size, others that are emerging within the provinces but which have so far been rather inconspicuous. No threshold was given on a lower limit of size, to indicate at what point city centres became town centres and thereby become of relatively less significance, for this would have introduced an arbitrary constraint that has no real relevance to the subject being treated. Some contributors do nevertheless indicate that future problems may well be more serious in larger rather than smaller city centres but that the degree in severity of these will also vary according to differences in urban setting and the socio-economic characteristics of the local economy. Secondly, on matters of definition, the city centre was taken to be what is conventionally regarded as the central business district or central area, namely that part of the city wherein there is the greatest concentration of retailing, office and service activities, generally tall buildings, high levels of pedestrian movement, traffic congestion and the architectural vestiges of much earlier periods of settlement. No precise spatial boundary was prescribed but it is recognized that there are really two components to the city centre, the inner core and the surrounding periphery or frame. Some of the papers, such as those on retailing and business services concentrate on the core area; others, like those on housing and the effects of renewal on employment concentrate on the frame. In the majority of cases, however, the city centre is treated in its entirety and the differences in its spatial structure are brought out only in the context of particular issues that need to be raised.

To provide some degree of integration between the various papers, the contributors were also asked to incorporate whenever possible four main themes. These involved providing some retrospective reviews of recent changes that have occurred within each particular topic; identifying the more important emerging and potential planning problems to be confronted during the next decade; suggesting what sorts of policies will need to be applied to alleviate these problems; and discussing the likely realistic nature of changes that will take place during the next decade and beyond. Clearly, these guidelines have been easier to follow in some cases than in others but while most contributors have kept fairly closely to the first two themes, there has been a more varied response to the last two, reflecting in part the proclivities of the people concerned and in part the inherent difficulty of their subject material. The contributors were also encouraged to draw on North American and continental European experiences to support any trends they may have observed and two papers refer specifically to lessons that can be learned from Copenhagen and Paris.

The topics selected for the conference and this volume represent a rather traditional or orthodox way of looking at changes within the city centre. Except for the papers on planning, property development, land-use structure and arguably that on traffic, there is no separate treatment given of the various agents of change, in terms such as political decision-making, the allocation of resources, the growth in corporate ownership of firms or consumerism and the role of pressure groups. These, and the underlying pressures for change, will have variable degrees of influence on different aspects of the form and functions of the city centre and are therefore dealt with in the context of individual subject areas. We are concerned at the end of the day with the manifestation of change in the built environment and socio-economic character of the city centre.

OUTLINE OF THE PAPERS

The first of the papers that follow, by Sir Wilfred Burns, is set apart as an introduction because it takes a more expansive view of the future than the others and elaborates on the new urban conditions within which the city centre will have to evolve. By virtue of his former position as Chief Planner at the Department of the Environment as well as his previous experience as the first City Planning Officer at Newcastle, Sir Wilfred is clearly well qualified to interpret how planning will change over the next few years and what its longer term objectives should be. The plan that he formulated for the city centre of Newcastle in 1961 epitomized the prevailing thinking of the day as to how the central area ought to be managed over the next two decades; writing in 1981, he provides us with a reflective account of how much of those earlier aspirations were able to be achieved and explains why, within a second generation of city-centre plans, there will be an emphasis on more modest aims rather than the pursuit of grandiose ideas.

The next four papers have been grouped together under the heading "scenarios on the environment" for they deal with a collective set of processes at work and the likely resulting form of the city centre.

John Holliday describes the sorts of issues being addressed and the types of policies being formulated in the new generation of city-centre plans that Burns has referred to. He reviews in particular the plans emerging for Birmingham, Leicester, Liverpool and Leeds, for which places he had examined the first generation plans in his own book on city-centre change a decade ago. He shows that the new plans display a much greater concern for socio-economic matters than their predecessors, with special prominence being given to the stimulation of employment and the provision of leisure-time facilities; but he also suggests that the long-standing problems on transport are still not being satisfactorily met, that there is perhaps now too much emphasis on conservation (that the pendulum has swung too far) and that the new plans for the 1980s continue to retain a strong physical basis to their proposals.

Michael Lee, dealing with likely trends in property development, reports that there is considerable uncertainty within the private sector as to how much and in what form investment will take place in the city centre in the next few years. This is because of the sensitivity of investment to inflation and interest rates, both of which have been highly volatile in the recent past. He thinks, however, that there will be a continuing expansion of office floorspace, although over time there will be profound changes in the nature of office activities as a result of the "chip" technology; and that there are exciting possibilities in the refurbishment of older properties in the frame of the city centre following the successful renovation of the old market hall in Covent Garden. The picture is less clear for retail development where the number and size of new schemes to be sought will depend on levels of durable-goods spending in the future.

Jeremy Whitehand can feel a little more confident in predicting changes in land-use structure and the morphology of the city centre, for these will reflect in part on investment and planning decisions already made and in part on the absorption of new development into existing building fabric that has a strong capacity to survive. However, he warns of the increased power of the major financial institutions and also local authorities to effect substantial and insensitive physical change, through the growth in their ownership of central area land. He suggests the need for a theory of townscape management, based around the delimitation of distinctive morphological regions within the city centre, which could be used as the basis for more effective policies to control the type and scale of physical change in the future and ensure the retention of important legacies from the past.

Barry Maitland's paper is likewise concerned with the built environment but from the point of view of the architecture that is imposed and the emerging character of the central area. He takes a much more philosophical approach to the interpretation of recent trends than the other contributors to this section, relating the dismal performance of past design concepts to the general fragmentation of both city and society and the disintegration of what he calls the public domain. Like Whitehand, he argues for a new theory, but in this case to encourage a new vitality within the city centre where there can be a mixing of people and activities in physical surrounds that are themselves varied and human in scale. He sees some promise of this in the recent work of Christopher Alexander, among others, and offers his own suggestions about the creation of a node structure. In more concrete terms, he sees the future city centre benefiting from more pedestrianization, the establishment of atrium buildings and mixed activity centres and new schemes that fit into the historical context of an area.

A further six papers follow that have been grouped under the heading "changes in functional activities" and largely comprise a systematic analysis of the major social and economic considerations for the future city centre.

Brian Robson and Wallace Pace provide a distinctive paper in two respects: first, in focusing on a specific issue involving the effects of redevelopment on employment and secondly, in the style with which they present their material and argue for a more positive approach to planning the less attractive fringe areas of the city centre. By reference to case studies of Newcastle, North Shields and Glasgow, they show that large numbers of people continue to be employed in mainly small businesses within these fringe areas but that substantial numbers of jobs have been lost through slum clearance programmes, new road developments and new shopping schemes. They suggest that policies should be implemented in future to protect those activities that are still surviving and to attract new services to the same types of locality. Their ideas are illustrated through a series of sketch diagrams, emphasizing the role that renovation can play.

John Goddard and Neil Marshall are also pre-occupied with the question of employment but from the point of view of the contributions that larger businesses will make during the next decade and in the context of office growth. Their perspective is different too to the extent that they see office growth as being dependent on wider conditions within the urban economy and the organizational and technological changes that will permeate the nation's business system as a whole. Their conclusions about the prospects for office growth in provincial city centres are rather pessimistic but they see two ways in which new development may be sustained; by encouraging locally-based industries to make greater use of locally-based services rather than transferring their demands to London; and by encouraging such industries to develop their own locally-based office activities as improved telecommunication facilities allow for a loosening of ties to headquarter offices generally located in London again.

David Thorpe presents a shorter paper on likely retail trends but is equally concerned over the future prospect of the major provincial city centres, which have lost sales in a relative sense in recent years to the suburbs and smaller town centres. He argues in more pragmatic terms that retailers in the larger city centres must be given greater planning support particularly through improved car parking facilities and improved accessibility to the wider, surrounding region. His justification for this is the important contribution which major retailers in these centres make not only to employment, but to the functional status of the centres, the quality of their built environment and the wide range of goods they provide at generally low prices. He amplifies these points in relation to Newcastle and Liverpool in which there are branches of the John Lewis Partnership.

Christopher Hamnett, in dealing with housing and social change, also sees a strong link between the trends that have been developing here and the structural and spatial shifts that have been taking place in employment. He focuses mainly on the case of London, however, which is the only city centre that retains a substantial residential population. He draws a comparison between the continuing decline in housing occupied by the lower socio-economic groups and the recent growth in middle-class residents, part of whom have contributed to the gentrification process and part to the emergence of high status areas within London. Drawing on much personal research, he also describes the decline in the private-rented sector of the housing market and the concomitant growth in owner-occupation.

Tony May's paper on future traffic problems takes as its frame of reference the shifts in transport policy objectives that have occurred in recent years. These have expanded from a simple concern to promote the efficiency and safety of movement to a wider consideration for the interests of non-vehicle users as well as motorists, the effects of energy constraints and the impact of transport planning on the environment. This means there are many different forms of traffic problems, but the severity of each of these, particularly with respect to the central area, are difficult to determine from inadequate data sources. May's general conclusion is that congestion, as perhaps the major problem, is not likely to get worse in the future although it is not likely to be substantially reduced either in view of the reluctance of local authorities to curtail the penetration of the car into city centres.

Peter Hills also finds it necessary to look at future public transport provisions in the context of the city as a whole. He suggests that, on the evidence of recent trends, and unless some radical changes in policy are applied, we are not likely to have an effective public transport system by the turn of the century. The basic reason for this is the general growth in incomes and the appeal of the car. He presents a "manifesto", however, on how these alarming prospects can be assuaged: through an extensive appraisal of existing services and the diversion of resources to those most viable; a strict curtailment on car journeys to and within the city centre; the use of informal services (such as mini-buses and shared taxis); and investment in other services that have a special consumer appeal.

There follows four papers that are case studies of particular city centres which, either because of the pressures for change being experienced there or the planning policies being directed to them, exemplify several of the common concerns for the future that have been described in the previous two sections.

Michael Bateman and David Burtenshaw examine the recent commercial pressures that have been experienced in the central area of Paris which have perhaps been more intense than in any other European capital. The enormous expansion in office developments in particular has been due not only to the growth of the quaternary sector of the economy but to the search for sites for international as well as national headquarter offices and the replacement of many buildings now unsuited to modern office activities. In the housing field, there are many parallels to be drawn with London; but fewer major retailing changes have been seen in recent years because of the establishment of several new regional shopping centres on the outskirts of the metropolis. The mixture of competition for sites, and the shifting attitudes of the public, are then discussed in some detail by reference to Les Halles.

Ole Kerndal-Hansen's paper focuses specifically on the "Ideplan 77" for the city centre of Copenhagen, for this constitutes one of the few visionary concepts that has been enunciated about the future social and economic regeneration of a central area. It gives emphasis to a concentration on piece-meal renovation which will accommodate a greater range of cultural activities at the expense of those commercial activities, such as convenience-goods shopping, which are better accommodated in the suburbs. The essence of the plan is the extension of pedestrianization to many side streets, the refurbishment of properties there to support new small businesses, and the development of theme quarters, where there will be groupings of like kinds of functions, such as those orientated to the teaching, selling or exhibiting of art and music. The plan has not yet been adopted by the local authority, however, and being specially adapted to the conditions of Copenhagen it may not be easily transposed to a British city centre.

Martin Foulkes deals with the question of future transport policies in London, but was placed, at the time of writing, in the awkward position of having to comment on these at a time when a new political party had just taken control of the GLC. He compensates for the difficulty of being able to forecast the outcome of new policies that have yet to be ratified by discussing the different scale problems that have to be kept in mind because of London's role as an international, national, regional and also local focus of different transport modes. As far as the local city centre transport connections are concerned, he foresees a greater emphasis on improvements to the underground service rather than bus services, especially in relation to the city. On other more substantive matters, he thinks a careful step-by-step approach will have to be taken.

The final paper in this volume brings us back to the case of Newcastle where Roy Angell, the present City Planning Officer, outlines the new draft Local Plan for the city centre which, like its predecessor in 1961, might well be seen in the years ahead as a model of contemporary thinking regarding the planning of a central area. The new plan gives stress to the replacement of large-scale redevelopment by more piece-meal infilling and renovation, and with higher priority assigned to the generation of new jobs, the conservation of important legacies, and the provision of more leisure-time facilities along the lines that both Burns and Holliday have alluded to. The new plan is distinctive too for the considerable amount of public consultation that went into its preparation, as is described at some length.

It seems fitting that a volume of papers concerned with "the future for the city centre" should begin and end with contributions from two persons who have been intimately concerned with the problems and prospects for Newcastle. As a city on the peripheral margins of England, Newcastle, perhaps more than any of the other provincial cities, has felt the need to assert itself and particularly through that part of its urban environment, the central area, wherein its inherent social and economic resources can best be displayed. Whether the current set of policies that will take it through the next decade and beyond are appropriate to its own destiny is difficult to say; but it is likely that they will influence those that are enacted in other parts of the country.

January 1982
Newcastle upon Tyne

R. L. Davies

ACKNOWLEDGEMENTS

The conference for which these papers were originally prepared was supported by a financial grant from the Institute of British Geographers. The support of the Urban Geography Study Group and the Geography and Planning Study Group of the Institute in organizing the conference and assisting with this publication is also gratefully acknowledged. Thanks should also be conveyed to a number of individual persons for their help at various stages: Miss Hillary Hill, Mrs Mary Davies, Mrs Doreen Morrison, Mr Eric Quenet and Mr Brian Allaker.

Permission has been given by the following people or agencies for the reproduction of diagrams or photographs: Professor A. W. Evans, University of Reading and Macmillan Ltd, London and Basingstoke for Fig. 28; The Transport and Road Research Laboratory, Crowthorne for Figs 30, 33, 34, 36 and 38; Dr M. J. H. Mogridge for Fig. 31; the Atelier Parisien d'Urbanisme, Paris Project No. 19-20 for Figs 40 and 41; the Institute for Center Planlaegning, Copenhagen for Figs 43, 44 and 45; Ordnance Survey for Figs 46 and 47; Greater London Council for Figs 48, 49 and 50; and Newcastle City Council for Figs 51, 52, 53, 57, 58 and 59.

CONTENTS

INTRODUCTION

Aspirations for the year 2000

SIR WILFRED BURNS

City centres have survived wars, economic crises, fashionable ideas—even the motor car. I propose to assume, therefore, that they will be with us at the turn of the century. My job as a public official is to deal with day-to-day practical problems and this means that my thinking always starts from where we are now. Speculation about ideal cities is for others who can tear themselves away from everyday reality. The future of the city centre for the year 2000 will be determined not only by the way in which we deal with present and emerging problems but also by the extent to which change is restricted by inertia—in buildings, in thought processes, in public attitudes and in public institutions.

This is not an apologia for ad hocery, for planners particularly have been trained to look to the future and at least try to reduce the risk of future generations having to pay a high price for our lack of vision, even if we are no longer so sure that we can plan for a better future. In considering present problems therefore it is important, in my view, to have some idea as to possible longer-term futures. My training and life-long experience does not allow me to join those who believe the future is so indeterminate that all we can do is deal with present problems in isolation and that any forward thinking is a waste of effort. Some vision is still, I believe, a prerequisite for a planner, but it needs to be kept in perspective.

This raises difficulties for some because vision is linked to politics. Planning is and always has been political because it is concerned not only with form and design but with priorities and the allocation of scarce resources. The planner therefore has to understand the political nature of his job and understand the political approach of his elected masters; he cannot, or should not, shelter behind a pseudo-scientific analysis when the real issue is "the public good"—a political issue without doubt. Those who want to change the nature of society generally, and some planners like many other people do, should not pursue their objectives in the guise of professionalism. My definition of vision is therefore rather more restricted than that adopted by some younger people today, but it is not so restricted as to reduce everything to pragmatic action.

I will make just one further point in this preamble, and that relates to very long-range forecasting. The subject of "Futures" was pursued rather vigorously some

THE FUTURE FOR THE CITY CENTRE
ISBN 0 12 206240 X

years ago and numerous books and articles discussed long-range planning techniques and propounded their scenarios for the future. With rapid changes in the world scene the interest in this kind of work seems to me to have waned somewhat. I hope I am only partly right in this view because we need to be aware of possible long-term alternatives if, in the shorter planning time-scale, we are to have plans that will help to avoid future disasters or that will be steps towards worthwhile achievements. Many American cities, for example, are quite different from European ones. The basic functions of an historic city centre have now gone or can often be better catered for elsewhere. It may not now be a transport node; it is unlikely to be a centre of religion; it need not be the main centre for the exchange of goods; it is not usually a place in which to live. We, in Europe, have therefore to beware of assuming that nothing can or will change in the longer-term future.

This is, of course, all a bit messy and certainly lacking in intellectual and theoretical rigour. Yet it is as I perceive reality and I make these introductory remarks not because I particularly want to debate them here but because it is as well to state one's position before tackling a subject of the kind set for me by the editors of this volume.

THE BUILDING BOOMS

In the early post-war years, and again in the late 1950s and early 1960s, we had great debates about city centres. The first boom (in ideas rather than investment) centred on the rebuilding of war-damaged towns. There was then an atmosphere that challenged us all to create a new and better world. Visions of that better world abounded. A Ministry book, *The Redevelopment of Central Areas*, published in 1947 said:

> the future prosperity of central areas of larger towns depends upon the solution of their traffic problems; and the provision in the plan for traffic circulation, including the waiting and parking of vehicles, must therefore be such as is likely to be sufficient for all vehicles and persons having business in the central area (Ministry of Town and Country Planning, 1947).

The plans for redeveloping the bombed centres of Plymouth, Exeter, Southampton, Coventry and Bristol were well known and much discussed. Coventry pursued the pedestrian precinct concept, Bristol changed the location of its centre, Plymouth favoured the monumental. All were radical plans pursuing new solutions to city centre problems.

The second boom, which grew out of the first, may have been encouraged by the same kind of idealism amongst planners and politicians but its driving force was purely materialistic. This was the age of the developer—the man who foresaw a continuing boom in living standards, spending power and property values. We all wanted more goods, new products and consumer satisfaction—the developer simply provided the framework for society to have what it was clamouring for.

John Holliday (1973) claimed that "Whatever the criticisms of post-war planning, the achievement is undeniable, unique during this century, and likely to stand in the next century as a monument to the aspirations and values of our society in the 1960s and 1970s". In the same vein I said in a paper in 1977,

> Many of our central area schemes faithfully reflected the spirit of the times—whether of blitz reconstruction, Festival of Britain, municipal timidity and aggrandisement or, indeed, rampant materialism. Society gets the kind of city centres it deserves and though glaring mistakes were sometimes made—as indeed is the case in all ventures—our city centres today are a fair reflection, I believe, of the quality of life we have pursued over the last thirty years or so (Burns, 1979).

To be fair I must add that Professor David Gosling, at the same conference, said, "The growing public disenchantment with the physical development of cities has in some part been due to the insensitivity of planners" (Gosling, 1979).

CONDITIONS TODAY

It is difficult to generalize about city centres when they vary so greatly in importance and character. But I judge that most of our city centres are today in better shape, physically at least, than they have been for many decades. The buildings of any architectural or historic interest are better cared for and appreciated than perhaps ever before (and I say this in spite of—perhaps it is because of—the great publicity that is given to the few cases of deliberate vandalism or neglect). Many of the commercial buildings are modern, even if sometimes ugly, and Victorian structures are progressively being revamped and put into good heart. Of course some major railway stations and docks are no longer required for their original uses, gas works have closed and old industries have died leaving problems—and opportunities. London is the major, but not the only, example of this type of challenge. There the clash of interests is fully illustrated by the current arguments as to how the riverside areas and the docks should be developed—whether in relation to the central area and London as a whole, or in relation to the local communities and their immediately pressing problems. There are still parts of many other central areas where redevelopment will continue to be required. But in general the physical conditions in central areas are now such that major rebuilding is unnecessary and major restructuring a virtual impossibility. What one is left with is the possibility of many small-scale redevelopment projects, along with refurbishing, infilling and adaptation. After some 25 years of major central area building activity we now face a similar period of more modest physical change in most towns. Public attention has now moved to the adjoining inner areas where quite different problems and, I believe, opportunities abound.

Quite apart from the physical characteristics, however, there are other factors that will limit the extent of change in the foreseeable future. People in the 1950s and 1960s, especially in the big cities, wanted change. Life, it was thought, could and should be better. People in the 1970s and 1980s seem to have had enough of change and want to keep familiar environments. The status quo is now revered. This may simply be the swing of the pendulum—too much change sets up an equal and opposite reaction—or it may be the result of disenchantment with modern architecture; in some cases it may be nothing more than nostalgia for a long-since departed way of life. Whatever it is—and no doubt it is a combination of a great many factors—public opinion is unlikely to countenance major changes in most central areas for some years to come and will slow down the rate of change generally.

The other factor is money. The most profitable redevelopment was, of course, tackled first. Profit can only come from increasing the return from the land, and this can only come through increasing the amount of floor space or increasing the rent from the space available. This in turn is substantially determined by changes in prosperity and personal spending. Few people these days would see much possibility of repeating the massively profitable developments of the boom period. And even where some redevelopment is admittedly necessary, support from public funds today is directed to more urgent priorities. But let us not over-emphasize the economic situation too much. The late Lord Holford, then Professor Sir William Holford, said in 1953 that "The economic outlook is far from favourable; and it may be partly for the reason that it has been black for so long that we can no longer afford to sustain the all-out effort" (Holford, 1953).

Nevertheless, the position today seems to be that we have little money for encouraging major change, not much of a stomach for it anyway and an existing physical fabric that in general is good, often modern, often historic and usually in sound structural order. The future would therefore seem to require us to concentrate our efforts on improvements and adaptations rather than on securing major change.

This, surely, has been the normal state of affairs throughout history interrupted only by wars and great fires. Roman towns, in some senses, are still with us; medieval towns even more so; Georgian towns are there in the flesh. Town-centre layouts and their accompanying buildings are remarkably resilient. We now buy goods that were quite unknown to our grandparents let alone ancestors, yet we might buy them in a medieval street and from premises that were built for selling quite different goods—indeed for supporting quite different uses. Lack of change in terms of building and layout does not therefore mean that functions will not change as people's tastes and aspirations change, or as the need for a business to be in a prime or secondary position changes.

Improvement and adaptation, if it is to be successful, requires a full understanding of the character and workings of the city centre. Comprehensive planning, which is just as necessary now as when comprehensive redevelopment was in vogue, thus follows naturally—though it is in fact much more difficult and much less glamorous. Comprehensive planning does not mean a fully detailed end-state plan. It means a framework of broad policies and then a great deal of hard thinking to capitalize on opportunities as they are presented.

SOME EXTERNAL FACTORS

A great many external factors will have an impact on the way in which city centres evolve in the future. I will consider only two—employment and energy.

First let us look at employment. The changes in employment structure in city centres that have taken place in the last few decades are clearly apparent to everyone; and the changes that are continuing to take place in the inner city areas around them are of special concern to people like myself. The two localities are interrelated, of course, and success or otherwise in alleviating the current inner area problems will undoubtedly have an impact on the city centre itself.

In 1980, Professor Tom Stonier predicted that there would be profound changes—as big as anything we have experienced before—to the post-industrial economy. Changes in the tertiary sector through a revolution in communication would result in less people being employed in offices even though vastly more work would be done. But even in 1969, Professor Suzanne Keller speculated that, ". . . dramatic innovation in the sphere of work is not the rising volume of complex jobs nor the further decline of the work week. It is the disappearance of work itself" (Keller, 1969).

We have seen the decline of the great ports and railway termini and the death or relocation of the great Victorian engineering industries. Are we now, as a result of microprocessors and other new technologies, to see the gradual decline of the white collar industries that are such an important feature of most of our cities? Are we going to see the development of more home-based work—and empty office blocks? That is one end of the spectrum of possibilities. At the other end of the spectrum is the possibility that nothing significant will change, at least within the 20-year period under review here. We had the computer developments of the 1960s and 1970s but the massive predicted changes in employment have not materialized so far. Is the world moving so fast that technological innovations will prove really significant for overall employment levels within two decades?

The straightforward response is that we do not know, but that should not absolve us from considering whether present plans might lead to the accentuation of the possible ill-effects of such changes if they occur, or alternatively give the next generation of planners sufficient flexibility to react constructively to them.

It is often predicted that the impact of the new technological revolution will result in the faster development of the personal services sector and in a much greater role for the so-called informal sector of employment. How relevant would city centre multi-storey office blocks be for that situation? In 1980 there was a strong demand for prime shop sites in many cities but not for offices, yet in London many vast new office developments continue to be proposed. The signs are not, therefore, very clear and many difficult questions remain. Nevertheless, whilst we may not be able to answer them we must surely keep them in mind as we consider the day-to-day problems of development and change in our city centres. Unpredictability simply emphasizes the need for retaining as much flexibility as possible.

I turn now to the subject of energy which poses another set of imponderables of great importance. Accessibility to and the functioning of central areas depend substantially on gas and oil. It is inconceivable that known reserves will have run out by the end of the century and we do not, of course, know what new reserves may be discovered; but we can be sure that by then there will be increased concern about conserving resources and developing new sources of energy. Conversion of coal to oil and gas will no doubt be seen as part of the solution. But will central areas need to be adapted to cope with other aspects of the energy problem? Consider space heating for example. Might there be a tendency to want to burn coal direct, especially having regard to the cost of fuel? What would that mean in the way of delivery and storage areas? Perhaps CHP (combined heat and power) will turn out to be worthwhile and we will then be faced with the problems not only of locating power stations but of installing the whole network of underground services. I am not predicting that these steps will be necessary, but I strongly emphasize that we need to be aware of what is happening so that we are prepared as far as is sensibly possible.

Of greater consequence may be an increasing shortage and cost of petrol for our cars. The motor industry will no doubt continue to ensure that vehicles will become more fuel efficient; the coal and/or industry will, if need be, develop plans for converting coal into petrol. There may also be new developments for vehicles using electric power and perhaps hybrid systems. But can we safely assume that all will be well for personal transport and so unwittingly distract attention from the possibilities for greater use of public transport in our cities? We will continue to have the love-hate relationship with the private car for a long time, and present difficulties in our national prosperity may be obscuring underlying trends and giving us a false sense of security in this respect. The debate about the proper role of public transport in our cities raged furiously for a long time; it will surely re-emerge in the future.

THE CITY CENTRE AS A PLACE

Our quality of life is affected by a great many things but there is little doubt that for many people the city centre is one of them. With more leisure, enforced or desired, our city centres ought to contribute even more to our quality of life. In our search for economy and efficiency we should not forget that they are great learning and experience centres. I do not refer to the location of educational establishments as such—though they may well be very relevant—but to the totality of experiences that are possible in a city centre that has a richness and diversity. So many city centres today, however, are in danger of developing into something rather like departmental stores that open and close at fixed times. Some major new shopping centres do in fact physically close and large parts of city centres are abandoned at a fixed time. Will this, I wonder, serve people well in the years ahead? Do we have to assume that the city centre is a daytime experience only?

The provision of living accommodation in city centres has, like the place of the car, been the subject of debate, if not a great deal of action, over many years. We seem to have tired of the debate and put the subject away in the filing cabinets of our minds. It may be that we should take out the file, dust it off, and consider its relevance in the light of conditions for the end of the century.

Part of the difficulty in creating the kind of lively city centres most of us no doubt want is the present level of violence and unsociable behaviour. Consideration of the factors that have resulted in our present state of affairs lies well outside the scope of this paper; yet we cannot step too far aside and deny all connection. There are many, for example, who believe that increased social unrest is inevitable unless we make substantial progress towards curing the ills of inner areas. Some believe that there is a strong linkage between crime and vandalism on the one hand and land uses and the physical arrangement of buildings on the other. Town planners and others concerned with land use problems may not be the most suitable persons to deal with these social problems but, as urbanists, we need to consider whether we know enough about them and whether we are making an appropriate contribution to their solution. If, for example, many parts of our city centres have become vast impersonal processing areas, we may feel that, at best, we are doing little to help. Perhaps more direct involvement of owners, occupiers, business organizations and the populace generally in the direct management of these areas would be a helpful contribution. Yet area management in this sense does not seem to be contemplated outside the direct management of enclosed shopping malls. Increased travel, leisure, and the growth of tourism must, I feel certain, push us into considering how the impersonal can be personalized and the unattractive be made more attractive.

There are many and deep societal issues that will in some way or other impinge on the changing functions, if not form, of city centres. They receive quite inadequate attention in professional debate today.

THE CENTRE OF PLEASURE

We love informality—and Camillo Sitte's influence still lurks at the back of our minds. Yet we cannot plan on any substantial scale for informality. We are impressed by classical formality but we do not seem to have the guts today to plan on this scale with real conviction—Milton Keynes' city centre may be the exception that proves the rule. It may in any event be irrelevant to discuss these contrasting basic approaches because of the practical considerations of the present age. If the city centre is to change slowly over time as it reflects new developments and reacts to new pressures, we are willy-nilly forced to adopt a more pragmatic outlook and simply seek to understand and underline existing character whatever it may be. And that, however modest, is in my view a good thing anyway. It means retaining uniqueness and creating, here and there, our own contribution to a city's uniqueness despite the ubiquity of our shoe shops and supermarkets. Unique features bequeathed from the past are precious elements in the quality of cities all over the world. In this country, for example, these include Princess Street and

Gardens, St George's Hall, Grey Street, Trafalgar Square and St James's Park; one does not have to mention the cities for they are identified by these unique features themselves. I have no doubt myself that the uniqueness of some post-war developments will turn out to be equally attractive symbols in future. For the future, however, I do not think that we will see many new major features; we will see new punctuation marks perhaps and more concentration on the appreciation of what is already unique.

We appreciate city centres in a personal way not only through seeing them but through the senses of smelling, touching, remembering, feeling. I am not sure that we have given enough attention to these matters since the days of Kevin Lynch, Gordon Cullen and others who pioneered the study of imagery. (For a recent statement on the importance of images, however, see Jarvis (1980).) Perhaps I could quote Professor R. Gardner-Medwin (1956):

> We are apt to forget that one of the foremost functions of a town centre is to give pleasure to those who live in towns. Among the pleasures of the eye we should count the contrasts between stimulating movement and secluded calm; between large and small, formal and informal enclosures; between the free forms of trees and the ordered geometry of buildings; between sun and shade, broad and narrow, high and low; between the ordinary and the theatrical.

But he went on to say

> what we have to realise about the reshaping of our existing centres is that the expanding city region, with its increasing volume of traffic and its greater assembly of people, demands a new concept of the scale of urban design, a scale far greater than we can hope to achieve by present methods of piecemeal development on the old street grids.

The last part of the quotation emphasizes my point. It was, of course, perfectly acceptable to argue in this way 20 years ago. Today we face different conditions. Most cities have passed through this phase of expansionism and have now returned to the piecemeal and the gradual approach to change. Whether the centres redeveloped on the basis outlined by Professor Gardner-Medwin are better or worse than before depends, as John Holliday (1973) says, "on what you mean. They may be less picturesque but they also have less disease, dirt and disorder. Some qualities of vitality, interest, character and variety have gone, especially those deriving from those who have lived and worked and owned property in the centre". If that be so, it makes the first part of Professor Gardner-Medwin's statement even more important.

I suggest that our approach to town centre development should be based on the underlying premise of giving pleasure by maintaining variety in scene and uses and experiences but without, I hope, feeling that bygone ages created all that was good and that our own contribution will necessarily be a poorer one. Each generation must make its own contribution to the form and functioning of our cities even though people of my generation think nostalgically about the friendly cobbler, tobacconist or saddle-maker and bewail the fashions that gave us bowling alleys, trendy boutiques, bingo halls and now sex shops.

A few rather more detailed points may be worth making in relation to developments that affect the character of city centres. Pedestrianization of shopping centres has proceeded slowly for well over 30 years. The resistance of shopkeepers in the early post-war years has now given way to much more general acceptance, indeed welcome, by retailers and public alike. But a great deal is still left to be done. I wonder why this is the case, when so much environmental benefit can apparently be achieved at such little cost. Have we lost the will or have the technical problems become so overwhelming? In new developments of whatever size the pedestrian area is taken for granted; indeed many shopping developments are now fully enclosed and, contrary to what I thought at one time, generally welcomed. But the vision of linked underground shopping centres (as in Vancouver) or linked deck access centres (London Wall and Newcastle) are unlikely to be repeated on a large scale in the foreseeable future for reasons that I have already given. We will, however, have retained our street markets in spite of all that was said against them.

We still have problems of satisfactorily integrating car parks with new developments. As the scope for redevelopment is reduced, the problems of coping with the stationary car, let alone the moving one, increase. Dealing with large lorries is equally difficult and changes in methods of retailing and warehousing have changed the nature of the problem.

I mention these few points to indicate that there are still many unsolved problems and much to think about at the micro- as well as the macro-level. Perhaps Konrad Smigielski (1973) had it right when he said "We know how to destroy and we know how to build on new lines. We still have not learnt how to develop a method whereby a continuous process of revitalization of our urban environment would be secured without destroying heritage".

I am conscious that I have not discussed mathematical models and quantitative assessments of traffic, floor space, profitability or even capital investment. This may be a disappointment to some, but I make no apology because in my experience this type of analytical work is so necessary that it invariably gets done: but in giving individual development proposals special scrutiny, there seems to be less attention directed at wider trends or the effects that will accrue from various policies.

CONCLUSION

I conclude this personal and idiosyncratic review of city centres therefore with my summary of some of the wider and possibly longer-term issues that need to be in our minds as we contemplate the more immediate matters that daily engage our attention.

(1) The future is largely determined by inertia in thought as well as in the existing built environment but modified by the day-to-day changes and developments in many diverse fields. Whilst long-range forecasting is now less fashionable, day-to-day changes need to be considered against ideas of possible long-term futures in which vision is still a component.

(2) Major city centre developments take place in fits and starts, but in more recent times major changes were necessary first because of war damage and secondly because so little development had taken place for so long that major restructuring had often become necessary.

(3) Most of our city centres are now, physically, in much better shape than they have been for many decades and as a result major rebuilding or restructuring is either unnecessary or impracticable.

(4) At the present time, in any event, the public does not welcome major changes and money is not available at least for public sector developments.

(5) Effort, in consequence, must be restricted to what has been called "creative adaptation".

(6) Nevertheless, we need to be aware of longer-term changes in society that may eventually have an impact on our city centres; amongst these may be:

(a) technological changes and the effect on employment and its location;
(b) energy policies and their effect on city centre and inner area servicing as well as traffic;
(c) leisure demands and changes in attitudes to the quality of life.

(7) The city centre has been and should remain an area that gives pleasure to all its users.

REFERENCES

Burns, W. (1979). *In* "Quality in Urban Planning and Design" (R. Cresswell, ed.). Newnes and Butterworth, London.

Cullen, G. (1961). "Townscape". The Architectural Press, London.

Gardner-Medwin, R. (1956). Paper Delivered at the Town and Country Planning Summer School.

Gosling, D. (1979). *In* "Quality in Urban Planning and Design" (R. Cresswell, ed.). Newnes and Butterworth, London.

Holford, W. (1953). Paper Delivered at the Town and Country Planning Summer School.

Holliday, J. (1973). *In* "City Centre Redevelopment" (J. Holliday, ed.). Charles Knight, London.

Jarvis, R. K. (1980). *Tn Plann. Rev.* **51**, 50-66.

Keller, S. (1969). Paper Delivered at the Town and Country Planning Summer School.

Lynch, K. (1960). "The Image of the City". MIT, Cambridge, Mass.

Ministry of Town and Country Planning (1947). "The Redevelopment of Central Areas". HMSO, London.

Smigielski, K. (1973). *In* "City Centre Redevelopment" (J. Holliday, ed.). Charles Knight, London.

Stonier, T. (1980). Paper Delivered to the Town and Country Planning Summer School.

PART ONE

Scenarios on the environment

ONE

City centre plans in the 1980s

J. C. HOLLIDAY

Within ten years city centre plans in the UK have changed from schemes involving expensive redevelopment to schemes which are modest and conservative in approach. This marked change, which is apparent in much of Western Europe, results from economic recession, cuts in public expenditure, changes in public attitudes to environment and some shift of central area functions arising from new development.

After the explosive changes of the 1960s and early 1970s, with their grand plans, a period of readjustment has been followed by a new series of plans very different in kind. They are no longer grand, but they are on the whole thoughtful and responsive to public opinion. Many of the earlier plans have failed to materialize or have been heavily amended. Today's plans are much more cautious about their objectives. Much of the achievement or failure of the earlier plans was dependent upon timing. Coventry and Birmingham began early and completed their ring roads; Liverpool and Leicester, starting later, did not. Liverpool, Tyneside and Glasgow have new metro systems. Other cities came too late to secure public funds, or, in the case of roads, to avoid public opposition.

This chapter draws mainly on the experience of some city centre studies by the author in the early 1970s (Holliday, 1973)—for Birmingham, Coventry, Leicester and Liverpool—as well as on plans completed or in preparation for Leeds, Bradford, Manchester and Glasgow. A number of other plans in the UK and elsewhere are also considered. The plans show fairly consistent changes in emphasis as compared with the 1970s, the most important of which are as follows:

(a) from master development plans to local plans as instruments of policy and management;
(b) from major development to conservation and selective, more modest development;
(c) from a context of city growth to one of city decline;
(d) to an emphasis on employment, including industrial employment;
(e) from expensive road and metro proposals to more modest road schemes and no new rail proposals;

PTO

THE FUTURE FOR THE CITY CENTRE
ISBN 0 12 206240 X

(f) to an emphasis on pedestrian ways and bus priorities;
(g) to a strong emphasis on the development of unique and attractive features in relation to visitors, tourists and industry.

In general the plans have moved from comprehensive schemes for offices, high buildings and multi-level roads to schemes which are trying to develop and exploit the character of centres, while struggling to solve problems of employment, public transport and housing.

THE CHANGING CONTEXT

Plans, planning and policies

The nature of planning has changed a great deal during the past 15 years. Although the statutory framework mainly requires attention to be given to land use and development, the end of the era of massive clearance and redevelopment in our old industrial cities now means that everyday management and a greater concern with resources provide the focus of activity. It is useful, however, to distinguish between planning and policy-making and, in the former regard, to note that there are two kinds of planning.

First, there is development planning, which is concerned with the process of construction and building and in which architects, engineers, town planners and developers play major roles. Secondly, there is management planning, which is concerned with the process of enabling change to take place within a heavily built up area that is not undergoing substantial physical change but where there may nevertheless be considerable changes of use and activity. This process requires different arts from those required for development planning.

Policies are essentially political but are often initiated by planners. They are the means for securing action in specific fields. For example, the change in approach taken towards the provision of high rise housing between the 1960s and 1970s represents a specific policy-decision which was carried out, often without the preparation of any plans. A similar case was the introduction of the 1972 traffic scheme which severely restricted car access to the centre of Nottingham. It is in such ways that politics can affect the planning process.

Our statutory planning system requires local authorities to prepare structure- and local plans—city centre plans are local plans—and the content of these plans reflects a process which combines policy making, development planning and management. In other words contemporary planning in the UK is complex and political in ways different from earlier planning, involving more continuous monitoring and review and closer liaison with the public and special interest groups. Statutory plans are required to include public participation which, combined with reduced public expenditure, has been a major reason for the switch to conservation. The public has brought the developers and professionals to heel.

Economic forces at work

Nearly all plans recognize the heavy decentralization of industry and population from their cities. (For an account of the wider implications of these processes on cities, see Cameron (1980).) The structure plans identify the amount of loss and examine city-wide effects. The local plans examine the effects on the centre, in particular falling employment. The effects of the retail revolution continue to be felt, whether as new developments within the city centre (as with the Arndale Centre in Manchester), or outside it. These are reflected in concern over vacancies and the fate of the less attractive fringes of the centre where closures are frequent. The office boom of the 1960s and early 1970s provided surplus space, but the spare capacity was declining in the late 1970s. As a result new proposals have appeared, on which many cities are now pinning their hopes for increased employment. However, with the recent decline in office employment in the public sector and with the micro-chip revolution underway, there is an absence of conviction about the future growth in office employment; a degree of uncertainty which is already recognized in the Leeds Central Business Area District Plan (1979), and more strongly in the Central Leicester District Plan (1980).

More important for employment perhaps, the plans recognize the growth of leisure and tourism with consequent possibilities for attracting new kinds of employers to the centre.

Declining public expenditure has also resulted in a severe cut back in public transport facilities. As the Manchester Report of Survey (1980) states, the city centre must make do with services mainly provided at the beginning of the century. Public utilities are in an even worse state, leading to major collapse in main shopping streets. Road proposals in the plans are small and no new metro system is envisaged. But the public outcry against the old plans and their massive renewal programmes has also been a major factor in slowing down the pace of change and encouraging not only policies of conservation, but an emphasis on public transport, on pedestrians, and on a more sensitive and varied approach to the environment.

Generally, economic forces are leading the planners to emphasize those attributes of central areas which have traditionally applied to capitals and historic cities, a fact which is perhaps unexpected from a set of plans concerned with our older industrial environments. When Birmingham can devote 25 pages to leisure and tourism in its Draft Written Statement (1980), something is changing.

Law and the organization of planning

The major change which occurred in the 1970s was the reorganization of local government in 1974, removing responsibility for preparing structure plans from the old county boroughs to the counties, which included the new metropolitan counties. Large cities therefore became "districts" and lost their powers to prepare city-wide structure plans, although in practice cities do prepare strategic policies and local plans covering the whole city; hence distinctions between the new types of plans are not always easy to make.

The Town and Country Planning Act 1971 requires that government approval be given to structure plans before it is given to local plans, except in approved cases coming under the Inner Urban Areas Act of 1978. The latest Department of Environment advice on the preparation of local plans (which can be district, action or subject plans), refers to four major functions. These are: (1) to develop the policies and proposals of structure plans and relate them to precise areas of land; (2) to provide a basis for development control; (3) to provide a basis for co-ordinating development and other uses of land; and (4) to bring issues before the public. These functions account for some of the format and approach of local plans. However, it is notable that whereas the statutory emphasis is physical, the local plans themselves are much concerned with economic factors.

The growth of central government concern over our large cities, particularly their social and economic characteristics, has been marked by the 1977 White Paper on Policies for the Inner Cities, which led to the Inner Urban Areas Act of 1978. Under this Act the powers for government to set up Urban Development Corporations to tackle severe inner city problems have led to their establishment in the Liverpool and London Docklands and proposals for these areas will affect central area plans when work gets underway. UDC's could well be set up in other cities adjacent to their central areas for they have, as some see it, the advantage of independence from local authorities, as did the New Town Development Corporations.

The third post-war attempt of a Labour government to secure better control over land led to the ill-fated Community Land Act of 1975 which was repealed by the Conservative Government in 1980. Although this measure had little impact on central areas, the conflicting ideologies of the political parties as regards land ownership and control remain as a central problem in all planning.

Against the background of these newer forms of legislation, some of the older powers have been repealed, especially where they have been seen to inhibit development in our old city centres. The Location of Offices' Bureau, established in 1963 to encourage the decentralization of offices from central London, was dissolved in 1980. Office Development Permits were abandoned in 1979 and there were relaxations in industrial development controls in 1976. These revocations may increase the possibilities of development generally, but they have also removed some of the teeth from government policies to help Assisted Areas.

Local government reorganization has inevitably led to tensions between county and district authorities. Both have responsibilities for the major city centres, because structure and local plans must fit, even though the political, financial and technical approaches are not necessarily the same. However, the Local Government Planning and Land Act 1980 gives more development control powers to the district councils, which should help in managing their central areas. Reorganization has also delayed some of the formal local planning work, as districts have waited for structure plans to be approved; and this has been one reason for the recent spate of plans, almost a decade after they were first called for. Although the local plans make reference to structure plan policies and the former mostly read as being in agreement with the latter, certain issues remain; for example, the role and provision of public transport, which has a major impact on detailed city centre planning but which is the responsibility of the county councils or passenger transport executives.

The other aspect to note regarding the organization of planning is the internal administrative structure to be found within the authorities, and in particular the role of corporate management. Although this development was a major part of the 1974 reorganization, some cities, for example Coventry, had pioneered such an approach to urban government some years before (Gregory, 1973). The coincidence of this approach with the economic recession of the 1970s was a major reason for the evolution of what we might now call management planning. The new style meant a closer look across the board at the responsibilities and services of departments, and an attempt to determine city-wide priorities and to allocate resources effectively.

The new local government system and the division of planning functions between districts and counties (in London between boroughs and the GLC) has been strongly criticized by many. Where large cities occur in shire counties, as with Leicester for example, there is some reason for regretting the division. In the conurbations, however, strategic powers which can relate several major centres together can be an advantage, although it may be that regional authorities would have provided a better planning framework than the constrained metropolitan counties. Certainly the problems of big city regions can be tackled more fairly where a major regional authority exists, as in Strathclyde.

CURRENT PLANS

Within the last year or two many cities have embarked on statutory plans for their city centres following the approval of structure plans. Few large cities, however, have completed their central area plans and one or two are not preparing them at all. Liverpool, which took a lead in the 1960s, is one of these. On the other hand, Birmingham produced its first ever central area plan in 1980. Very few city centre local plans are on deposit or have been approved by the Department of the Environment: only Rochdale, Ipswich, Brighton, Leicester, Gillingham and a few of the London boroughs are at these stages. A few plans, however, have been adopted by local authorities independently.

The areas covered by the plans or proposed plans are very varied. Edinburgh's newly started plan will embrace only the old and new town conservation areas, whereas Birmingham's plan includes a large area of inner city industrial land. In general, however, the plans cover the CBD's only and do not include adjacent areas which in several cities are now the subject of separate inner area policies.

The plans are paperback statutory working documents, in contrast to some of the hardback glossies of the 1960s and 1970s. But at the same time exhibitions and leaflets show the improvement in public relations and a recognition of the need not only to sell but to share issues with the public. Many contain a great deal of research and hard analysis, although some stereotyped assumptions remain and there is commonly an absence of deep perspective to give a sense of historic forces and likely futures.

Aims and objectives

The overriding purpose of all the local plans is to promote the central area in every possible way. The structure plans express the same intention and provide the context in which emphasis can be given to city centre schemes while control can be exercised over outlying retail and other developments which may harm the economy of the centre. The big cities stress the regional importance of their centres and often their international significance—for example, Birmingham, with the National Exhibition Centre at the eastern edge of the city. To quote from the Birmingham Central Area District Plan (1980):

> The long-term aims of the City Council and West Midlands County Council for the Central Area are set out below in *priority order*:
>
> 1. To enhance the role of the Central Area as a regional centre for commerce, retailing, public administration, cultural facilities and entertainment.
> 2. To assist the economic wellbeing of industry located in the established industrial areas within the Central Area.
> 3. To enhance the potential of the Central Area as a place in which people would wish to live.

The aims of the Leeds Central Business Area District Plan (1979) are:

> (a) To enhance the City Centre's regional role.
> (b) To retain and whenever possible increase job opportunities.
> (c) To make the best use of available road space and improve access within the City Centre for pedestrians and vehicles.
> (d) To further protect and enhance the built environment.
> (e) To upgrade the Riverside.
> (f) To extend the range of leisure facilities, including open space.
> (g) To encourage housing provision.

The Manchester City Centre Local Plan Report of Survey (1980) neatly summarizes the changes between 1968 and 1980:

> implicit in the City Centre Map (1968) was a belief that in the face of evergrowing pressures upon the City Centre there was a need to be "restrictive", and to "channel", or in some cases even "deflect" activity. To this extent our objective would now be fundamentally different with the whole emphasis being on the "promotion" of the regional centre and the "encouragement" and "nurturing" of activity. Apart from the much changed world in which the City Centre Map now finds itself, the great weakness of many of its proposals—which found expression in numerous advisory

schemes—was that they did not relate well to the existing fabric of the City. Moreover they depended upon wholesale and large scale change and needed to be implemented as a whole in order to be coherent.

There is no doubt about the general concerns and objectives of central area plans, and policies are now formulated to ensure that the city centres get all the aid they can. In this context many of the plans are concerned with the image and quality of the city centre, which is reflected in a host of small proposals and some well publicized developments aimed at industry as much as at visitors and tourists. Liverpool, amongst others, now produces a glossy leaflet (including "review" quotes from the press) on the planning context for development in the city centre; a leaflet which could have come from a tourist board. Sadly the reality of a visit is disillusioning.

Employment, industry and offices

Employment is now a major issue in all plans, perhaps most strikingly seen in the encouragement given to industry, which received little attention in most earlier plans. Several major city centres show a decline in employment. For example, in Manchester, there has been a reduction in the central area workforce from 167 000 in 1961 to 108 000 in 1971 to 105 000 in 1979. In most places the areas covered by the plans have changed and precise figures cannot be given, but the trend is there nevertheless. The heavy falls in manufacturing employment were offset to some extent in the 1970s by increases in office employment and most plans, probably optimistically, look to further office growth as a means of maintaining job levels. The inclusion of industrial areas in a few places—for example, the Jewellery district with its 42 000 jobs in Birmingham—indicates the importance being given to all forms of employment. Many plans contain proposals for Industrial Improvement Areas and almost all are concerned with the refurbishment of old premises. The objectives are jobs at all costs, subject to not degrading adjacent environments and combined with improvements in the industrial environment whenever possible. The Leicester Plan, for example, includes a policy which gives presumption in favour of the location of industry over 25 per cent of the area. The issue of how to deal with old and to some extent unused property is clearly brought out in Nottingham (City Council, 1980), where the Lace Market accommodates 40 per cent of the central industrial floor space and is also a conservation area.

There is some justification for optimism about the relative health of office employment in spite of the reservations expressed earlier, but the general absence of hard analysis on the impact of the microchip is an example of failure to look at the future. The optimism comes from such facts as the high level of rents and demand in Liverpool and the 600 overseas companies located in Manchester, although in the latter city there was a 12 per cent decline of office employment between 1971 and 1977, combined with the provision of 490 000 m^2 of new floor space between 1966 and 1980. Types of office accommodation receive much attention in the reports of survey of plans, recognizing a demand for small office suites and a problem of vacant upper floors.

New office complexes of which a number are still being conceived often provide opportunities for undertaking comprehensive redevelopment and in such cases the importance of including housing and other uses with them is stressed. The lessons of major single-purpose office developments have been learned to some extent. Particularly where local communities exist, as in London's Coin Street area, proposals have become major political issues.

Shopping

While battles over "out-of-town" and suburban hypermarkets continue, the wider issue of where most shopping centre resources should be concentrated seems to have been settled by central and local government policies aimed at retaining these within existing central areas. As a result, all our old city centres remain healthy and fairly buoyant. All the plans reviewed in this chapter aim to continue to consolidate the core shopping areas of the city centre. Fringe areas are discounted in many cases and the concern over the growing incursion of offices, savings banks and other uses into major shopping streets is expressed in strong policies to stop them. At the same time proposals for large new shopping developments are not part of most plans.

Discount warehouses are variously treated. Leeds provides an interesting example. The plan proposal allows discount warehouses (provided that they do not sell food) to be located within two areas of the prime shopping area but outside the main core. In justification the plan states (Leeds City Council, 1980):

> The City Council recognizes that retail discount warehouses can offer wider variety and choice to shoppers and can have benefits in terms of competitive prices. The City Council, however, considers that if any further discount warehouses are established in the City they should be accessible to the whole community and not just to those households with cars. Clearly the City Centre is the most accessible location in the City and therefore other things being equal it would be an appropriate location for the development of discount stores, particularly those selling furniture and electrical goods. In fact this type of retailing activity, because of its trading methods will require a fringe location outside the core shopping area, where land values are lower and adjacent car parking can be provided. Also there is little doubt that it would present direct competition for shops selling similar products within the core shopping area. However the Department of the Environment advise (Development Control Policy Note—13) that it is not the function of land use planning to prevent or to stimulate competition among retailers or among methods of retailing, nor to preserve existing commercial interests as such but it must take into account the benefits to the public which flow from new developments in the distributive and retailing trades.

Not all plans are so clear in their policies and in many cases the emphasis given to the public interest remains an important issue to be resolved.

An interesting development in Leicester is the acceptance of factory shops provided that sales are restricted to products of the type produced in the factory.

But no shop front can be established unless the factory is in the shopping core.

Plans, on the topic of shopping, are now on the whole more responsive to the market and less predictive than they used to be. Consolidation is the key word.

Population and housing

The decline of population continues in almost all the city centres which have been studied. Decline has sometimes been essential as in the case of Glasgow where severe overcrowding in slum conditions had to be dealt with. In contrast, some cities with a stronger heritage of high quality residential accommodation such as Edinburgh have retained high levels of central area population. But our industrial cities have fared badly. The population in Manchester's city centre declined from 4000 in 1961 to 1000 in 1978; in Coventry, despite strong policies to arrest the trend, the population fell from 4850 in 1961 to 3250 in 1979. Others show the same story.

Most plans are concerned to provide for small households in the city centre. Students, old people and the young all present a demand which is not met, but proposals are vague, as there is little land and the problems of converting the upper floors of old shopping streets remain unsolved. New high rise housing is not countenanced, nor has it been in some cities for nearly ten years. One of Britain's pre-war show pieces, Quarry Hill in Leeds, has been demolished and the site is in reserve for a proposal of regional significance. Post-war flats have also been demolished near city centres although some complexes have proved to be successful. Mixed development provides a few opportunities for new housing, but the majority of English cities seem to have sold out their often fine central residential areas to commercial projects. Conservation has emphasized the preservation of architectural and historic features but not the social structures.

In England further attempts at removing central area housing are likely to face resistance, as already seen, most notably in London. The designation of general improvement areas (GIA's) and housing action areas (HAA's) has resulted in some up-grading of homes and environments.

A private development in the Glasgow Eastern Area Project—not the most attractive residential quarter—has sold well and experience from continental Europe suggests that most people's roots are a strong motive force for attracting residents back to the city centre. The classic case of social conservation in Bologna is discussed later. Political philosophy, technical values and timing are determining the fate of population and housing in city centres. In England purpose is varied and often weak, and it shows in the plans. The Leeds plan doubts whether a reversal of population decline can actually be brought about, but a more general view is that such trends should be reversed.

Transport and pedestrians

The most striking contrast in failure and achievement since the 1970s has been in policies directed at transport systems, particularly in road proposals. The time at which proposals were made and the determination of the city concerned have generally been the causes of this variation. Birmingham had proposals for a ring road in 1914. It pursued a modified scheme and completed it in the 1970s. Leicester produced an extravagant scheme in 1964; but little has been built. Today's plan for Leicester shows a very modest improvement in roads—but with no more multi-level junctions. The schemes for Liverpool have again changed over the years. But some cities are still pursuing fairly ambitious road proposals, as for example in Glasgow (Glasgow City Council, 1979) and Bradford (Bradford City Council, 1980).

The central issue is still the balance between public and private transport. All plans adopt a rather uneasy and pragmatic approach to the problem, although heavy subsidies for public transport are continued. Bus and taxi priorities are now well established, while Nottingham continues with its more radical central core barrier system aimed at restricting the private car. At the same time control over the provision of private car parking has been reduced almost everywhere for fear of frightening off potential employers. Leeds and Bradford are considering more staggering of working hours, and Leeds is investigating the possibilities of car pooling, as well as safeguarding a corridor for possible future light public transport, surely a wise step and one of the few examples of long-range planning in a cautious and conservationist set of plans.

Heavy vehicles seem to face few restrictions although there is a general mood to bring in tighter controls on their road usage. The increase in pedestrian streets has been significant, although less than many would like, and they are almost universally successful for shop owners and shoppers. Some mixed pedestrian/bus ways have been tried, as in Newcastle and Coventry, but in Coventry the almost total exclusion of traffic in the central precinct is now causing problems with safety at night. Perhaps some mix of transport and pedestrians could have advantages, despite the obvious risk of accidents. The comprehensive high-level pedestrian ways begun in Liverpool and one or two other cities have been abandoned. Cyclists receive little attention.

City centre plans are still failing to come to terms with transport issues. The early schemes were too ambitious; today's too cautious. Opportunities to capitalize on the energy problem and its implications have not been grasped, although they are well recognized in Glasgow's Draft Survey (1979).

Leisure, tourism and education

Since the earlier plans there has been some striking development in leisure and tourism. All surveys and plans have substantial sections devoted to what is a growing industry which holds out hope for the future of our city centres. We can thank the recession and public opinion for the opportunity to capitalize now on some of the fine remaining historic buildings and areas in our city centres. The national tourist movement, grants for hotels and other leisure purposes, the establishment of new local authority departments, have all given force to the possibilities of exploiting the economic potential of tourism.

Most plans refer to new or proposed developments which will be well known to the public. Sports centres, theatres and specialist museums all feature prominently. Hotels and restaurants have blossomed, if rather expensively, and bright lights, water, open space, trees, pedestrian ways and cleaned historic buildings are all part and parcel of the plans.

The consideration of proposals for conference centres is also a strong feature, especially in regional city centres, and particularly where such developments as the National Exhibition Centre in Birmingham have already become successful. There are clear possibilities for new development along North American lines, and where universities and polytechnics exist within central areas conference facilities are already being developed. In contrast the opportunities to provide new forms of educational facility have been exploited hardly at all, nor do they feature in the plans. Surely the changing world demands new concepts about the role and place of education? Certainly the growth of the campus in the centres of our cities should not be thought of in isolation by either the city or the educational institute.

The environment and conservation

> The primary proposal for the built environment is to maintain the identity and sense of place of the City Centre by protecting that building fabric and style which makes Leeds a distinctive and attractive City while encouraging high quality new building and adapting the environment to those commercial and other activities which are vital to the identity and function of the City Centre (Leeds City Council, 1979).

> A good environment, full of variety and interest and well maintained can be a major factor in attracting private investment of all kinds. The identification of measures for improving the physical environment of the Central Area is seen as a particularly important element of the District Plan if the aims and objectives are to be achieved (Birmingham City Council, 1980).

So read the first proposal of the chapter on environment in the Leeds Plan and the opening section of the chapter on environment in the Birmingham Plan. It is here, and in the other plans, that one finds the elements which have traditionally belonged to the planner. Now, however, the basis for proposals is not so much the architectural values which pervaded the earlier plans, but the recognition of social and economic benefit and its exemplification in the Image of the City, captured in Lynch's (1960) classic work of that name, and subsequently developed in the field of environmental psychology.

The proposals range from the mundane to the spectacular. Clearing waste land, cleaning canals and controlling noisy and dirty uses find their place next to protecting fine historic buildings, extending conservation areas and harmonizing townscapes. The struggle of the 1970s is now largely won and the evidence seen earlier in the improvement programme for Grey Street in Newcastle upon Tyne is now visible across the UK, for example in the fine terraces on the west side of Glasgow's city centre. In contrast are the new trees and open spaces in the run down east side.

Overbuilding is still a concern, and specifications regarding plot ratios (the relationship between site area and floor areas) still feature in the plans as do controls over height. Bradford, for example, has a draft policy which includes the presumption:

> Against any new building which would be visible either above adjoining and nearby buildings, as seen from street level, or conspicuous from more distant viewpoints. This policy will be particularly relevant within elevated areas of the City Centre and within the building-dominated street corridors. Each proposal shall be treated on its individual merit in terms of its potential townscape contribution, such as the termination of views (Bradford City Council, 1980).

Although generalized policies are included in such plans, there is an absence of strong positive new design proposals based on relating practical possibilities to architecture and city image. Instead most cities still rely on utilizing their legacies from the past, which includes bad as well as good. The pendulum seems to have swung too far. But it is nice to see wildlife now featuring as a special topic in city centre plans.

LESSONS FROM HOME AND ABROAD

It is in the nature of the development industry that technologies and designs dating from one period show great similarities, especially in this age of rapid communication. Plans share this characteristic and it is difficult to point to any one of the plans studied and suggest that it represents a breakthrough or marks a new starting point. (The Covent Garden Plan (Greater London Council, 1978) is significant but not as a general city centre plan.) Of course the quality is variable, reflecting the variation of human skills, and the content is variable, reflecting the variety of environment. It is probably true to say that whereas the plans of the 1970s tended to reflect the uniformity of new development, the plans of the 1980s tend to reflect the variety of existing environment. This must surely be a gain, although ultra-conservatism may tend to stifle new thinking.

Planning for our city centres seems to have passed through two stages over the last 20 years and is now moving into a third. First, there was the pre-occupation with the nineteenth century inheritance; secondly, there came a period of massive demolition, much of which was socially necessary, and some not; now we are witnessing a process of slow management towards city centres which will likely become more attractive places to visit. We have avoided the excesses of the USA in terms of tarmac deserts and the commercial decline of central areas through the implementation of strong policies on controlling suburban shopping schemes and attempts, though not yet successful, to control the motor car. The city centre in Britain is still the major focus of most of our activities.

However, many central area fringes are a mess and much of the recent development in these localities is soulless, some of it irretrievably so. We shall have to wait some decades for the renewal of the latter. The more general problems of the fringes are best seen in the context of the inner city. The boundary between the city centre and its surrounding tracts is a frontier area, vulnerable and economically risky. It is an area about which the new plans say little and its omission shows a failing to develop wider planning concepts, particularly on a social theme.

The implementation of plans has always been part of post-war planning exercises, but the plans of the 1980s show little advance over those for the 1970s or before. This in part reflects the failure of central and local government to relate economic and physical resources. The Scottish situation is better than the English and Welsh. Northern Ireland cannot be compared at present. Our system of central financial control and allocation is inadequate for really effective local government. But it also must be said that local government is unresponsive to urgent problems and beset by political ideology in which planning and other services become political footballs. How can we sensibly tackle a housing problem in this situation? Therefore, our ability to implement quickly and efficiently is weak by virtue of the system.

The process of estimating and budgeting in cities—Glasgow's rateable value for the year 1979-1980 was nearly £211 million—is difficult when the local councils do not know from one year to the next what central government will provide, and when central government contributes such a high proportion of total expenditure (approximately 60 per cent in English cities).

The potential of the plans is that there is a good deal of consensus about the need to develop the economic and environmental benefits of our city centres. Slow and steady progress is there in spite of the recession. Shopping holds up remarkably well, small industries and crafts have room to develop and, with current redundancies and aid from government, there are new opportunities for putting entrepreneural skills to work. Many private individuals are prepared to invest in central areas and good opportunities exist for combining public and private investment, although the examples we have seen in this latter regard are rather few.

The traditional compromises of the British are found in the task of devising clear cut policies for transport. Colin Buchanan's publications—*Mixed Blessing* (1958) and *Traffic in Towns* (1963)—clearly illustrate the essential problem. Although the plans show a slow movement towards putting the car in its place, there is no imaginative development of small-scale transport technology in pedestrian streets or attempts to bring pedestrians and vehicles into some kind of safer harmony in the same street. The lack of vision applies especially to the fringe areas. It is as if planning was too frightened by the experience of the 1970s, or perhaps it is the general state of the economy which is at the root of the matter. This can be measured to some extent by comparing our own cities with those abroad.

The plans discussed above are a very limited set. They exclude London, the New Towns, the smaller but often more rapidly growing towns of the UK and examples from abroad. What can be learned from other plans? From the UK not very much perhaps because of the common political and statutory system. Of course there is an exciting new centre at Milton Keynes but this is on a green field site. In London the boroughs experience the same problem as the provincial cities in dealing with an old fabric and often strong community action. Covent Garden, an approved local plan, was a watershed in planning in this respect. No longer the clean sweep and the new office quarter. Across the Channel the same trends are evident; that is, public hostility to mass clearance and support for a strong conservation movement. This is well documented by Appleyard's book on *The Conservation of European Cities* (1979). Pedestrian centres abound, especially in Germany, and Munich has one of the best. Paris, characteristically, has imaginative new "cities" around its periphery and the Pompidou Centre shows how animation can be brought into old centres.

The technology of planning and development has strong limitations in meeting the needs of communities, especially when pushed and financed by commerce. The USA has shown what commerce and cars can do to the health of the city centre. However, some impressive efforts are now being made to restore city centres in American cities as places worth visiting for pleasure, and worth living in. The developments in Philadelphia have been widely reported (Cresswell, 1979). Baltimore's Charles Centre and Inner Harbour Development, and Boston's Quincy Market also show what can be done. But the retail core has largely gone to the suburbs in many cities to be surrounded by other new developments which in the UK would go to the old centre. So the political philosophy of the USA has been to sacrifice many city centres of their traditional West European form. Instead they are being reconstructed with new kinds of agencies and developments.

At the other end of the political spectrum the socialist city of Bologna has not only rejected the continued large-scale commercialization of the centre at the expense of the resident community, but has also adopted a conservation policy which, unlike those in the UK, emphasizes the protection of dwellings and a high population as well as historic monuments (Baudarin, 1979). Life is conserved with the fabric. There is a strong decentralization of administration and of decision-making in the city, all of which contributes to new political approaches towards the centre. The conservation is cultural in the sense that the interests of existing central area residents are protected. They are not all displaced by a gentrified population.

It can be argued that people will eventually leave the often low-quality housing in Bologna as has indeed occurred in Venice. On the other hand, there are many examples in Central London where the local culture is preferred to traditional planning solutions. The Covent Garden Plan has overwhelming social objectives and standards are a matter of interpretation. Other left-wing authorities in Europe have failed to conserve the culture of their centres, so Bologna is a special case, and it has been left to pressure groups to act.

Some lessons have been clearer than others. While we learnt from the USA on the matter of commercial decentralization and to some extent prevented the destruction of our city centres, we did not learn about people in city centres until people themselves produced the political force. Planning, as required by the Department of the Environment, is still too physical in its approach and although public participation provides some opportunity for change, the local planners and politicians do not include strong policies on the social aspects of life in city centres.

Nevertheless, although there are criticisms, the record of UK planning comes out fairly well as compared with other countries. Of course, British towns lack the life and gaiety of some European countries, but this is a matter of national culture, not town planning. One task ahead for planning is to develop the fringes of the centres in an attempt to get back some of the residential qualities which our centres have lost.

CONCLUSION

Given that the consolidation of the commercial core has by and large succeeded, most opportunities for the future may well lie at the fringe, both spatially and in terms of the impetus for life and activity. The core is dominated by business. Populations have been pushed out. Planners have lost confidence after the architectural and road engineering visions of the 1960s and 1970s. If our centres mean anything they mean liveliness and opportunity as well as pomp and circumstance. It is this life which needs encouraging, and planning legislation and technique with its heavy land-use emphasis will not do it.

Much of this life is to be found in all the small entrepreneural efforts which are taking place—in workshops, gardens, murals—and which are both creative and enjoyable. They are traditional back-street activities brought out into the open, and they need encouraging. Land and buildings must be designed to help. Resources from Whitehall are short, but people's resources are boundless, given the opportunities; which means houses and small spaces to develop.

City government has to learn how to regenerate rather than how to provide a service. It must share the learning with people, not act paternally. The great traditions of local government make this difficult, but it must be done.

Plans for the future should take as their starting point life as well as the economy. Livelier plans could be prepared regardless of convention. There are signs that this is happening and that plans for the late 1980s will again achieve some vision to excite the imagination. This is a challenge for us all.

REFERENCES

Appleyard, D. (ed.) (1979). "The Conservation of European Cities". MIT, Cambridge, Mass.

Baudarin, F. (1979). *In* "The Conservation of European Cities" (D. Appleyard, ed.). MIT, Cambridge, Mass.

Birmingham City Council (1980). "Central Area District Plan, Draft Written Statement, Discussion Document". Birmingham.

Bradford City Council (1980). "City Centre Plan, Draft Policies and Proposals". Bradford.

Buchanan, C. (1958). "Mixed Blessing: the Motor Car in Britain". Leonard Hill, London.

Buchanan, C. (1963). "Traffic in Towns". HMSO, London.

Cameron, G. (ed.). (1980). "The Future of the British Conurbations". Longman, London.

Cresswell, R. (ed.). (1979). "Quality in Urban Planning and Design". Newnes and Butterworth, London.

Glasgow City Council (1979). "Central Area Local Plan, Draft Survey and Issues Report". Glasgow.

Greater London Council (1978). "Covent Garden Action Area Plan". London.

Gregory, T. (1973). *In* "Cities and City Regions in Europe" (J. Holliday, ed.). Report of Conference, Lancester Polytechnic, Coventry.

Holliday, J. (ed.). (1973). "City Centre Redevelopment". Charles Knight, London.

Leeds City Council (1980). "Central Business Area District Plan, Written Statement". Leeds.

Leicester City Council (1980). "Central Leicester District Plan, Written Statement". Leicester.

Lynch, K. (1960). "The Image of the City". MIT, Cambridge, Mass.

Manchester City Council (1980). "Manchester City Centre Local Plan, Report of Survey". Manchester.

Nottingham City Council (1980). "The Central Area, Position Statement". Nottingham.

TWO

Property development in the 1980s

M. LEE

The last ten years were not by any means the easiest times for property investment and development, although they may have been golden for some. The decade started quietly enough, yet soon produced one of the giddiest property booms of recent decades. But trees never reach the sky; the boom was followed by spectacular collapse and a slump in values and investment. By early 1975 values and outlook suggested that the apocalypse had arrived. The last few years of the decade saw a slow return in values and investment activity, but this has drawn much fuel from the persistence of price inflation.

The broad economic history of the decade can be encapsulated simply by a few key indicators. In 1970, the inflation rate was 6·4 per cent; in 1980, it came to 18·4 per cent, after touching 25 per cent in 1974. The pound sterling in 1970 bought only the equivalent of 27p in 1980. Interest rates at the end of 1970 were 7 per cent; at the end of 1980, they were 14 per cent, falling from a record 17 per cent set in autumn of 1979. Unemployment in June 1970 was 2·6 per cent of the workforce or some 600 000 jobless; by mid-1980 the rate had risen to 6·9 per cent or 1 700 000 unemployed. The rate has since increased to 11·1 per cent with 2 700 000 unemployed by mid-1981 (NIESR, 1981).

The inflation and interest rate form the two critical components in any property investment decision. Because of the residue basis of most valuation and appraisal techniques, the impact of either of these factors upon property investment decisions is exceptionally volatile even when a narrow range of expectations is explored. In stable economic circumstances, it does not much matter whether the "real rate" of interest is calculated by reference to the most recently known estimate of price inflation in the past or to expectation in the future during which interest payments are due. But the recent past has produced little stability in the rates of inflation, and much depends for the future upon how developers' expectations may be formed.

There is little cause to expect much improvement in this picture in the immediate future. The current forecasts, from various macro-economic modelling techniques, range widely from the merely pessimistic to the highly gloomy. There is the apocalyptic Cambridge view that:

THE FUTURE FOR THE CITY CENTRE
ISBN 0 12 206240 X

> our national output including oil this year will be no higher than in 1976. Investment has fallen, unemployment has doubled, inflation is still above 10% and for most people the tax burden is much higher. The oil has not merely been wasted, it has been used to destroy our economic base . . . . reflation sufficient to halt the rise in unemployment and enlarge the area of dynamism in industry would lead to a financial deficit on the balance of payments of the order of £10 bn . . . . if the economy will not turn, the government must (CEPG, 1981).

More moderately, the National Institute's outlook sees no

> real signs of an increase over the period to the end of 1982. At the same time unemployment is expected to rise throughout the period to reach 3 million . . . . we also expect the fall in the rate of consumer price inflation to taper away with inflation of some 10·5% in the last quarter of this year and 8·5% by the last quarter of next (NIESR, 1981).

The main variation on this gloomy theme has come from some sections of the Treasury relying on the cyclical model of the economy. The leading indicators since the end of last year suggest a bottoming out of the slump by the summer of 1981, which on cyclical forecasts offers the prospect of an eventual up-turn (*Economic Trends*, 1981).

The outlook for the first few years of the decade and even possibly for some time thereafter must inescapably be highly uncertain. The critical factors, of inflation and interest rates, linked classically to the severe problems of unemployment bear particularly heavily upon property development. The first and certain forecast therefore for property development in the 1980s generally, and for city centres in particular, is that high uncertainty will be constant. With this, there will emerge during the decade the inevitable repetition of boom and slump. This is the machine which will continue to drive development. As always, timing will be crucial.

THE CITY CENTRE

The city centre forms the core of the property development market. It is the major concentration of values and all prime investment opportunities. In this context, the centre is defined as the hard commercial core, the Central Business or the Central Shopping Area. The wider framework of the city centre, touching onto the inner city or twilight area, is not yet seen to be within the main line of commercial development. The two zones meet at the point where the central core expands. Such expansion creates wider conflicts, outside the immediate scope of an appraisal of property development within the central core.

In contrast to the acute picture of uncertainty and difficulty in property investment during the past decade, a reflection on the physical nature of those that were completed looks more encouraging.

Undoubtedly, the extent of development within centres has been substantial. It is immediately apparent from the change that can be observed within major streets such as Victoria Street in London or in the sky line of the City. There has also been the maturation of major new shopping schemes in a number of major city centres, including the Arndale and Market Place, Manchester (with 110 000 m^2 gross shopping space), Eldon Square, Newcastle (70 000 m^2), Bond Street and Trinity Street, Leeds (50 000 m^2), St John's, Liverpool (49 000 m^2), and the Broadmarsh and Victoria centres in Nottingham (93 000 m^2) (Davies and Bennison, 1979).

It is true, however, that much development of major new shopping schemes during the 1970s concentrated upon the lower-order centres in smaller towns and on the peripheries of major cities. The suburban locations, with a growing population, attracted most development. It was not perhaps until the later years of the decade that developers' activities became more precisely focused on the core areas of the major centre.

Despite the dismal economic picture shown in the key economic indicators, there are others which substantiate the success of these developments. For the shopping schemes, from 1970 to 1980, consumer expenditure on clothing grew in volume by 3·0 per cent annually, on furniture by 2·6 per cent and on radio and electrical goods by over 9·0 per cent. Total employment in non-industrial occupations, mainly the services which must include a substantial office employment sector, also grew over the decade by some 14 per cent or about 1·6 million new jobs (NIESR, 1981). The city centre has retained and enhanced its strength. It has acted as an economic redoubt, within the surrounding decline of the industrial and manufacturing activities of the wider urban frame.

In reviewing the prospects for the next ten years, the principal components of commercial development in the city centre, offices, shopping and leisure or social facilities, can be looked at separately.

OFFICES

The office block is the single most characteristic city centre building of the twentieth century. It has, in the first three-quarters of the twentieth century, come to dominate the central area sky lines and functions, and is as typical of the era as the railway station or city halls were characteristic of the last century or perhaps the cathedrals and castles were in medieval times. With the use of sky, rather than ground space, the office block has produced a highly intense concentration of economic activity.

There are the conventional limitations in data for measuring the pace of development in the commercial office sector. Few statistics relate precisely to this special function. The aggregate floor space data that are available cover both public and private uses and include the usually much smaller-scale customer-oriented office uses. The occupational statistics for typical office work cover employees in industrial and other commercial sectors as well as those in office blocks; while the industry sector data refer to far too specialist functions, leaving aside the free standing industrial head office. Yet the common feature of all these series is the strong suggestion of long-term sustained growth, which physically is manifest in the large city-centre office blocks.

The longest specific series of data on the expansion of office floor space come from the United States. In Manhattan CBD, private gross office floor space grew by 2·9 per cent annually between 1900 and 1970, with a faster 3·5 per cent growth from 1960 to 1970. In Dallas, the growth rate from 1950 to 1970 amounted to 6·8 per cent with a slower 3·7 per cent during the 1960s (Armstrong, 1972). These orders of magnitude are similar to the long-term growth rates of indicators for Great Britain, such as the long run increase in clerical occupations over the 50 years from 1920 (Ministry of Labour, 1968 with 1971 data added).

Imposed upon the long-term trend, however, has been a high amplitude cyclical pattern, with office floor space moving over a three to five-year cycle from surplus to shortage in most city centres. The recurrent surplus has often prompted the argument that saturation has been reached, and that future expansion is dubious.

Apart from the deficiency of data on long-term trends, there are also little data for Great Britain on office floor space classified by type of function, showing the division of space between national head office, middle market or local market functions.

The headquarters office exports services from any metropolitan area. The market area is international and national, and the degree of complexity in the office operations is greater than in any other office activity. The operations require highly specialist functions. The economies of scale emphasize concentration within a metropolis for the support that can be obtained in labour, ancillary services and inter-firm communications. The middle market offices cover the regional and sub-regional markets. Their location and concentration tend to reflect most closely regional and sub-regional population distributions. Finally, the local or branch office is typical of the smaller cities and towns where direct customer contact is often critical.

These simple basic features of the office function in city centres will clearly remain significant and important over the next decade shaping the location and pace of new development. Dynamic changes in the economy will vary the relative stress upon different sectors or segments of the market. But these apart, the major question mark over future office development is the impact of the "silicon chip" or whether the micro-electronic revolution will radically or abruptly change the role of the city-centre office. It would be wholly wrong to minimize the probable impact of micro-electronics upon the current state of economic technology.

Its implications are without parallel. First, the development of the silicon chip with further development still in prospect, makes the micro-computer or a micro-electronic control process device, a commonplace machine. It brings the prospect of a virtually unlimited capacity to measure, to memorize, to apply and to store information. There is no reason why any process which can be logically defined should in future require the continuous involvement of any of the work force beyond the stage of definition and construction of a computer-controlled system.

Further, the capital investment for each application of micro-electronics is very small and is diminishing. The product, which is in a sense a brain of incalculable power, is cheap and has the capacity to transform by orders of magnitude the versatility, sophistication, relevance and flexibility of administrative and commercial systems. Concurrent with this transformation, the systems afford scope for delegation in the most remarkable fashion. The skills for operating such systems may in the long term be no more sophisticated or specialist than the ability to use a telephone, tune a television set or play Space Invaders!

Also, because telecommunications of all sorts represent an area where micro-electronics finds a particularly potent and productive application, the new technology will underwrite its own expansion. It affords the prospect of an extremely rapid rate of technological dispersal. Finally, coincident with this, there have been developments in related fields, particularly in fibre optics and laser technology, which further enhance and reinforce the potential applications of micro-electronics (Lloyd, 1981).

The potential for change is clearly enormous. The problem is to forecast the precise nature and range of commercial activity which may result. It is too easy just to consider say the typing pool, the filing room or the clerical section which may well become quite obsolete. The difficulty in forecasting is to judge the form and kind of functions that will replace them.

The popular version anticipates widespread dispersal of commercial activities with greater speculation as to what will occur in the way of domestic or cottage industry offices. Such development is feasible, but should be considered as only one of many possible new forms. It would represent a further example of the persistent trends to dispersion which all city-centre functions have to overcome.

The new technology should undoubtedly simplify much current office work. The change can therefore be classified as a substantial reduction in costs of current conventional office and commercial activity. The effects will therefore be those which usually follow a cost reduction. These include the spread in application of existing systems to wider markets than currently served. The high proportion of households currently without bank accounts, for example, is likely to be substantially reduced and, alongside this, there would be a more general spread of financial services. Further, with the simplification of information handling allied to a significant cost reduction, there will be a progressive willingness to explore more fully and more rigorously any of a variety of problems which now depend upon hunch or judgement. Existing administrative systems themselves would also become capable of controlling the basic material or activities more thoroughly than previously. These developments can help to take the place of those traditional procedures which have been removed by the destructive impact of micro-electronics. They may indeed more than cover the loss. This prospect has been the broad characteristic of most technological change.

But over and above this, the office does not exist merely to handle information. The city centre is primarily a market place; it creates the market wherein exchange takes place. The classical function will persist. High concentration will remain essential to reduce risks in exchange and to achieve the propinquity essential for negotiation. There is no reason to suspect that there should be any change in this process which, at any level both within and between organizations, demands personal contact.

Therefore, for the future, the forecast is for change but not for decline. The scope for increased specialization is enhanced by the new technology. There remains the prospect for continued expansion of the office function in city centres.

The hierarchy of office centres in Great Britain is more sharply pointed than with many other city-centre functions. London, for example, dominates far more heavily in office floor space than it does for shopping. The main interest for the next decade is to consider how this hierarchy may change, and whether growth will continue to be highly centralized or whether relative growth could be faster for second-order cities.

The new technology offers far more scope and far greater opportunity for delegation and dispersal of conventional office functions than exists at present. Yet the determinant factor in the extent of relative growth in office space between the capital and the second-order cities is likely to be shaped by the general tendency in the economic system regarding the mix between centralized or command economics and decentralized or market economics. The former would emphasize heavy concentration within London, and the latter would favour the provincial cities. The economic tendency for the past century has favoured centralization; it is only with the re-birth of the attitude known sweepingly as monetarism, that decentralized market-orientated development has now become a major economic objective.

Perhaps, therefore, among the more interesting aspects of office development in the next decade, may be the evidence which it might afford of any change in the growth prospects of different sizes of city centres wrought by the new approach to economic management.

Also, the new technology brings with it a change in levels of skill requirements. The implications are great for the composition and the commuting draw of the city-centre workforce. With the spread of micro-electronics systems, the centre may recruit from its immediate residential surrounds, from the older inner city zones, rather than rely, as it has for the past century, upon the outer suburbs and dormitory areas.

SHOPPING

The role of the city centre as a market place is most evident in its shopping facilities. In this respect, the central shopping area has traditionally been distinguished from the surrounding suburbs by a concentration upon durable goods rather than convenience or food shopping.

The major change in shopping during the past decade has been the establishment of large-scale hypermarkets or superstores within district shopping centres or on free-standing "edge-of-town" sites. The rate of growth in this form of retailing and its concentration within existing suburban shopping centres has been largely determined by planning constraint. Within retail planning, the past few years have been dominated by conflict over the optimum form or location of such large new stores.

Initially, there was widespread concern that such developments would undermine the strength of the established city centre and suburban shopping hierarchy. The arguments stemmed more from planning orthodoxy, particularly regarding the dangers inherent in dispersal of urban functions, than from any detailed evaluation of hypermarkets or superstores as retailing facilities or developments in their own right.

The policies espoused in structure plans have, virtually without exception, resisted free-standing developments in principle or where possible guided their location into established centres. New free-standing developments have, with few exceptions, been carried out only after the delays and costs of planning enquiries (Lee and Kent, 1978).

Much of the dispute, so far as it might bear heavily upon shopping in the city centre, has been ill-founded. The hypermarket or superstore is concerned principally with food or convenience shopping; it does not conflict with the prime durable-goods or comparison-goods shopping function of the city centre. The conflict is manifest only in the manner in which a large-scale hypermarket or superstore might draw its trade; they draw sub-regionally, much in the way a city centre may draw. The trade attracted, however, is not that characteristic of the city centre, but comprises in the main large-scale bulk food purchasing. The prime conflict in the possible diversion of trade has been with the smaller district or suburban centres and not with the major city-centre shopping areas (Lee and Kent, 1979).

Therefore the city centre has not been challenged severely by recent trends in retailing or new forms of shopping development. The exception was the possibility which emerged briefly during the early 1970s of establishing new free standing sub-regional durable-goods centres. Several projects were fought to inquiry around Manchester, Nottingham, Oxford and Birmingham. Each of these proposals were in the event rejected by the Secretary of State, generally on the grounds of land-use objections which were not overridden by the force of need.

The sole successful project for a new free-standing major durable-goods shopping centre was the Brent Cross centre in north-west London. The centre opened for trading in 1976, some 12 years after the initial planning application was submitted and exploration into its potential impact was made. Yet, despite the high degree of success that Brent Cross has enjoyed, there is no evidence of adverse impact upon the established suburban shopping hierarchy and certainly not upon the West End or central shopping facilities in London (Downey, 1980).

The reasons behind this result provide pointers to the likely trend for major city shopping centres over the next decade. Two reasons appear to be responsible for the success of Brent Cross and the ability of the established city centres to sustain shifts of trade or to house substantial new developments in the face of growing competition from smaller centres within the hinterland. The first is the overall heavy volume of shopping generated by city residents, while the other is the increase in durable-goods spending per person (Bennison and Davies, 1980).

The city centre involves a heavy concentration of durable-goods spending drawn from a wide hinterland. This draw is regional or sub-regional. The hinterland population served is substantial. With shifts of population in cities and general dispersal to the suburbs and dormitory towns, the central shopping area has tended to retain and indeed increase its overall population support. Unlike inner city shopping centres, the commercial core has not suffered generally from a depletion of trade; it has rather extended its territorial sphere of influence within which there has actually been population gain. Its close-in shopping centre competitors, in contrast, have suffered a population loss within their traditional hinterlands, and consequently have exhibited signs of decay.

Given the extended hinterlands of the city centres, their retail sales volumes have been maintained by a moderate proportion of draw from the total volume of sales generated by the population served. Although there have been significant shopping developments in the suburbs or small town centres in the sub-region, which might be important within any city centre's immediate trade area, these developments have not had a serious debilitating effect on trade.

The losses from shifts to outlying new centres have also generally been more than offset by increased volumes of retail spending per person of the hinterland population. Growth in disposable income has been concentrated in higher volumes of retail spending in durable goods rather than on convenience goods. Within this broad sector there has been a heavier emphasis upon the higher quality or comparison element in durable-goods spending. This is precisely the type of retail spending that tends to be drawn to major rather than second-order shopping centres.

It is true that the general pattern, with population dispersal and improved local shopping facilities, is for the outlying centres to grow faster than the city centre. But given the initial far greater volume of sales to be found in the city centre, even a slow growth here represents a substantial increase in retail sales volumes upon which substantial new developments may be based.

The future of shopping in city centres therefore depends largely on trends in durable-goods spending. This in turn is a function of the level and rate of economic growth. Because of the wide extent of a city centre's trade area, it is well positioned to take advantage of any improvement in the economic situation. It requires only small shifts in the levels of potential drawn against the power of local centres to create a volume of retail sales which can justify significant new development.

The opportunities for individual cities vary. Unlike office development, where the cities are to some extent competing for the same function, the shopping centre relates more closely to the individual sub-region. The prosperity of the sub-region shapes individual city prospects.

LEISURE AND SOCIAL FUNCTIONS

The broad range of leisure and social functions established by the private sector goes far to shaping the popular image of a city centre. It plays a significant role, too, in shaping the hierarchy of centres. In measuring relative strengths, much depends upon the weight attached to any particular facility or function. As a general impression, the hierarchy is again sharply pointed, with London overwhelmingly dominant. The relative strengths and precise rank in the hierarchy of Glasgow, Birmingham, Manchester, Leeds, Liverpool or Newcastle are not easy to judge. Also, again impressionistically, there would appear to have been a tendency during the past ten years for the second-order centres to improve their complement of facilities and perhaps for changes to have occurred in their relative rank position.

This sector of development has not traditionally attracted heavy investment from commercial property developers. The buildings are highly specific in form without scope for flexible use. Also, the level of profits is highly dependent upon the quality of the operator and his ability to attract the public. In the past, much of the investment in leisure and social facilities in the city centre has come from the operator developer, rather than from the conventional development company.

The risks are high, and the sector represents perhaps the most volatile use within the city centre. Fashions change as witnessed by the history of support for theatres and musical halls, cinemas, bowling alleys, leisure complexes to discos and now the roller skate disco. No doubt this volatility in tastes and fashions will continue during the next decade.

There is, however, one trend, which grew in strength during the past decade, that has great significance for the relationship between investment and the environmental quality of city centres. This is represented by the conservation movement, or what has been called, more cheerfully, the "history industry".

The source of this trend or widespread change in attitude is not easy to fathom. There is most certainly a strong element of disillusionment with the achievements and social implications of much of the development produced by the last 30 years of formal planning. There may be a more philosophical base, shaping an appreciation of the individual within the context of his environment, which stems from the holistic view. There might also be a failure of nerve within the populace or a sense of impending doom for modern urban society. The prospect of the nuclear holocaust provides the rational base for this fear; the imminence of death recalls the past.

Whatever the source, the conservation movement is among the most important for shaping the pattern of development. The need to enhance and to conserve the best of the inherited environment is commonly accepted by virtually all engaged in planning and development for major city centres. Undoubtedly, the interests of development and conservation create severe conflicts with the majority of major redevelopment schemes.

But the more encouraging feature is the growing interest in re-cycling old buildings and areas, renewing their physical environment and changing their functions. The classic, and the forerunner of many others, has been the GLC renewal of Covent Garden Market. The success of this scheme is virtually self-evident. It operates firstly as a "speciality shopping centre", and in this role attracts a volume of shoppers in relation to size far higher than major city-centre developments. This in turn is reflected in values and returns so that the whole renewal project represents a most attractive investment. But beyond this, the Market attracts many people simply just as a place to be (Donaldsons, 1980). It has become within a few months of opening a focal point for London, complementing such historical locales as Trafalgar Square or Leicester Square. The Covent Garden Market now provides a strong sense of theatre for its visitors, which enhances the experiences of a visit to this part of London.

CONCLUSION

Interest in property development acts as a barometer of the expectations in national economic trends in the city centre as much as elsewhere. During the 1980s there seems no reason why the three- or four-year cycle in property investment should not continue despite the lower profile of "stop-go" in national economic management, but such medium-term fluctuations are likely to be set within the context of a generally lower level of new construction compared with the previous two decades. This reduction in activity is partly a reaction to the previous intensity of new building and redevelopment coming both from the industry itself and from the conservation lobby, but is also rooted in the lower average rate of economic growth expected for the 1980s.

The significance of general economic trends varies between the main sectors. Shopping development is particularly sensitive to changes in disposable incomes, though the emphasis of the city centre on durable goods and the accessibility of city centres to wide catchment areas will help to bolster up the retailing element there. The office development sector is less predictable for individual city centres because swings in the nature of central government economic management affect not only the overall level of investment but also its distribution between the capital and provincial cities. Moreover, in this context are the unknowns attached to the implications of new telecommunications and information-processing innovations.

The greatest uncertainties, however, relate to the leisure and social sector because of the fickleness of its fashions and fads. Essentially because of this, the property development industry has not been so concerned with this sector, but the lessons of Covent Garden have been learnt rapidly by the investment community. The development or improvement of similar areas may prove to be the most interesting and attractive trend to be seen in city centres over the next ten years.

REFERENCES

Armstrong, R. (1972). "The Office Industry". Regional Plan Association, MIT Press, Cambridge, Mass.

Bennison, D. and Davies, R. (1980). *Progress in Planning* **14**, 1-104.

CEPG (1981). "Economic Policy in the UK". Gower, Aldershot.

Davies, R. and Bennison, D. (1979). "British Town Centre Shopping Schemes". Unit for Retail Planning Information Ltd, Reading.

Donaldsons (1980). "Covent Garden Market Survey". Donaldsons, London.

Downey, P. (1980). "The Impact of Brent Cross". GLC, London.

Economic Trends (1981). February 1981, p.68. HMSO, London.

Lee, M. and Kent, E. (1978). "Planning Inquiry Study Two". Donaldsons, London.

Lee, M. and Kent, E. (1979). "Caerphilly Hypermarket Study Year Five", Donaldsons, London.

Lloyd, I. (1981). *Personal Computer World* **4.4**, 110.

Ministry of Labour (1968). "Growth of Office Employment". HMSO, London.

NIESR (1981). *Economic Review* **96**.

THREE

Land-use structure, built-form and agents of change

J. W. R. WHITEHAND

City centres tend to undergo more rapid physical change than most parts of urban areas but, nevertheless, they change slowly by the standard of the individual human life-span. Major changes to city centres involving the construction of new streets and buildings represent enormous investments of capital and generally require a long life in order to be economically viable. This has a pronounced stabilizing effect on the townscape that enables us to forecast with some confidence the main physical characteristics of most city centres some decades in the future. These characteristics for the most part already exist. They comprise a cumulative record, albeit an imperfect one, of the processes that have been at work over past decades and often centuries. It is apparent, however, that though many of these processes are likely to continue, by definition we cannot forecast the discoveries that underlie so many of the innovations that characterize the development of a society and directly or indirectly affect its townscapes. Thus an element of speculation inevitably enters into any consideration of even the near future.

In spite of this, the considerable research that has been undertaken in recent years on the processes and agents affecting the townscape has yielded generalizations that are relevant to a variety of city-centre conditions and many of them provide us with valuable bases upon which to view the future. This research also identifies the importance of certain enduring attributes of the city-centre townscape that may well provide a basis for making the major intellectual leap from monitoring developments and identifying those that are likely to continue into the future to formulating principles for managing change and suggesting possible procedures for their implementation. Our approach will therefore be to summarize the main sorts of morphological changes, both secular and cyclical, going on in city centres, mainly within Britain, to consider the main agents responsible for these changes, and to assess the probability of their continuance in the short- and medium-term. At the end of the chapter some ideas about managing townscape change in city centres will be discussed briefly.

THE FUTURE FOR THE CITY CENTRE
ISBN 0 12 206240 X

DIFFERENTIAL RATES OF CHANGE AMONG TOWNSCAPE ELEMENTS

For quite fundamental reasons that are unlikely to change in the foreseeable future the different elements that make up the townscape of the city centre change at different speeds. This is partly related to the time-lag between changes in function and those in form that is a general characteristic of the cultural landscape. It is particularly manifest in the occupation of buildings by land uses for which they were not designed. More generally, however, a spectrum of susceptibility to change can be recognized, with structures entailing a large capital investment, such as street systems, changing rarely and those involving a relatively small capital investment, such as shopfronts, undergoing quite frequent changes. Seldom are any of these changes the result of physical decay. Their root cause is the endless succession of changes in society generally and in local circumstances in particular.

If we take a long-term view it is possible to recognize certain recurrent features in the speed of change of different types of forms that have remained in evidence in spite of major changes in the functioning of society. The rarity of changes to the street system is apparent from a comparison of successive editions of Ordnance Survey plans. Even in exceptionally radical reshapings of central areas, such as took place in Newcastle upon Tyne in the mid-nineteenth century (Wilkes and Dodds, 1964), or in Birmingham in the 1950s and 1960s (Sutcliffe and Smith, 1974, pp.399-411), or indeed, if we extend our field of view beyond Britain, in cities whose centres were almost razed to the ground by bombing (Blacksell, 1968), the large majority of street lines have remained unaltered. The building fabric is on average less resistant to replacement, although in Europe, where building life-spans well in excess of 100 years are quite normal (Whitehand, 1978, p.84; Holden and Holford, 1951, p.173; Buissink and de Widt, 1967, pp.245-246), buildings would seem to survive longer than in the United States (Hoyt, 1933, p.335). Alterations to the existing fabric, as distinct from complete replacements, are comparatively frequent. Extensions to buildings and façade changes are both more numerous than complete building replacements and, if all alterations to buildings are combined, building replacements are numerically insignificant by comparison (Buissink and de Widt, 1967, pp.243-244; Sim, 1977, fig. 4.2), although individually their cost and impact on the townscape is usually substantially greater.

Changes of building user and, in parts of the city centre, changes of use occur more frequently than building replacements. Most buildings are occupied by several users during the course of their lives, and the arrival of a new occupier increases the likelihood of physical change to the premises. Most building replacements are associated with a change of site user. It seems likely that office users occupying the smallest amounts of space are more mobile than average (Cowan *et al.*, 1969, p.95) and that there is variability in the mobility of retailers according to the types of goods sold (Dorey, 1981). However, since mobility appears to be inversely related to the scale of operations, the changes to the townscape that these movements engender are not commensurate with their numbers. But where a building passes from one use to another the probability of a substantial change to the building fabric, especially internally, is inevitably high.

Most of these generalizations about the incidence of different types of changes are based on observations covering long periods. For a proper understanding of the mechanisms underlying these regularities, however, it is necessary to consider the social and economic forces that are at work. When we do this it becomes apparent that the superficially rather simple regularities that we have recognized in the townscape are the product of a complex web of functional relationships that is constantly changing. Many of the changes so far referred to are caused by changes in the sizes of business and/or changes in the amounts of space required for different types of land use, which are in turn related to national economic changes and rises or falls in the population catchments of individual city centres. Shifts in the relative abilities of different categories of land use to compete for specific sites may result, for example, from an expansion or contraction of city-centre functions as a whole or from a general change in demand for a particular use, as in the case of the declining demand for cinemas and churches. Some of the forces at work are social as much as economic, the long-term trend for residential premises in upper floors to become vacant being a case in point (Institute of Advanced Architectual Studies, 1978). A major change, and one that is fundamental to the whole structure of the economy in the case of Britain, is the gradual shift in emphasis from manufacturing to services and the associated shift towards a demand for offices rather than factories, workshops or warehouses (Cameron and Evans, 1973).

Viewed in this way land-use structure and built-form appear as the outcome of social and economic changes. But changes in built-form in turn have major ramifications for the way in which activities are distributed. For example, an effect of recent comprehensive redevelopments has been to aggravate the tendency for certain specialized activities to be displaced from central sites by comparatively unspecialized shops whose high turnover enables them to afford the high rents of the new premises (Allpass and Agergaard, 1979, pp.255–256).

AGENTS OF CHANGE

Although the purpose for which structures are used may be viewed as a prime determinant of built-form, which in turn affects land-use structure, this circle of causation is over-simplified. In particular if we are going to extend our time perspective into the future and, indeed, go so far as to suggest how change should be managed, we must consider the many agents that are responsible for the process of change or at least intervene in it. Not only is the link between user and built-form complicated by the frequently dynamic nature of one compared with the static character of the other, but even at the time of construction the influence of the user may be indirect or non-existent. The prime interests at work are often those of developers and investors. The tradition of erecting new structures on speculation goes far back into history and its incidence in British city centres has tended to increase in recent decades, at least by comparison with the first half of this century. In his study of nine town and city centres in West Yorkshire between 1945 and 1968, Bateman (1971, p.26) revealed that the median proportion of private-sector redevelopment (by total floor space) that was speculative was two-thirds. In the case of office development in the City of London, Barras (1979b, pp.50-53) found that a similar proportion of schemes with over 10 000 m^2 of gross floor space were speculative during the 1970s: this compared with about one-half in the 1950s and 1960s, although by the end of the 1970s users were again tending to increase their share of development. How far these figures for West Yorkshire and the City of London may be taken as representative of British town and city centres is not clear. Information on the number of private-sector redevelopments (including major reconstructions) in the central area of Newcastle under Lyme suggests a rise in the speculative proportion from one-quarter in the period 1955-1964 to one-third in the period 1965-1974 (Ross, 1979).

Speculative redevelopment tends to be dominated by a handful of companies operating on a national scale. It is a reasonable inference that six development companies accounted for well over one-half of the major shopping schemes (those with over 4645 m^2 of gross floor space)—the large majority in town and city centres—undertaken in Britain between 1965 and 1978 (Hillier Parker Research, 1979, p.33), and Barras (1979b, p.55, App.2) has shown that six development companies accounted for about one-half of the major office redevelopments (those with over 10 000 m^2 of gross floor space) in the City of London between 1959 and 1979. The predominance of national firms in redevelopment generally was already apparent in the study of West Yorkshire town and city centres by Bateman (1971), in which he revealed that the median proportion of private-sector redevelopment (by total floor space) undertaken by national firms was two-thirds.

There would seem to be few central areas in which the public sector has undertaken more than a small share of redevelopment (Bateman, 1971; Ross, 1979). As far as shopping schemes are concerned, the two largest development companies (Town and City Properties and Ravenseft) between 1965 and 1978 were each responsible for nearly twice the number of major schemes (those with over 4645 m^2 of gross floor space) as all the local authorities together (Hillier Parker Research, 1979, p.33), although it should be noted that in this count joint ventures between a local authority and a developer were recorded under the name of the developer. In the large majority of cases local authorities lack staff with the requisite skills (Department of the Environment, 1975, pp.43-45) and, given the present government policy towards local authority expenditure, it seems unlikely that this position will change significantly in the near future.

Redevelopments for owner-occupation are, like speculative redevelopments, being undertaken predominantly by national firms. In central Liverpool in the 1970s major national stores dominated retail redevelopment outside the one major shopping scheme (City of Liverpool, 1980, p.16), and in the town centres of Newcastle under Lyme (Ross, 1979) and Watford (Whitehand, in preparation) redevelopments for owner-occupation are also largely by national firms. The domination of redevelopment in traditional city-centre shopping streets by a dozen or so major chain-stores is a familiar feature, and when it is coupled with the fact that a high proportion of speculative redevelopments are being carried out by a small number of companies, it is apparent that the bulk of city-centre redevelopment in Britain is being undertaken by just a few dozen organizations. Because there is a continuing tendency for mergers and take-overs to occur among property companies and chain-stores, it seems unlikely that development activity will become less concentrated in its organization in the 1980s.

The interests in city-centre property are more complex, however, than such a simple numerical account of developers might suggest. Allowance must be made for the part played by other interests, notably those of land- and property-owners and financial concerns. Information on land ownership is difficult to assemble for England and Wales. The amounts of land owned by local authorities vary widely from total ownership in central Huddersfield—although here the existence of long leases seriously limits the scope for the local authority to exercise a major influence on the townscape in the near future (Bateman, 1971, pp.34-35)—to cases in which local authority ownership is largely confined to the sites of certain public buildings. Intermediate positions such as in Birmingham, where approximately one-third of the central area is owned by the local authority (City of Birmingham, 1980, Plan 3.5), are probably more normal. On the whole, however, the direct involvement of local authorities in city-centre redevelopment has not been in proportion to their ownership of land in these areas. For example, in the City of London, the Corporation owned at least part of the site of about one-third of the office redevelopments with over 10 000 m^2 of gross floor space that took place between 1959 and 1979 but was involved in redevelopment itself in only one case (Barras, 1979b, p.61).

Determining land ownership among private owners is particularly difficult but it is evident that city-centre land is becoming increasingly concentrated in the hands of major national concerns. Financial companies now constitute the largest single category of landowner in the City of London, judged by the number of sites they owned among those that were developed between 1959 and 1979 (Barras, 1979b, pp.107-113). The increasing proportion of buildings (as distinct from land) owned by major national concerns is revealed by an examination of the owners specified in applications to undertake redevelopments or other major changes to the building fabric. Data for the town centres of Boston, Lincolnshire (Pain, 1980, p.32), Newcastle under Lyme (Ross, 1979) and Watford (Whitehand, in preparation) all show a marked rise in the proportion of non-local owners in the 1950s and 1960s, although there would appear to have been comparatively little further change in the 1970s.

The main recent trend has been the increasing ownership of property by insurance companies and pension funds (Ambrose and Colenutt, 1975, p.52; Barras, 1979a, p.43). For example, between 1964 and 1979 insurance companies increased the proportion of their holdings that were in land, property and ground rents from less than one-tenth to over one-fifth (Central Statistical Office, 1964-1981), most of their property holdings being freeholds in city centres (Department of the Environment, 1975, p.23; Massey and Catalano, 1978, p.114). In the City of London, financial institutions are increasingly dominating the ownership of office redevelopments either by undertaking redevelopments themselves or by purchasing sites and completed properties from development companies (Barras, 1979a, p.34), the Co-operative, Norwich Union, Pearl, Prudential and Standard Life being among the insurance companies known to be active (Barras, 1979b, p.73). On a national scale, between 1965 and 1978 the Norwich Union acted as a developer in ten shopping schemes of over 4645 m^2 of gross floor space, almost all in small- or medium-sized town centres (Hillier Parker Research, 1979, pp.3-32). By 1978 financial institutions owned about one-third of the equity of Town and City Properties and Hammerson (Barras, 1979b, p.74), two of the three main developers of shopping schemes (Hillier Parker Research, 1979, p.23). Overall their importance has increased relative to that of the property companies, whose role seems to be increasingly one of acting as the development agents of insurance companies and pension funds, at least as far as major schemes on prime sites are concerned (Barras, 1979a, pp.37-38). Thus the growth in the funds of insurance companies and pension schemes and the consistently better returns from property than from other investments over the past two decades (Department of the Environment, 1975, p.23; Economic Intelligence Unit Ltd, 1977, p.7) have been major factors underlying the scale of city-centre redevelopment. If these funds grow further during the 1980s, as seems probable, then in the absence of significant industrial growth it is a reasonable assumption that they will continue to be channelled into commercial property.

While the interests that owners, users, investors and, to some extent, developers have in property tend to be long term, there are other agents responsible for change in the townscape whose interests tend to be primarily confined to the changes themselves. The most important of these are architects, shopfitters, construction companies and consulting engineers. It would seem from the studies of Watford and Boston that the architects submitting plans for town-centre changes were increasingly from outside the towns concerned during the period from the 1920s to the 1950s, levelling off since then at just under one-half from outside the town in the case of all plans (except minor alterations) in Boston (Pain, 1980, p.21) and at about four-fifths in the case of additions to floor space and structural alterations in Watford (Whitehand, in preparation). Judging from these two town centres, shopfitters appear to have operated on a non-local scale ever since they developed as a major separate trade in the 1920s. In the case of building contracting, the data for Watford town centre (additions to floor space and structural alterations only) reveal a marked increase in the proportion of builders from outside the town, which has been more pronounced in the post-war period than the comparable trend in the case of architects and building owners and is still continuing at the present time. Consulting engineers undertaking work in the town centre have been almost entirely from outside the town since they began to take a prominent part in the construction process in the 1950s. At the top of the urban hierarchy, in the City of

London, construction work became increasingly concentrated in the 1970s in five companies—Trollope and Colls, Higgs and Hill, Wimpey, Laing, and McAlpine (Barras, 1979b, p.66). But as far as the development process is concerned the role of the construction companies has diminished, at least by comparison with the 1950s and 1960s. By the 1970s they had been replaced by financial institutions, with their growing demand for property as an investment, as the main partners of property companies (Barras, 1979b, pp.51-53).

Going on at the same time as these changes in private enterprise have been changes in central government and local authorities. The nature of the cause and effect relation between "planning" and private enterprise is difficult to disentangle. There is little doubt that one of the effects of the Town and Country Planning Acts has been to add further to the scale of the already large changes stemming from the increasing size of the organizations interested in property: the combining of changes to the road system with redevelopment has certainly been facilitated. Nevertheless, the impression, though difficult to quantify, is of planners responding to the agents and processes already considered rather than acting as a positive force (Department of the Environment, 1975, p.40). Formal comprehensive plans for city centres have tended to be slow to emerge and in many cases they are largely a recognition of existing patterns and trends. Despite its major central redevelopment schemes, Birmingham has never had a formal comprehensive plan for its central area (City of Birmingham, 1980, p.1), and much the same is true of Glasgow, where redevelopments in the commercial core have been on a comparatively minor scale. There would still seem to be substance in the view of Ambrose and Colenutt (1975, pp.178-179) that land-use planning is largely treated as a matter of designating areas in terms of land-use categories essentially to accommodate observed trends in population and employment. Whether Barras (1979b, p.95) exaggerates when he suggests that the main effects of central and local government planning policy on office development in the City of London are to reinforce underlying market trends is not readily resolved. The high proportion of new shopping centres being located in existing town and city centres would certainly seem to be attributable in part to local and central government planning policies, although as with other redevelopments the concern of developers and chain-stores to protect their existing property interests in town and city centres is almost certainly a factor (Bennison and Davies, 1980, p.23). Clearly there is the scope for a more positive role by local authorities where they own the freehold of large parts of city centres (Department of the Environment, 1975, p.37), although it is most improbable that there will be a sizeable increase in the amount of redevelopment undertaken directly by local authorities while central government restraints on their expenditure continue.

THE AMOUNT AND CHARACTER OF SECULAR CHANGE

Taken together, the various changes in the agents responsible for change during the post-war period are bringing about major changes in the land-use structure and built-form of British city centres. Changes in the scale of operations and in economic and social objectives are reflected in the townscape. In gross terms the main land-use change in the post-war period is the growth in floor space devoted to offices, especially professional and scientific services, insurance, banking and finance, and public administration (Ambrose and Colenutt, 1975, p.21; Barras, 1979b, pp.7–18), reflecting an increase in both office employment and the amount of space per office worker. In contrast, declines in floor space in industry and wholesaling, already evident at least 20 years ago (Alexander, 1974b, p.139), appear to be continuing, in the latter case reflecting in part a decreasing dependence of retail establishments on separate centrally-located wholesaling facilities (Davies, 1976, p.158), and in both cases reflecting the increased demand for central office space (Cameron and Evans, 1973). Retailing occupies an intermediate position, with many city centres undergoing moderate increases in floor space but some experiencing declines. The West Midlands County Structure Plan reveals the extent of the variability between major centres within a single region (West Midlands County Council, 1980, p.108). At the national scale, the great variation between city centres in the extent of their changes in retail turnover (City of Liverpool, 1980, p.5) suggests that a pattern of considerable variation in changes in their amounts of retail floor space is likely to continue.

These changes in the admixture of city-centre land use are being accommodated by a variety of forms of building adaptation and redevelopment. In the case of offices the main increases of floor space are resulting from the construction of new, large and generally free-standing office blocks, particularly on sites formerly occupied by lower-density offices or by warehouses, industrial establishments and transport installations. In the City of London this is further accentuating the domination by offices, which by 1978 comprised three-quarters of the City's floor space, and is restoring floor-space concentrations to their pre-war levels (Barras, 1979b, p.14). Indeed in the City of London and in Manchester the limited scope for further major office redevelopments in the core office area is forcing new schemes farther out into the zone around the core which is largely occupied by warehouses and small factories (Barras, 1979b, p.34; Catalano and Barras, 1980, p.72). This is happening in spite of a slackening in the demand for office space by users, and largely reflects the growing demand by financial institutions for office property in city centres as an investment, the limited number of sites in such areas ensuring the growth of rents and the increased value of existing investments (Barras, 1979b, p.95). Thus it would seem that the investment policies of the financial institutions are having a major effect on the scale and location of new office building—probably more so than the demands of building users. One of the effects on users, particularly in the City of London, is to reduce the number of small units of accommodation that are available, thereby further increasing the rents of small businesses and displacing them from central sites (Barras, 1979b, p.31).

In the case of retailing the major variety chain-stores have continued to undertake their own redevelopments of key sites. But the main additions to floor space during the last decade have resulted from shopping schemes intended for more than one, usually many, tenants. Bennison and Davies (1980, p.98) have put forward reasons for doubting whether this boom in the creation of shopping centres will extend beyond the mid-1980s but its impact on the townscape is already considerable and by no means confined to the sites that the schemes occupy. Although retailing is the most common single former use of the sites that have been developed in this way, considerable amounts of land formerly in other uses are incorporated (Davies and Bennison, 1979, p.228). Furthermore, on average less than 8 per cent of all tenants of town-centre shopping schemes formerly traded on the site (Davies and Bennison, 1979, p.230) and the character of the new retail uses differs considerably from that of those displaced. Many specialized retailers, such as antiquarian bookshops, stamp dealers, antique shops, art dealers and musical instrument shops, that are able to afford the rents in old property are unable to meet the high rents that generally obtain after redevelopment (Allpass and Agergaard, 1979, pp.255-257). The same is true of craft and specialist services (Amos, 1973, p.190; Galley, 1973, p.219), and it has been estimated that about half of the industrial firms whose sites are taken over for such schemes close down (Amos, 1973, p.190). The tenants replacing them tend to comprise a much higher proportion of shops selling high-turnover goods of a type available in large suburban centres, leading to the suburbanization of city centres discussed by Allpass and Agergaard (1979). Thus the variety of goods and services available is being reduced (Davies, 1976, p.291), small traders are being displaced and the socio-cultural role of the city centre is diminishing (Davies and Bennison, 1978, p.118; Allpass and Agergaard, 1979). A further problem is the integration of shopping schemes into the townscape, because they have a tendency to be inward looking, sometimes presenting a blank face to the established streets on to which they have a frontage. They are also tending to attract retailers away from existing streets, some of which are suffering as shopping streets from an excessive influx of "service trades", such as employment agencies, travel agents, betting offices, estate agents and building societies, which may have the effect of isolating parts of streets from the main pedestrian flows (Davies and Bennison, 1978, p.119). The new shopping schemes are also highlighting the existing problems of traditional shopping streets, notably their frequently great length—in contrast to the compactness of most shopping schemes—exposure to weather and traffic, and difficulties of service access (Davies, 1976, p.185).

The new shopping schemes, even more than the new office blocks, are bringing major land-use change and physical renewal. But going on simultaneously is a great deal of other change that is more widely spread over the city centre. Some of this involves the small-scale replacement of individual buildings or small groups of buildings, but a great deal consists of the much more numerous other types of change that the building fabric undergoes, notably change of use, façade changes, and the extension of existing buildings.

As far as building replacement is concerned, surprisingly few attempts have been made to assess the life-spans of city-centre buildings and the speed with which buildings of different types and ages are being replaced. Tables of building depreciation such as those of the United States Department of the Treasury (Cowan, 1963, pp.69-70) are a far from satisfactory guide because of the great variations that occur over time and space. For example, buildings over 150 years old still survive in sizable numbers in the city centre of Glasgow, with only a small minority of sites having undergone as many as three redevelopments since their initial development in the late-eighteenth and early-nineteenth centuries (Whitehand, 1978, pp.84-85). In contrast, Hoyt (1933, p.335) estimated that in the central business district of Chicago, much of which was initially developed at about the same time as central Glasgow, few sites had not been occupied by at least three different buildings and one exceptional site had undergone five redevelopments. It is evident that age alone is a poor indicator of the likelihood of building replacement (Bourne, 1967, p.143). Although the replacement of new buildings is rare, relatively new buildings in one part of the city centre may be more susceptible to replacement than old buildings elsewhere. The probable effect for the city centre as a whole is a rise and then a fall in the death rates of buildings of particular ages, the death rates of old buildings tending to fall eventually below those of younger buildings because they are on average on sites less susceptible to redevelopment, notably outside the prime shopping and office areas (Whitehand, 1978, pp.90-91). This tendency is being increased by a policy of seeking to conserve old buildings and is complicated in various ways; for example, by variations in existing floor-space concentrations and therefore in the extent to which extra floor space can be created by redevelopment within the constraints of plot-ratio controls. Victorian office buildings, representing much of the finest surviving commercial architecture, are especially vulnerable (Sim, 1977, pp.170-171, 183, fig. 7.1; Whitehand, 1978, pp.90-91), particularly because of their comparatively low floor-space concentrations, although the size of the accommodation they offer may be appropriate for many small firms. Conservation policies constitute an amelioration of this problem but not yet a solution.

The role of individually minor, but in aggregate important, changes to the fabric of buildings has been even less studied than complete building replacement. Buissink and de Widt (1967, p.246) in their study of central Utrecht over the period 1910-1961 found that buildings in shopping streets were consistently and markedly more prone to frontal alterations than buildings in other streets, a similar result later emerging from Sim's study of façade changes in central Glasgow between 1950 and 1969 (Sim, 1977, p.48). Within the shopping streets they also found that buildings in the most central streets were consistently more prone to frontal alterations than buildings in more peripheral streets, a finding with which both Sim in Glasgow and Alexander (1974b, p.152) in Perth, Australia subsequently concurred. Buissink and de Widt also found that buildings in shopping streets had consistently more internal alterations than those in other streets, although in this case the difference was comparatively small. Differences between streets in the rate of frontal alterations seem bound to persist in the foreseeable future, related as they are to the more intimate connection in retailing than in any other city-centre function between the attraction of trade and the external appearances of buildings.

Such spatial patterns of change may well have their parallels in the distribution patterns of the activities of the various agents of change. There is more than a suggestion in the case of the Boston central area that the works of local architects are on average located less centrally than the works of architects from outside the Boston area (Pain, 1980, pp.59-67) and that this is associated with a more peripheral distribution of locally-owned buildings, although this subject awaits a full investigation for town and city centres of varying types and sizes.

With all these variables probable differences between the central areas of different towns and cities must be borne in mind. Bateman's research revealed a number of inter-urban variations within West Yorkshire alone; for example, he discovered wide variations in the proportions of redevelopment for different uses (Bateman, 1971, p.12). It is probable that many of the other characteristics that we have observed, but for which data for more than one or two cities are lacking, are also subject to considerable variability.

FLUCTUATIONS

The temporal trends and spatial patterns that have been referred to, some of them with a history extending over the post-war period and sometimes much longer, must not obscure the fact that many types of changes in city centres are, and will continue to be, very uneven over time. This is inevitable given the long life of physical structures. Some fluctuations are very long-term. For example, it was commonplace for British city centres to undergo major redevelopments associated with major road building, and occasionally railway construction, in the nineteenth-century—Birmingham and Newcastle upon Tyne are examples—but not to undergo further major redevelopments on this scale until well into the post-war period. It would not be surprising if cities such as Birmingham that have been subject to major redevelopment schemes in their commercial cores in recent years underwent no further changes of this type until well into the twenty-first century. Even where the replacement of physical structures throughout Victorian and modern times has been overwhelmingly piecemeal, as in the commercial core of Glasgow, there have still been major long-term fluctuations in its incidence (Whitehand, 1978, pp.86-87).

Superimposed on these long swings have been marked short-term fluctuations which, despite inter-city and regional variations, are evident in national aggregate figures for commercial building. Thus the value (at constant prices) of new orders obtained for commercial construction in Britain reached a peak in 1964, fell to less than two-thirds this figure by 1967, rose to another peak in 1971, fell to little more than half this value by 1975, and then rose again at the end of the 1970s (Department of the Environment *et al.*, 1972, p.62, 1980, p.6). These data do not distinguish between new building and the great variety of alterations that take place. Data for central Huddersfield suggest that alterations may be less erratic than the construction of new buildings in their incidence over time, at least at the scale of the individual town centre (I. A. Thompson, personal communication), a finding that would seem to hold for building generally (Warren and Pearson, 1937, p.121;

Lewis, 1965, pp.335-340). Time series of building completions naturally show a time-lag relative to plans submitted and orders obtained by contractors, and the peak year for the opening of shopping centres was actually 1975 (Bennison and Davies, 1980, p.16), the lowest year of the decade for new orders for commercial buildings (Department of the Environment *et al.*, 1980, p.6). The redevelopment of sites on speculation, as in the case of many office blocks, combined with a lag of three or four years between the drawing up of plans and building completion, are major factors underlying the short-term cyclical element in city-centre redevelopment (Barras, 1979b, p.41). The marked fluctuations in speculative office building are underlain by a more stable pattern of bespoke office building (including that for owner-occupation) which, as in bespoke building generally (Whitehand, 1981), comprises a higher proportion of developments initiated in slumps than of those initiated in booms.

Arguably, in the case of the cycles in office redevelopment, there has been a tendency for public policy to reinforce the peaks and troughs (Barras, 1979a, p.49; 1979b, pp.30-31). Thus in the City of London the development charge and building licence regulations of the 1947 Town Planning Act held back the post-war redevelopment boom until the early 1950s, the introduction of Office Development Permits to some extent delayed the beginning of the second boom in the late 1960s, the end of which was followed in 1973/1974 by the new Labour government ordering a review of this policy and its strict enforcement in the interim, and the abolition of Office Development Permits by the Conservative government in 1979 has encouraged a new speculative boom and added fuel to the most recent resurgence of activity.

The extent of this latest boom and inter-city variations in its incidence will depend on a variety of factors, including the extent to which the oversupply of office space from the previous boom has been whittled down and, in the absence of exchange controls, the extent to which pension funds invest in real estate abroad. The continued flow of international capital into the City of London is likely to maintain the growth in demand for prime space from the financial sector in that city, and the further concentration of the headquarters' of firms in south-east England is likely to maintain the demand for office space in that region as a whole. But in the public sector, which was a major user of speculative redevelopments in most provincial cities during the boom of the early 1970s, the reductions in expenditure will severely curtail the demand for office space (Barras, 1979a, p.51). However, the demand for property by users has a far from perfect correlation with the demand for property as an investment, and there is not a simple relation between cycles of redevelopment and the general state of the economy. The strength of the speculative element in commercial property development, for which no major substitute shows any sign of emerging, almost guarantees the continuation of the cyclical tendencies which, at least in building generally, have existed in some form for as long as there have been reliable records (Lewis, 1965, pp.10-41).

These cyclical tendencies are sometimes more pronounced on the ground than appears from data aggregated for whole city centres, because there is a tendency for an area once selected to receive the concentrated efforts of developers until its potentialities are exhausted, whereupon activity shifts to another location (Bourne, 1967, p.175). A "neighbourhood effect" of this kind is evident in shop redevelopments (almost entirely individual shops) in central Glasgow, although not in office redevelopments (Whitehand, 1978, pp.92-93), and the tendency for such an effect to exist in alterations to the façades of buildings has been observed in small town centres (Pain, 1980, p.48; Luffrum, 1981, pp.172-173).

INNOVATIONS

The unevenness that characterizes the development of city centres is by no means simply historical repetition. Although the continuance of fluctuations seems inevitable, each future cycle will differ in some way, much as cycles have done in the past. One reason for this is the adoption of innovations. Apart from their effects on the whole process of change, these tend to endow particular booms and slumps with their own characteristics.

Included among these innovations are the controls and laws that govern change. The changing legislation relating to building is one instance. For example, present daylighting codes and controls over building heights and plot ratios combine to make it difficult to develop a small site (Cowan *et al.*, 1969, p.111). Often fundamental but, because legislation is not necessarily involved, sometimes indeterminate, are changes in planning fashions. Major among such changes has been the swing from a widespread espousal of comprehensive redevelopment in the first 25 years after the war (Hall, 1963, p.203) to the present approach which is more concerned with adapting and supplementing what already exists.

Even more significant in some respects are technical innovations, particularly in the construction industry, communications and retailing. It has been estimated, for example, that the introduction of business machines has been responsible for an increase of about 3 per cent per year in the amount of space needed per office worker (Ambrose and Colenutt, 1975, p.21). Furthermore, there is the growth of agents of change that are largely new, at least within property development. Looking back over several decades one may note, for example, the rise to prominence of the shopfitters in the 1920s, the consulting engineers in the 1950s, and the insurance companies and pension funds in the 1960s. It would be surprising if another agent of change did not rise to importance before the end of the century.

Perhaps most obviously, there is the advent of new types of land use in the city centre, sometimes entailing the erection of purpose-built structures. For example, the cinema came and largely went within well under a century (Atwell, 1980), and the multi-storey car park appeared, at least on a large scale, in the 1960s and is likely to be with us in large numbers until well into the twenty-first century. These and many more innovations add qualitative variety to the trends and fluctuations that characterize the city centre and require taking into account in any balanced appraisal of change and how it can be managed.

MANAGING CHANGE

The processes at work in city centres and the land-use patterns and built-forms that are resulting on the ground and seem likely to emerge in the future must ultimately be evaluated according to the quality of the environment that they provide. The interests that are crucial here are those of the people using city centres, both as individuals and as communities. Ironically, despite its fundamental importance this perspective has received comparatively little attention in our discussion so far because it has on the whole impinged on the processes creating city-centre townscapes only indirectly: the interests of those living and working in city centres are filtered by the various agents having a formal role. When these interests are examined, however, a number of problems come into sharper focus.

The scale and to some extent the character of changes in the 1980s are unlikely to be determined primarily by how they fit into the existing fabric or by the needs of the inhabitants of the cities concerned. Even the requirements of potential occupiers of buildings are likely to be subsidiary in many cases. Particularly important will be the policies of the financial institutions in maintaining and enhancing the value of their city-centre property interests. The incidence and type of development will be influenced by events apparently far removed from what is visible to the average city-centre user, notably the investment decisions of insurance companies and not least the attractiveness of the United States for the investment of pension funds. Townscape problems are likely to be minor influences by comparison. These include the destruction, long before they are worn out physically, of buildings into which enormous amounts of economic and cultural capital have been invested, their replacement by massive structures out of scale with the existing townscape and often with the needs of users, and the ousting of smaller firms providing specialist goods and services. All these processes are leading to less diversified and culturally impoverished city centres. They are aggravated by the enlarged scale of land- and property-ownership, which stems in part from the increased powers of local authorities to acquire land. This has increased the facility with which major road-system changes are implemented in conjunction with redevelopment and has given scope to a kind of functional logic that is all too frequently divorced from human experience of form on the ground.

The main reaction to these developments is to be seen in the growth of the conservation movement. Unfortunately the effectiveness of this movement is hampered in two crucial respects, both of which reflect a national propensity to put short-term economic gains before long-term social and cultural ones. First, it lacks an effective means of implementation: although the conservation emphasis in the recent spate of local planning documents on city centres is unmistakeable (see for example, Norfolk County Council, 1978; City of Birmingham, 1980), local authorities lack both the financial means and the staff with the requisite skills. Secondly, and even more fundamental, it lacks a theoretical basis—a theory of townscape management that can give direction and coherence to the way in which conservation problems are tackled. The first of these problems raises issues well beyond the scope of this chapter, but the second can be treated as an extension of our treatment of changes in land-use structure and built-form, although the events of the 1970s and 1980s and their manifestations in the townscape necessarily become details on a much broader canvas.

The effects on the landscape of the processes and agents that we have discussed have a number of important attributes that a theory of townscape management needs to take into account. In addition to having a considerable lasting quality relative to the individual human life-span, each change in the townscape embodies something of the efforts and aspirations of the society responsible for it. Thus the townscape reflects not only the society occupying it at that time but also previous societies. In this way it is conditioned by culture and history. This is especially true of the townscape of the city centre which it could be argued is in a sense a particularly representative area of a city and nearly always the part of it that has existed the longest. The city centre may be viewed morphologically as part of the stage on which successive societies work out their lives, each society learning from, and working to some extent within the framework provided by, the experiments of its predecessors. Seen in this way townscapes represent accumulated experience, those with a high degree of expressiveness of past societies especially so, and are thus a precious asset (Conzen, 1966, 1975).

This asset is increasingly under threat not just because so many of the agents of change are intrusive rather than outgrowths of the local economy and society—for an element of intrusiveness in city centres goes back at least to the beginning of the industrial era—but also because the scale of many individual developments has become so large that they cannot readily fit harmoniously into a townscape founded on a system of traditional, often medieval, plots and their derivatives. This enlarged scale, by no means always in accord with the interests of occupiers of city-centre premises, has been engendered to a considerable extent by changed investment policies in combination with local authority powers. The consequent discord in the townscape is accentuated by the increasing role of consulting engineers and associated changes in constructional materials. Until the 1960s the keynote of city-centre development was transition: in cases of abrupt change, and there were many, the scale was often sufficiently similar to that of previous developments for them to blend in. The combination of a heavy concentration of investment funds in commercial property, local authority involvement (and hence large areas in single ownership), and new materials and technology has changed this.

The problems that this situation poses for townscape management are of major proportions even by comparison with those faced in the Victorian era. Their significance is not lessened by the fact that the townscape asset that is at risk is often experienced unconsciously and is not susceptible to direct measurement in terms of economic benefits. Apart from the basic and practical level at which the townscape provides orientation, the nature of this asset is two-fold. First, the combination of forms created by the gradual adaptation, modification and replacement of elements in city-centre townscapes has aesthetic value. Secondly, and perhaps most importantly, the city-centre townscape is an intellectual and, in a broad sense, educational asset. It is, as Conzen (1966, 1975) has pointed out, an important means by which both individual and society can orientate in time. Through its high density of forms a well-established city-centre townscape provides a particularly strong visual experience of the history of a city, helping the individual to place himself within a wider evolving society, stimulating historical comparison and thus providing a more informed basis for decision making. The continuity that it represents gives those who live in it a sense of the historical dimension of human experience, which encourages a less time-bound and more integrated approach to contemporary problems. Clearly this historical and geographical appreciation cannot be divorced from the practical utility of the townscape and is intimately related to emotional and aesthetic experiences.

To a varying degree these attributes of city-centre townscapes are related to the way in which the townscape encapsulates the history of a society in a particular locale as it is transformed by additions and subtractions; the way in which it "objectivates the spirit of a society" (Schwind, 1951; Conzen, 1966, 1975), viewed not at a moment in time but as a historical phenomenon. This suggests that variations between city-centre townscapes in their historical expressiveness provide a basis for determining conservation priorities. A major aspect of this, and an important contribution of geographical townscape analysis, is the recognition of townscape units reflecting the nature and intensity of the historical expressiveness of various parts of the urban area. Conzen (1975, pp.98-99) has shown how such units can be identified. Put simply, in his scheme individual maps of land and building utilization, building types, and the historical development of the town plan form a basis for establishing a hierarchy of boundaries between areas ranging from the smallest cells, comprising, for example, just a few plots distinctive from those in their immediate vicinity, to major subdivisions of the urban area, having only the most basic characteristics in common and normally encompassing many streets. Superimposition of the three delimitations provides the basis for the recognition of composite morphological regions, which constitute a framework that can be used to ensure that future changes are incorporated harmoniously into the existing fabric.

Clearly this approach looks to the past for its guiding principle and finds it in the historical unfolding of the townscape. It recognizes new functional needs but requires that they respect the existing townscape as a tangible record of the endeavours of past societies in a particular locale. It is founded on a long-term view of human endeavour. By emphasizing the historical and geographical context of each change in the townscape and by laying stress on the long-term repercussions of decisions affecting the townscape it draws attention to the responsibility that a society has for its future generations.

There are, of course, familiar elements in this perspective. In a sense it seeks to restore that sense of geographical identity that was once taken for granted but which the industrial revolution and its aftermath have partially destroyed. The view of future city-centre townscapes that is recommended is thus essentially conservative, the accent being not on wholesale clearance and comprehensive redevelopment but on transformation, augmentation and conservation. This is not a panacea for the many problems outlined earlier. The piecemeal approach that is to some extent necessary involves financial costs as well as social gains. In practice a balance has to be struck and Alexander (1974a) has suggested ways in which this may be effected.

While it is inevitable that in the foreseeable future the pace of change in city centres will to a considerable extent be determined by economic conditions, in the light of the processes at work and in particular their character and outcome in the post-war period it would be irresponsible effectively to leave decisions about long-term social assets largely in the hands of organizations whose concern for history is slight and whose connections with the environmental effects of their policies upon those who use city centres is frequently tenuous. There is thus a large gap between the way in which British city-centre townscapes appear to be evolving in the 1980s and our suggestions as to the principles that should govern the management of change. But if the views on conservation expressed both in the academic literature of the last decade and in recent city-centre planning documents carry any force then that gap should at least be smaller than it was in the 1960s and 1970s.

ACKNOWLEDGEMENT

This work was aided by a grant from the Social Science Research Council.

REFERENCES

Alexander, I. (1974a). *Progr. Plann.* **3**, 1-81.

Alexander, I. (1974b). "The City Centre". University of Western Australia Press, Nedlands.

Allpass, J. and Agergaard, E. (1979). *In* "Growth and Transformation of the Modern City" (I. Hammarström and T. Hall, eds), pp.233-264. Swedish Council for Building Research, Stockholm.

Ambrose, P. and Colenutt, B. (1975). "The Property Machine". Penguin, Harmondsworth.

Amos, F. J. C. (1973). *In* "City Centre Redevelopment" (J. Holliday, ed.), pp.175-206. Charles Knight, London.

Atwell, D. (1980). "Cathedrals of the Movies". Architectural Press, London.

Barras, R. (1979a). "The Returns from Office Development and Investment". Centre for Environmental Studies Research Series 35.

Barras, R. (1979b). "The Development Cycle in the City of London". Centre for Environmental Studies Research Series 36.

Bateman, M. (1971). "Some Aspects of Change in the Central Areas of Towns in West Yorkshire since 1945". Department of Geography, Portsmouth Polytechnic, Occasional Papers 1.

Bennison, D. J. and Davies, R. L. (1980). *Progr. Plann.* **14**, 1-104.

Blacksell, M. (1968). *In* "Urbanization and its Problems" (R. W. Beckinsale and J. M. Houston, eds), pp.199-217. Basil Blackwell, Oxford.

Bourne, L. S. (1967). "Private Redevelopment of the Central City", University of Chicago Department of Geography Research Paper 112.

Buissink, J. D. and de Widt, D. J. (1967). *In* "Urban Core and Inner City" (W. F. Heinemeyer, M. van Hulten and H. D. de Vries Reilingh, eds), pp.237-255. E. J. Brill, Leiden.

Cameron, G. C. and Evans, A. W. (1973). *Reg. Stud.* **7**, 47-55.

Catalano, A. and Barras, R. (1980). "Office Development in Central Manchester". Centre for Environmental Studies Research Series 37.

Central Statistical Office (1964-81). "Financial Statistics". HMSO, London.

City of Birmingham (1980). "Birmingham Central Area District Plan: Draft Written Statement". City of Birmingham, Birmingham.

City of Liverpool (1980). "Shopping: Trends and Opportunities". City of Liverpool, Liverpool.

Conzen, M. R. G. (1966). *In* "Northern Geographical Essays in Honour of G. H. J. Daysh" (J. W. House, ed.), pp.56-78. Department of Geography, University of Newcastle upon Tyne, Newcastle upon Tyne.

Conzen, M. R. G. (1975). *Giessener geogr. Schr.* Anglo-German Symposium in Applied Geography, 95-102.

Cowan, P. (1963). *Trans. Bartlett Soc.* **1**, 55-84.

Cowan, P., Fine, D., Ireland, J., Jordan, C., Mercer, D. and Sears, A. (1969). "The Office". Heinemann, London.

Davies, R. L. (1976). "Marketing Geography". Methuen, London.

Davies, R. L. and Bennison, D. J. (1978). *Estates Gaz.* **246**, 117-121.

Davies, R. L. and Bennison, D. J. (1979). "British Town Centre Shopping Schemes". Unit for Retail Planning Information Ltd., Reading.

Department of the Environment (1975). "Commercial Property Development". HMSO, London.

Department of the Environment, Scottish Development Department, Welsh Office (1972). "Housing and Construction Statistics" Part 1. HMSO, London.

Department of the Environment, Scottish Development Department, Welsh Office (1980). "Housing and Construction Statistics 1969-1979". HMSO, London.

Dorey, N. M. (1981). "Retail Change in Reading, Berkshire 1896-1976". Unpublished B.A. Dissertation, University of Birmingham.

Economic Intelligence Unit Ltd (1977). "An Analysis of Commercial Property Values 1962-1976". London.

Galley, K. A. (1973). *In* "City Centre Redevelopment" (J. Holliday, ed.), pp.207-233. Charles Knight, London.

Hall, P. (1963). "London 2000". Faber and Faber, London.

Hillier Parker Research (1979). "British Shopping Developments". Hillier Parker May and Rowden, London.

Holden, C. H. and Holford, W. G. (1951). "The City of London". Architectural Press, London.

Hoyt, H. (1933). "One Hundred Years of Land Values in Chicago". University of Chicago Press, Chicago.

Institute of Advanced Architectural Studies (1978). "The Underuse of Upper Floors in Historic Town Centres". Institute of Advanced Architectural Studies, University of York, Research Paper 15.

Lewis, J. P. (1965). "Building Cycles and Britain's Growth". Macmillan, London.

Luffrum, J. M. (1981). *Urban Geogr.* **2**, 161-177.

Massey, D. and Catalano, A. (1978). "Capital and Land". Edward Arnold, London.
Norfolk County Council (1978). "Norwich Central Area Plan". Norfolk County Council, Norwich.
Pain, R. J. (1980). "Changes to the Building Fabric of the Town Centre of Boston, Lincolnshire, 1918-1977". Unpublished B.A. Dissertation, University of Birmingham.
Ross, G. R. (1979). "The Interaction of Function and Form in the Pattern of Building Replacements in Central Newcastle under Lyme, Staffordshire 1920-1975". Unpublished B.A. Dissertation, University of Birmingham.
Schwind, M. (1951). *Dte geogr. Bl.* **46**, 5-28.
Sim, D. F. (1977). "Patterns of Building Adaptation and Redevelopment in the Central Business District of Glasgow". Unpublished Ph.D. Thesis, University of Glasgow.
Sutcliffe, A. and Smith, R. (1974). "Birmingham 1939-1970". Oxford University Press, London.
Warren, G. F. and Pearson, F. A. (1937). "World Prices and the Building Industry". John Wiley, New York.
West Midlands County Council (1980). "West Midlands County Structure Plan". West Midlands County Council, Birmingham.
Whitehand, J. W. R. (1978). *Geogr. Annlr.* Ser. B, **60**, 79-96.
Whitehand, J. W. R. (1981). *Erdkunde* **35**, 129-140.
Wilkes, L. and Dodds, G. (1964). "Tyneside Classical". John Murray, London.

FOUR

The future townscape

B. S. MAITLAND

Most analyses of the city centre are concerned with the nature and influence of the economic, social and technological forces which shape its activities and, as a kind of by-product, generate its built-form. But we know that built-form, once generated, itself modifies the possibilities for those activities; that, far from being a neutral container, it in fact constitutes the most elaborate cultural product, able either, by its coherence and convenience, to stimulate and enrich the life for which it forms a context, or else to constrain and impoverish it. It is with this reciprocal effect that the urban designer is concerned. This chapter considers some of the ways in which changes in the built-form of the city—the future townscape—may modify its impact, first by examining some of the major problems which urban designers have identified and then by reviewing a few of the responses which have emerged in recent years. Because the theoretical basis for future action is important, the chapter goes on to examine a number of contrasting theories which are current, before concluding with a brief examination of some new developments in the design of the city which may provide significant pointers for the future.

KEY PROBLEMS

We have no agreed picture of the ideal pattern of built-form in the modern city, such as was shared by the contemporaries of the fifteenth century painter of "The Ideal City" in the Palazzo Ducale at Urbino. Instead both the design professions and the public express unease at a variety of individual aspects of the characteristic patterns of recent development. If one were to attempt to draw out of these a central theme, it might be a sense of the fragmentation of the contemporary city, with the consequential impoverishment of its component parts. There have been a number of tendencies to reinforce this belief among which the increasing specialization of the parts has been significant. This specialization of forms for specific purposes has arisen out of progressively more demanding aspects of the "internal" brief for these buildings, that is to say, the functional brief of the client irrespective of context. And such internal elaboration has been accompanied by the apparent ability of these

THE FUTURE FOR THE CITY CENTRE
ISBN 0 12 206240 X

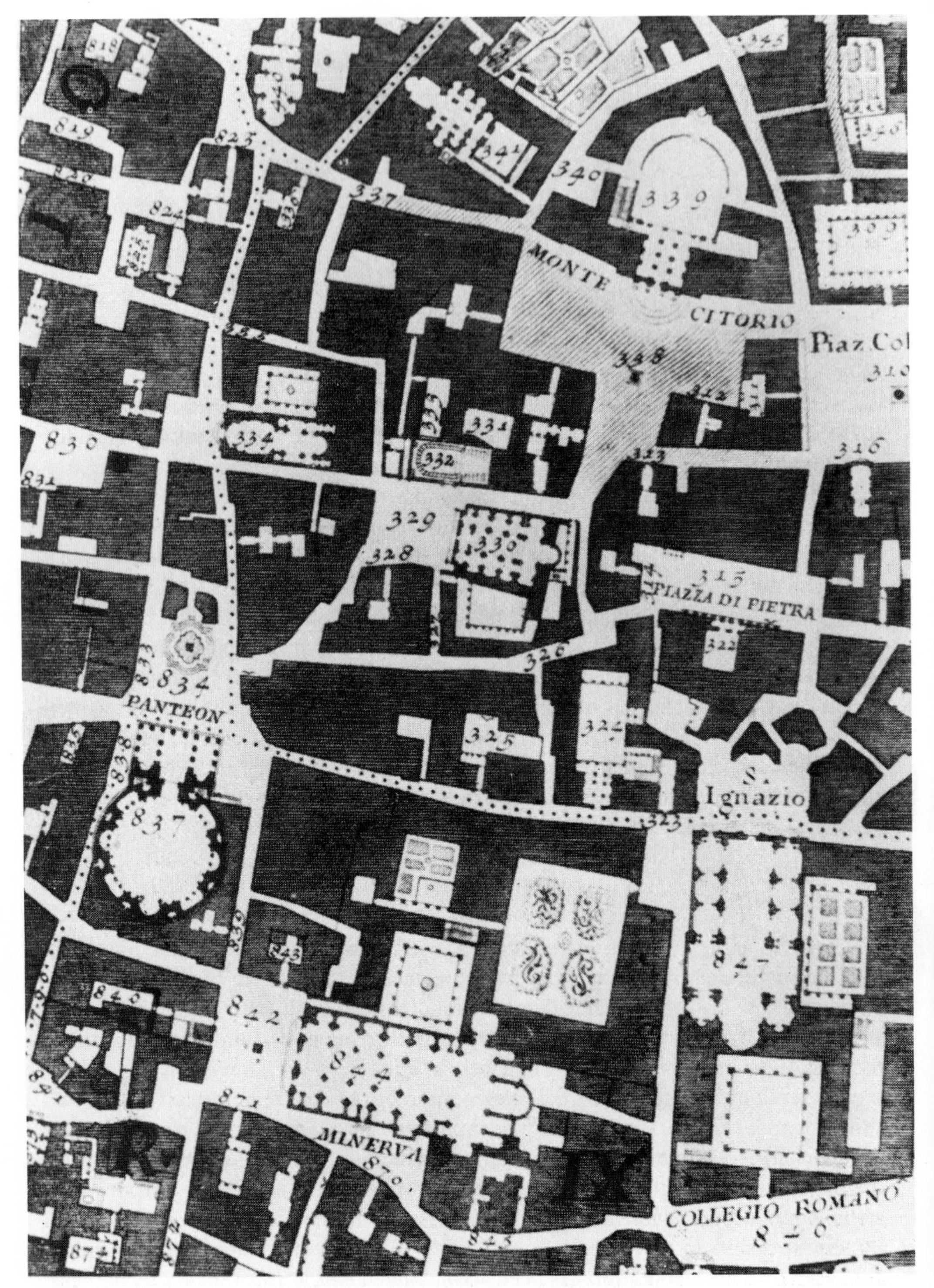

Figure 1. Section of Nolli's plan of Rome, 1748.

urban components to exist free of their traditional urban context. The out-of-town shopping centre is perhaps the most dramatic illustration of these tendencies, in which the most central and most gregarious element of the historical city takes up a peripheral, isolated location and, in response to a new formulation of its brief, adopts an introspective organization, impeccable in terms of its development logic but totally oblivious of its surroundings. The other components of the city have been similarly affected by this tendency, with a result which is vividly demonstrated by two contrasting illustrations. The first is part of Nolli's 1748 plan of Rome (Fig. 1), in which he shows the city as two contrasting territorial zones, private spaces all shown black, and the public domain, whether outdoor streets and piazzas or else the indoor spaces of public buildings, shown as a continuous network of white. In contrast, an aerial view of Los Angeles suggests rather that the city has become a loose federation of isolated private domains, in which the public domain has ceased to have any significance that Nolli would recognize, beyond that of crude circulation. In Britain, although the federation tended formerly to be more tightly packed, a similar isolation of elements and inconsequentiality of intervening space occurred in recent times. And this apparent disollution of the public realm was felt by some to reflect and reinforce destructive aspects of society which tended to an almost pathological isolation of both the activities of life and of social groups, as in Richard Sennett's (1970) analysis in which the term "community" becomes a euphemism used by sectional interest to cover the expulsion of dissimilar uses and social groups from its territory.

Unease at this fragmentation of the city fabric was compounded by certain physical characteristics of new urban building projects. The scale of their implementation, for example, seemed to some observers to modify the terms under which the city has traditionally been formed to such a degree that its integrity was threatened in a new way. For whereas the city has always been formed and renewed in packages of varying size, in the past that variation was comparatively modest and was contained within a common framework of plots, blocks and streets. Now, however, the scale of implementation of the urban project was enormously increased, and its forms governed not by a common framework, but by the internal logic peculiar to its specialized use. The phenomenon is graphically illustrated by the plans before and after the construction of the Eldon Square and Arndale Shopping centre developments in Newcastle and Manchester, two of the largest central area projects to be implemented in the UK (Fig. 2). Not only is there a dramatic jump in the scale of building, but again patterns of frontage and outlook have been inverted. A similar phenomenon occurred with other building types, and most dramatically perhaps with urban housing in the public sector, which seemed to reinforce a further impression, that the new scale of development was determined not by any change in the way people intended to use these facilities, but rather in the power of the development agencies responsible for their implementation, and hence the charge, voiced by Habraken (1972) and others, that they represented, not the patterns of a living community, but rather the diagrams of an institutionalized brief.

Further difficulties accompanied the implementation of such projects. Conceived as fixed end states, even where they had to be phased in execution, they tended to ignore the reality of the city as a continually evolving process, which must therefore rely upon patterns of development which can be sustained over periods of time. This condition often proved unexpectedly difficult to fulfil, while the prolonged

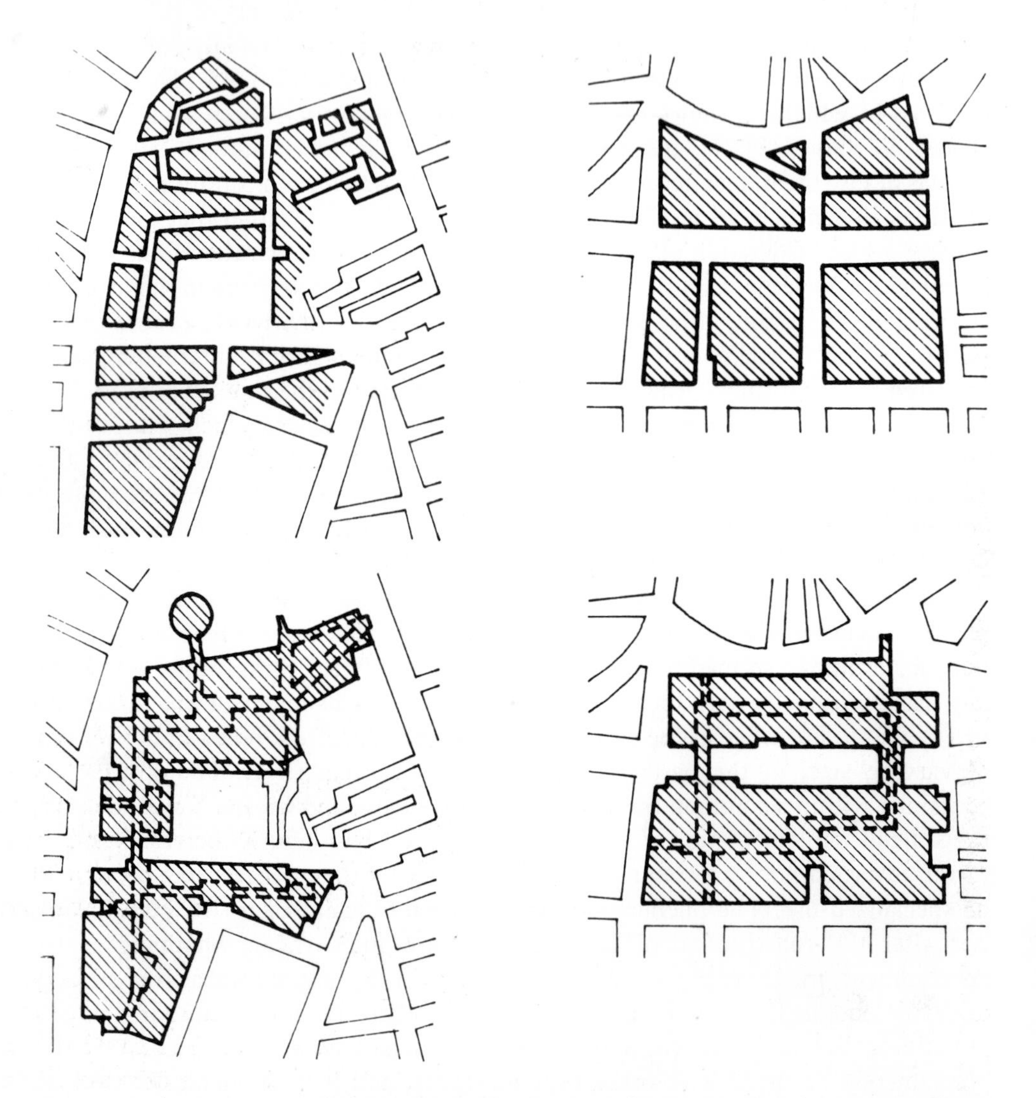

Figure 2. Comparative plans before and after the development of Eldon Square Centre, Newcastle (left) and Arndale Centre, Manchester (right).

development periods of large projects, with accompanying sterilization of adjoining land required for possible future growth, led to painful gestation periods. Because it was rightly innovatory, searching out new approaches to these problems, the town centre of Cumbernauld provides a particularly poignant illustration of this last difficulty. The celebrated 1961 image of the town centre provided a powerful vision of the goal to be achieved, in which a layered multi-use facility would act as the complex heart of the town. By 1967 with the completion of Phase I, a slice of that heart had been constructed, with car parking at the lowest levels, serving shopping above, and housing at the top of the section. Already the reservations of large areas of land on either side of the centre for possible future expansion tended to isolate it from the housing areas of which it was intended to be the focus. Then with Phase II the first stages of a metamorphosis occurred. The requirements for shopping altered, and instead of continuing the Phase I form, a Woolco store was built with car parking at the same level as the sales floor to ease trolley access. No housing over the retail space was included. Then with the third phase a further shift occurred, with the car parking now located on the roof of the shopping areas. Thus the original construction pattern was completely inverted in response to changing circumstances over a development period of some 15 years.

The fragmentation of the city fabric, the absence of a common scale of development, and problems associated with growth and decline, all seemed to be symptoms of a failure to evolve humane and flexible containers for city life. The examples I have used to illustrate this are drawn from the more thoughtful and innovative urban projects of the 1960s, and for that reason expose the tendencies particularly honestly, but they were accompanied by a much larger body of banal work which suggested that urban townscape had degenerated into an incoherent and hostile assembly of isolated packages of arbitary form and size, indifferent to their context.

PRACTICAL RESPONSES

Now if this pessimistic analysis is correct—if, through structural changes in society, in the form of the buildings it requires and in the way urban projects are implemented, the public domain really is effectively shattered—then we may say that urban design, which is primarily concerned with the shaping of that public domain, is pointless and that townscape, as Gordon Cullen once lamented, has indeed degenerated into a trivial choice of cobblestones and bollards. However, there have been many attempts to compensate for these tendencies, and among them we might comment on three common approaches. The first is the establishment of pedestrianized streets, at first sight little more than a technical solution to a problem of circulation, but actually achieving rather more than this. For as projects such as that based on the Strøget in Copenhagen, or in the centre of Leeds, became progressively enlarged to form a network extending throughout the centre of the city, it was possible to see them unifying and reintegrating parts of the core previously isolated by traffic arteries. In addition the streets themselves were no longer simply circulation routes, but became positive settings for public life. In Munich the pedestrianization of the main shopping area on Kaufingerstrasse and Neuhauserstrasse led to the creation of a unified public space 700 m in length with an average width of 22 m and including several squares, which added a new element to the life of the city, as shown by the great numbers of people who crowd into it and the variety of events and entertainments which occur along its length.

Now as a technique for urban design such an approach has its limitations. Beyond the medieval gates which mark the ends of the Munich scheme a ring road defines its limits and isolates it from the surrounding city. To extend a sense of coherence and continuity to the public realm over the city as a whole, an alternative strategy was developed in the form of an urban design plan which aimed to provide a unifying context for individual decisions. An early example of this was adopted by Oscar Niemeyer in the early years of the new city of Brasilia, to ensure conformity in the output of various architects working in the central area. In a paper setting out this policy in 1959 he argued that historical towns had achieved unity through the repetition of restricted solutions, whereas modern architecture had "fallen away from this ancient virtue, and become reduced to a conglomeration of structures, some of them of great merit, considered individually, but having nothing in common with one another and presenting as a group a deplorable picture of confusion and lack of harmony". This fall from grace could only be corrected by the imposition of a stringent artificial control to take the place of the former limitations. "It may be," he wrote, "that Brasilia will exercise a salutary influence on Brasilian architecture in the field of city planning, by disciplining the use of masses and open spaces and by restoring among architects the concern with unity."

The chilling tone of this passage was reflected in the buildings which the policy engendered, and subsequent design guides have generally not felt it necessary to take such a universally disapproving view of the state of existing cities, but rather have sought out those aspects of their development which might be encouraged and those which should be suppressed. This approach was adopted, for example, by the San Francisco Department of City Planning (1970) in its preparation of citywide "urban design guidelines" as a framework for more detailed urban design plans at district and neighbourhood levels. The framework depended first upon an analysis of the city as a set of fairly discrete "design units", identifiable by the distinctive natural or man-made character peculiar to each. This definition of "visual districts" indicated the qualities of each part of the city which could be enhanced, and urban design guidelines were then formulated to achieve this.

Such an approach, permitting exceptions but offering a consensus view of the particular qualities of a city which each new development should respect, was obviously a more flexible form of urban design control than the Brasilia example. However, like most such regulatory documents, it shared some of the historical pessimism of that policy, being based on the view that some distinctive quality had been, or was about to be, lost, and that restrictive legislation would be necessary to save it.

Taken a little further, this view produced a third category of response to the fragmentation of the city, in which the most important task of urban design was seen to be the conservation, not just of particular buildings, but of whole townscapes. And where the townscape possessed outstanding qualities of architectural consistency this response could provide a common ground for widely

Figure 3. Architects drawing of proposed development in the Lanes Area, Carlisle, 1981.

Figure 4. View of the Old Quarter of Warsaw.

divergent groups, as in the New Town area of Edinburgh, where a voluntary survey of all 11 000 properties in the 310 hectare area was carried out by the Edinburgh Architectural Association, and a New Town Conservation Committee formed, with members from central and local government, voluntary bodies and residents' associations. This Committee then secured what amounted to an urban design plan based on total conservation and restoration, channelling advice and grants to a large number of individual conservation projects and appointing a full time executive Director, Desmond Hodges, whose Conservation Centre in a shop in the New Town exhibits the work of the Committee, provides advice on the maintenance and repair of Georgian details, and acts as a central clearing house for the collection and re-use of salvaged building elements (McWilliam, 1978).

The New Town of Edinburgh is an outstanding example, but the question of conserving certain characteristics of existing towns gradually came to be an issue wherever redevelopment was mooted. At Carlisle, proposals for commercial development in the Lanes area has been a controversial issue for some 20 years, during which time several of the frontages which conservation groups argued should be retained have fallen down. In current proposals framed by Keith Scott of Building Design Partnership (Fig. 3), these elevations are reconstructed as frontage to new buildings hidden behind, providing an interesting acknowledgement to the sentiment and value attributed by people to the continuity of another urban context even where that continuity is known to be consciously contrived. Perhaps the most dramatic demonstration of this lies, not in this country, but in Poland. Visitors to the old quarter of Warsaw (Fig. 4) might regard it as an outstanding example, like Edinburgh New Town, of urban conservation, until they are reminded that this was totally destroyed in 1944, and that they are in fact looking at an exact replica of the old city, painstakingly achieved from architectural students' measured drawings, Canaletto paintings and old photographs, an extraordinary tribute to the affection and loyalty which citizens can invest in the built-form of their city. But the knowledge that it is a replica raises uncomfortable sensations. It is an act of intense nostalgia, in which the public realm has been lovingly mummified. It reminds us of the power of urban design to engage people, but is ultimately a sterile model for us, lacking the ability to accommodate in built-form the acts of the living.

URBAN DESIGN THEORIES

A number of designers have attempted to frame more coherent urban design philosophies which can accommodate those patterns of change to which we have referred. These ideas avoid some of the limitations in the strategies we have discussed and provide a possible basis for the future townscape. Being concerned with the coherence of urban form, such theories may be said to be formal in nature, in the same sense that language or mathematics constitute consistent formal systems. As in those disciplines, a comprehensive urban design theory must define both the elements of the system, and also the rules for their association—that is, both a vocabulary and a grammar. In addition, and unlike mathematics, say, but in common with architecture, a formal system valid for urban design purposes must have the further quality of a structural correspondence with the functional organizations which will inhabit it, because its purpose is to provide a setting for everyday life. Now it can be argued that many of the attempts to frame a coherent urban design philosophy in the past have failed to meet these criteria. They may have concentrated on defining the vocabulary of the city, as did Kevin Lynch (1960) with his famous study identifying paths, edges, nodes, districts, and landmarks as the fundamental elements of urban design, or alternatively, as did Gordon Cullen (1961) with his townscape analyses, studying the sequential nature of the experience of towns and hence their underlying grammar. Three recent theories, though very different, each provide a consistent formal solution which might supply a way forward.

The first is that developed by Melville Dunbar for Essex County Council and contained in the Essex Design Guide, first published in 1973. In effect the Guide reconstructs a vernacular language, defining its grammar and vocabulary as appropriate to two conditions, rural and urban, and hence providing a common basis for unlimited local variations. The intention is thus to take the principle of urban design control beyond both the rigidly restrictive edicts of Brasilia and the somewhat loose formulations of city "character" in San Francisco, to recreate the conditions of a genuinely creative tradition. In basing its position on the observation of preferred existing models, and then refining from them a universal language of design, the Essex Design Guide has much in common with the second theory of design, that of the Rationalist school, although with very different results.

As with the Guide, so the Rationalists reject the urban solutions of the post-war period as an unqualified disaster, responsible for "a cultural tragedy to which there is no precedent in history" (Krier, 1978) and by its servitude to speculators an instrument in a greater destruction of European cities "both physically and socially than in any other period of their history, including the two world wars". Their model for study is the traditional nineteenth century European city, with its pattern of streets, squares and quarters, providing "desirable models of collective life", typical configurations of the public realm as carved out of the urban material available, of whatever use. Idealized and purified of their contextual associations they could then be reapplied to specific conditions. Robert Krier's project for the centre of Leinfelden and Leon Krier's for Echternach (Fig. 5), for example, both proposed monumental systems of public spaces of this kind across the fabric of existing towns.

Both of these theories then take historical models as a basis for the rediscovery of an effective strategy of urban design. Although the principal author of the third, Christopher Alexander (1977), would certainly claim to base his on observations of existing urban forms, this historical dependence is absent from his proposal for what he describes as a "Pattern Language", the theory and applications of which he has set out in three books.

The scope of the theory is certainly utopian in scale: "The books are intended to

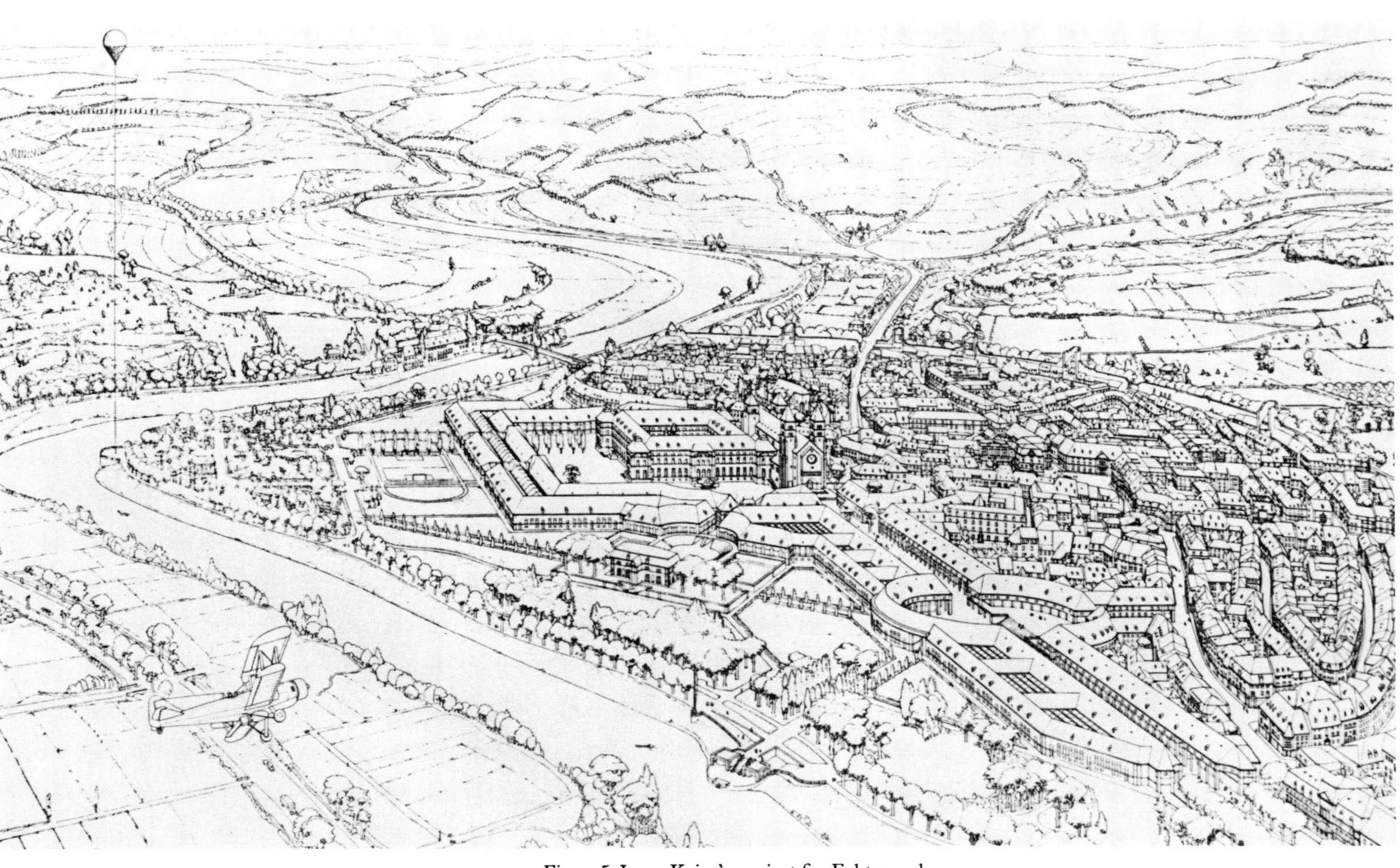

Figure 5. Leon Krier's project for Echternach.

provide a complete working alternative to our present ideas about architecture, building and planning—an alternative which will, we hope, gradually replace current ideas and practices."

Ranging from the global arrangement of regions down to the minutiae of domestic construction, they set out a menu of preferred solutions to the main design problems encountered through all the scales of environmental design. These 253 patterns are interrelated, not as a fixed sequence, but rather as a network in which each is contained by or related to a number of larger scale patterns "up" the network, and in turn contains smaller scale patterns "below". For example, pattern 31 "Promenade", is related to the larger scale patterns 8 "Mosaic of Subcultures", 12 "Community of 7000" and 30 "Activity Nodes". The statement of the problem which makes pattern 31 necessary runs: "Each subculture needs a centre for its public life: a place where you can go to see people, and to be seen."

A discussion of the problem then follows, concluding with a statement of the proposed instruction, pattern 31: "Encourage the gradual formation of a promenade at the heart of every community, linking the main activity nodes, and placed centrally, so that each point in the community is within 10 minutes walk of it. Put main points of attraction at the two ends, to keep a constant movement up and down."

In turn this pattern leads to others in the network, including 32 "Shopping Street", 33 "Night Life", 58 "Carnival", 63 "Dancing in the Street", 100 "Pedestrian Streets", 121 "Path Shape", and so on.

Arbitary or even quirky as some of the individual patterns might appear, the mosaic they create, of humane injunctions logically interrelated, forms perhaps the most comprehensive and appealing of urban design theories to date, because

> These patterns can never be "designed" or "built" in one fell swoop—but patient piecemeal growth, designed in such a way that every individual act is always helping to create or generate these larger global patterns, will slowly and surely, over the years make a community that has these global patterns in it (Alexander *et al.*, 1977).

These three urban design theories then illustrate the wide spread of ideas now current. They are all sustainable as coherent formal systems, and in addition all three have a great deal to say about the relationship of the formal system to the reality they serve. Krier (1978), on behalf of the Rationalist school, has argued that his model must be "part of an integral vision of society, it has to be part of a political struggle or else it will merely be reduced to a style". The Essex Design Guide on the other hand seems to belong to what one observer has described as "that grand and endlessly running British cultural project to make the institutions of the present day seem like those of preindustrial, agrarian, village society" (Hill, 1980), while Alexander's urban design patterns are embedded in a network which includes regional and even global strategies in such a way that "every individual act is always helping to create or generate these larger global patterns".

TOWARDS A CONCEPTUAL STRUCTURE

Now we might ask whether it is really essential or indeed practical to adopt such comprehensive programmes in order to achieve an effective form of urban design. We could argue that such theories set out to achieve a maximum level of control over the built form of the city and that, given the intractability of urban design problems in the past, it might be wise to establish, by contrast, a minimal position as a basis for action. Such a minimal conceptual structure ought to recognize and strengthen the underlying characteristics of the public domain in existing cities and should acknowledge those tendencies which have been described as weakening and fragmenting it. Thus we might hope that our formal structure would act as a scaling device, providing a city-wide framework appropriate to the way in which the city is used, irrespective of the way in which it is made. Secondly, the structure should have the ability both to survive, and to provide a comprehensible context for, change in the urban fabric, whether that change be the internal piecemeal renewal of the urban core, the generation of a new green field settlement, or the decline of an established area now bypassed by new industrial and transportation patterns. That is to say that the formal structure should not only be able to accept change, but should itself reflect the way in which change occurs. Thirdly, we might hope that our design structure would relate and reconcile the increasingly isolated and specialized single-use zones which the modern city generates.

If it is indeed possible to make such a general proposition about urban structure, and the way it can respond to change, we might expect to find evidence of it in the existing urban fabric itself. In fact an increasing amount of attention has been paid recently to this point, with a number of research projects undertaken into the quantitative and qualitative evaluation of conventional urban components and their arrangements. And we might expect to find these traces most clearly in areas of established building which have undergone relatively unpremeditated cycles of development. I should like to sketch the outline of a possible minimal structure which is developed from such a study.

The mass of construction which makes up a city contains variations of use and levels of activity which articulate that urban mass both functionally and visually. This differentiation tends to occur around points of focus, or nodes, which generally relate to local intensifications of form (crossroads for example). The frequency of these nodes is thus a basic characteristic of the city, and the network they produce creates a fundamental structure in terms of both our use and understanding of it. Node frequency is dependent in part upon the level of surrounding activity, and hence upon such variables as density of land usage, but it is also related to the tolerance or ability of the pedestrian to move about the city. The latter relatively invariant factor makes it possible to postulate a "standard" or "median" node interval which will operate within a middle range of activity levels, and indeed analysis of a great number of older towns suggests that an interval of about 200 m does commonly occur. In certain cases, however, as within the densely packed mass of certain medieval walled towns for example, this might reduce as far as 100 m, while low density suburban areas often lack significant functional differentiation below 400 m.

The generic net of nodes at 200 m intervals exists, however, only as a first approximation to an urban structure, subject to modification by a number of factors. In older settlements topography acts upon this model in quite specific and predictable ways to adapt it to the local case. Again, important routes passing through the net produce dominant linear sequences, or "strings" of nodes within the general pattern. The combination of these two factors then produces an enormous variety of specific solutions. The example of the small Bavarian town of Landshut may serve to illustrate just one possible variation (Fig. 6). The town stands on land contained by a curve of the Isar to north and west, and high ground to south and east, and is based upon one major street, Altstadt, along which, from the river bridge at its north end to a city gate at its south end, the major public buildings are ranged at 200 m intervals to form a classic string, reinforced by monuments and interspersed with commercial uses. Parallel to this, and 200 m to the east, a second street, Neustadt, accommodates secondary commercial uses, its length again articulated into major intervals of 200 m lengths by fountains, and connected by numerous cross streets to the Altstadt to form a double-string or "ladder" arrangement.

It should be noted that, although the node structure is closely related to the distribution of uses within the town it is also independent of any specific economic or social configurations. Thus, in the medieval hill towns of Umbria, for example, it expresses itself in the pattern of churches and associated piazzas, whereas in nineteenth century English industrial towns a corresponding pattern is traced through the rows of terrace houses, but now by corner shops and pubs.

What the node structure does is to describe a hierarchy of accessibility and activity levels, and hence also of land value, privacy and susceptibility to change, across the urban mass. To take the case of the industrial towns for instance, houses occurring at node points would become converted to corner shops, and then, as the patterns of retailing coarsened after 1950, reconverted back to residential use or perhaps changed to some service trade. When slum clearance and redevelopment occurred, the more expensive shops and pubs on the node locations would often remain, presiding over a wasteland until the fabric filled in again around them.

Although the node structure may appear as a rather general strategic idea, it carries quite specific and detailed implications for local decisions about land use, for example, or the size of development packages, or the appropriateness of particular architectural statements. Avoiding prescriptions which are rapidly overtaken by cultural, technological or economic events, but rather, by attempting to identify the essential feature of the way cities are actually used and perceived, setting out a matrix within which unpredictable events can naturally occur, it is possible to describe the structure as "minimal".

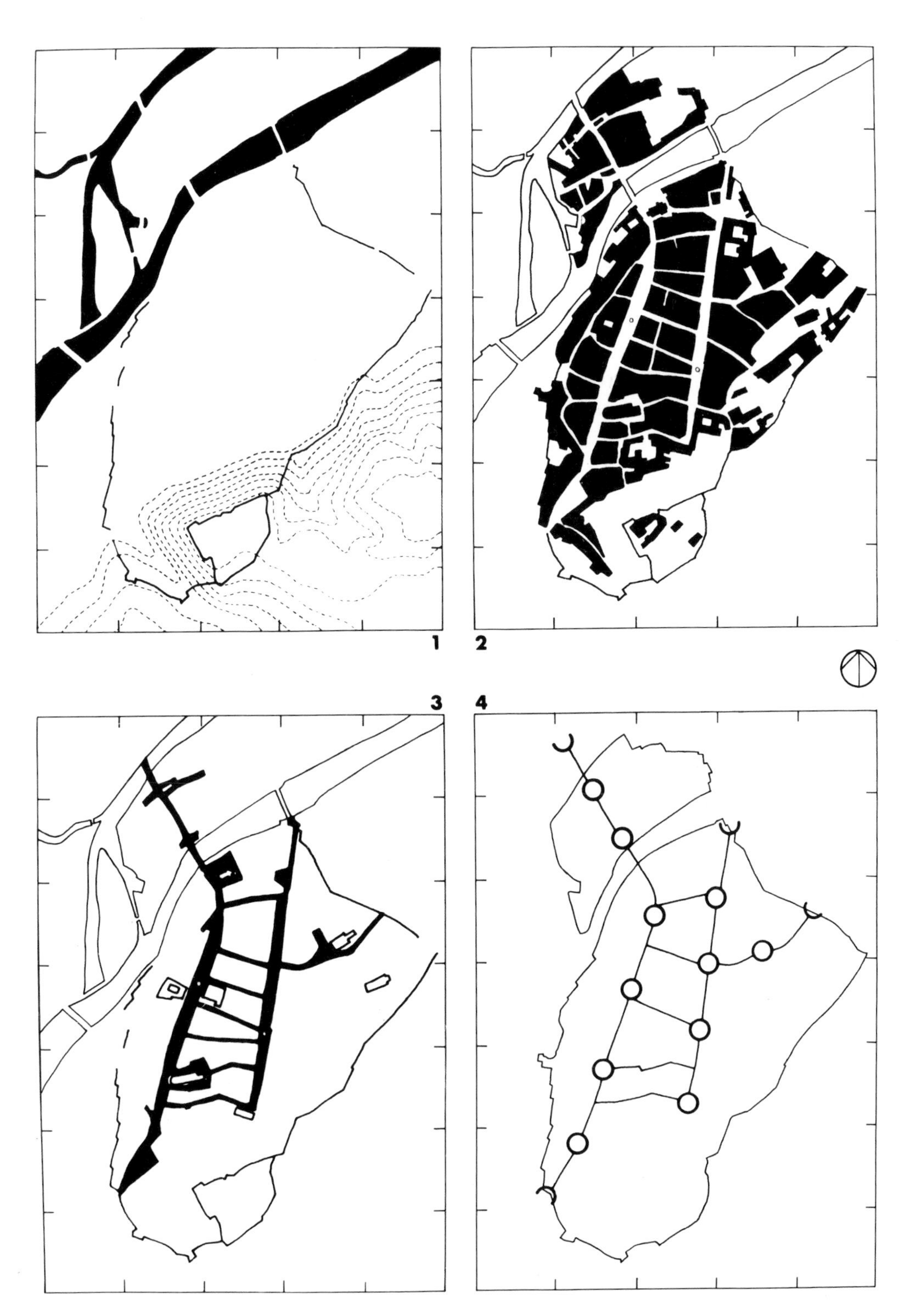

Figure 6. The site and structural characteristics of Landshut.

NEW DEVELOPMENTS IN THE TOWNSCAPE

Whether or not any of these theories of urban design will be found to have relevance in shaping the future townscape, we can still speculate on the way in which it may develop. There are a number of factors in the present situation which may affect that development. A review of a few of these can help to draw out the conclusions of this chapter.

Earlier it was suggested that part of our difficulties arose from the evolution of new, specialized urban building types. That evolution continues, and while we search for more appropriate solutions to the problems of the 1960s and early 1970s, we may find that new variants have altered the terms of that search. Indeed it could be thought that this may already have occurred, and that while the earlier stages of speculation tended to encourage the isolation and functional exclusiveness of urban components, new tendencies may, through the further evolution of the same commercial and technical considerations which formed the earlier types, result in an encouragingly more integrated and complex pattern of uses and spaces in the city. For example, atrium buildings, primarily developed in North America but increasingly of interest in this country (Saxon, 1979), extend the earlier notion of enclosed single-use malls into elaborate internal spaces of truly urban scale, in which the concept of public space as a theatre for, and physical manifestation of, the life of the city is given a new and powerful expression (Fig. 7). They have interesting implications for energy conservation in the city, and moreover, allow, as in the traditional city, varieties of use to co-exist and to establish rich symbiotic patterns of activity.

Examples of atrium buildings tend to be confined to dense metropolitan sites, but there is evidence of similar attempts to reconstitute urban activities at a less intensive level too. In the recently completed Orton township centre at Peterborough, for example, the now familiar shopping mix of a district centre facility—a major superstore supported by a range of standard shop units and a larger DIY outlet—is transformed into a true district centre by the addition of a range of other uses normally dispersed and isolated throughout the community. Chief among these is a community school which, in a development of the Cambridgeshire village schools concept, opens its library, gymnasium and workshops to the town (Fig. 8). The spaces around these buildings are not separated out from the other pedestrian spaces forming the township centre, so that school playground and town square become one and the same. Other social and welfare facilities are included in the mixture of uses making up the centre, as is single person housing on upper floors, with the effect of creating a truly integrated centre with a convincing urban townscape character.

The Orton township centre is the latest in a series of experiments in mixed use facilities at Peterborough, and its success has depended upon the Development Corporation's determination to carry it through in both estates management and architectural terms. Increasingly, however, in response to consumer pressure and

Figure 7. View of an atrium building in North America. The Omni Center, Atlanta, Georgia.

competition from neighbouring centres, we may expect conventional existing centres to be forced to question their success as integrated management and townscape exercises, in which such a re-examination of the traditional and often sterilizing rigid boundaries between institutionalized uses may play an invigorating part.

Figure 8. View of the Orton Centre, Peterborough. Chief Architect: K. Maplestone.

A second prediction about the future townscape which we might make concerns its architectural character and the technology selected to achieve it. Twenty years ago there was a fairly universal view as to the general architectural character of the future city. It would be of frame construction, with lightweight, non-loadbearing infill panels, and with flat roofs, and this general description would apply broadly to all building types. Today this unitary sense of appropriate technology is replaced by at least two dramatically opposed visions of the future. Housing, schools and community facilities it seems are appropriately housed under pitched roofs, with brick, tile and timber construction, while offices, factories and leisure centres are clad in the latest taut metallic skins. Shopping centres fluctuate uneasily between these poles, appropriately enough because, as the final wrapper for the consumer durables they contain, they must indulge both myths of the good life to which these technologies refer: at once they must provide the consumer with access to the latest, most sophisticated technology, while at the same time reassuring him that the product is wholesome and free of all artificial preservatives.

Because it seems unlikely that a new unitary conviction will replace these

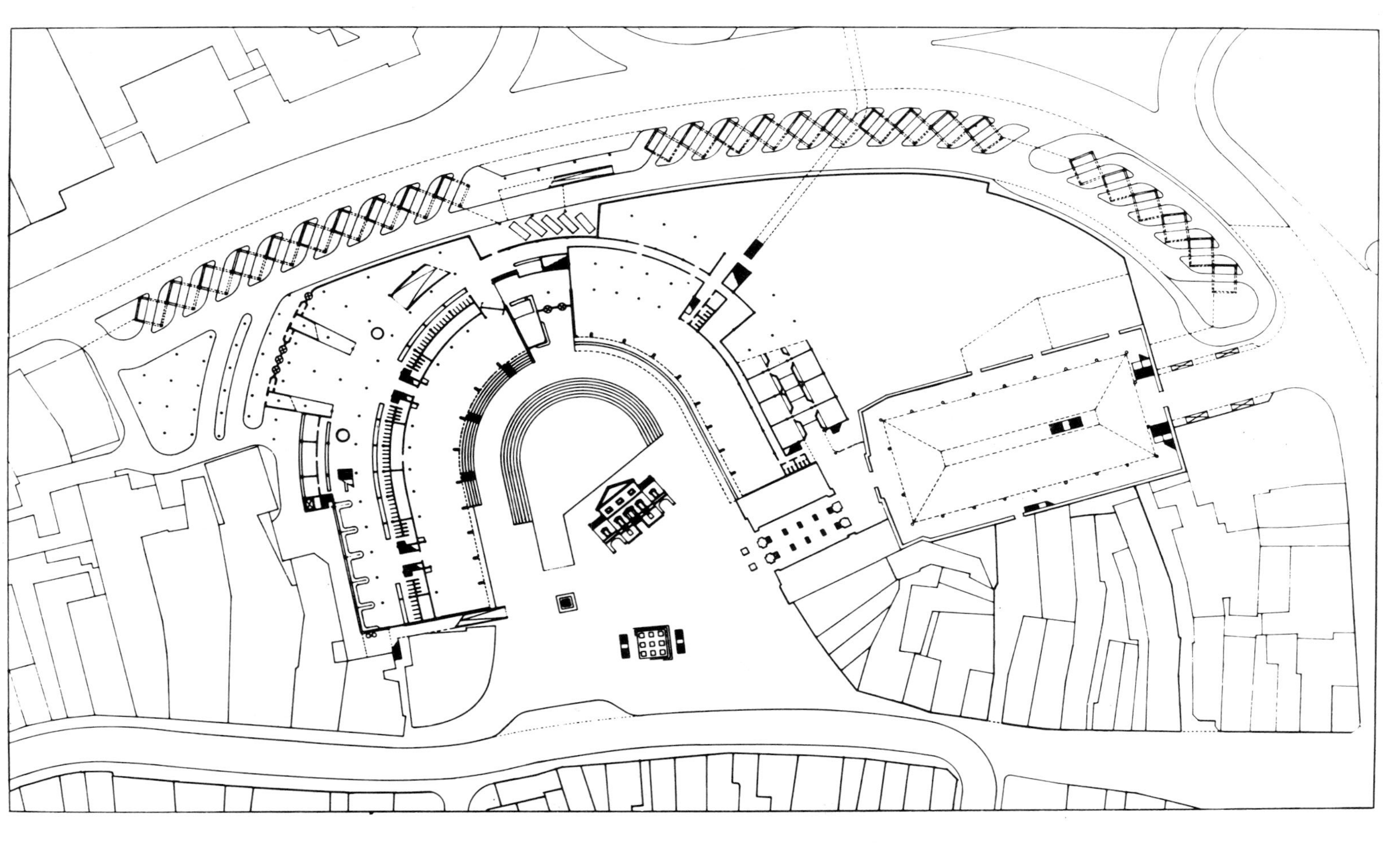

Figure 9. Plan of the Derby Civic Centre project by James Stirling and Partner.

divergent architectural vocabularies, we should perhaps recognize this in our view of the future townscape. Such an argument has been explored by Colin Rowe (1978) in his book *Collage City*, in which he recommends as a model for the city, not the single obsessive creation of the palace of Versailles, but rather the multiple and complex assemblage of Hadrian's Villa at Tivoli, with its recognition of a multi-valent architectural world.

In such a world the most important point of understanding is that each new statement falls within a context established by what has gone before, rather than, as at Versailles, ignoring that context, and this provides us with a third observation about the future townscape. Although there may be little consensus about the preferred form of the city, there is a new and widely shared conviction among thoughtful designers about the importance of context as a determinant of good design. This conviction is present in all of the theories outlined earlier, as well as underpinning the strategies of conservation, urban design plans and pedestrianization. It does not mean that new projects must imitate the forms of their neighbours, but rather it implies that, in addition to the internal brief generated by the client, each project has an obligation to recognize and then respond to and reinforce the positive urban characteristics of its location. This attitude is exemplified by James Stirling's (1975) project for Derby Civic Centre (Fig. 9), in which the whole building programme was bent (literally) to an urban design purpose, the recomposition of an historic central place which had been shattered by traffic and highway works. In this way, an "historical" urban design intention does not need to be accompanied by an historicist architectural vocabulary.

The invention of new urban components, an acceptance of a multi-valent urban townscape, and a greater regard for context, do not perhaps amount to a comprehensive programme for the formation of the future city centre. They may, however, provide us with clues as to its likely progress, and perhaps allow us some grounds for optimism that, although we may no longer possess a single unitary conviction about that progress, we can hope that it will adopt richer and more sympathetic patterns than in the immediate past.

REFERENCES

Alexander, C., *et al.* (1977). "The Timeless Way of Building", Vol. 1; "A Pattern Language", Vol. 2; "The Oregon Experiment", Vol. 3. Oxford University Press, Oxford.

Cullen, G. (1961). "Townscape". The Architectural Press, London.

Essex County Council (1973). "A Design Guide for Residential Areas". Essex County Council.

Habraken, N. J. (1972). "Supports: An Alternative to Mass Housing" (translated by B. Valkenburg). The Architectural Press, London.

Hill, R. (1980). *Marxism Today* Nov., 21-25.

Krier, L. (1978). *In* "Rational Architecture". Archives d'Architecture Moderne.

Lynch, K. (1960). "The Image of the City". The Technological Press and Harvard University Press, Cambridge, Mass.
McWilliam, C. (1978). "New Town Guide: The Story of Edinburgh's Georgian New Town". New Town Conservation Committee, Edinburgh.
Modulo (1959). **2**, 12.
Rowe, C. and Koetter, F. (1978). "Collage City". MIT Press, Cambridge, Mass.
San Francisco Department of City Planning (1970). "Preliminary Report No. 8: Urban Design Plans".
Saxon, R. G. (1979). *Arch. Rev.* March, 161-163.
Sennett, R. (1970). "The Uses of Disorder: Personal Identity and City Life". Penguin, Harmondsworth.
Stirling, J. (1975). "Buildings and Projects 1950-74". Thames and Hudson, London.

PART TWO

Changes in functional activities

FIVE

Renewal and employment

B. D. ROBSON and W. PACE

"Renewal": Make new or as good as new, resuscitate, revivify, regenerate: patch, fill up, reinforce, replace; . . . begin . . . or give anew (. . . grow young again . . . grant or be granted continuation); become new again (Oxford English Dictionary).

This chapter has two principal objectives: *first*, briefly to highlight the over-simplistic weaknesses of past abstractly "modelled" approaches to the *promotion and control* of renewal in central areas—especially in terms of their adverse impact on the scale and structure of vital economic and employment activities. *Secondly*, to advance a case for the development in future renewal of the central and closely related inner areas of our cities of a more "organic" approach to the *conservation and promotion* of complex activity patterns geared to satisfying with greater economic and social benefit than hitherto, the innate needs and potentials of those areas and the resident and working communities whom they serve.

Our argument is substantially based on the findings of a series of major operational urban design and management studies carried out by an interdisciplinary unit of the Departments of Architecture and of Town and Country Planning in the University of Newcastle upon Tyne, which was established in 1973 at the joint request of the Presidents of the R.I.B.A. and R.T.P.I., who reflected the growing public and professional concern about the insensitive effects of much post-war urban renewal activity. The findings of these studies have led us to conclude that each urban place possesses "uniquenesses" in the properties of its physical, sensory, and economic and social activity elements and in the qualities and opportunities which result from their interaction in time and space which, if ignored, will cause any policy established for the future development and management of that place to either miscarry or at least seriously under-achieve.

In advancing our argument for a more inductively-based approach to renewal, we do not seek to deny the operational value of the substantial established body of deductively-determined urban theory, but would suggest that the true value of that body of knowledge lies in its capacity—as a provider of measures of "general tendency"—to throw the "uniquenesses" of environmental situations into sharper but balanced relief. What we would deny, however, is the operational efficacy

THE FUTURE FOR THE CITY CENTRE
ISBN 0 12 206240 X

of standardized "instant" or "plug-in" models of urban renewal, which have characterized much of post-war city-centre planning and which represent, in their real sense, sub-optimal substitutes for creative analytical thinking.

HISTORICAL PRECEDENTS

Historical examination of urban structures demonstrates a natural process in which most emergent urban activities have sought, at least initially, to establish themselves in central area locations in close proximity to a wide range of other activities. But whereas over time some activities have consolidated and expanded within their initial central location others have migrated away from it. Thus it may be observed that the central area reflects in heightened perspective the very essence of the city—the need for "mutual accessibility"—and that because of its inherent and derived "convenience" attributes, it both attracts and retains those activities which serve the city as a whole, especially those which require a high degree of inter-personal contact; whereas those activities for whom mutual convenience of access *within* the enterprise has become the prime consideration, migrate over time to locations of inferior centrality. In our submission post-war planning has so interfered with this natural process that central areas no longer so readily attract new growth activities, whilst the outward migration of established central area activities has so increased that it is possible for Allpass *et al.* (1967) to define a Central Business District function as "A function which has not yet left the CBD."

For example, post-war plans have in effect completed this process (which gained momentum in the inter-war years) under which previously substantial residential populations have transferred to suburban estates. These in turn have encouraged new growth industries to locate initially in suburban locations, thus leaving multiple-deprived inner area communities over-dependent on declining industries with their diminishing and low paid job opportunities; and encouraged the development of district shopping centres which have deprived central areas of their traditional staple resource, namely the supply of convenience and lower-order durable goods.

Shopping facilities are an important determinant of the quality of life for communities and are an important source of employment—for example in Tyne & Wear, the total of 50 000 jobs in shops represents 10 per cent of the total employment of the County. Formal schemes of development and redevelopment by development companies acting in concert with local authorities have been the most apparent feature of central area renewal throughout the 1960s and 1970s; but it is the structural economic changes which these schemes have brought with them that are the most significant. Whereas gross shopping floor space and unit size have increased, total shop employment has tended to decrease, and at the same time the proportion of female employment has risen significantly in relation to that of men, as has part-time relative to full-time employment. Many of these larger shop units are occupied by branches of national multiple firms which do not integrate fully into the local regional economy in the sense that, unlike their locally-based predecessors, they do not draw upon and sustain locally produced goods and services. Standardization of goods has increased and it is noteworthy, for example, that in the public participation exercise for the Newcastle City Centre Local Plan there was strong public opinion against further northward expansion of the major new Eldon Square Shopping Centre and more support for encouraging fuller use of existing building conservation stock in the southern part of the city centre for smaller shop unit accommodation, which would "increase the range of choice of goods available and the attractiveness of the centre as a whole". Many major centres have great difficulty in securing and even retaining specialist quality goods shops. Thus the redeveloped centres of Birmingham, Coventry and Bristol have difficulty in attracting regional shopping populations away from the old established specialist shopping centres of Leamington Spa and Cheltenham.

Another substantial feature of post-war central area renewal has been the proliferation of office developments associated with the major national growth in "white collar service" activities and employment. In general terms this growth has been beneficial, but four cautionary notes should be sounded for the future. *First*, much of this growth in "white collar" activity has been absorbed in speculative office developments which, as future generations are likely to discover, are less adaptable to changing needs than is the under-employed reserve of existing building conservation stock in city centres which could otherwise have accommodated this expansion. *Secondly*, these new office developments are not exclusive to city centres, as a significant amount of new office floor space has been permitted in suburban district centres. *Thirdly*, this growth in "white collar" sector activity has tended to favour female employment and has not succeeded in offsetting the net loss of male job opportunities in the other main industrial sectors. *Fourthly*, the fact that the rate of growth in "white collar" activity in the Special Development Areas (such as the north-east of England) has tended to lag behind that for the nation as a whole, means that they are still over-dependent on other regions for the provision of vital financial, business, professional and scientific services, and this is an impediment to truly self-sustaining economic growth in those areas. Putting these four factors together, it will be important, particularly in the development areas:

(i) to focus future office developments on the main city centres which, as the dominant regional providers of higher order goods and services, are best placed to compete nationally for scarce investment resources, and contain substantial reserves of suitable but presently under-utilized building conservation stock; and

(ii) to increase the number and range of male employment opportunities in city centres—which represent the point of maximum accessibility advantage for a wider region.

The aspect of post-war central area renewal policies which has received the greatest and most sustained adverse reactions has been the measures adopted to resolve urban congestion—land-use zoning and urban motorway construction.

From early in the century it has been conventional planning wisdom that a significant contributor to urban congestion was the intimate locational inter-mixture of activities of different kinds, and that this could be resolved by the enforcement of clear-cut land-use zoning provisions. The weaknesses of this principle as applied in post-war central area renewal policies will be dealt with more fully later, but it will be helpful to indicate three of the more salient ones now. *First*, in its application this principle has tended to ignore the differences in operational characteristics and requirements of finer groupings of activities within the same land-use class. *Secondly*, there has been a tendency to regard ground floor activities as the effective dominant use and to disregard the significance and operational requirements of upper floor activities of a different kind. *Thirdly*, application of the principle has weakened the ability of activities of different kinds to afford close mutual support and desirable reinforcement of each other.

The provision of relief highways in city centre renewal has a much longer history, but government adoption of the recommendations of the Buchanan Report on *Traffic in Towns* (1963) opened the way to full-blooded urban motorway schemes which generally were proposed to be routed through the supposedly "soft" zones of transition between central and inner city areas. Where these motorways were actually constructed they resulted in the destruction of substantial numbers of small- to medium-size business and industrial enterprises of the kind which we are now encouraged to (re) provide as a contribution to national economic recovery and fuller employment. Along the planning-blighted, proposed routes of motorways which have not been proceeded with, a more immediate complex situation has arisen. Large numbers of existing firms unwilling to continue with substantial operational investment elected to leave these areas, to be replaced by enterprises prepared to accept insecurity in return for lower rentals which offset low profit margins. Many of these adventitiously located enterprises have become valuable contributors to the economic and social welfare of central and inner city areas but, with the abandonment of motorway proposals in favour of public transport priority policies, they are now vulnerable to activities which can afford to pay higher site costs. This raises the question of whether, in addition to "enterprise zones" which protect new enterprises from the full operation of public taxation and planning controls, there would be merit in introducing another class of "zone" within which both existing and new enterprises would in effect be protected from the unfettered operation of the open property market.

It is in many respects fortunate that local authorities are no longer in a financial position to engage in the blanket and prescriptive approaches to urban renewal which have been common in city centres since the war. It is important now to redirect attention to improving the quality and effectiveness of the social and economic environments of our central and inner city areas, but on a more selective and more sensitively informed basis than hitherto, and with physical adaptation and change, as the servants, and not the determinants of those ends.

In the past few years there has—especially in the more enlightened authorities—

been a silent revolution in the planning process which has become less long-term and regulative and more immediately entrepreneurial in its orientation. Planners are increasingly expected to interpret the organic processes of change in specific situations in terms relevant and specific to that situation. They are increasingly required to possess the creative ability to identify opportunities suggested by a close appreciation of the needs, potentials, resources and aspirations of actual working and resident communities. They are increasingly required to posses the persuasive skills of collaborational management necessary to secure acceptance and implementation of those opportunities presented by other agencies and private individuals and groups—reserving scarce local authority investment resources for the initial pump priming of implementation, and thereafter to carry out those elements of renewal projects which are beyond the economic or constitutional competence of others to undertake.

We now turn to the bases on which those new skills and understanding should be developed.

CONCEPTUALIZING THE URBAN RENEWAL PROCESS

Planning for the city centre and adjacent areas in the future needs to relate more to those natural organic processes that have led to the mixing and overlapping of land uses within these locations. This requires an alternative conceptual approach to the rigid design blueprints of past plans and we can take as our starting point the ideas of Christopher Alexander. In his book, *A City is Not a Tree*, Alexander (1965) suggested that the pattern of activities to be found in an urban area can be looked at in terms of its being the spatial manifestation of a complex set of interactions and linkages at work. This is represented in a simplistic way in Fig. 10, where the numbers denote a variety of activities, the lines in the lattice-type arrangements the inter-linkages that operate between them, and the lines in the plan form of the diagram a series of locational fields in which they might be found. The overlap between these locational fields indicates the potential interaction that can occur between the activities in a spatial context.

This can be contrasted with the type of design concepts used in the deliberate segregation of land uses in the past. Figure 11 is a scaled down original masterplan of a successful New Town. Industry is given great incentive to locate in New Towns with heavy subsidy, very cheap land and a young overspill population.

There is, however, no possibility of overlap within this model without which many activities and services cannot locate at all, let alone build up linkages. Essentially it constitutes the "tree concept" that Alexander has been critical of. This concept has been endemic among those concerned with city planning in an endeavour to simplify that which is essentially a complex matrix of activity. The high employment in inner areas occurs in those parts of cities which have survived this process of imposing zoning and a separation of uses.

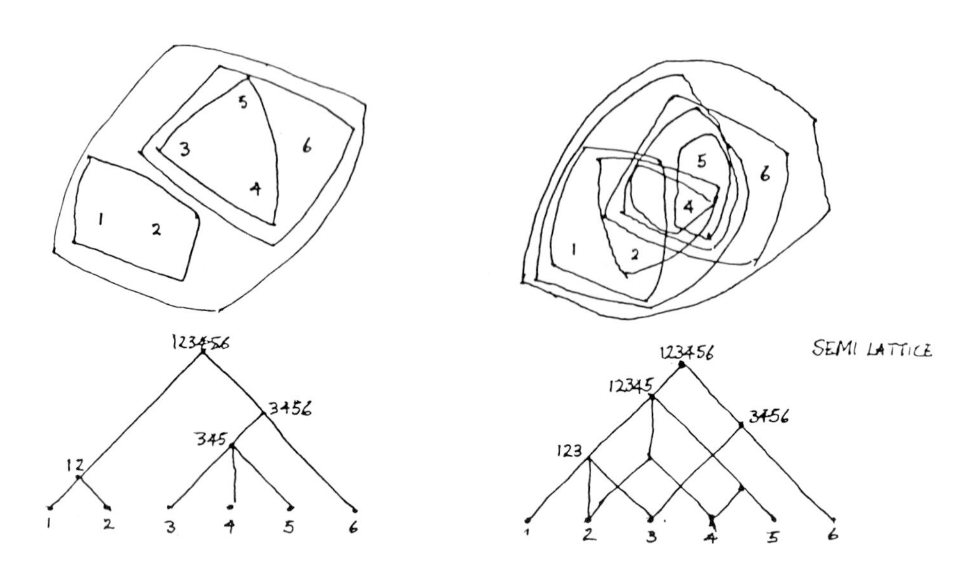

Figure 10. Sketch of alternative levels of interaction within a town.

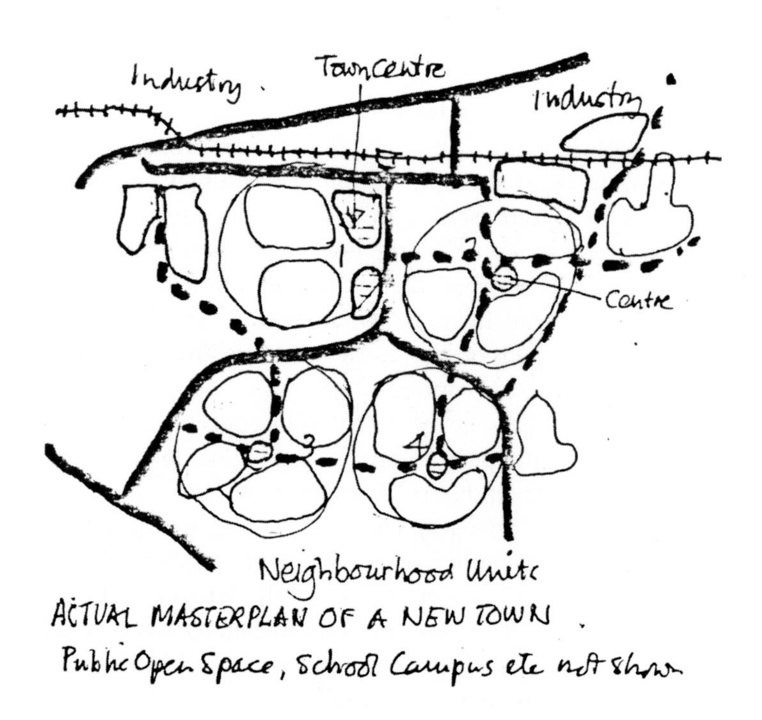

Figure 11. Sketch of a typical master plan for a new town.

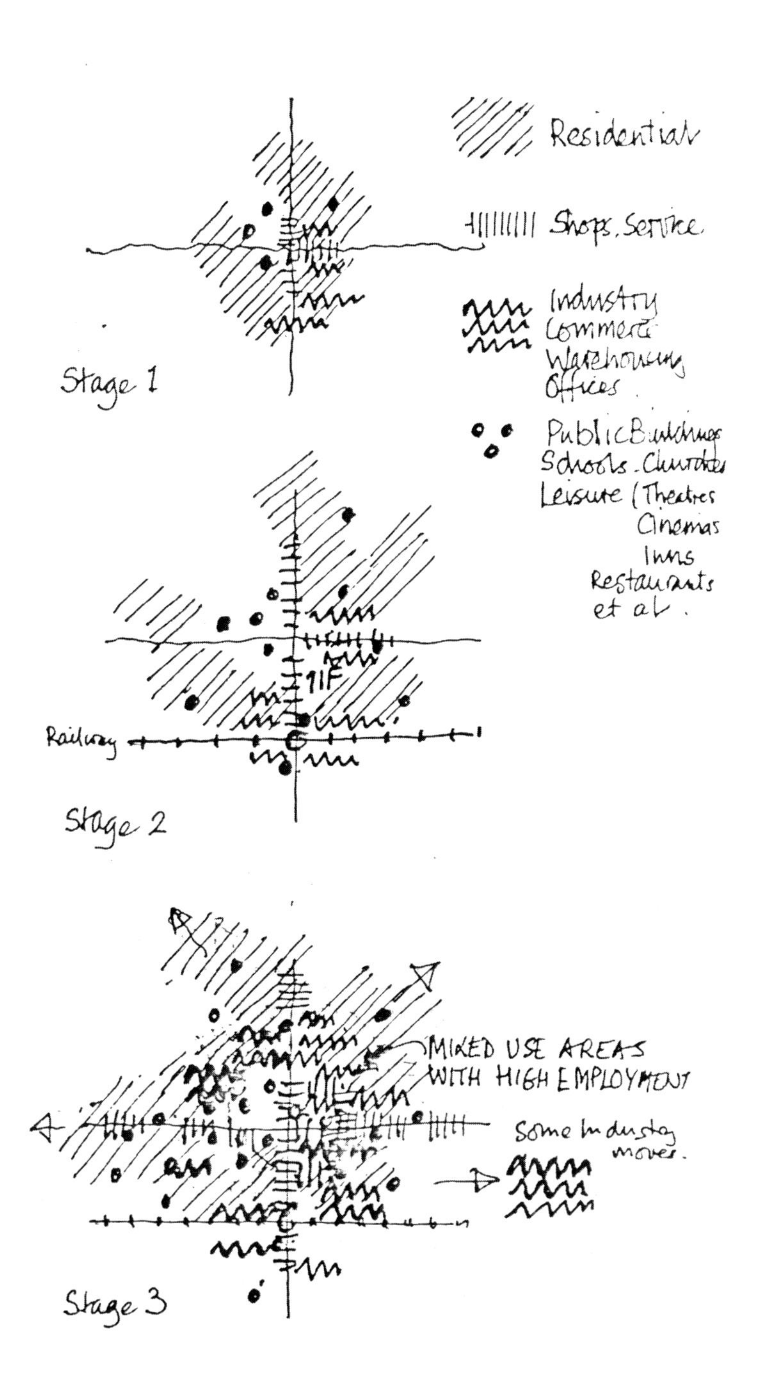

Figure 12. Sketch of the typical development of old settlements.

It is not really possible to draw adequate diagrams of old developed settlements as they are essentially all different. But stages 1, 2 and 3 (Fig. 12) are intended to show in broad terms the typical development of a town as it expands and all uses require more space. Some such as offices and entertainments may be new uses which only come in when the town is large enough. At stage 3, provided redevelopment and road schemes have not interfered, there will be substantial overlap areas of mixed use between residential, shopping, entertainment and industry, containing an element which has grown because of networks to *all* the overlapping uses. These sorts of areas will be found in most large towns or cities as well as in small towns.

These areas frequently have the following characteristics:

(a) High employment density.
(b) Most of the employment not registered or known by the local authority.
(c) A slightly run-down appearance.
(d) Cheap accommodation.
(e) Great vulnerability—because of b and c—these are the "grey areas" ripe for ring roads, parking lots or clearance for no clearly understood motive. This of course destroys not only the activities within the area but in destroying the linkages with areas inside and out also adversely affects other areas and the general economic health of the town. Even when such an area is cleared for redevelopment of a positive nature the result may not be advantageous from an employment point of view.

In the area of the new Eldon Square development in Newcastle, for example, although the scheme is much more intense and integrated with the city fabric than most developments of this sort, the employment that has been created is slightly less than what previously existed. It has of course the advantage of bringing a number of multi-national retailers of quality into the city, but this is a mixed blessing when many of the older shops and services of an indigenous nature were "priced out" and in many cases went out of business altogether. (Some managed to re-locate, either in the new green (retail) market in the new complex or in older cheap accommodation elsewhere. Exact figures for the amount of relocation are not known to the writer but estimates vary between one-third and one-half.)

The cogent point about these indigenous shops and services is that they were locally owned in most cases and frequently used local wholesaling and manufacturers, so that the money was "ploughed back" into the area, whereas in the case of the multi-nationals it goes elsewhere and is only marginally (if at all) concerned with local networks and linkages.

It is not the intention to be overcritical towards what must be one of the better indoor shopping centres in the world but to make the point that if this has not improved the employment situation, how much deterioration must have occurred with less well considered schemes, not to mention the great losses by the "empty clearance" road works and SLOAP* which is so often the result. Several thousand jobs were probably lost in the great swathe demolished between Shields Road and the "Byker Wall", for example, in the eastern part of the inner city of Newcastle. The writer suggested during discussions prior to the Eldon Square development that a planned move for the existing activities ought to take place to other parts of the city to bolster the conservation and other areas. This was sympathetically regarded by Ted Dickson, then Deputy City Planner, the concept being to "rehouse" at a peppercorn rent initially.

The basic problem is that new developments appeal to developers (obviously) and to financial officials such as Treasurers and Estates personnel whose job it is to obtain maximum rates and returns regardless of employment or service to the public.

In order to reinforce and develop the study of inner town and city overlap areas and their employment potential, it is now proposed to examine briefly certain aspects of projects for three such areas carried out by the Newcastle University Urban Design Team, in 1978, 1979-1980 and 1977 respectively for (a) a section of the south-west "centre periphery" of Newcastle (other "periphery" areas of the city centre are currently being studied); (b) the Glasgow Cross and "Enochs" area; (c) North Shields Centre. This will be done via a series of notes and sketch diagrams.

SOME CASE STUDIES

Newcastle: south-west periphery

A Newcastle University survey team recorded 4657 people working in the area (Fig. 13) which, given that this represented about 80% of the total, suggested an overall figure of about 5600. The area itself comprises 21·5 hectares, therefore yielding a gross employment density of 260 persons per hectare or 104 per acre. There is also a considerable residential population living above shops and pubs and the area encroaches into the Summerhill/Rye Hill residential districts. The Crown Metropole housing scheme on Clayton Street provides accommodation for 600 people. An interesting additional factor is the range of property values in the area which are high in the northern part of Newgate Street, medium in upper Clayton Street and become progressively lower in the Westgate Road/Blackfriars quarter and towards the south where there is blight due to possible motorway or other major road developments.

This means that numerous activities only exist because of the low values, but in other cases spontaneous relocation and continued commercial use have settled on a more permanent basis, the blighting being of such long standing that occupiers have

*SLOAP = space left over after planning.

become "immunized" against the likelihood of redevelopment. (The medium low values in Clayton Street have of course been in existence ever since it was built.) The effect has been in total to produce what could be said to be a spontaneous "Enterprise Zone" but one in which the traditional interaction between commerce is possible and where multi-use encourages services, pubs, cafes and "local" shopping.

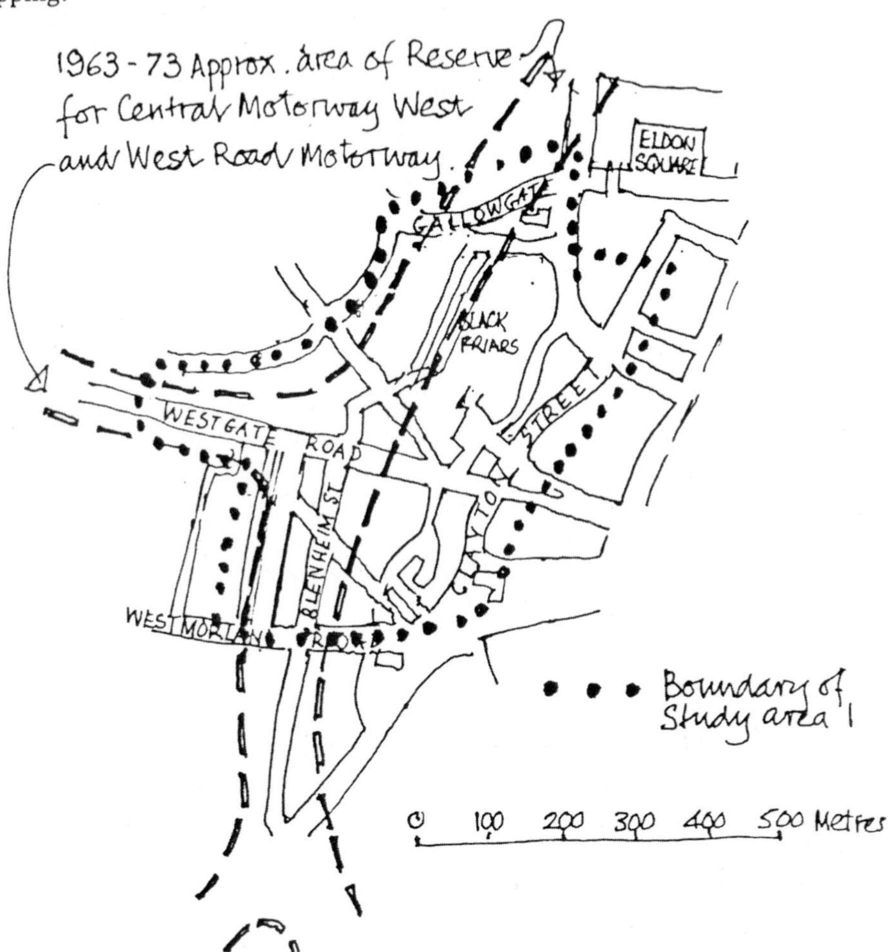

Figure 13. Sketch of the south-west periphery of Newcastle upon Tyne.

Glasgow Cross area study

The Glasgow Cross study brought several points into prominence (Fig. 14). There was a major blighting problem because of the projected East Link Road. There was also a social problem with gangsterism and meths drinking. There was considerable dereliction, most of the tenements having been demolished leaving shop premises only at ground floor level.

The area had been assumed to be neither Central nor part of the Glasgow East

Area Renewal Programme and did not feature in plans for either. The survey by the Newcastle University Team in 1979 found however that:

(a) There were numerous activities operating in the area because of its location as an overlap between the central and inner area—needing ready access to the former.
(b) That the Barrows were very significant in the location of many small industries, services and shops.

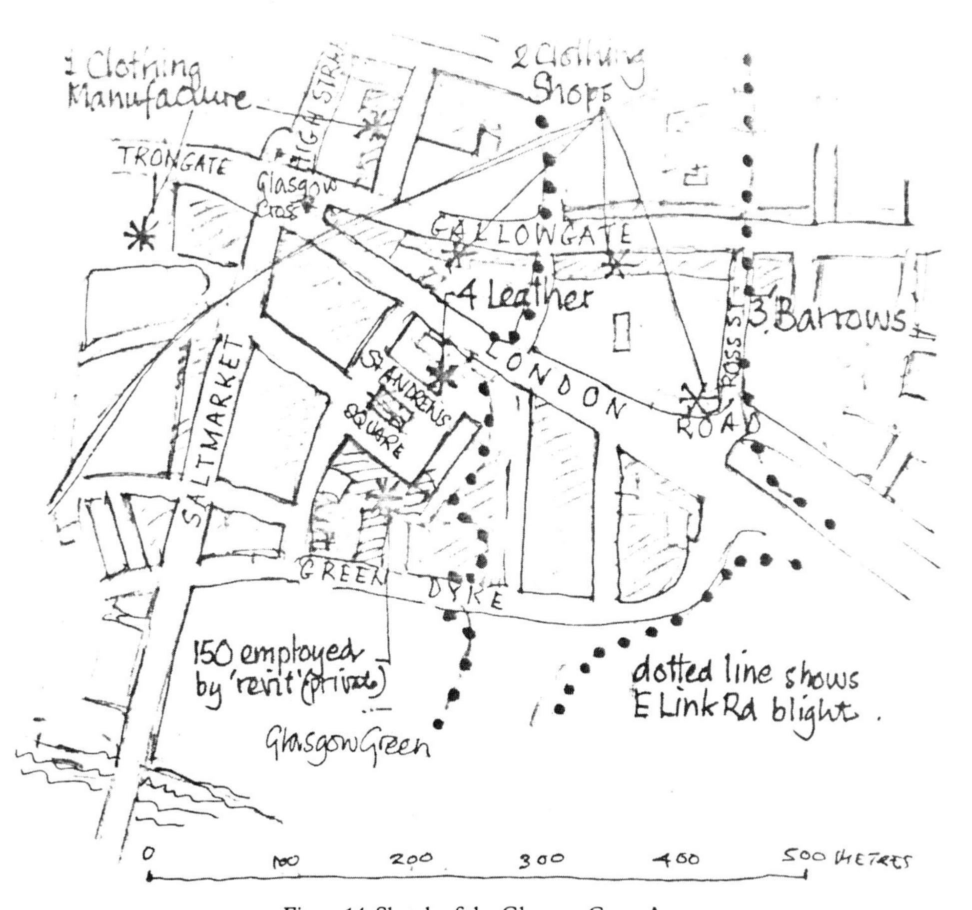

Figure 14. Sketch of the Glasgow Cross Area.

(c) That there was a definite matrix of activities.
(d) That there was a demand for accommodation from small businesses wishing to set up, as well as from some of longer standing. (Revitalization of 4-5 storey listed buildings on one side of St Andrews Square for lettable commercial premises produced an employment in this block alone of over 150 within a year of the property being purchased.)

A specific example (Fig. 15) will help to illustrate these points.

A considerable amount of clothing was manufactured in the Cross area and in the adjacent Enochs area. This "exported" to national wholesalers but also sold "2nds" direct to the Barrows. A specialist firm of leather workers employing 28 people was located in St Andrews Square. Because of their central location they sold:

(a) to those who sought them out visiting Glasgow;
(b) to the adjacent clothing manufacturers (belts and buttons);
(c) 2nds to the Barrows and local shops.

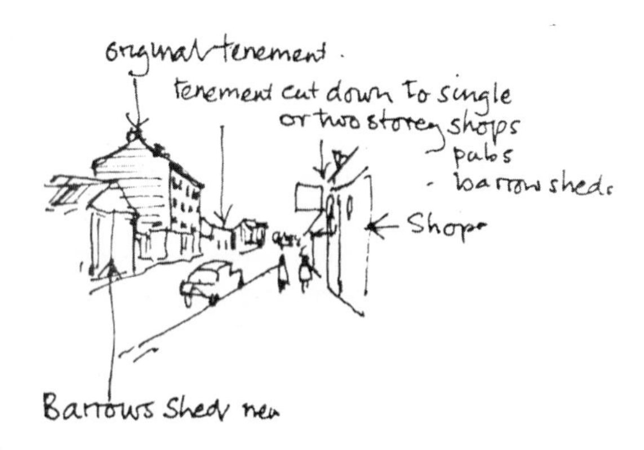

Figure 15. Sketch of a typical street in Glasgow's Cross Area.

The leather goods manufacturer was typical of many who found the need for a fairly central location, but equally or more important formed part of an "activity network". They could not in fact have survived as businesses without their regular supply to the clothing trade—precarious under late twentieth century economic conditions—which in turn relied on a local network for the supply of belts and buttons, thread and servicing, sewing machines and inexpensive centrally located premises. The role of the Barrows and lower-end of the scale clothes retailing was very important and was enough to cross the threshold of viability in some of the manufacturing businesses.

An attempt was made by the Newcastle University Team to develop an interactivity matrix related to this part of Glasgow. This has obviously been complex and is not complete even now. It did attempt, however, to show which commercial and other activities were interdependent and went far enough to prove that interdependence was more than just an hypothesis. If a certain activity was removed through insensitive redevelopment, for example, a whole further range of activities went with it, to the employment deficit of the area. Other activities on the other hand were "footloose" and could be relocated if necessary, although there were few longer established businesses in the area which had not formed local linkages of some sort, and even many of the newer ones had located there because of proximity to the centre.

In Glasgow East, the removal of much of the residential accommodation had lowered the viability of quite a lot of "local shopping" and many pubs and cafes relied largely on the Barrows and on the large working population for survival. Since the survey was done it must be said that the proposals for the East link road have been scaled down to an extent where it should be possible to keep the Barrows Market linkages and avoid displacing much of the local commercial and industrial activities. Also, there has been quite a lot of housing revitalization in the Saltmarket area.

The necessity of an exhaustive door-to-door survey in determining essential "roles" of part of a larger city is amply illustrated by the "Enochs" area survey, carried out by the Newcastle University Team in 1980 (Fig.16). This area in fact overlapped the Glasgow Cross survey area in so far as the revitalized Saltmarket was by then coming into occupation. A casual pilot study, and data drawn from general local sources, gave an impression of shopping with run down office accommodation above—although this was largely unoccupied (Fig. 17).

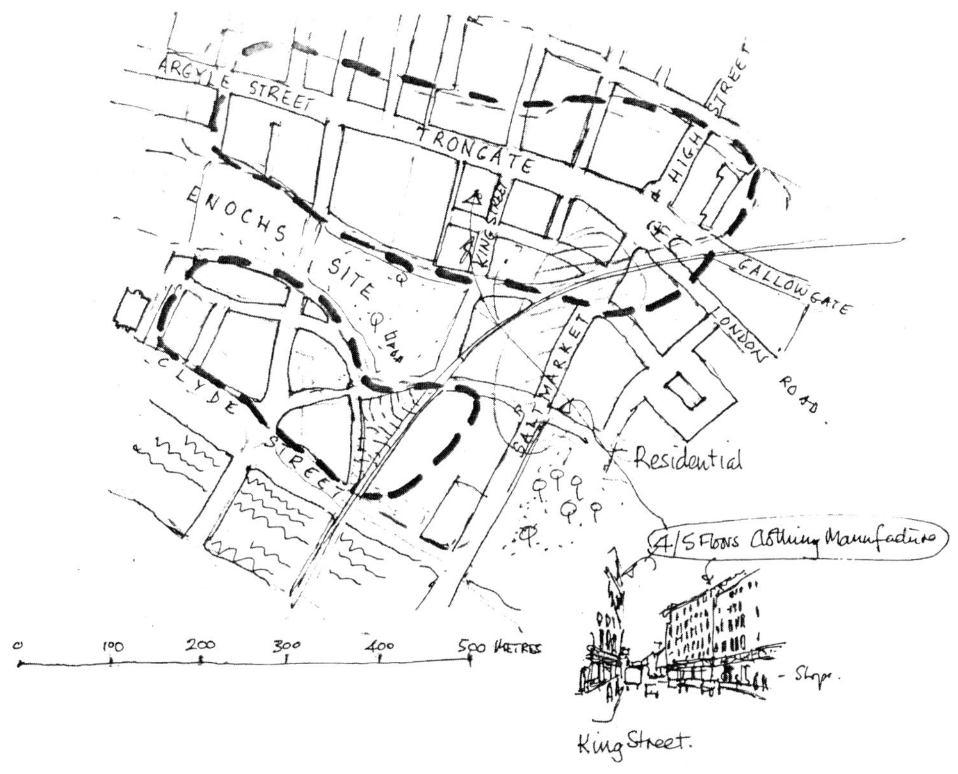

Figures 16 and 17. Fig. 16 (left) Sketch of the Glasgow Enochs Area. Fig. 17 (right) Sketch of a typical street in Glasgow's Enoch's Area.

The detailed survey, however, produced a total working population of 10 000 in the areas ringed on the plan (about 0·5 km^2 in total), almost half of this number being employed in manufacturing.

North Shields centre

This area comprises mainly shops and services. Prior to the development of a new shopping centre, there were 124 shops of which 42 were engaged in food trades. The traditional centre has therefore acted as both a sub-regional and local focus of shopping with 8000 people living within 10 min walking distance of it. There were 62 service establishments in 1977, comprising a mixture of cafes, pubs and specialist

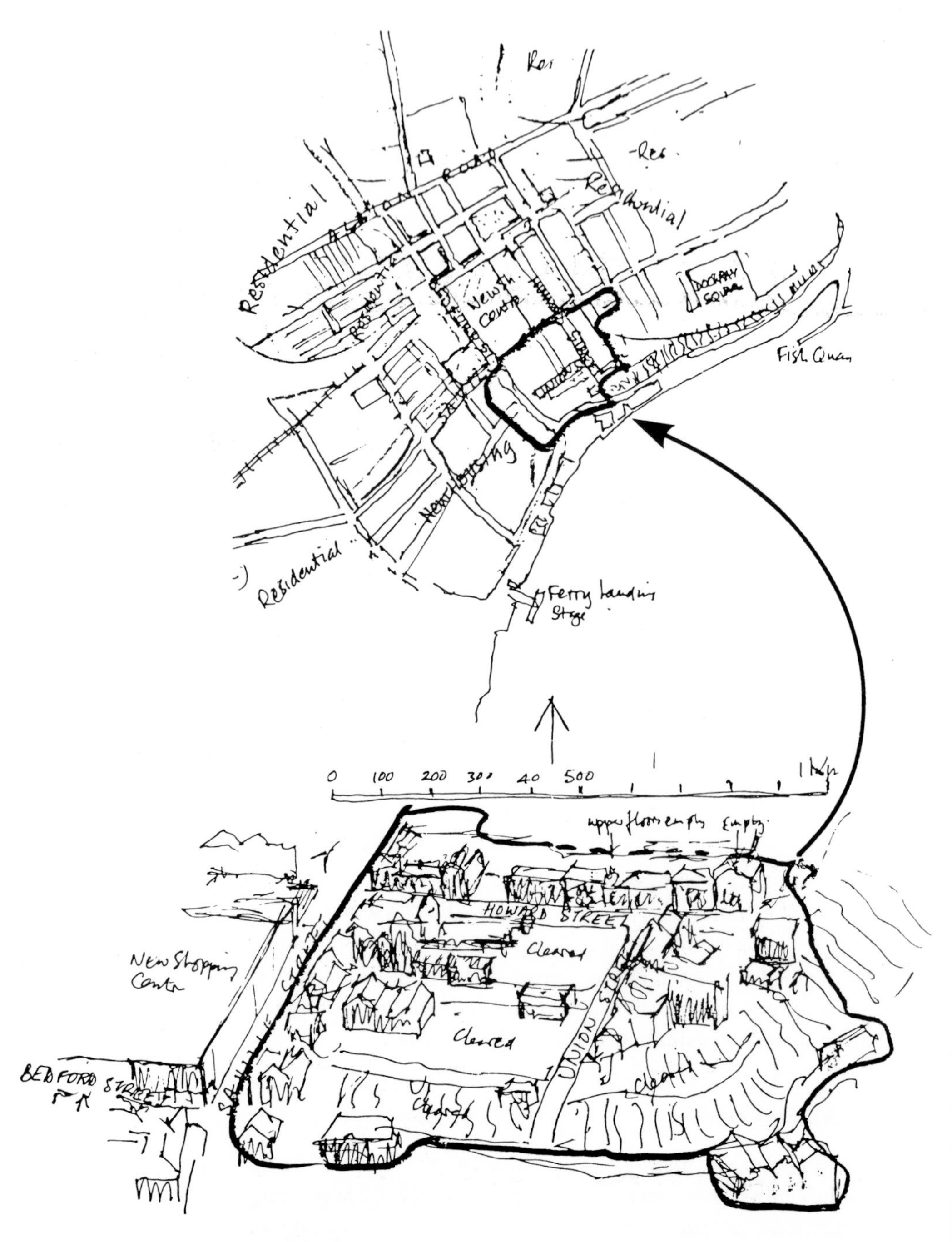

Figures 18 and 19. Fig. 18 (above) Sketch of the town centre of North Shields. Fig. 19 (below) Sketch of part of the redevelopment area of North Shield's centre.

activities. These, together with the shops, rendered a significant amount of employment; and the contribution made by retailing and allied activities to employment generation are in general often neglected.

The area shown outlined in the 1/10 000 plan (Fig. 18) was blighted by proposals for a new Civic Centre and looks 75 per cent derelict (Fig. 19). It was found from a door-to-door survey to employ over 400 people, 40 per cent in light and service industry, 40 per cent in services and shops and 20 per cent in offices. All activities required both a central location (the industries being linked to other uses and usually having a "retail outlet") and cheap accommodation. This small part of the periphery of North Shields, to quote from the report, "despite its derelict appearance, thus supports a large labour force. In the whole of North Tyneside there are only eleven employers employing more than a total of 300 workers." The areas of mixed shopping and service industry around the town centre thus perform an employment function equal to that of large industries. An employer proposing to employ 300 would be treated with respect and offered many incentives to locate his business within the town; but conversely the local authority has plans to redevelop most of the areas around the town centre. This is inconsistent policy especially in view of the unemployment problem. It is suggested that the function of the town centre mixed use area needs to be strengthened and confidence enhanced by

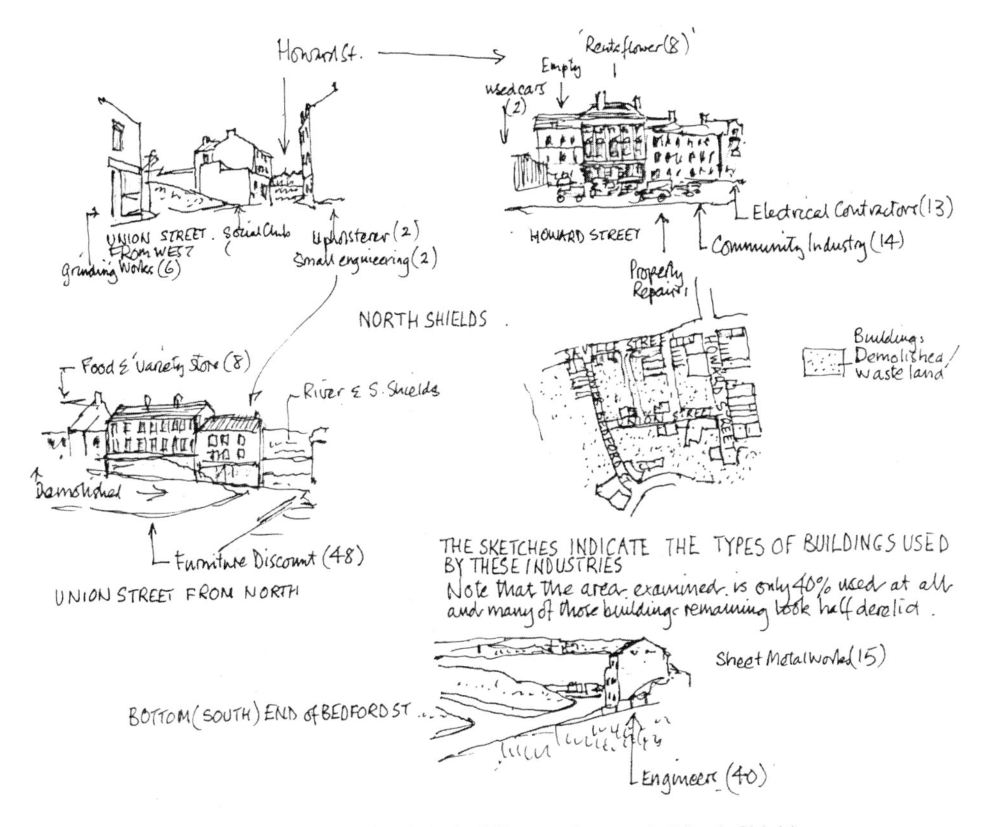

Figure 20. Sketches of various buildings and streets in North Shields.

positive local authority policy. (It is encouraging that because the publication of the report the Planning Officer has carried out a major review of policy, and proposals for a more conservation-orientated approach have been recognized as allowing many activities to remain and flourish if sensitively handled in detail.)

Some indication of the present level of blight conditions to be found within the central area are shown in Fig. 20. Since the survey in 1977 several more buildings have become blighted.

SPECIFIC PROPOSALS

Conservation can be a positive planning tool if the priorities of conservation are the retention of: (a) activities, (b) resources, and (c) heritage, in that order.

The fact that high employment exists in areas overlapping inner and central areas of towns and cities has, it is hoped, been convincingly demonstrated. This has been shown to rely on (a) especially in the form of closely knit activity patterns with linkages to other activities and to central and inner areas. The resources of existing building fabrics, historically significant or otherwise, lie in their being highly adaptable and inexpensive, but as has been emphasized they are highly vulnerable. Where (c) is involved there is more chance of (b) being preserved, but there is a great danger that if architectural heritage values are overemphasized without consideration for (a) and (b) these activities may be jeopardized by being "priced out" or removed as unsuitable.

North Shields

In the report on the North Shields centre the proposals by the Newcastle University Team suggested that the main area of shopping and related services, service

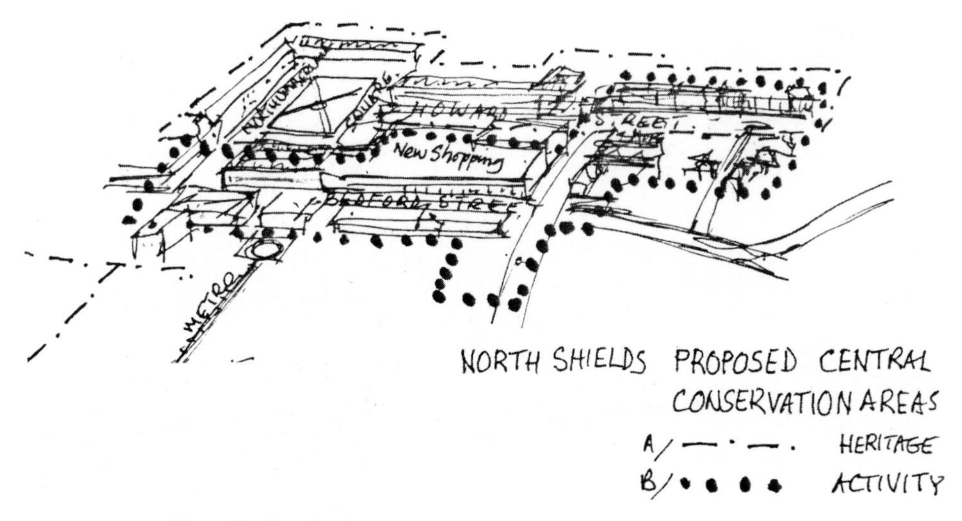

Figure 21. Sketch of the proposed conservation area of North Shields.

industry and small-scale manufacturing should be treated as an Activity Conservation Area. This is shown in Fig. 21.

The areas of overlap between these kinds of conservation are where the greatest discretion and flexibility are called for. The Chief Planning Officer has discussed with the authors the possibility of the New Civic Centre/Council Offices being in converted premises and infill in Howard Street. This could certainly be preferable to the wholesale blighting which a new Civic Centre has caused elsewhere, but even on the small scale should be seen in the light of the potential relocation of those activities that would be displaced in the immediate area before work commenced.

Glasgow St Andrews Square

Figure 22 shows buildings (listed Grade 2) bought and renovated by Tom Keen for industrial and commercial purposes. Table 1 gives a breakdown of employment at the time of the survey when renovation was half complete and did not include buildings at the rear (a Cooperage etc.). The buildings taken over by Tom Keen were given a "five year permission". Work commenced in 1978 and was about half complete at the time of the University Team survey. The premises were filled as soon as complete, working from the ground up.

Conversion was really a matter of waterproofing, providing goods lifts, fire escapes and fireproofing. The planning officers were concerned that more was not

Figure 22. Sketch of St Andrews Square, Glasgow (East End).

TABLE 1

Employment in St Andrews Square (Nos 36, 38, 40, 42, 44), Glasgow, 1978

Nature of business	Full-time	Part-time	Mostly off premises but full-time
Clothing manufacture	13	—	2
Clothing wholesale	2	—	—
Dental manufacture	3	2	4
Shopfitter/advert. (2 firms)	20	—	7
Wholesale paper/education supplies	11	10	2
Sign manufacture	18	—	3
Printers	2	3	—
Alarm systems	4	—	2
Janitorical supplies	2	—	4
Upholsterers (3 firms)	18	—	6
Cash registers	2	4	4
Dress designers	4	—	—
Manufacturing Coopers	18	—	—
Piano repairs	2	—	2
	119	19	36

Note. There were two distinctive classes of occupier. Because of Tom Keen's monthly tenacy many of the occupiers (nearly all) were newly formed activities. Many hoped to move to their own premises later so that the venture had the nature of a nursery. Others such as the Coopers had set up plant and intended to stay. Nearly all stressed the necessity to be near the centre.

Figure 23. Sketch of St Andrews Square, Glasgow (East End).

being done on "heritage restoration" in view of their historic and architectural placing, but if these buildings had not been taken over when they were they would have very likely become quite derelict. From the "activity point" of view, these buildings (Fig. 23) and their new uses had in fact turned the tide of evacuation from a previously blighted area.

It has been suggested that this is a clear case for partnership between user/developer and the local authority, who could provide extra monies or carry out works themselves on stonecleaning, renovation of porches, railings etc.

EMPLOYMENT DENSITY

The illustrations shown earlier regarding Glasgow and Newcastle indicate a high gross density of employment in overlap areas. Table 2 amplifies this. The Industrial Estates of Team Valley (established nearly 50 years) and Teesside (approximately 16 years old), are compared to emphasize the enormous difference in employment density between new and old areas. For example, the Newcastle area and Glasgow have densities four times that of Team Valley and 13 times that of Teesside Estate.

These figures reinforce claims about "mixed use areas" engendering additional employment activity, but still understate the difference in employment density. The gross areas include a resident population of 1500 in Glasgow, 4000 in Covent Garden and nearly 25 000 in Edinburgh, plus churches, art galleries, museums, and particularly in Edinburgh, considerable areas of gardens and public open space and parks.

It is not within the scope of this chapter, nor necessary to a highly responsible readership, to deplore the prodigal waste by modern industrial development of our main resource—land; and the basic inefficiency of dispersal has been extensively criticized by others, notably Bruce Alsopp (1974). In the context of inner city employment, however, this factor is critical. The interrelationships and close knit linkages between activities can only be sustained if gross employment density is high. This needs special emphasis because of the national penchant for low density "Noddyland", which while being prevalent in housing (the Crown Development in Newcastle being a happy exception to this), is of disease proportions in industry; and it would be tragic if "Enterprise Zones" and other attempts were doomed by the "single storey SLOAP" syndrome.

What is clear is that much of the industry involved and most of the services lose nothing by operating on upper floors, though provision of goods lifts and adequate fire escapes are obvious priorities in revitalization (see the St Andrew's Square revitalization which proves that it is economic to do this).*

Figure 24. Sketch of an old commercial building, Glasgow.

* The fact that a commercial entrepreneur could so readily provide these services up to required standards (granted fairly minimal), keep listed buildings in operation and have a demand which "swallowed up" accommodation as soon as converted and still make a profit, is surely significant.

TABLE 2

Comparisons of gross employment density in various central areas

Part of town surveyed	Area surveyed (ha)	Total employment	Employment density (gross) persons/ha (acres)	Date and source of survey
Newcastle S.W. centre	21·5	5600	260 (104)	1978 Newcastle Unversity Team
Glasgow Trongate/Saltmarket	50·0	11 000	220 (88)	1979 Newcastle University Team
Covent Garden GLC action area	48·0	28 500	590 (236)	1975 GLC
Edinburgh New Town conservation area	318·0	53 659	170 (68)	1977 Edinburgh City Planning
Newcastle Team Valley trading estate	275·0	15 580	57 (23)	EIEC March 1981 Inc Fruit Market EIEC Personnel, NCB etc.
Teesside industrial estate	134·0	2902	22 (8)	EIEC June 1981 Inc "lease" and "sold" Estate laid out 1964-1965

The Glasgow clothing industry was mostly concentrated in those very well glazed, early nineteenth century commercial buildings (Fig. 24) for which the city is famous. In fact most of the people working there, questioned by the team in Glasgow, Newcastle and other towns and cities, expressed a preference for an inner location. The high intensity of use, apart from working linkages of the "go across the road and get another gross of wee brass buttons" type, puts the people working there within minutes of public transport, shops, pubs, cafés etc., which they could not get "out on the prairies".

The corollary to the revitalization of multi-storey buildings in inner areas for commerce, industry—both manufacturing and service (mixed with retail outlets, pubs, cafés and housing of course)—is that new premises for these uses should be "flatted" and should also be as flexible as possible. It should be a sobering thought to us all—particularly architects—that only old buildings appear to be suited for a variety of purposes. (The RIBA Long Life, Loose Fit, Low Energy Project attempts to move the emphasis to flexibility and mixed use of building structure.) The microchip could call into question quite a lot of office space (though the small "users" in these sorts of areas are less likely to be affected) and the pressure to make multi-storey car parks more flexible has been well publicized over the past few years (as it is obvious that a change in transportation emphasis or merely a change in traffic management could make these massive and expensive structures moribund overnight).

While some of the case-study areas examined showed a fairly active use of upper floors it was evident that others showed considerable under-usage. This was generally, though not exclusively, in the cases where there was a shopping demand for the ground floor, and access to the upper floors was via the shop. Clayton Street in Newcastle illustrated this point very well. Some shops, notably furniture shops, have taken advantage of the cheap accommodation of the upper floors engendered by access difficulty. A furniture shop could be said to be half retail and half warehouse and in several parts of the town—the most extensive being Chapmans on the east side of the centre, retailers have turned this to advantage. (It will be noted that Clayton Street has a large number of furniture shops.) In other cases, however, this has been a great disadvantage and this has apparently always been so. A very venerable eye-witness told the writer that he recalled "pigeons roosting in upper floors in Clayton Street which had never been let since Grainger built them!" It is here that local authorities could very beneficially act as agents for renewal.

Included in the University recommendations for Newcastle was a specific proposal for a new commercial building to be combined with a shopping pedestrian-way using a then vacant shop, joining Clayton Street to Low Friar Street—all on vacant land (Fig. 25). Access to the new building was to be combined with access to upper floors for eight units on each floor.

In consideration of a planning application for a new office building in Fenkle Street, the Conservation Area Advisory Committee suggested that a similar approach be followed, as all the upper floors are currently underused or unused. Regrettably this step has not been taken.

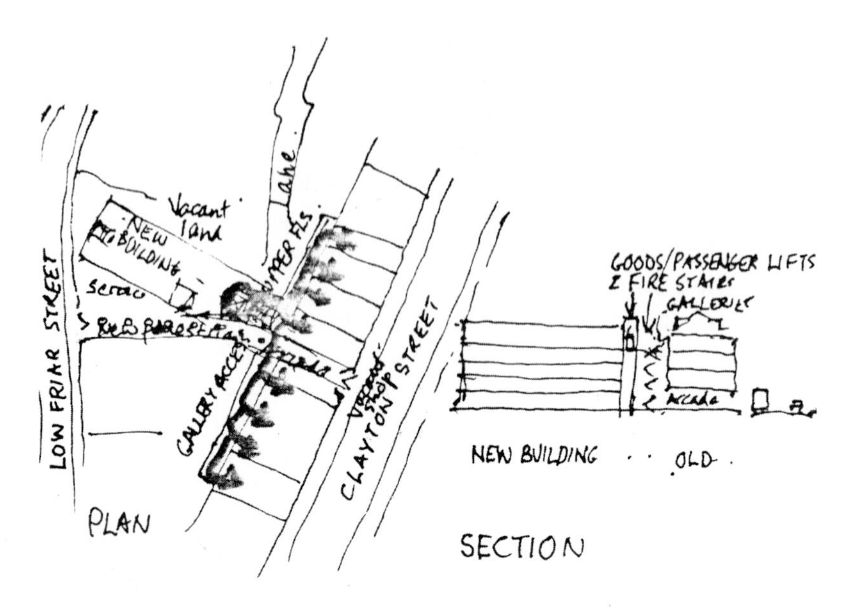

Figure 25. Sketch of access improvements to building on Clayton Street, Newcastle upon Tyne.

CONCLUSION

To summarize, it is hoped that this chapter might draw attention to the following:

"Overlap" areas. These areas offer enormous employment potential. Planning policy should seek to enhance and reinforce them, both because of the employment prospect and because the approach taken in these areas usually gives clues to the successful planning of other central and inner areas.

Mixed use. Overlap areas are most successful when there is a major residential population either within or immediately adjacent to them without physical barriers. The actual commercial uses include manufacture, service industry, services and warehousing as well as specialist and other shopping facilities. The "multi-use" by different sections of the public, of those activities within easy distance of other activities, opens up many additional enterprises which would otherwise not exist at all.

Time or cyclical use. The foregoing is particularly true if the time available for their use is extended. When the market still existed in Covent Garden, for example, shops, services, pubs and cafés were used (a) by the market people early in the morning (the traffic "problem" which caused the move could be said, viewed in this way, to be non existent); (b) the resident population; (c) the people working in the area; and (d) the theatre and restaurant crowds in the evening.

High employment density and multi-floor activity. Without these the areas will not work.

Low property values. These are perhaps the most difficult of all features to control. It depends to a large extent on whether we want active lively areas of real value to cities or developments for investment.

Conservation. To be primarily concerned with activities and buildings as a resource to house them rather than in beautification or facelifting.

Part-time employment. It has been found that a significant amount of employment in these areas (as much as 30 per cent) is part-time and a smaller though still significant number are employed "off the premises", either servicing "in the field" or being self-employed—sometimes at home. It is not clear to the writers how much of this is reflected in local and national employment figures, but it is suspected that a large proportion is frequently underestimated as is probably true for full-time employment in small-scale activity.

Intimate knowledge. The tremendous potential of these inner/central overlap urban areas can only be realized by a really intimate knowledge of how they work—activity by activity, property by property. Person by person might be too much to ask but there should at least be an attempt to assess the personal nature of the activities, how they interrelate, who uses them, who works in them, where do most workers live, how do they get there, and so on.

This knowledge also offers positive clues to the planning of both central and inner areas and in the present climate of low development pressures there are plenty of people available to undertake such surveys. (Architects have been found to enjoy it, and do it very well!)

The Newcastle University Team referred to in this chapter is the Urban Design Section run jointly by the Department of Town and Country Planning and the School of Architecture.

REFERENCES

Alexander, C. (1965). "A City is Not a Tree". Harvard University Press, Cambridge, Mass.

Allpass, J. *et al.* (1967). *In* "Urban Core and Inner City" (M. H. M. van Hulten, ed.). Brill, Leiden.

Allsopp, B. (1974). "Towards a Humane Architecture". Muller, London.

Buchanan, C. (1963). "Traffic in Towns". HMSO, London.

Edinburgh Royal Burgh, Department of Planning (1981). "Edinburgh New Town Conservation Committee Reports 1977-1980, Employment Survey". Edinburgh.

Glasgow District Council (1978). "Glasgow East Area Renewal—Plans and Reports, Article 4: Central Area Directions". Glasgow.

Greater London Council (1978). "Covent Garden Action Area Plan". London.

Newcastle City Council (1978). "Choices For the Future". Newcastle upon Tyne.

North Tyneside M.B.C. (1978). "North Shields Central Area Plan—Report of Survey". North Shields.

Sarbartz, K. (1981). "Convent Garden". University of Newcastle, M.Sc. thesis, Newcastle upon Tyne.

SIX

The future for offices

J. B. GODDARD and J. N. MARSHALL

The central premise of this chapter is a simple one that is often neglected, namely that the future for office development in the city centre is inextricably bound up with that of the city region which it has grown up to serve and the place of that region within the national and even international urban system. In many of the discussions of the city centre this area is abstracted from its specific spatial and historical context. Moreover, because the demand for the space and locational conditions offered by the city centre is principally generated by business activities, the future of this area must be seen in the context of the changing structure of business organizations within the economy as a whole.

This standpoint suggests that although the city centre is a readily identifiable physical component of the urban fabric, in the long run the demand for the structures it provides will be determined by economic factors. Nevertheless, while the principal thrust of the argument suggests that the main direction of causality is demand driven, it will also be suggested that the supply of business services by city-centre offices can perhaps shape the pattern of future demand at the margin. It is on this margin that urban and regional planning initiatives designed to preserve the role of a particular city centre must operate.

A secondary concern of this chapter is with the impact of developments in communications technology on the city centre. This theme is treated as secondary because it will be argued that the impact of new technology on the city centre will arise indirectly through the way in which organizations making use of advances in technology choose to restructure themselves spatially. It will be suggested that such restructuring will flow from economic and organizational considerations; new communications technologies will facilitate new locational patterns that arise from broader organizational requirements—for example, for greater centralization of control or greater local autonomy.

THE FUTURE FOR THE CITY CENTRE
ISBN 0 12 206240 X

THE CITY CENTRE IN BRITAIN IN ITS HISTORICAL AND SPATIAL CONTEXT

A well developed central business district is a feature of all the major cities of Britain. The growth of office service functions in the centres of cities like Birmingham, Manchester, Glasgow, Leeds and Newcastle was historically linked with the growth of manufacturing industries in these cities and the surrounding regions. A wide range of institutions such as stock exchanges, merchant banks and solicitors supported the needs of local industry. The position of London, in view of its international trading role, was unique even before the Industrial Revolution. More recently, the importance of the metropolis *vis-à-vis* the provincial centres has grown in response to a number of developments. The increasing concentration of ownership of industry has meant the creation of more and more national as opposed to regionally organized companies. These companies have come to rely increasingly on the major financial institutions such as the Pension Funds rather than the private investor for their capital requirements. They are becoming more involved with central government and with international investment. As a consequence there has been an increasing need to locate head office functions in London. Early developments in communications technology, particularly the telephone, and reductions in the constraints on long distance business travel facilitated the spatial separation of production activities in the regions and control functions in London. As will be demonstrated later in this chapter it is likely that these trends will continue into the future.

One feature of the process of industrial concentration needs particular mention in the context of the city centre, namely that it has frequently occurred through the acquisition of smaller companies by larger companies. National companies already possessing a London headquarters have been able to acquire companies with a headquarters in a provincial centre. The growing spatial concentration of headquarters in London and their relative decline in the provincial centres is primarily due to this process rather than to provincial companies deciding to set up London headquarters. The process of centralization over a short time period can clearly be seen from Table 3 which shows that London contained 567 of the headquarters of 1000 of the largest UK companies in 1977, while over the previous five years provincial areas and in particular the North-West (principally Manchester) lost headquarters (Goddard and Smith, 1978). Although the number of headquarters of larger firms in London has declined marginally, this is chiefly the result of local decentralization to areas in the South-East outside London. Other research has shown that the larger the company the greater the likelihood of headquarters being located in London. Thus 86 per cent of the companies ranked 1-100 have their headquarters in London compared with 32 per cent of those ranked 900-1000 (Westaway, 1974).

The concentration of ownership in industry has further implications for the provincial centres through its impact on production activities located in their

TABLE 3
Regional size distribution of companies in 1977, and absolute change from 1972 to 1977

Planning region	Rank 1-500 Number	Rank 1-500 Absolute change	Rank 501-1000 Number	Rank 501-1000 Absolute change	Rank 1-1000 Number	Rank 1-1000 Absolute change
Greater London	304	-11	221	30	525	19
Rest of the South-East	46	13	51	4	97	17
East Anglia	4	0	7	-2	11	-2
East Midlands	11	-5	22	-5	33	-10
West Midlands	36	4	49	-7	85	-3
North-West	26	0	51	-15	77	-15
Yorkshire and Humberside	30	0	42	-9	72	-9
South-West	11	1	10	0	21	1
Wales	0	-2	4	-1	4	-3
Scotland	23	1	31	4	54	5
Northern Ireland	1	1	1	0	2	1
North	8	-2	11	1	19	-1
Total	500	0	500	0	1000	0

TABLE 4
Location of major business service supplier by ownership status,[a] Northern Region manufacturing establishments

Ownership status	Location of service: Northern Region	Location of service: Non-Northern Region	Total
Independent	69 (72·6)	26 (27·4)	95 (25·8)
Subsidiary	11 (24·4)	34 (76·1)	45 (12·2)
Branch	51 (22·4)	177 (77·6)	258 (62·0)
Total			368 (100·0)

[a] Source: Marshall (1979a).

hinterlands. Research undertaken in the Northern Region has indicated that locally owned companies purchase the majority of their business service needs within their region—this may be taken to mean primarily from firms located in the city centre of Newcastle (Table 4). In contrast, manufacturing establishments owned by firms with headquarters outside the region meet more than three-quarters of their needs for business services from outside the region, either from company headquarters or from specialist service firms near to these headquarters. So the suggestion is that the extent of local ownership of industry within the sphere of influence of a particular centre will have an important bearing on the proportion of business it can attract. Moreover, as local firms are transferred to non-local ownership, the businesses they have generated locally may also be moved away.

Taken together these trends have meant a relative decline in office employment in the main provincial centres compared to the national economy as a whole (Table 5). The figures shown in Table 5 are for city regions and therefore take account of the possible local decentralization of office activities. The only exception in this respect is London where decentralization has occurred beyond its city region boundary to

TABLE 5

Office employment and office employment change, Metropolitan Economic Labour Areas (MELAs), Great Britain, 1966–1971

Ten MELAs with highest proportions of office workers as % total employment			Ten MELAs with lowest proportions of office workers as % total employment		
1	London	36·3	117	Doncaster	16·4
2	Crawley	34·6	118	Port Talbot	16·2
3	Hemel Hempstead	32·3	119	Scunthorpe	15·9
4	Stevenage	32·2	120	Ayr	15·4
5	Watford	30·8	121	Workington	15·0
6	Walton & Weybridge	30·8	122	Kings Lynn	14·7
7	Letchworth	29·7	123	Barnsley	14·7
8	Harlow	29·6	124	Hartlepool	13·8
9	Worthing	29·0	125	Mansfield	13·2
10	Reading	28·5	126	Rhondda	12·9
Ten MELAs with largest relative increase in total office employment			**Ten MELAs with smallest relative increase/decrease in total office employment**		
1	Basingstoke	81·8	117	Newport	3·1
2	Milton Keynes	60·1	118	Sheffield	1·7
3	High Wycombe	45·5	119	Liverpool	1·6
4	Dunfermline	44·4	120	Manchester	0·9
5	Worthing	41·6	121	Perth	-1·7
6	Harlow	40·3	122	Hereford	-2·3
7	Hemel Hempstead	36·8	123	Halifax	-2·5
8	Dewsbury	33·1	124	Aberdeen	-3·9
9	Great Yarmouth	32·6	125	Rhondda	-4·7
10	Crewe	32·2	126	Ayr	-5·7

Source: Urban Change Project, Department of Geography, London School of Economics.

small- and medium-sized towns in the South-East. In general an analysis of the employment data presented in Table 5 suggests an inverse relationship between office employment growth and distance from London (see Goddard, 1978). Most of the towns with the highest proportion of office employment are in the South-East peripheral to London and do not include any of the large cities. An examination of office employment change between 1966 and 1971 shows that most office employment growth has been occurring in smaller centres and has been chiefly in the southern part of the country. So while there is evidence that manufacturing activity is growing in small- and medium-sized towns throughout the country (Fothergill and Gudgin, 1982) the growth of service functions has been confined to areas south of the Severn/Wash axis.

The net employment changes described above can in theory be broken down into their various components—the setting up or closure of independent establishments or of branches, their *in-situ* contraction or expansion and their migration in whole or in part from one location to another. As has been the case with industrial location studies most attention has been focused on office movement, particularly from London. However, if experience in the field of industrial location is anything to go by, then new openings and closures and *in-situ* change are likely to be the most significant components of the net changes in an area. Employment growth in existing offices in provincial conurbations will be investigated; however, it is notable that most of the evidence suggests that office relocation has been local or intra-regional in character. For example, 82 per cent of the firms relocated from Central London through the efforts of the Location of Office Bureau between 1963 and 1976 were confined to the South-East and 38 per cent to Greater London. Because the main motivation for movement is expansion it can be anticipated, given the decline in economic activity in the economy as a whole, that the level of mobility likely to occur in the near future will be much reduced.

Communication considerations play an important part in relocation decisions. Previous research has shown that it is less communication intensive and lower level jobs that are relocated (Goddard and Morris, 1976). While greater use of telecommunications may reduce constraints on mobility, when communication costs are weighed up in relation to other costs, it can also be demonstrated that the savings that arise at a distance of approximately 100 miles from London are likely to be minimal (Goddard and Pye, 1977). Provincial centres can therefore not expect a significant increase in office jobs resulting from inter-regional transfers.

This brief review suggests that the prospects for office developments in the centres of provincial cities are limited. The remainder of this chapter will examine in more detail two possibilities that could have a marginal positive impact on this situation. First, consideration is given to the possibility of improvements in the supply of business services in provincial centres influencing demand by encouraging industry within the city region to make greater use of local facilities. The arguments will be presented using evidence of a detailed study of the supply and demand of business services in Birmingham, Manchester and Leeds. The second possibility to be examined is that more widespread use of telecommunications, by reducing travel constraints, might encourage manufacturing organizations already located in the regions to develop their office activity *in-situ*. Here the argument will draw primarily upon a major study of the potential for telecommunications in offices in the Northern Region of England.

THE SUPPLY AND DEMAND FOR BUSINESS SERVICES IN THE CENTRES OF PROVINCIAL CITIES

The preceding discussion has emphasized the impact of manufacturing industry demand on service activities. For example, it has been suggested that the internalization of service demand within multi-site manufacturing firms may have a detrimental impact on service firms in the city centres of regions which are dominated by branch manufacturing plants. Implicit in this argument is an assumption that service sector firms are locally linked and dependent upon manufacturing industry. The logic of this perspective is that the causal relationships operate vertically downwards in the diagram shown in Fig. 26. The following two sections argue that the development of the service sector in provincial city centres is in fact more complex. It suggests that manufacturing industry demand is not necessarily the most important determinant of variations in business service supply. It will be argued that the spatial pattern of manufacturing industry service purchases in part reflects locational differences in the distribution of service activity. Moreover, it will be suggested that external control is an important feature of the business service sector and that the way multi-site business service firms organize themselves over space can influence the supply of services. Finally, it will be argued that not all business services are locally linked and dependent upon their local industrial base; certain services generate regional exports. All of this is not to suggest that the effect of manufacturing industry demand on the supply of services is unimportant; rather the relationship between the service and manufacturing sectors in the provinces is likely to be two-way with changes in the composition of each affecting the other over time in historical rounds of investment (see Fig. 26).

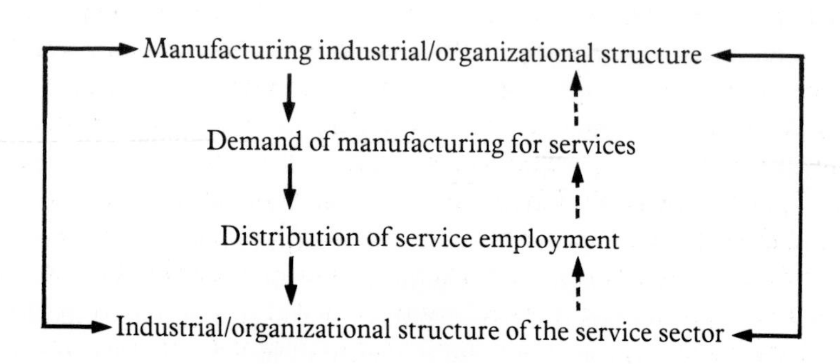

Figure 26. Manufacturing industry demand for business services.

Manufacturing industry demand for business services

In order to provide some substance to the above argument reference is made in this section to a survey of the demand for business services by manufacturing establishments located in the West Midlands, North-West and Yorkshire and Humberside regions. A postal survey was designed to be representative of the size and sectoral composition of establishments in each region. A final response of 357 establishments was obtained or 24·4 per cent of those approached. (Further details of the methodology are given in Marshall (1980).)

The first point to note is that manufacturing firms meet the bulk of their business service needs from within their own organization (57·3 per cent of their total requirements), and only 19·1 per cent of this total from company sites outside the establishment in question. Therefore, in discussing business service demand it is important to remember that companies outside manufacturing account for only a small proportion of the total supply. Nevertheless, any general developments that alter the propensity of companies to use non-company services are likely to have important implications for the city centre. In so far as external services are used to supplement internal services when peaks of activity arise, then periods of recession are likely to severely affect independent service firms. Alternatively, business may drop to such a level that internal departments within manufacturing establishments can no longer be justified and so external services are called upon. Finally, it should be stressed that the actual and perceived quantity and quality of services available locally may influence the decisions of companies to service a particular manufacturing site locally, from headquarters or from an independent service firm adjacent to the headquarters.

If attention is focused upon those services purchased outside the company, the survey reveals a highly localized pattern of buying, with 78·8 per cent of purchases being obtained from within the manufacturing establishment's own planning region and 15·2 per cent in the same local authority district. Taking all major service suppliers to the manufacturing establishments together, Manchester proved to be the main centre for service purchases, followed by Birmingham and then Leeds (Table 6). Not surprisingly, London is most important for more specialized services like insurance, stock-broking, advertising, market research and consultancy.

What is particularly interesting is the variation in the extent to which service expenditure is confined to the same region as the establishment. In spite of its size, the North-West region exhibited the lowest degree of regional self containment. Establishments in the North-West appear to purchase fewer services within their immediate locality, with only Manchester and Liverpool accounting for more than 3 per cent of the total regional expenditure—although Manchester does account for some expenditure originating in the Yorkshire and Humberside region and in the West Midlands. In contrast, a greater number of other service centres in addition to Leeds and Birmingham appear to be significant in these latter two regions.

There are many explanations for these variations. One important consideration is the difference between regions in terms of industrial structure. For example, firms

TABLE 6

Location of the most important non-company supplier of business services

	Locations with more than 1% of total service activity	
	N	*(%)*
Manchester	257	15·2
Stockport	19	1·1
Liverpool	42	2·5
Sheffield	76	4·5
Bradford	84	5·0
Kirklees	28	1·7
Leeds	160	9·5
Hull	32	1·9
Birmingham	238	14·1
Dudley	31	1·8
Wolverhampton	26	1·5
Stoke	92	5·4
London	176	10·4
	1268	75·0
Total number of suppliers	1691	100·0
Number of establishments	284	

in the chemicals industry (a sector which is important in the North-West) tend to purchase from outside their own region. This is because firms in this industry tend to have an above average population of non-production workers on site and these meet routine service needs, like accountancy; at the same time such establishments are also heavy spenders on higher order services like advertising, a service which is highly concentrated in London. In contrast, establishments in the woollen and worsted industry, which is highly localized in Yorkshire and Humberside, tend to have relatively few office workers on site and purchase a high proportion (53·3 per cent) of even their routine services from outside the company, and only 8·8 per cent of these come from sources outside the region.

Organizational as well as sectoral differences are important in shaping the pattern of business service purchases. Large externally-owned branch establishments that are part of multi-site companies and are mass producing components for other factories in the company group are most likely to purchase business services from within the company. What non-company expenditures such establishments do generate are most likely to be made outside the local region. These findings therefore clearly confirm the suggested effect of external control on the demand for business services within a region.

The specific regional implications of these original considerations are highlighted by the fact that 66 per cent of establishments in the North-West are branches compared with 42·9 per cent in Yorkshire and Humberside and 48·6 per cent in the West Midlands. Nevertheless, even when these differences in organizational structure and size of establishment are allowed for, statistically there is still less local purchasing in the North-West. This appears to be related to the greater degree of intra-company servicing within the North-West which is in turn influenced by the location of the company headquarters. Thus Table 7 shows that branch plants which have a headquarters within their own region are more likely to purchase services from outside the company than those with headquarters in London. The higher level of containment of service expenditure recorded in the West Midlands as compared with the North-West may be attributed to the fact that more branch plants are controlled from within the former region.

The ownership and organizational status of manufacturing firms also has an important bearing on the type of service organizations used. Table 8 suggests that branch plants and externally-owned firms purchase more of their services from the branch offices of national business firms than do head offices or independent firms. This reflects the corporate decisions of multi-site industrial enterprise to meet the service needs of their manufacturing establishments throughout a company via one national service organization. So as the external control of manufacturing industry grows in provincial areas an increasing leakage of service expenditure to national business service companies can be expected in provincial cities.

TABLE 7

Internalization of service activity by branch plans with a head office in differing locations[a]

	Location of head office		
Source of service	Local	London	Other locations
Own company (%)	70·7	90·7	78·9
Other companies (%)	29·3	9·3	21·1
Number of establishments	22	19	22

[a] A chi-square statistic is significant at the 5 per cent level.

TABLE 8

Type of service organization used by manufacturing establishments in the survey[a]

	Type of manufacturing establishment			
	Status (%)		Ownership (of single site firms) (%)	
Type of service organization	Head office	Branch	Externally owned	Independent
Regional	46·6	34·8	42·6	61·8
National	53·4	65·2	57·4	38·2
Number of establishments	104		178	

[a] A chi-square statistic is significant at the 5 per cent level.

TABLE 9

Location of service suppliers to establishments in service centre and non-service centre locations[a]

Location of service purchases	Service centre location	Non-service centre location
Own Local Authority (%)	26·1	9·3
Own region (%)	81·1	76·0
Other regions (%)	18·9	24·0
Number of establishments	318	

[a] A chi-square statistic is significant at the 5 per cent level.

TABLE 10

Proportion of establishments in business service centres by region[a]

Region	Service centre	Non-service centre	Number of establishments
North-West	25·6	74·4	137
Yorkshire and Humberside	73·3	26·7	90
West Midlands	59·1	40·9	110

[a] A chi-square statistic is significant at the 5 per cent level.

All of these findings are particularly depressing for the future of office services in the provincial centres as they by and large emphasize the importance of organizational considerations which are largely outside the control of local planning initiatives. However, there is one important spatial factor that has not so far been considered. The absence of secondary service centres in the North-West region outside Manchester and Liverpool and the lack of a well developed urban hierarchy is an important additional factor accounting for the high degree of leakage of service expenditure from that area. This suggestion is reinforced by Tables 9 and 10. For the survey as a whole, manufacturing establishments were classified as to whether or not they were located in a service centre, with service centres being defined as local authority districts which accounted for more than 1 per cent of the major non-company service suppliers to survey firms. Table 9 reveals that firms located outside service centres spend a higher proportion of their purchases in other regions while Table 10 indicates that the North-West has a much higher proportion of establishments located outside service centres. Clearly then, spatial variations in the distribution of service activity can influence the corporate purchasing patterns of manufacturing enterprises.

The supply of business services

The discussion so far has emphasized the influence of demand from manufacturing industry as a principal determinant of the prospect for business services in the provincial city centres. This section examines the markets of 378 offices which provide specialized business services in the centres of Birmingham, Manchester, and Leeds. The services are: accountants, finance companies, insurance brokers, solicitors, advertising agencies, computer bureaux, architects, consultant engineers, and management consultants; and the offices represent a 25·2 per cent response to a postal questionnaire of a random sample of addresses (for details of the methodology, see Marshall, 1981).

It is clear from Table 11 that private manufacturing industry accounts for only a little over a third of the total market for these business services. Although industry is the major customer, private individuals, distribution, nationalized industry, central and local government and other business service firms are all important sources of revenue. Moreover, if account is only taken of the three largest customers of the establishments, insurance, banking, and finance and other business services account for the largest proportion of non-private customers. In other words, service to manufacturing industry is spread over a large number of relatively small clients while services to other parts of the service sector are dependent upon a limited number of key clients.

TABLE 11
The market of business service firms

Source of income	Proportion of income
Private individuals	17·8
Nationalized industries and public utilities	6·6
Manufacturing industry and construction	36·5
Central and local government	10·5
Retailing, wholesaling, distribution and general service firms	16·4
Business service firms	8·3
Others, e.g. mining and quarrying	3·9
	100·0
Number of firms	351

One may conclude from these figures that the future for business services in the city centre may not be so reliant on manufacturing industry in its hinterland as has been assumed. In addition, the analysis of the market areas served by the offices in the centres of the three cities studied suggests a significant national component, with 19·4 per cent of total income coming from customers located more than 50

TABLE 12

The proportionate distribution of the income of offices in each business service

Income from location (%)	Accountancy	Advertising	Insurance	Computing	Solicitors	Finance	Architecture	Consultant engineers	Management consultants	Significance
1-10 miles	51·9	40·6	47·1	21·8	70·5	59·6	52·3	36·7	33·9	[a]
National	12·9	24·0	11·4	32·0	4·8	19·5	16·5	17·9	24·7	[b]
N	15	32	19	12	6	8	38	52	43	
Total *N*					225					

[a] A Kruskal-Wallis analysis of variance is significant at the 5 per cent level.
[b] A Kruskal-Wallis analysis of variance is significant at the 10 per cent level.

miles away and 3·5 per cent from overseas. There are of course variations between the various services (Table 12). Solicitors, finance companies and insurance brokers depend more on industry and commerce in their local areas. Solicitors, for example, gain 70·5 per cent of their business from locations within 10 miles. This compares with only 21·8 per cent for computing bureaux. Therefore, any decline in the hinterland of the city centre is likely to have a variable impact on different services.

The reaction of service firms to changes in the level of demand will depend very much on their size and organizational characteristics with large branches of national organizations having the greatest propensity for survival. While business service establishments are on average small—40·2 per cent employ less that ten people—a significant proportion (48·5 per cent) are part of multi-site organizations. In terms of organizational status 67·3 per cent are branch offices and 71·5 per cent of these have their headquarters in London or the South-East. So external control is an important feature of the service sector as well as manufacturing industry.

In terms of employment, branches of national companies account for nearly a third of the total number of jobs provided by the survey establishments. These are mainly new openings of branches—relocation of establishments is relatively unimportant. Over the period 1976 to 1980, and excluding new openings, branch establishments have experienced a 35·5 per cent increase in employment compared with a 19·1 per cent increase in establishments set up *de-novo* in the centres prior to this five-year period. While this contrast may be partly attributable to the longer average length of establishment of local firms (27·9 years) compared with branches (13·5 years) it does suggest that national companies have been responsible for capturing a significant share of the market once held by local firms in these centres. It is not readily apparent as to whether this employment will be rapidly shed if business contracts. Nevertheless, the survey does suggest that the rate of establishment of new branches has declined recently with only ten new openings over the period 1976 to 1980, the lowest for any four-year period since 1961 to 1965. This decline in mobility is similar to that experienced in manufacturing industry and, as in the case of industry, many presage a reduction in employment growth in already established branches.

There are important variations in experience between Birmingham, Manchester and Leeds, with the latter centre recording the highest rate of employment growth in surveyed firms. A number of factors could explain these differences. First, the different mix of fast and slow growing services in each centre; Leeds, for example, has an above average share of fast growing services like computing and management consultancy. Nevertheless, there are substantial differences in growth rates for similar services in each of the centres (Table 13). A second consideration could be differences in the ownership structure of services. Birmingham, for example, has few of the fast growing branches of national companies. This may be because national firms can service the West Midlands from London and do not need to open an office in Birmingham. In contrast, Manchester is frequently used as a base for serving the north as a whole with 33 per cent of its employment in branches of national companies and 38·1 per cent of its business generated from outside the

TABLE 13

Percentage employment change in individual business service activities in provincial conurbations, 1976–1980

Type of service	Manchester	City Leeds	Birmingham	Total	*N*
Accountancy	9·5	42·7	23·4	18·8	27
Advertising	15·8	83·5	26·0	28·8	38
Insurance	163·4	59·1	39·5	77·5	40
Computing	94·3	518·3	58·9	100·0	24
Solicitors	34·4	18·1	12·2	20·1	16
Finance	85·5	129·0	12·6	55·6	22
Architects	27·1	-13·3	23·3	8·6	50
Consultant engineers	18·8	21·4	29·1	23·5	62
Management consultants	50·1	158·5	56·3	62·8	49
Total	32·2	39·1	30·9	32·9	

North-West region. However, Manchester does appear to be losing some of its market to Leeds with branches of national companies recording a 127·8 per cent increase in employment in that city over a four-year period compared with only 33·8 per cent in Manchester. This may reflect a recognition on the part of national firms that the market in Manchester is saturated and that they can effectively

TABLE 14

Type of business market associated with variations in employment performance

Types of market serving	Employment performance		
	Low	Intermediate	High
Metal working and engineering industries	20·9	17·1	13·0
Clothing, leather and textile industries	5·9	3·9	3·5
Other manufacturing, mining and construction	20·4	22·2	25·2
Intermediate growth services	21·3	25·7	17·7
Fast growth services	31·5	31·1	40·6

N = 253

A chi-square text is significant at the 7 per cent level.

Key:

Metal working and engineering

VI	Metals	XI	Vehicles
VII	Mechanical engineering	XII	Metals NEC
VIII	Electrical engineering		

Textiles, leather and clothing

XIII	Textiles	XV	Clothing
XIV	Leather		

Other manufacturing, mining and construction

II	Mining	XVI	Bricks etc.	XX	Construction
III	Food	XVII	Timber		
IV	Coal and petroleum	XVIII	Paper		
V	Chemicals	XIX	Other manufacturing		

Intermediate growth services

XXII	Transport	XXVII	Public sector
XXIII	Distribution		

Fast growth

XXI	Gas etc.	XXV	Professional and scientific
XXIV	Insurance, banking and finance	XXVI	Miscellaneous services

compete with Manchester in northern markets to the east of the Pennines from Leeds.

The final factor accounting for variations in the performance of different services in each of the centres is the nature of their markets. Considering the sample as a whole, offices whose three main customers are in metal working, engineering and footwear, leather and clothing are characterized by lower than average employment growth for their service (Table 14). Those firms selling primarily to insurance, banking and finance, and basic industries such as mining, chemicals and construction appear to have grown more rapidly. These contrasts feed through differentially to the respective city centres with the worst overall performer, Birmingham, exhibiting the greatest market dependency on metals and engineering, and Leeds doing particularly well with regard to the share of its market in growing service markets such as insurance, banking and finance. The relative insignificance of the clothing and textile industries as a market for business services in both Leeds and Manchester is indicative of the lack of emphasis placed by these traditional sectors on the buying-in of specialist advice. These findings, therefore, confirm that the nature of industry within the hinterland of a particular service centre does have some bearing on its growth prospects.

In the preceding discussion "performance" has been measured simply in terms of employment growth. However, with developments in office technology an increasing share of a particular market could be gained without the creation of additional jobs. In the case of the surveyed offices this would appear not to have been true in the past two years with growth in output being broadly matched by employment growth. Those offices which increased employment more than the average for their service increased output in the same manner (the relationship between employment growth and output growth is statistically significant at the 5 per cent level). Nevertheless, there are important exceptions to this generalization with output in a number of offices growing more quickly relative to other offices in their sector than employment. This suggests that employment growth in certain offices is being slowed down by improvements in productivity. However, it is unlikely that this improvement is related to the introduction of new labour-saving technologies. Only 1·5 per cent of offices considered that new technologies had affected their employment during the last two years. Qualitative information from interviews with a small sample of firms indicate that improvements in work methods may be the most important factor accounting for this increased efficiency. Nevertheless, during the immediate future, labour saving technology is likely to have more impact, with 11·5 per cent of offices considering it likely to reduce employment in the next two years. Therefore, there may be a future decline in the rate of business service employment growth in provincial conurbations irrespective of the market considerations that have already been discussed.

TELECOMMUNICATIONS AND OFFICE LOCATION IN THE CITY CENTRE

Given that one of the principal activities of business services is the exchange as well as the processing of information it would be reasonable to ask what impact new telecommunications technology will have on business efficiency and therefore employment. Such developments might affect not only the service provided but also service users. Could telecommunications, for example, facilitate a greater decentralization of administrative autonomy to lower levels in the corporate hierarchy, therefore stimulating a growth of office employment outside London and the South-East, in particular increasing the demand for business services in provincial conurbations?

To answer this question, we must look at the existing patterns of business communication in relation to corporate structure and office relocation. Unfortunately, most research on office communications and office location has been concerned with the detached head office or independent business service firms, and hence divorced from the wider corporate context. Nevertheless, these studies all demonstrate the importance of communication factors in office location decisions. Offices that have moved or are about to move from London are less communication intensive than their counterparts who have remained. Similarly, relocated offices have fewer communications with other firms in London than the non-movers (Goddard and Morris, 1976).

The fact that most office moves from London have been confined to south-east England can largely be explained on communication cost grounds, particularly when these costs are viewed in the light of other office costs, notably, clerical, labour, and office rents. Thus, while communication costs increase linearly with distance, the savings on rent and salary level off about 60 miles from London; it is only the less communication-intensive functions that can economically move longer distances (Goddard and Pye, 1977). It is therefore not surprising that it is principally the routine functions in both the public and private sector which were dispersed to cities such as Liverpool, Newcastle and Teesside.

However, these conclusions assume that all communications remain with London. Yet, a firm moving to Manchester for example, might replace business service contacts with London firms by new contacts with Manchester suppliers, thereby reducing travelling costs. Significantly, many of the longer-distance movers in the Goddard and Morris study went to provincial conurbations and had more communication with their immediate locality than firms moving shorter distances. This latter group also tended to represent a dispersal of routine functions heavily controlled from a head office remaining in London, such control necessitating frequent travel back to the capital. Changes in corporate organization, for example giving greater autonomy to relocated offices, could reduce this need to travel to London and increase the potential for longer-distance relocation of the firms.

But what of the effects of substituting telecommunication for business travel? In what ways could this reduce the constraints on long distance relocation? Most of the research on the use of new telecommunications technology has focused on the individual meeting and it is extremely difficult to generalize such findings to the level of the communications requirements of different office functions, of different types of office organization, or of different locations. Nevertheless, the laboratory experiments of Short *et al.* (1976), suggest that the use of different communication media (audio or video) does not affect the outcome of meetings as much as might be expected. In particular, their results imply that video systems are not significantly different in effect from the much cheaper audio-conference systems. Evaluation of actual field usage of audio systems suggests that these are most satisfactory for such tasks as giving or receiving information, asking questions and exchanging opinions but less satisfactory for getting to know people, bargaining, or persuasion (Pye and Williams, 1977). In general, most of this research suggests that expensive video systems have little to offer over audio-conferencing facilities enhanced by document-transmission devices.

But from the population of meetings going on in different types of office in different locations, what proportions have characteristics which make them suitable for transfer to telecommunications? Various attempts have been made to answer this question. In 1972, approximately 6000 civil servants subject to the relocation of government review were asked details of one recent face-to-face meeting involving people from outside the respondent's "block of work" (a small organizational unit unsuitable for further subdivision) (HMSO, 1973). Respondents were asked to indicate whether the meeting required face-to-face contact and, if not, the primary and secondary reasons for making that judgement. On the basis of their responses the meetings were allocated to three classes—those suitable for audio-graphics or video substitution, and meetings not suitable for transfer. The results of this analysis suggest that only a third of the meetings really needed to be carried out face-to-face. A similar method was used to classify 344 meetings recorded by individuals in decentralized offices (Goddard and Morris, 1976). The results of this study also indicate a considerable potential usage of audio systems.

In a further investigation of 145 office establishments selected at random in three regions throughout the UK, managers were asked to recall details of up to 10 meetings involving someone outside their workplace. On the basis of a series of detailed evaluative scales describing what went on in 3160 business meetings, and using previous experimental work in which individuals were asked to perform different meeting tasks using different media, an exercise allocated 45 per cent of the meetings to audio media, 8 per cent to video and 47 per cent to the face-to-face category (Short and Williams, 1977).

It is difficult to evaluate the implications of these sorts of findings because no attempt was made in the various studies to control for the range of organizational and spatial situations in which their investigations were carried out. A further weakness of such studies is that they have concentrated upon relocation from London, ignoring the possible contribution more widespread use of telecommunications could make to extending the range of office functions performed in firms already operating outside the capital; in other words the possible contribution of telecommunications to *in-situ* expansion of office employment rather than to transfers.

Some of these deficiencies have been remedied in a recent study of the communication needs of office activities in the Northern Region of the UK (James *et al.*, 1979). Although this study did not have an urban focus, the findings do have important implications for Newcastle as a regional office centre. The investigations involved surveys of business travel by plane and train between Newcastle-Durham-Teesside and London of business contacts maintained by 285 managers in a selection of large manufacturing companies in the Northern Region of England. By comparing the results of these surveys with previous investigations some indication of locational variations in the potential for telecommunications substitution can be obtained.

Significantly, the frequency of communication recorded in offices outside London is lower than in the capital. The lowest levels of contact are recorded in offices that have decentralized from London, confirming that these are a relatively atypical group of routine functions. There is an important contrast in the number of meetings between the North and London with a much lower number taking place in the former area. There is a similar number of telephone calls in the two locations which suggests that the telephone is already used to a considerable extent in the North to overcome barriers on distance.

Unfortunately no telecommunications-substitution estimates are available for central London. However, the figures for the civil service dispersal study can be included because they refer to London-based staff. Taken together the figures suggest that there is significant scope for the use of audio-conferencing techniques or telephones as a substitute for face-to-face meetings in all locations, especially in the Northern Region. In the North more than three-quarters of existing meetings could be conducted by telecommunications (Table 15). Not surprisingly, meetings involving long-distance travel are less substitutable (28 per cent of the total from the travel survey).

In the Northern Region study it is possible to identify differences in telecommunications-substitution potential between meetings held in various types of location and between various types of participants. In the case of long-distance travel there is clearly a greater potential for telecommunications-substitution within multi-site companies as compared with single-site companies, within the manufacturing sector as compared with the service sector, for meetings held in the North-East as compared with the South-East, and for top management as compared with middle management (Table 16).

The results of the survey of meetings in the sample of northern manufacturing firms reveals some contrasts chiefly because this survey also covered local communication and contacts with places elsewhere in the UK and overseas (i.e. not just with London and the South-East as in the case of the travel survey). Here we see that meetings held in the respondent's own workplace are more substitutable

TABLE 15

Telecommunications substitution potential: comparison of business meetings recorded in different surveys

<table>
<tr><th>Survey</th><th>Telephone and post (%)</th><th>Audio (%)</th><th>Video (%)</th><th>Face to face (%)</th><th>Sample size</th></tr>
<tr><td>1 Inter-regional travel</td><td>6</td><td>21</td><td>1</td><td>71</td><td>1759</td></tr>
<tr><td>2 Northern Region manufacturing establishments</td><td>25</td><td>54</td><td>0</td><td>21</td><td>615</td></tr>
<tr><td>3 Decentralized offices</td><td>13</td><td>38</td><td>27</td><td>22</td><td>344</td></tr>
<tr><td>4 Random sample 4 regions</td><td colspan="2">45</td><td>8</td><td>47</td><td>1377</td></tr>
<tr><td>5 Central London civil service</td><td>3</td><td>40</td><td>23</td><td>34</td><td>6397</td></tr>
</table>

Sources: Surveys 1 and 2, James *et al.* (1979); Survey 3, Goddard and Morris (1976); Survey 4, Tyler *et al.* (1973); Survey 5, Communications Studies Group (1972).

Note: Each of the surveys quoted in this table used different procedures for sampling establishments, individuals and meetings and for allocating these meetings to communication channels. In terms of allocation procedures, surveys 1, 2 and 4 and 3 and 5 used similar methodologies (see Pye and Williams, 1977; Goddard, 1980).

TABLE 16

Telecommunications substitution potential: travel by rail and air between the North-East and South-East regions (in rank order)

Company organization of workplace
1 Multi-site companies
2 Single-site companies
Sector of workplace
1 Manufacturing
2 Services
Occupation of respondent
1 Top management
2 Top management support
3 Technical
4 Sales
5 Line management
Location of meeting place
1 North-East
2 South-East

Note: All differences in communication mode allocation are significant at the 0·1 per cent level and are ranked in order of substitution potential within each category.

Source: James *et al.* (1979).

TABLE 17

Telecommunications substitution potential: meetings recorded by managers in Northern Region manufacturing establishments (in rank order)

Status of meeting place
1 Own workplace
2 Another workplace of respondent's own company
3 Workplace of another company
4 Elsewhere (e.g. hotel)
Location of the meeting place
1 UK outside South-East and Northern Region
2 South-East
3 Northern Region
Commercial relationship between respondent and other participant(s)
1 Supplier
2 Customer
3 Non-commercial (e.g. Government Department)
Intra-/inter-corporate relationships
1 All participants in meeting from respondent's own company group
2 All participants from company group other than that of respondent

Note: All differences in communications mode allocation are significant at the 0·1 per cent level and are ranked in order of substitution potential within each category.

Source: James *et al.* (1979).

than those held on neutral ground (Table 17). Also, somewhat surprisingly, contacts outside the company are more substitutable than those within the company; in addition local meetings are less substitutable than those involving longer or more difficult travel. Therefore, although the potential for using telecommunications within a large company is greater because compatible equipment may be available in all sites, these meetings tend to be of a higher-level nature than those which occur with other organizations.

The significance of these findings for the space economy in general and the city centre in particular are far from obvious. Contacts taking place in a peripheral area like the North are of a more routine character than those occurring in London and therefore potentially substitutable by telecommunications. This is particularly so for those meetings involving persons travelling from London and the South-East. Because of the routine nature of the managerial functions performed by branch plants in peripheral areas, more widespread use of telecommunications provides the opportunity for greater "remote control". On the other hand, the finding that top management meetings are more substitutable than those of lower-level staff—chiefly because of the need of the former to deal with "physical problems"—suggests that high-level functions could be dispersed. Alternatively, it could be argued that because functions like production management need to be in close face-to-face contact with production itself, what decentralization does occur could be mainly in this low-level type of function with top management using telecommunications to control manufacturing from a remote headquarters. It should also be noted that the use of telecommunications is more difficult in the service sector and it is service-sector office employment which is most heavily concentrated in the South-East. Also of particular significance for the provincial centre is the finding that the opportunity for the use of telecommunications is considerably greater in contact between areas outside the South-East including overseas. Business travel by plane and train between the provinces and London is fairly easy, but across country the car is the only realistic alternative. Many organizations maintain London offices chiefly as a base for bringing together executives from throughout the country. Greater use of telecommunications could ease cross-country contact and thereby facilitate more decentralized modes of working. But this will only take place where multi-site organizations have adopted more developed systems of management for other reasons.

Finally, what of the smaller single-site company? The study of such companies in the North suggests they have poorly developed office functions and depend more on the immediate locality for service linkages (Marshall, 1979a,b). Small single-site enterprises tend to predominate in the less communication-intensive sectors with top management relatively more involved in travel than is the case in multi-site companies. It is just possible that greater use of telecommunications could enable such companies to maintain more effective long-distance contacts both within the UK and internationally. In other words, the development of small- to medium-sized companies, wherever they are located, need not be so constrained by business communications problems as might have been the case in the past. Of course this again suggests that ease of personal communication, which was at one time a particular benefit of the large urban agglomeration, will cease to be the attraction that it once was.

However, these conclusions are tentative, especially with respect to the city centre. This is partly because all of the studies of telecommunications quoted have been primarily concerned with inter-regional issues. A growth of office functions in the region does not necessarily require a growth in the centres of the provincial conurbations. In the case of office functions within manufacturing industry any dispersal that does occur is likely to be to production plants rather than to detached regional headquarters' offices. Given the rundown of manufacturing in the inner parts of provincial cities, such dispersal is likely to be to suburban and semi-rural locations. In so far as detached office functions in the pure service sector are concerned (i.e. functions which might prefer a central location because of the need for access to a large labour force—insurance, banking and finance and public administration) it is already apparent that capital is now being rapidly substituted for labour. So the employment prospects from this sector are likely to be limited.

This points to a final caveat, namely that the work that has been reviewed has concentrated upon the possible impacts of telecommunications on inter-personal contact. It has been traditionally assumed that this is the area where new technologies and of organizational adaptation is often grossly overestimated. In spite of all the gloomy scenarios presented in this chapter, the provincial city centre and government. The greater significance of audio-conferencing systems as opposed to the video phone indicates that new technologies designed to deal with the higher-level communications are less relevant than simpler alternatives. It is therefore highly likely that the biggest push for more decentralized modes of work will arise from developments in man-machine communications rather than man-man communications.

CONCLUSION

From the discussion presented in this chapter it will be apparent that it is extremely difficult to isolate the independent effects of organizational and technological change on the city centre. This problem is compounded by the inertia of the built environment, coupled with the constraints imposed by existing industrial and institutional structures. Scenarios which seem reasonable in the abstract context of the national economy or even in the context of an individual industry, business service or company, fall apart when projected onto the specific realities of particular places. When reviewing the research on the city centre, one is struck by the absence of these place-specific considerations. Many studies tend to ignore the existing realities of physical transport systems, the distribution of homes and workplaces, the structure of public and private organizations, or the labour constraints on the introduction of new techniques. In consequence, the speed of diffusion of new technologies and of organizational adaptation is often grossly overestimated. In spite of all the gloomy scenarios presented in this chapter, the provincial city centre may survive simply because of inertia and defensive investment designed to protect existing interests.

REFERENCES

Communication Studies Group (1972). "Interim Report for the Hardman Commission". Communication Studies Group, B/72145/RD.

Fothergill, S. and Gudgin, G. (1982). "Unequal Growth". Heinemann, London.

Goddard, J. B. (1978). *In* "Spatial Patterns of Office Growth and Location" (P. W. Daniels, ed.). Wiley, London.

Goddard, J. B. (1980). *Futures* **12**, 90-105.

Goddard, J. B. and Morris, D. (1976). *Progr. Plann.* **6**, 1-90.

Goddard, J. B. and Pye, R. (1977). *Reg. Stud.* **11**, 19-30.

Goddard, J. B. and Smith, I. J. (1978) *Envir. Plann.* **10**, 1073-1084.

HMSO (1973). "The Dispersal of Government Work from London", CMND 5322.

James, V. Z., Marshall, J. N. and Walters, N. (1979). "Telecommunications and Office Location". Final Report to the Department of the Environment—Centre for Urban and Regional Development Studies, University of Newcastle upon Tyne.

Marshall, J. N. (1979a). *Reg. Studies.* **13**, 531-557.

Marshall, J. N. (1979b). *Envir. Plann. A* **11**, 553-563.

Marshall, J. N. (1980). "Spatial Variations in Manufacturing Industry Demand for Business Services: Some Implications for Government Economic Policies". Discussion Paper No. 35—Centre for Urban and Regional Development Studies, University of Newcastle upon Tyne.

Marshall, J. N. (1981). "Business Service Activities in Provincial Connurbations: Implications for Regional Economic Development". Discussion Paper No. 37—Centre for Urban and Regional Development Studies, University of Newcastle upon Tyne.

Pye, R. and Williams, E. (1977). *Telecommun. Policy* **1**, 230-241.

Short, J., Williams, E. and Christie, B. (1976). "The Social Psychology of Telecommunications". Wiley, London.

Tyler, M., Cartwright, B. and Collins, H. A. (1973). "Interactions Between Telecommunications and Face-to-Face Contact: Prospects for Teleconferencing Systems". Long Range Intelligence Bulletin 9, Telecommunications Systems Strategy Dept, UK Post Office.

Westerway, E. J. (1974). *Reg. Stud.* **8**, 57-73.

SEVEN

Changes in the retail sector

D. THORPE

Before examining the current problems and future prospects of retailing in the city centre it is instructive to explore something of the history of retailing in this environment in the last 20 years.

THE PAST

In 1961 there were major differences in the size of the retail sales of the top city centres. It is true that both Carruthers (1967) and Thorpe (1968), in separate exercises using the 1961 Census of Distribution, recognized seven major centres. As Fig. 27 and Table 18 show, however, the range of sales between these centres was considerable. Not only were sales in the largest of these centres 65 per cent higher than in the smallest, but there was also a substantial gap between the fourth and fifth ranking centre. Below these seven top centres Carruthers recognized another four as a separate group and then counted the remaining 36 (38 if he included Scotland) as his third ranking group. Thorpe's assessment of the 1961 situation was that, after the first seven (*regional*) centres, the next 22 (*sub-regional*) centres were probably sufficiently similar not to warrant any sub-division and that, below them, a group of *area centres* existed which had distinctly more important functions than the basic *major centre*.

By the time of the 1971 Census the situation had clarified and simply in turnover terms those in Carruthers' second group of centres had pulled clear of the rest of the sub-regional centres and have achieved, or were in the process of achieving, a dominance over their sub-regions which they had not formerly achieved. Furthermore, most of the remaining sub-regional centres in Thorpe's 1961 classification had pushed ahead of centres with lower turnovers. A few centres rose substantially in rank (e.g. Watford) but the majority of the more lowly ranking sub-regional centres made little headway. Thus many of these centres were in danger of being overtaken by the more rapidly expanding area centres. In more detail, groups of centres at that date appeared to be:

THE FUTURE FOR THE CITY CENTRE
ISBN 0 12 206240 X

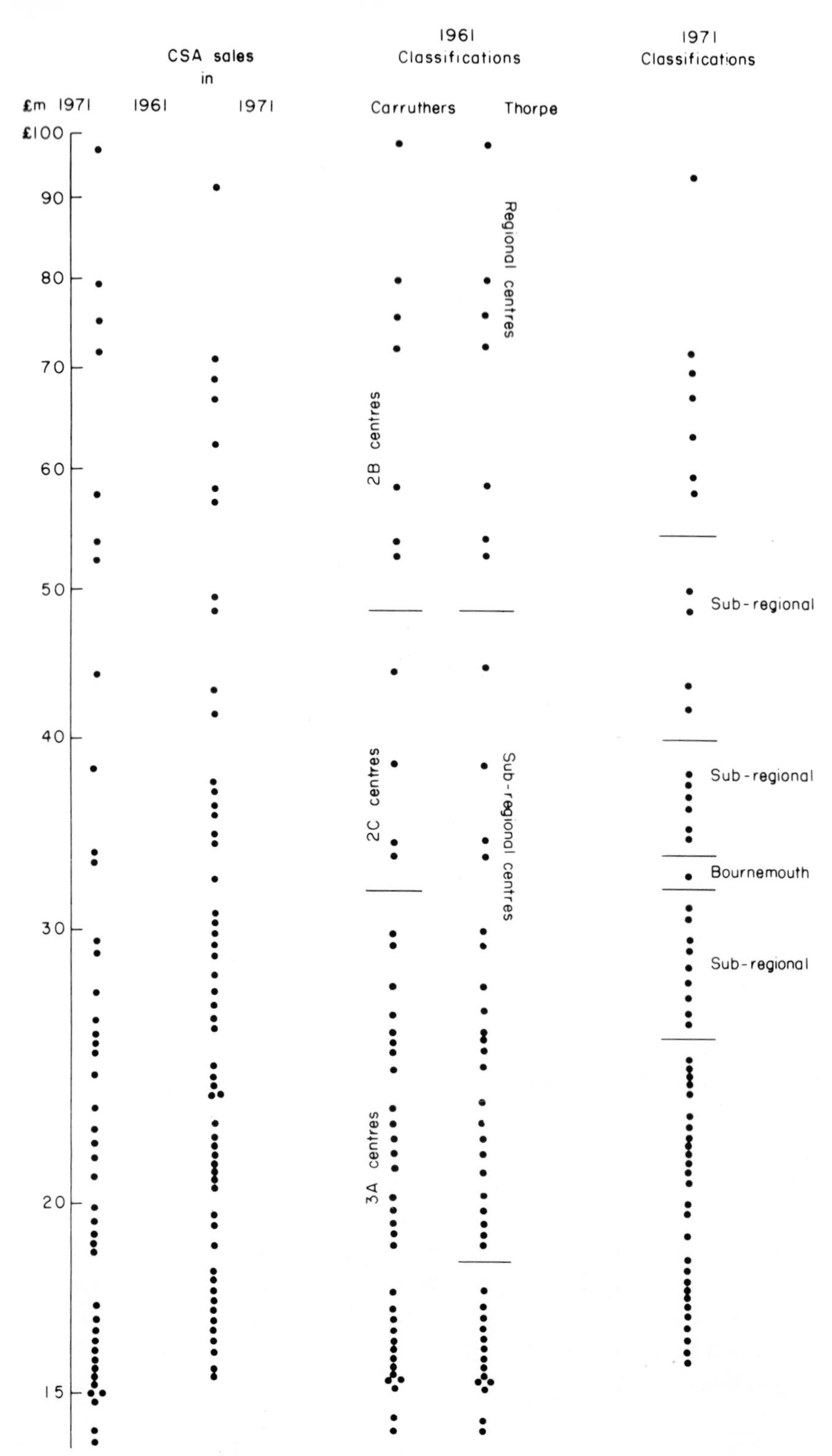

Figure 27. Rank placements of central shopping areas by comparison goods sales.

TABLE 18

Central shopping areas in rank order of comparison—goods shops sales (M£) (1971)

	1961	1971
Glasgow	96·86	91·75
Liverpool	79·18	70·50
Birmingham	71·41	68·69
Manchester	74·94	66·64
Newcastle	53·45	62·20
Edinburgh	52·46	57·97
Leeds	58·68	57·92
Sheffield	38·32	49·11
Nottingham	44·12	48·20
Bristol	29·55	42·70
Cardiff	33·94	41·49
Leicester	33·94	37·58
Southampton	25·17	36·70
Wolverhampton	26·16	36·06
Hull	29·13	35·34
Plymouth	24·04	34·43
Reading	21·35	34·32
Bournemouth	21·78	32·40
Sunderland	22·91	30·66
Norwich	19·80	30·19
Brighton	16·83	29·96
Coventry	25·45	29·10
Bradford	27·43	28·76
Swansea	22·20	27·92
Aberdeen	24·89	27·04
Watford	15·27	26·77
Derby	20·64	26·77
Doncaster	18·81	25·60
Chester	15·84	24·01
Guildford	12·16	23·77
Dundee	18·80	23·63
Middlesborough	19·51	23·59
Blackpool	18·94	23·53
Cambridge	16·26	22·31
York	16·54	21·79
Exeter	15·70	21·49
Southend	13·72	21·37
Oxford	15·13	21·02
Ipswich	12·58	20·75
Stockport	10·32	20·53
Preston	16·12	20·40
Newport	15·13	19·45
Bolton	17·11	19·20
Northampton	14·14	18·57
Bath	13·15	17·81
Cheltenham	13·72	17·71
Hanley	13·01	17·38
Gloucester	13·01	17·07

(a) *The regional centres* which remained sizeable but were becoming more and more similar in their roles and in the problems that confronted them. These centres were Glasgow, Liverpool, Birmingham, Manchester, Newcastle, Leeds and Edinburgh. Only in Newcastle and Edinburgh did sales grow in real terms during 1961-1971.

(b) *The sub-regional centres (full ranking)*, all four of which (Sheffield, Nottingham, Cardiff and Bristol) enjoyed growth in real terms. In 1961 the gap between them and the next lowest ranking centre was indistinct for Leicester had sales higher than Bristol. By 1971 Bristol's sales were 14 per cent higher than Leicester's and higher than Cardiff's.

(c) *The sub-regional centres (normal ranking).* All these centres except Leicester (the others were Southampton, Wolverhampton, Hull, Plymouth and Reading) enjoyed significant growth in real terms.

(d) *Bournemouth,* like Bristol with two central shopping areas, would be probably best viewed as a distinctive kind of centre.

(e) *Other sub-regional centres (limited potential).* Although some of these centres grew substantially in real terms the majority of them would appear to be limited in their growth either because of their geographical position or the proximity of more powerful centres. These centres were Sunderland, Norwich, Brighton, Coventry, Bradford, Swansea, Aberdeen, Watford, Derby and Doncaster.

The above classification is based on the last statistical evidence available and so is more than ten years out of date! During the 1970s major developments have taken place in Manchester, Newcastle, Edinburgh, Nottingham and Cardiff. Birmingham and Sheffield were both enjoying the benefits of major schemes completed in the second half of the 1960s. Even though the scale of some of these developments has been substantial it seems unlikely that they will have resulted in great changes to the classification. The differential growth in the period 1961-1971, and the subsequent attentions of city-centre developers, has probably mainly resulted in each centre being able to establish what might be thought to be a normal role in its natural catchment area. The degree to which developments since 1971 have added to the overall sales volume of a centre rather than redistributed custom already attracted to a centre is, in the absence of data, open to dispute. However, given the state of the economy in 1981, the scope for additional development schemes of any size in the provincial cities with regional or sub-regional status is likely to be very much the exception rather than the rule.

It is a salutory warning when looking at the 1980s that, of the regional centres during the period 1961-1971, when the volume of comparison goods sales in Great Britain rose by 31 per cent (Lee, 1977), only Newcastle and Edinburgh achieved an increase in sales volume. Furthermore only nine of the top 29 centres achieved a sales increase higher than the national rate. For 1971-1981 it is likely that much the same story would emerge if statistics were available, even though nationally the volume of comparison goods sales will have risen by something like 41 per cent in this period (22 per cent from 1971 to 1976 and perhaps 15 per cent from 1976 to 1981).

Rents are notoriously dangerous as an indicator of a centre's true prosperity because they depend on "a market" which is influenced by a very small number of transactions relative to the total number of shops in a given centre. They thus reflect the desire of particular traders to gain entry to a city centre rather than the price at which all the shop premises in a centre might be sold if a large number of retailers wished to vacate their premises. Thus when estate agents claim that in a given centre rents are very high, any real appreciation of that claim would need a record of the number of transactions on which it was based. However, in very broad terms the relative (and absolute?) decline of a number of major city centres is apparent in the Investors Chronicle/Hillier Parker Rent Index (1980) (Table 19). Thus, after adjusting for general changes in shop rents, the regional centres experienced a decline of 15 per cent or more whereas the sub-regional centres and some selected area centres experienced a growth of 30 per cent during the period 1965-1978.

TABLE 19

Index for groups of centres divided by the All Centre Index (expressed as % of 1965 relative position[a])

Centres grouped by size of 1971 sales	1972	1974	1977	1978
1 Birmingham + Manchester + Liverpool	90	94	85	83
2 Newcastle + Leeds + Croydon	97	98	89	85
3 Nottingham + Sheffield	118	107	91	90
4 Cardiff, Kingston, Leicester, Bristol, Southampton, Plymouth, Norwich	123	133	124	129
5 Watford—Hull, Doncaster, Brighton, Guildford	113	131	136	131
6 Hounslow—York (and 8 others)	100	109	101	100
7 Ashford, Blackburn (and 12 others)	82	93	96	96
8 Orpington, Durham (and 7 others)	88	81	83	83

[a] i.e. by 1978, adjusting for general changes in rents, rents in the first group had fallen by 17 per cent on their 1965 level or in the fifth group had risen by 31 per cent.

Source: Investors Chronicle/Hillier Parker Rent Index (1979).

THE FUTURE

If the recent past of the provincial major city centres has been one of either absolute or relative retail decline, it might be asked whether this matters and in any case whether the past is any guide for the future. These questions come to the heart of this volume of essays. What then are the factors leading to such decline? If we come to believe that it does matter and that we expect some continuation of past trends, what then can be done about it?

Problems

The continuing problems of retailers in the major city centres would seem to be:

(a) a declining immediate support population;
(b) a particularly rapid relative (and perhaps absolute) decline in the spending power of that population;
(c) the rapid growth of retail floor space within their catchment areas;
(d) a disproportionate rise in the expenses of city-centre traders, particularly rates, at a time when sales might be static or falling;
(e) the difficulty of ensuring good accessibility to all groups of potential customers;
(f) the difficulty of providing a pleasant clean and enjoyable environment for those using the city centre.

The first two of these problems are changes largely outside the control of local or central government, and will continue to be the prime conditioning factors which determine the prosperity of city centres. However, city-centre performance during 1961-1971 was by no means a direct function of changes in the characteristics of catchment area populations. Some cities benefiting from improvements in accessibility were able to buck the trend. Others, as a result of large increases in alternative shopping provisions, had performances substantially worse than might have been anticipated. Since 1971, these two factors, accessibility and the scale of alternative shopping provision, have probably become of even greater significance. In the 1980s this trend will grow in importance. There could now be some real danger that substantial city centres will be threatened in a way which could have a serious impact on their role. This is by no means inevitable, but if it is to be prevented local and national government will have to work closely with city-centre traders in order to ensure that the problems outlined above are minimized.

The importance of the city centre

The decline of city centres is a source of concern not only for the major retail groups, but also for those concerned with wider issues such as:

(a) the employment opportunities provided by city centres;
(b) the regional attractiveness afforded by city centres;
(c) the quality of the built environment in city centres;
(d) the competitive interaction of city-centre shops resulting in keen prices for a range of goods much wider than any hypermarket would want to or plan to stock.

(i) Employment

Retailers in city centres offer jobs in a location of great significance for the urban economy as a whole. Inner city residents generally have only a short bus ride to the city centre and so depend, and will probably increasingly depend, heavily on such jobs. A run down in the city centre's role can therefore have serious consequences to the beleaguered inner city. It is worth noting that city-centre retailers offering a wide variety of goods and services make a more extensive use of labour than, say, would be characteristic in an automated hypermarket. Furthermore, city-centre stores in provincial regions compete for custom not only with shops in off-centre locations but also with Central London or those in foreign tourist resorts. Maintaining the buoyancy of the city centre therefore has employment implications for the regional economy.

(ii) Regional development

When Sir Wilfred Burns was City Planning Officer in Newcastle in the early 1960s he placed great importance on the strategic role for north-east England of an attractive regional centre. It was argued by many that one of the factors inhibiting regional development was a potential shortfall between the quality of local retail services and those which a potential mobile industrialist's wife had come to expect in Bond Street or Oxford Street. The service given to the North-East in this respect by Fenwicks and Bainbridges (the two main Department Stores in Newcastle) must have been considerable. The same consideration applies to other regional centres and would seem to be as important now as it was 20 years ago.

(iii) Built environment

The seven regional centres lie in the centre of major conurbations which owed most of their growth to the industrialization of the nineteenth century. The physical environment of many of these conurbations is still impoverished. Yet the city centres generally have an attractiveness and a dynamism which makes a great contrast to the dereliction of inner city areas or the drabness of much of the inter-war and post-war housing characteristic of such areas. The contrast, for instance, between Liverpool city centre and extensive areas of the rest of Merseyside is one which strikes most visitors to Merseyside. These regional centres are able to achieve this environmental impact only if carefully nurtured and in particular, in the present context, if retailers find trade sufficiently sound to maintain buildings to a good standard.

(iv) Retail function

In retail planning circles it has become fashionable to describe the advantages of new forms of retailing: for instance the discount warehouse and the hypermarket. In an ideal world it might be desirable for the consumer to have available as wide a variety of forms of shop as possible. In a period, such as the early 1970s, when retail sales were likely to grow far more rapidly than retailers' costs it was just feasible to believe that most parts of Britain could afford such choice for the consumer without substantial offsetting penalties. The 1980s will not be such a period. It should be recognized that the balance of costs and benefits is now very finely tuned. In addition to the employment, regional strategic and urban environmental roles of the city centre we should not lose sight of its unique retail roles. The choice between an excellent regional centre and more hypermarkets or discount warehouses is one which is not often posed properly.

The city centre has a primary and a subsidiary retail role. The subsidiary role is to cater for the needs of those employed in the centre in offices. It is important for the primary role of the regional centre as the destination of the special shopping expedition that this subsidiary role is conducted in such a way as not to harm the environmental attractiveness of the shopping streets. This is particularly true if office employment in city centres is likely to fall in the long term. The regional role is simple, yet seemingly now not always understood. It is the provision of a range of shops in one place which compete with each other in an intense way. This affords the consumer the possibility of visiting more than one of these shops to make direct comparisons. This role is therefore one in which competition is highly developed and not obscured, if that is the right word, by surface car parking or promotional advertising. There is little possibility for a city-centre trader of benefiting from a localized monopoly created by loss leading on one product or products to attract shoppers. The role extends further in that if the spending power of a region is concentrated to a reasonable degree in one centre there is a chance that the variety of goods on offer will be substantially greater than if a decentralized pattern of trading appears.

Newcastle upon Tyne

It will perhaps help to clarify these themes if a brief look is taken at two of the cities in which the John Lewis Partnership operates department stores. In Newcastle, the 1961–1971 period, as we have seen, saw some growth in sales volume aided probably in part by the improvements in the sub-regional road system. The opening of the Eldon Square Centre in 1976 with its 8073 m^2 of gross leaseable area was a major element to digest into the city.* Bennison and Davies (1980) have already indicated some of the implications of this development, but it is probable that a good number of years will be needed before this digestion process can be completed.

For the Partnership a major implication has been an increase in its rates bill (see Table 20). Thus although Bainbridge's sales have risen, operational costs have risen substantially as a result of the move. Economically it is therefore vital that sales continue to increase. Fortunately the City appears to understand this and can see that its city centre is of such value to the people of Tyneside and north-east England as a whole that care should be taken not to harm it by over-development.

Equally there is an understanding that improvements in accessibility are of

* The John Lewis Partnership is represented in Newcastle by Bainbridge's Department Store which relocated into the Eldon Square Centre from a position on Grainger Street.

TABLE 20

Rates bills in city centres

	Bainbridge Newcastle		Cole Bros. Sheffield		G H Lee Liverpool		John Lewis Edinburgh		Comparison goods price index
	Actual	1973 = 100	Actual	1973 = 100	Actual	1973 = 100	Actual	1973 = 100	1973 = 100
1973	59 352	100	74 153	100	127 066	100	74 247	100	100
1974	79 897	135	99 364	134	140 856	111	84 767	114	117
1975	121 329	204	121 610	164	156 291	123	113 245	153	140
1976	121 443	205	132 733	179	163 207[a]	128	122 995	166	157
1977	249 720[b]	421	149 788	202	186 537[a]	147	138 744	187	180
1978	287 871	485	159 428	215	190 953[a]	150	159 498	215	198
1979	331 804	559	183 157[a]	247	231 260[a]	182	191 123	257	227
1980	438 859	739	251 080	339	323 123[a]	254	259 872	350	253
1981	549 846	926	335 911	453	379 886[a]	299	394 621	531	266
1981 (if still in old building)	271 420	457							

[a] Excluding the effect of additional gross rateable value on some additions to the stores.
[b] Time at which Bainbridge relocated to Eldon Square.

continuing importance. Tyneside is fortunate that it has funding for its Metro-Rail system. This it is hoped will provide an increasingly attractive transport mode for those who are prepared to shop without their car. At the same time, however, there are many who are not prepared to do this, particularly people who may well spend disproportionately large amounts. Thus car parking in the city centre for shoppers (i.e. with modest charges for a short stay rising to penal charges for a long stay) is a vital ingredient in its continued viability. The experience of the 1970s has been that it is no good taking doctrinaire stances on car parking. Towns which try to restrict shoppers from using their cars will find that their city centres decline. By all means explore all possible ways of making alternative transport arrangements attractive but under-provision of car parking, penal charges or other restrictive policies will not lead to a switch of allegiance to other modes of transport but rather a switch to other towns or to foreign holidays. In the planning stages of Eldon Square there was considerable pressure to keep down the number of car parking spaces in the development, but eventually such pressures were at least partially overcome. However, Central Newcastle, like most city centres, is still inadequately provided with car parking.

One of the benefits of Eldon Square is that as a managed shopping centre there is at least one part of the shopping centre under constant environmental control. Whilst climatic control confers great benefits, particularly during a north-east winter, there are probably as great benefits for the city environment in the careful maintenance and daily cleansing of the malls in the Centre.

Liverpool

In Liverpool the Partnership store is G H Lee. The St John's Centre is not comparable with Eldon Square but considerable improvements have been made over the last ten years in car parking availability and the street environment. For instance, during a recent survey by the Liverpool Stores Committee it was found that there were many citizens of Liverpool who simply enjoyed being in the city centre because of its vitality. Even, or perhaps particularly, for those who are unemployed, this was seen as a major service to the community. Unfortunately one of the reasons for the high pedestrian flow in Church Street is that some of those who are unemployed find that visiting the centre is the most attractive way of spending the time that lies heavily on their hands.

However, unlike Newcastle, Liverpool is under some pressure, for the accessibility of the city centre to an important part of its catchment area is deteriorating. This deterioration is not so much a feature of physical conditions but of pricing policy of the Mersey tunnels. For Liverpool city centre the Wirral is a particularly important part of its catchment area owing to the disproportionate spending power located there. Because it is apparently government policy that estuarine crossings (but not ordinary roads or other bridged or tunnelled routes) that provide local benefits should be covered by tolls, the Mersey toll authority is having to raise progressively the level of tolls simply in order to cover debt charges on capital provided in part almost half a century ago. The available evidence suggests that this is becoming an increasing deterrent for those who make personal discretionery trips through the tunnels (e.g. shoppers). The danger is that the city centre, being thus deprived of part of its support population, will become increasingly less able to fulfil the functions outlined above as being so important for the vitality of provincial regions.

SOLUTIONS

There are many different possible futures for the city centre. If we had been considering this in the 1960s, the range would, however, have been even wider. Then we might have thought of anything from considerable growth to modest decline. Now all the pointers suggest that growth at best will be limited and that there is a possibility of substantial decline. Which of such futures is the trend is a worthless question to consider. There is a general consensus that any substantial decline would be unfortunate (to say the least). There is then a need to ensure that all possible solutions are explored and that action occurs to overcome as many as possible of the environmental handicaps to the vitality of the city centre. Time is running out.

Accessibility is the initial key. Amos, writing in 1973 on Liverpool City Centre, commented "the disproportionately large investment in highways has done much to undermine the strengths of the central area and this should, and could, now be reversed".

Car Parking is the next vital ingredient. Borg (1973) has described the complicated history of proposals for pedestrianization and places for additional car parking in Central Birmingham. Nearly ten years on there are still city centres in which similar debates occur. Borg commented that what was at risk

> if retail shopping disappeared from the centre . . . would be a devastating void in the city's heart . . . if the shops go there will be a tendency for some work places to go with them, or near them, and the dismantling of the city centre will have begun. Will it then be possible to retain interest in those somewhat fewer social, recreational and cultural centres that remain, or that have been renewed?

Environment forms a third element. Given that it is possible to reach the city centre and then to park, it is important that the visitor's experience is as attractive as possible. According to Smigielski (1973)

> a walk in the central area of Leicester today would give an impression that the city has undergone a recent bombardment by enemy action; [whereas] a city should be built for the convenience and satisfaction of the people who live in it and for the great surprises of strangers (Sansovino, 1460-1529, quoted by Smigielski).

This is a general theme of importance for the city centre. It is, however, of special importance for the Regional Shopping Centre. There is now a growing body of evidence that the quality of the environment is of major importance in its influence on the shopping trip and expenditure. City authorities and shopkeepers have a combined responsibility to ensure the continued improvement of the environment.

Finally, in a society in which resources are limited there may well be a need for a more careful evaluation of competing developments and a reconsideration of the distinctions, which may become greater and greater, between those twin, but often opposed, pillars of retail planning of demand and need. In this context it is worth noting that those involved in city-centre development have widely differing interests. To some extent the chapters in this volume will reflect this fact. Developers, and their agents the major firms of estate agents, seek to discover new sites for their next project without necessarily any concern for the overall health of the centre in which a site is identified. This applies to all forms of development, not only shopping. The major firms of estate agents are in a particularly difficult position here, for although they may well make their experience available to local authorities as property advisers, ultimately they are dependent on a changing property market. In the 1960s and 1970s change may well have been an appropriate norm. In the 1980s and 1990s it may well be that society will benefit most from stability.

Local authorities have many different roles in the city centre. It may become increasingly difficult for them to resolve conflict between their town planning functions, their corporate financial interests and general strategic functions. Even in the financial context there could well be problems in resolving optimum long-term strategies.

When confronted by such difficulties it is to be hoped that the degree of dialogue which now exists between local authorities and city-centre retailers and other private sector employers will be reinforced so that plans will increasingly reflect the reality of commercial life.

REFERENCES

Amos, F. J. C. (1973). *In* "City Centre Redevelopment" (J. Holliday, ed.). Charles Knight, London.

Bennison, D. J. and Davies, R. L. (1980). *Progr. Plann.* **14**, 1-104.

Borg, N. (1973). *In* "City Centre Redevelopment" (J. Holliday, ed.). Charles Knight, London.

Carruthers, W. L. (1967). *Reg. Stud.* **1**, 65-81. Investors Chronicle-Hillier Parker Rent Index (1979). Research Report No. 4, London.

Lee, M. (1977). "Shopping Centre Data". Donaldsons, London.

Smigielski, W. K. (1973). *In* "City Centre Redevelopment" (J. Holliday, ed.). Charles Knight, London.

Thorpe, D. (1968). *Urban Stud.* **5**, 165-206.

EIGHT

Housing change and social change

C. HAMNETT

The last hundred years and more have been generally characterized in both Britain and North America by rapid urban growth, suburban expansion and central area redevelopment. One consequence of these developments is that the central areas of most large western industrial cities are commonly conceived of today as being dominated by what are termed central area land-uses, in other words, retailing, offices and other commercial functions. Central areas are rarely thought of as performing any further significant residential function and, in consequence, the residential role of the city centre is today a largely neglected area of study.

It is the intention of this chapter to attempt to correct this understandable, and to some extent, justifiable myopia by an examination of the changing residential function of the city centre with particular reference to London. First, however, it is necessary to make some preliminary observations on attempts to forecast or predict the future, be it of the city centre or any other object of urban analysis. We shall not attempt to do this systematically as this has already been attempted elsewhere (see Hamnett, 1974). The key point to be made is the simple one that any attempt to predict or forecast the course of future events will prove inadequate if it is ahistorical or asocial. The legacy of history cannot be ignored. As Peter Hall (1966) has tellingly put it: "No-one is more a prisoner of history than he who is unaware of it." The basic contention of this chapter is that any attempt to foretell the future requires, even within the limits of such an exercise, to be adequately grounded in an understanding of changing current circumstances, their determinants and precursors.

Where the urban scene is concerned, this in turn necessitates an analysis of wider social structures and processes. The city does not exist in a vacuum: it is an integral part of the economic, political and social structure of society. Settlement patterns are not independent entities, external to and autonomous of the structure of social organization. Whilst there is a complex interplay between the two, spatial patterns are, in large part, socially produced. It is imperative, therefore, not to fall into what A. N. Whitehead has termed "the fallacy of misplaced concreteness", reifying changing spatial distributions and functions as if they occurred independently of their own volition, rather than as the outcome of the interplay between existing

THE FUTURE FOR THE CITY CENTRE
ISBN 0 12 206240 X

spatial structures and changing social processes. Thus, just as changes in the extent, shape and function of central areas must be related back to the economic and other forces which have produced them, so too it is crucial to anticipate the effects of new developments such as the increasing flow of money into pension funds or the growth of the microchip. As de Jouvenal (1967) has put it, society is stable so long as the same repetitive patterns and mutual relations are maintained. To the extent that these are not, "episodic and periodic deformations of the social surface can occur", which destroy our structural certainties. The task and problem of forecasting is "to apprehend, at their origin, those shoots which as they grow will deform the familiar social surface and produce swellings, fractures and cracks".

Considering the residential future of the city centre in the light of these points, no apology is made for devoting the bulk of this chapter to past and present changes, because it is only after this has been done that any sensible assessment of future developments can be made.

CENTRAL AREA COMMERCIAL DEVELOPMENT AND RESIDENTIAL DISPLACEMENT

Most western city centres are no longer generally considered to perform any significant residential function. This image is broadly correct, except for a number of major metropolises such as London, New York, San Francisco and Paris and, to a lesser extent, several older cities such as Amsterdam and Edinburgh where a major residential function continues. What residential areas there were in the centres of many large cities have been gradually squeezed out or forcibly displaced by the process of central area commercial development. As an official Report of 1857 noted of New York:

> As our wharves became crowded with warehouses and encompassed with bustle and noise, the wealthier citizens, who peopled old "knickerbocker" mansions, near the bay, transferred their residence to streets beyond the din: compensating for remoteness from their counting houses, by the advantages of increased quiet and luxury. Their habitations then passed into the hands, on the one side, of boarding house keepers, on the other of real estate agents; and here, in its beginning, the tenant house became a real blessing to that class of industrious poor whose small earnings limited their expenses and whose employment in workshops, stores, and about the wharves and thoroughfares, rendered a near residence of much importance. . . . This state of tenanting comfort did not, however, continue long; for the rapid march of improvement speedily enhanced the value of property in the lower wards of the city, and as this took place, rents rose and accommodation decreased in the same proportion.

The description of the residential location behaviour of low income city-centre workers might well have come straight from Alonso, but this state of affairs was commonplace rather than exceptional. As Engels (1972) put it in a now familiar quotation:

> The growth of the big modern cities gives the land in certain areas, particularly those which are centrally situated, an artificial and often colossally increasing value; the buildings erected on these areas depress this value, instead of increasing it, because they no longer conform to the changed circumstances. They are pulled down and replaced by others. This takes place above all with workers' houses which are situated centrally and whose rents, even with the greatest overcrowding, can never, or only very slowly, increase above a certain maximum. They are pulled down and in their stead shops, warehouses and public buildings are erected.... The result is that the workers are forced out of the centre of the towns towards the outskirts; that workers' dwellings in general, become rare and expensive and often altogether unobtainable, for under these circumstances the building industry, which is offered a much better field for speculation by more expensive houses, builds workers' houses only by way of exception.

As Banfield (1975) describes the process:

> What was happening in New York (and elsewhere as well) was the expansion of the city outward under the pressure of growth at its centre. Typically, land closest to the point of original settlement (always the point most accessible to waterborne transportation) became the site of the central business district. General accessibility to wharves, markets, shops and offices, and later to railheads, meant that commercial and industrial activities had to be located there .... As the central business district grew, it absorbed the residential neighbourhoods adjacent to it .... Most of the housing taken over in this way was torn down to make room for factories, stores and offices.

In consequence, the resident population of the city centre has generally been in a process of continual decline since the mid-nineteenth century.

Residential decline in central London

In Britain, this tendency is perhaps most clearly exemplified by the City of London. The wealthy residential focus of London had already started to move westwards towards Westminster from the late seventeenth century, but the City of London still had a resident population of 123 000 in 1841 and even as late as 1861 it numbered 112 000. By 1881, however, as a result of large-scale Victorian office development, this had declined to 51 000 and by the turn of the century there were but 27 000. By 1971 the resident population of the City stood at only 4000, but the subsequent redevelopment of the Barbican site increased this to almost 6000 by 1981 (Gray, 1978; Morrey, 1973).

As Olsson (1976) comments, "The office building as a specific type was a nineteenth century invention and its proliferation a Victorian phenomena." He quotes Edward l'Anson (1812-1888), probably the best-known city architect, who commented on its novelty in a paper read to the RIBA in 1872:

> When I first began on the New London Bridge approaches, previous to 1840, city offices as now constructed were not thought of; the houses were built as shops and dwellings, or as warehouses, and it was the same in Moorgate Street. Since that time, however, a distinct type of construction has been evolved which is now, perhaps, nearly perfect.

Olsson also quotes T. R. Smith and W. H. White who in a paper read to the Society of Arts in 1876 cited specialized office buildings as one of the

> remarkable and suggestive modifications in town buildings . . . made within the present century . . . . The huge blocks of offices for merchants and professional men now to be found in the City . . . are comparative novelties . . . . Little more than fifty years ago a great many merchants resided east of Temple Bar often over their counting houses. Even at that time a few houses were let in separate floors, and used as offices; but buildings erected expressly for offices were unknown, and one of the first houses planned and constructed for that purpose was a block of offices in Clements Lane, built about 1823. During the last twenty years the growth of this class of buildings has been enormous.

The extent of nineteenth century residential displacement by commercial and other development has been ably recorded and analysed by Steadman-Jones (1971) and, more recently, in the case of Tolmers Square, Euston by Nick Wates (1976). Brown (1980) argues that whereas there was a 1 : 1 correspondence between residential and office floor space in the West End in 1971, this is now being threatened by the continued extension of "mixed development" schemes on the South Bank, in Covent Garden and elsewhere with an office/housing ratio of 4:1 which can "only exacerbate an already dangerous imbalance" whereby vital city-centre services are being threatened by a shortage of decent accommodation for low paid service workers. Westminster City Council have imposed tight planning controls on office uses in the borough but these are being strongly challenged. As will be shown below, however, the supply of rented housing in central London faces a much more severe threat than that from commercial takeover, which may in any event be a declining force. Just as the office as a specialized land-use and built-form came into being in the mid-nineteenth century, developments in employment and occupational structure, aided by microchip technology may well result in the gradual demise of large-scale office cores in the last two decades of the twentieth century. De Jouvenal (1967) pointed to the dangers inherent in trend projection or extrapolation when he wrote, "The trouble with prolongation of a tendency is that the reversal of the tendency is not anticipated." The tendency to view the future through the blinkers of the present is endemic and can easily serve to blind us to the growth of new shoots and structures which de Jouvenal refers to.

The central area as defined today for census purposes includes not only the City of London but all of the City of Westminster as far north as Paddington Station, a small part of Kensington, the southern part of Camden including Bloomsbury and Holborn and small parts of northern Lambeth and Southwark. It is therefore wholly incorrect to associate the city centre of London solely with the contemporary financial district of the City of London. Central London has consisted of two cities for over 300 years just as Manhattan has its specialist financial district in the downtown, its midtown shopping and entertainment area and its uptown prestige residential areas.

The three central boroughs have seen a considerable reduction in resident population over the last 70–100 years, but they still have a major residential function (see Williams *et al.*, 1972). Westminster was the first to reach its population peak in 1871 with 524 000 residents, subsequently declining by just over half to 240 000 in 1971, an annual average rate of decline of some 0·5 per cent. This rate speeded up in the decades 1951-1961 and 1961-1971 when it lost approximately 30 000 people per decade, an average annual rate of some 1·2 per cent per annum in 1961-1971 compared to just under 1 per cent in 1951-1961. Camden and Kensington both reached their population peaks later in 1901 with 377 000 and 250 000 respectively. By 1971 Camden's population had fallen to 207 000 and Kensington's to 188 000, giving average annual rates of decline over the 70-year period of 0·64 per cent and 0·35 per cent respectively. Kensington's overall rate of population decline has been slow, its population remaining virtually static until 1939. It only declined suddenly in the decade 1961-1971 when, like Westminster, it lost 30 000, an average annual rate of decline of 1·4 per cent. Camden too showed a rapid rate of decline in this period of some 1·6 per cent. Much of this decline represents the reduction of overcrowding in the boroughs from their previously high levels—for example, the number of persons per room falling in Westminster from 0·74 in 1961 to 0·64 in 1966. However, population decline in such desirable, attractive and accessible a residential area as central London will not continue indefinitely. It is much more likely to stabilize at more acceptable density levels related to the tenure mix and the price of space. (See Hamnett and Randolph (1982) for a full discussion of 1961-81 population trends in central London.)

The role of central London as a high status residential area

Central London has long been recognized as one of the highest status residential areas in London. The City of London performed a similar role until as late as 1700 but its premier position had been undermined with the permanent establishment of the court at Westminster and it was usurped from the early seventeenth century onwards with the development of Leicester Square and other areas in the 1670s and after. The final nail in the coffin of the City as a prestige residential area was the Great Plague of 1665 and the Great Fire in 1666, both of which increased the impetus of westward development (Gray, 1978). The development of the West End as a high-status residential area continued through the eighteenth and early nineteenth centuries (Prince, 1964) and it has never lost this position despite the subsequent waves of suburban development.

Whilst many areas of inner London experienced in the 1960s and 1970s the phenomenon known as gentrification, with higher income, managerial, professional owner-occupiers tending to replace, if not actively displace, lower income, working class renters (Hamnett and Williams, 1979, 1980), it has been the existing high status central London boroughs that have witnessed some of the largest absolute and proportionate increases. Thus whereas Islington has built up a legendary reputation as a gentrified borough, showing an increase of 1400 or 23 per cent in its economically active professional and managerial males, this still only raised the proportion of this social group from 6·6 per cent to 11·5 per cent of the borough total. In the three central London boroughs of Camden, Westminster and

Kensington by contrast, the proportion of professionals and managers was already 19, 25 and 27 per cent in 1961, and by 1971 this share had increased to 24, 30 and 33 per cent respectively. The significance of these figures becomes apparent when it is realized that no other borough in inner London had more than 16 per cent of its economically active residents classified as professionals and managers in 1971.

HIGH STATUS RESIDENTIAL AREAS IN THE CENTRAL CITY AND RESIDENTIAL LOCATION THEORY

The existence of a body of high status city-centre residents in London is by no means a unique anomaly, even in Britain. Edgebaston in Birmingham has long been known, as has Edinburgh New Town, and the Park in Nottingham. For a wide ranging review of these quarters see Simpson and Lloyd (1977). In the USA the existence of high status groups in Manhattan was discussed by Hoover and Vernon in 1959. The work of both Rapkin and Grigsby (1960) on Philadelphia and Abu-Lughod (1960) on New York, Chicago and Philadelphia was concerned solely with these groups, and Schnore (1965, p.84) commented on: "the persistence of elite groups near the centre of many (American) cities". The general characteristics of these groups and their residential locations have been outlined by Hamnett (1973).

The existence of such a substantial amount of high status residents in the city centre poses problems for traditional residential location theory, as does the gentrification of other areas of inner London and elsewhere. Burgess recognized no central high status areas at all, whilst both Hoyt and Alonso viewed them as atypical, small-scale anomalies. As Senior (1974) points out, Burgess assumes the existence of a high income preference for peripheral areas and Hoyt assumed the existence of a strong preference for newer structures. Hoyt did however accept that: "de luxe high-rent apartment areas tend to be established near the business centre in old residential areas".

Alonso (1964) recognized the existence in the United States of "a substantial minority of the well-to-do that does prefer accessibility to space", noting that they live in luxury apartments or town houses in the central areas. None the less, Alonso elevated preference for space to the "key variable of the structural theory", forcibly stating that "Taste or preference for space are possibly words too weak to denote what is really meant by this key variable of the structural theory. Rather, the nature of the demand for space in this country seems to be a deeply engrained cultural value." Alonso is thus sceptical of the efficiency of urban renewal efforts to attract middle and high income groups back to the central and inner city. Unless there is a change of taste, and a greater preference for accessibility over space, the urban renewal movement can only skim "a narrow and specialized sector of demand which will soon dry up" (Alonso, 1964). Berry (1980) takes a smilar view, arguing that "the prospect for wider inner city revitalization appears to be bleak".

Harvey (1973), however, has pointed out that

> since the shape of the bid-rent curve for the rich is really a function of their preference for space relative to transport costs . . . the spatial structure of the city will change if

> the preferences of the rich group change . . . (as) . . . the rich can always enforce its preferences over the poor group because it has more resources to apply either to transport costs or to obtaining land in whatever location it chooses.

Simmonds (1968) has also observed that, "A shift in middle class norms regarding the values of access to downtown could be more significant than all the urban renewal to date." Significantly, Zeitz (1979) commented a decade later that private urban renewal, as she terms gentrification, "is the first success among many efforts to rehabilitate inner cities". Gentrification has thus come to be seen as very important in the US since the late 1970s.

Explanations of high status city-centre residential areas

Where then does this leave traditional residential location theory? Evans (1973) comments that "The high income households who locate, at, or near, the city centre provide one of the most interesting problems in the analysis of patterns of residential location . . . (though) . . . Many American authors seem to imply that no such households exist or that, if they do, they are at a suboptimal location." In a sophisticated extension of Alonso's work incorporating both differential incomes and differential income-elasticities for space, Evans was able to derive a model which predicts the existence of a substantial body of high income city-centre residents with a low income-elasticity for space (Fig. 28). Evans claims that "even this simple theory roughly predicts the distribution of households by income in the large British or American city". Figure 29, taken from Evans, shows the geographical distribution of income recipients by income classes in the New York Metropolitan Region. As can be seen Manhattan contains a high proportion of both the high and low income groups.

Moreover, from figures shown in Table 21, Evans (1973) claims that a similar pattern exists in the major British cities, with the highest income groups being over-represented in the conurbation centres. The very high income group comprising professional self-employed persons (SEG 3) was found to be particularly strongly concentrated in the conurbation centre and was under-represented throughout the rest of the conurbation. The next highest income groups (SEG 1: employers and managers of large organizations; and SEG 4: professional employees) were over-represented in the conurbation centre and in the outer area of the conurbation but were under-represented in the central city outside the conurbation centre. Meanwhile, the lowest income group (SEG 11: unskilled manual workers) is over-represented in the conurbation centre, with its proportion in any area declining with increasing distance from the centre.

How are the variations in the geographical distribution of socio-economic Groups 1, 3 and 4 between the conurbations to be explained? They result, says Evans (1973) "from variations in the income distribution between the conurbations, with the population of London having a higher average income than that of the other conurbations". He goes on, however to look at the role of social agglomeration, arguing that:

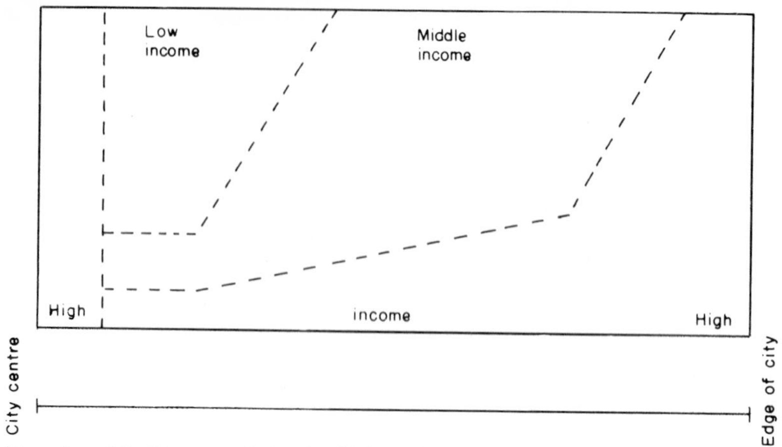

Figure 28. Evans' model of the population in different income groups and their variation with distance from the city centre.

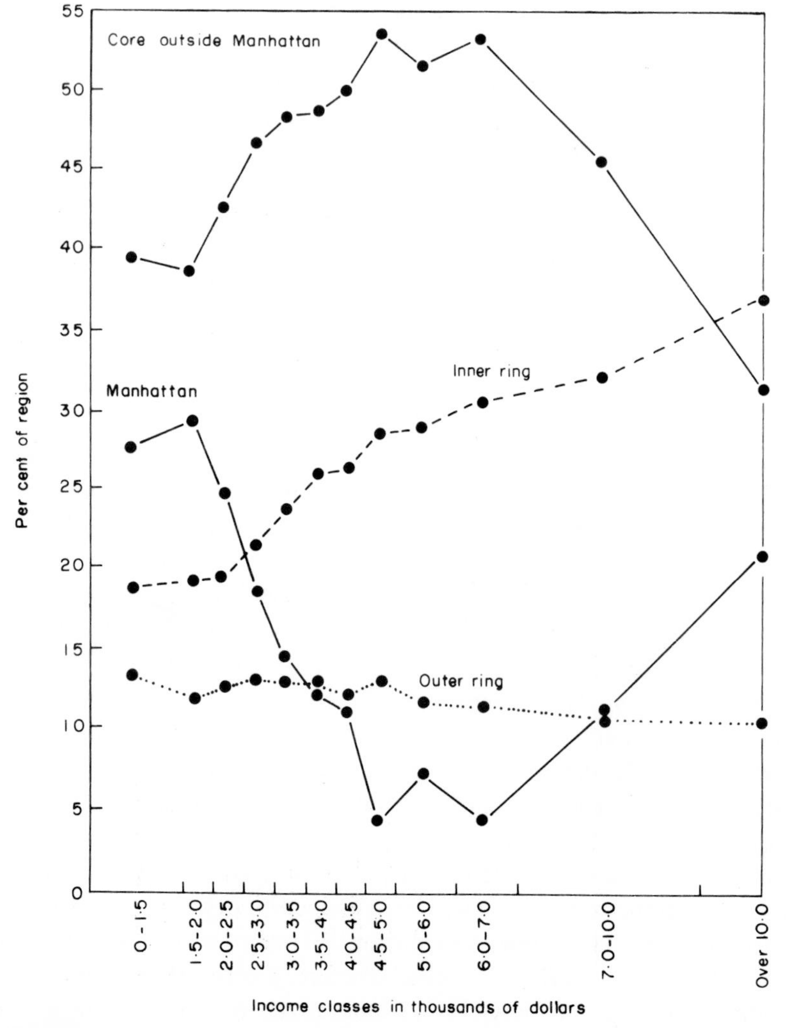

Figure 29. Geographical distribution of income recipients by income classes, New York metropolitan region, 1949.

TABLE 21

Geographical distribution of socio-economic groups in the British conurbations, 1961

	Group 3[a]			Groups 1 and 4[a]			Group 11[a]		
	Conurbation centre (%)	Rest of central city (%)	Rest of conurbation (%)	Conurbation centre (%)	Rest of central city (%)	Rest of conurbation (%)	Conurbation centre (%)	Rest of central city (%)	Rest of conurbation (%)
Greater London	2·1	0·7	0·9	9·4	5·7	10·2	11·1	11·2	6·4
West Midlands	1·9	0·5	0·5	7·9	5·0	7·2	13·1	8·1	7·2
South-east Lancashire	3·3	0·5	0·7	5·9	4·5	7·2	23·3	10·9	9·3
Merseyside	2·9	0·6	0·6	7·4	4·9	7·8	22·4	15·1	12·1
Tyneside	3·8	0·7	0·5	5·3	6·2	6·2	18·0	11·8	11·3
Clydeside	0·7	0·5	0·9	4·3	3·8	5·9	20·7	12·8	11·1

[a] See text for definitions of socio-economic groups.

Source: Evans (1973).

> As the size of the city increases, so the number of people in the high-income group who wish to live near the centre increases, and a viable neighbourhood becomes feasible. Moreover, as the size of the city increases, so the distance from the centre to the edge of the city increases, and so the cost of giving up proximity to the centre increases relative to the benefit of living in the high-income neighbourhood at the periphery. For both these reasons, the large city is likely to have a high-income neighbourhood at, or near, the centre, while in a small town all members of the high-income group will locate in the outer part of a sector of the city.

This and other accessibility explanations rest on the notion that the increasing size of metropolitan areas leads to increasing time/distance commuting costs, one response to which is recentralization. As such, they have quite a long and respectable pedigree.

Thus, Alonso (1964) observed that, "As metropolitan areas have grown bigger and roads more congested it may be that some have come to feel that the commuting trip is too long and have returned to central locations." Richards (1963) argued in a similar vein that, "One would anticipate that accessibility desires would vary over time in large, growing urban areas. As the population increases and the city grows outwards by accretion, the problem of accessibility becomes more important to urban inhabitants . . . certain individuals become willing to substitute amenities on the outer fringe to satisfy their desire for accessibility to the inner core." The Milner Holland report (1965) related this thesis specifically to London: "The sum of the waste of time and effort and money and discomfort attendant on this arrangement (commuting) is immeasurable, and it has had its own reaction. There are some who have bought old houses in the inner parts of London rather than face such a daily journey."

There is, no doubt, some truth in this thesis, but it is not without major defects, not the least of which is that it ignores other possible causes of residential centralization. This is perhaps not surprising in that the explanation is firmly embedded in a trade-off type of reasoning with its in-built assumption that a space-accessibility continuum exists where more of the one implies less of the other. This type of explanation shares most of the deficiencies of trade-off theories, even the more sophisticated variants such as Evans. Both variations and changes in income-elasticity for space are incorporated as exogenous, unexplained assumptions. Any element of a process-based explanation is lacking, because "causal" factors are specified only indirectly through location as with revealed preference theory.

The role of employment structure

A more likely explanation of the observed relationship between city size and the proportion of centrally located higher income groups is that of employment structure. Ley (1980) argues that the growing service categories of "quaternary" office employment tend to be concentrated in the largest metropolitan centres, predominantly in what Jefferson referred to as primate cities. Ley points out that Paris contains the headquarter offices of 90 per cent of France's major corporations and half of its national civil service jobs, and Paris has experienced major gentrification in the central city. London's primacy, says Ley, is equally marked, with 62 per cent of Britain's top 500 industrial corporations being located there, with its quaternary employment (administrators and professionals) being four times as great as the combined total for the remaining five British conurbations in 1971, and with its quaternary employment growth between 1966 and 1971 being 12 times greater than the total of only 3000 for the other five conurbations combined. According to Ley (1980), the quaternary sector bears out Jefferson's dictum that "the most skilled workers in every science and art" are to be found in primate cities, these groups being characterized by extreme geographical concentration at both the national and intra-urban scales.

This argument would seem to be borne out by most of the evidence on changes in the employment and socio-economic structure of London and, to a lesser extent, the other conurbations. The upward shift in the socio-economic structure of central and inner London during the period 1961-1971 has already been referred to and it would seem to be strongly related to differential changes in employment structure and migration. The employment losses in the conurbations which began in the early 1960s have been most intense in London (Fothergill and Gudgin, 1978; Danson *et al.*, 1980). They have been characterized by losses in manufacturing employment and skilled manual employment, though, as Cameron and Evans (1973) have showed, the centres of conurbations began to lose service employment as well as early as 1961-1966. These losses were concentrated in the distributive trades, transport and communication and miscellaneous services, whilst professional services, insurance, banking and public administration still showed increases. In London, manufacturing employment as a whole decreased by 342 000 between 1961 and 1971, whilst employment in the finance, banking and insurance sectors increased by 207 000 and in the professional and scientific sector by 101 000. Daniels (1979) has also shown that, whilst the number of office clerical workers declined in the conurbation centres during 1966-1971, the number of administrators, managers and professionals generally increased, particularly in London. The only question mark over these developments has been raised by Lomas (1979) who suggests that, in aggregate, even these growth categories went into decline in central and inner London over the period 1971-1976. It is unclear, however, from Lomas's figures whether or not these declines include or exclude clerical employment. Until the detailed results of the 1981 census are available it will be impossible to know for sure whether the tendency for professional, managerial and other high status jobs to increase in the conurbation centres has continued in recent years.

Whilst there is no necessary causal link between changes in employment structure and gentrification, the increases in purchasing power and education levels of many centrally located quaternary workers may well generate a higher direct demand for centrally located housing close to work and the cultural and entertainment facilities which such groups tend to patronize more than average (Abu Lughod, 1960). They are what Heiinemeyer (1966) referred to as "urban core enjoyers". Ley (1980) also points correctly to the importance of demographic factors, notably the growth of one- and two-person childless households which are now in a majority in many central cities (Hamnett, 1983).

The growth of these predominantly young, childless, professional, managerial and administrative groups who have positively sought central and inner city residential locations has served to put pressure on the existing high status West-End residential areas in London, the result being a displaced demand for large, cheap, accessible housing in other areas of inner London, notably in parts of Hammersmith, Camden and Islington and, latterly, further out.

TENURIAL CHANGE AND GENTRIFICATION

The existence of a substantial amount of cheap, accessible, privately rented housing in the inner city provided a springboard for gentrification to take place. Prior to the onset of gentrification there was little effective demand for middle class owner-occupied housing in the inner city outside the pre-existing high status residential areas. As Williams (1975) has shown, there was also little possibility of transferring privately-rented housing into owner-occupation until the mid-1960s. The subsequent shift in the occupational structure of the population and the lucrative transfer of privately rented working class housing into middle class owner-occupation can therefore be seen as an example of the integration of a variety of disparate spatially fragmented and imperfect housing sub-markets into one large middle class owner-occupied housing market. As Smith (1979) has put it, "A theory of gentrification will need to explain the detailed historical mechanisms of capital depreciation and the precise way in which this depreciation produces the possibility of a profitable reinvestment."

Although cheapness plays an important part in the earliest stages of gentrification, thereafter prices rise rapidly towards the levels prevailing in other gentrified areas (Chambers, 1974). The rapid change in price differential has a marked effect upon the type of gentrifier who can afford to buy in at different stages in the process. Evans (1973) summised such a process and Chambers would appear to validate it through her evidence that gentrifiers in education, research and the arts had moved in earlier than those in the employers and managerial categories.

The essential mechanics of the process have been brilliantly summarized from the individual's perspective by Frayn (1967) in his novel *Towards the End of Morning* where he writes:

> They decided to find a cheap Georgian or Regency house in some down at heel district near the centre. However depressed the district, if it was Georgian or Regency, and reasonably central, it would soon be colonized by the middle classes. In this way they would secure an attractive and potentially fashionable house in the heart of London, at a price they could afford; be given credit by their friends for going to live among the working classes; acquire very shortly congenial middle class neighbours of a similarly adventurous and intellectual outlook to themselves; and see their investment undergo a satisfactory and reassuring rise in value in the process.

Social and tenurial segregation

Glass (1963) summarized the impact of these changes as follows:

> One by one, many of the working class quarters of London have been invaded by the middle classes—upper and lower—shabby modest mews and cottages . . . have been taken over when their leases expired, and have become elegant, expensive residences. Larger Victorian houses, down-graded in an earlier or recent period—which were used as lodging houses or were otherwise in multiple occupation—have been upgraded once again . . . . Once this process of "gentrification" starts in a district it goes on rapidly until all or most of the original working class occupiers are displaced and the whole social character of the district is changed.

Ten years later, Glass (1973) went even further to suggest that

> London is now being renewed at a rapid pace—but not on the model about which we are so often warned. Inner London is not being "Americanized": it is not on the way to becoming mainly a working class city, a "polarized" city, or a vast ghetto for a black proletariat. The real risk for inner London is that it may well be gentrified with a vengeance, and be almost exclusively reserved for selected higher-class strata.

These predictions were supported by Hamnett (1976) who found on the basis of a ward-level analysis that inner London was *not* becoming socially polarized at that level in the sense that the high and low socio-economic groups were both increasing at the expense of the intermediate non-manual and skilled manual groups. The socio-economic structure of London appears rather to be undergoing an upward shift. This is not to say, however, that polarization and sharper social divisions are not occurring at the sub-ward level, as Jones and McEvoy (1978) have argued *vis-à-vis* racial segregation. Indeed, Tindall (1971) has suggested that whatever else is happening, increasing segregation is occurring at the micro level.

> The turn of the century seems likely to see the whole of inner London parcelled out either into council blocks . . . or into highly expensive and inevitably exclusive owner-occupied property. The gain in overall appearance and repair may be considerable, the loss in flexibility and the possibility of having space for those who are neither well off nor clever, will be immeasurable.

The importance of this tenurial polarization cannot be emphasized enough. The national decline of the private-rented sector from its 1914 peak of 90 per cent of households to its current level of 12 per cent is known well enough. What is less well known is that inner London, and central London in particular, has long been a bastion of private renting. In 1961, inner London (defined as the 12 ILEA boroughs) had 63 per cent of its households renting privately and the percentages for Camden, Kensington and Westminster were no less than 74, 82, 83 per cent respectively. The 1960s saw a considerable decline in private renting to 21 per cent nationally by 1971. In inner London, however, the overall figure was still 50 per cent of households, whilst the three central boroughs were 62, 76 and 70 per cent respectively. The 1970s have seen the intensification of the decline in private-rented

TABLE 22

Household tenure by borough in central London (per cent)

	1961			1971			1977		
	Local authority	Owner-occupied	Privately rented	Local authority	Owner-occupied	Privately rented	Local authority	Owner-occupied	Privately rented
Camden	15·5	10·8	73·7	24·0	14·2	61·8	32·9	21·7	45·4
Kensington	6·3	11·4	82·3	7·7	15·9	76·4	12·8	28·8	58·4
Westminster	10·5	6·3	83·2	20·0	10·0	70·0	28·7	16·2	55·1
Average	10·7	9·3	80·0	17·5	13·2	69·3	25·4	21·3	53·3

accommodation, with the National Housing and Dwelling Survey of 1977 recording percentages for the three boroughs of 45, 58 and 55 per cent respectively. As Table 22 shows, these declines have been mirrored by sharp increases in the local authority and owner-occupied tenures.

The 1981 census yields aggregate figures on the tenure split for the three central London boroughs of 28 per cent of households in local authority housing, 24 per cent in owner-occupied housing, and 47 per cent in privately rented accommodation. These changes have had and will have a far more dramatic effect on the central London housing market than any amount of commercial invasion of residential areas. It is not without significance that a *Guardian* item of 24 March 1981 reported that the Church Commissioners are going to sell off properties in their 160-acre Maida Vale to tenants. More than 2000 properties are involved with a collective market value approaching £100 million. So too, the *Estates Times* of the 12 June reported the first sales of luxury flats in the Barbican development in the City of London. Developed as a prestige publicly rented scheme only 10–15 years ago, the City of London clearly sees the financial advantages of sale at prices between £30 000 and £165 000.

The flat break-up market in central London

Over the last three years the author has been engaged in research on the "break-up" of previously privately rented blocks of purpose-built flats for individual owner-occupation. These blocks, mostly built within ten years of the turn of the century or in the mid- to late-1930s, constitute a surprisingly high proportion of the central London housing market. On the basis of rent office data some 1300 blocks have been identified containing some 43 000 flats and we estimate that in 1966 before the start of widespread break-up these predominantly unfurnished flats constituted 45 per cent of all privately rented unfurnished dwellings in Camden, 44 per cent in Kensington and an astonishingly high 65 per cent in Westminster. These figures have subsequently been precisely verified by an OPCS special tabulation which lists purpose-built multi-dwellings by tenure and by ward and borough for the 1966 census. As a percentage of the total private (i.e. non-local authority) dwellings, flats in such blocks constituted 26 per cent in Camden, 24 per cent in Kensington and 42 per cent in Westminster. Quite clearly any image of central London's private residential market being dominated by Georgian and Victorian private houses and bijou mews cottages must be substantially revised.

The average block size in the three boroughs is 33 flats per block, but the size distribution is highly skewed, with the great majority of flats being in a relatively small number of large blocks with up to 500 flats or more. In Camden, for instance, half the blocks had less than 20 flats but they contained only 12 per cent of all flats.

On the basis of a systematic analysis of rent office records for the three boroughs we estimate that no more than 12 600 of the 43 000 flats are still currently registered.

Knowing that large commercial landlords tend to register the rents in those blocks, we estimate that only about 30 per cent of all such flats are still conventionally rented, the remainder either having been sold, being held vacant pending sale or having been transferred into the ultra-high rent, company or holiday let sector of the market outside the Rent Act. By this latter trend we mean rents for good quality, centrally located flats of between £5000-£8000 per annum. These rents should be compared to the average registered rent in purpose-built privately rented flats in Camden and Westminster in 1980 of £1500 per annum.

If one seeks the reason behind the recent spate of sales there is little need to look further than at the inflation of central London housing prices in the 1970s. The average sale price of purpose-built flats in mid-1980 in the two boroughs was £52 000 and, including the data for Kensington, £90 000. This corresponds to the price for the average four room flat. Even on the lower figure of £52 000 the average rent yield on vacant possession capital value is under 3 per cent. On the higher figures it is 1·6 per cent. This should be compared to the 11 per cent tax free return from building society deposit accounts in 1980. Without going into detail about the financial and economic background to this (see Hamnett and Randolph, 1981a, b), there is a compelling financial motivation to the landlord to sell the property into owner-occupation either to sitting tenants at a discount or at full vacant possession value on the open market. Thus, when a flat falls empty either by the death or movement of the tenant—which may be induced by cash offers of up to £8000—flats are scarcely ever relet as this would be to lock up the landlord's potential capital gain for an indeterminate period owing to security of tenure. The privately rented tenants who remain in such blocks of flats constitute a relict tenantry in a relict tenure. Virtually no new tenants are entering the blocks, the new owner-occupiers being younger and more affluent professional, executive or managerial households. Many of the buyers are foreign. Savills the London Estate Agents estimate that upwards of 40 per cent of the flats they sell go to overseas buyers, mostly Arabs and Americans. Another large London estate agent has calculated that in 1980, 25 per cent of flats up to £50 000, 50 per cent of flats priced between £50 000 and £150 000 and 75 per cent of flats selling for more than £150 000 go to overseas buyers. The tenant body by contrast is ageing and relatively poor, the great majority of tenants having moved into the blocks over ten years ago.

Although these changes are dramatically changing the demographic and, to a lesser extent, the ethnic character of the blocks, they are not totally changing their socio-economic composition. The residents of the blocks have always been predominantly middle class to upper class in occupational and income terms with a generous sprinkling of the titled and the famous. What is happening rather is that these characteristics are being intensified as a new generation of open market buyers earning £15 000-£30 000 per annum or more move into the blocks. Where the sitting tenants purchase there is, of course, no social change, merely a tenurial one.

We have been able to make a relatively precise analysis of the social composition and characteristics of the residents by virtue of the very size of the blocks, some 85 of which were large enough to constitute complete enumeration districts (EDs) in

1971. Overall, the 85 block EDs represented 102 separate blocks of flats and constituted, by virtue of their larger than average size, 27 per cent of all identified flat units in the three boroughs.

Aggregate analysis of the census data for these 85 EDs has revealed that the residents of these blocks are even more atypical than the central boroughs as a whole. Thus, looking at the socio-economic profiles of the blocks compared to the boroughs, some 40 per cent of the households in blocks in Westminster were headed by professionals and managers compared to 25 per cent in Westminster as a whole. In Kensington the contrast is even more marked; 45 per cent of households being professional and managerial compared to a borough-wide figure of 27 per cent. Intermediate non-manual workers were also over-represented in the blocks compared to the borough figures, whereas all the manual categories were substantially under-represented, only 16 per cent of all block households being manual compared to borough-wide figures of between 27 per cent in Kensington and 37 per cent in Camden.

Where the household size and demographic structure of the blocks are concerned, the 85 EDs had a lower (10·5 per cent) proportion of households with children under 14 than did the boroughs as a whole (17·1 per cent). Similarly, the proportion of pensioner households was significantly higher than the borough figures, with those EDs possessing 18·7 per cent one-person pensioner householders compared to a figure for all central boroughs of 14·5 per cent. It cannot be stressed too strongly that not only are the characteristics of the residents of the blocks atypical in relation to the boroughs as a whole, but that, as Daly (1971) has shown, the characteristics of the population of most of the three central boroughs is atypical in relation to Greater London as a whole. By surveying some 25 of these blocks in early 1981, it has proved possible to make some assessment of the changes which have taken place. Most significantly, the percentage of households in such blocks renting privately has declined from 90 per cent in 1971 to just under 50 per cent (excluding vacant flats) and we have reason to believe that bias in the pattern of non-responses, principally from foreign owners, is such as to understate the extent of current ownership. The preliminary results of the survey have also, as expected, shown a marked upwards shift in the socio-economic composition of the blocks, virtually all of the residents now being non-manual, and the great majority in the professional and managerial groups.

CONSEQUENCES AND FUTURE CHANGES

The housing market of central London is undergoing a rapid transformation. From its total dominance by privately rented accommodation only 20 years ago, it is conceivable that within ten years the largest tenure type will be owner-occupation. The inner city is likewise becoming polarized between owner-occupied and local authority housing. The consequences of such a shift are only too apparent. With the exception of ultra-high rent, company and holiday lets, privately rented accommodation is, to all intents and purposes, effectively unobtainable in central London, as far as purpose-built blocks of flats are concerned. As a result, demand is inevitably displaced into other sectors of the declining privately rented market. Competition for scarce rented accommodation is intense in the remainder of London and the difficulties facing young migrant households coming into London to take up employment would seem to be intensifying. Whilst the number of resident owner-occupiers letting furnished rooms to students and others may be increasing, this in no way compensates for the loss of the traditional home for young mobile households.

Despite the recent building for sale of owner-occupied flats in central Manchester and the purchase of the "Piggeries" in Liverpool for conversion to owner-occupation, it seems unlikely that the trends which are so marked in London will become prevalent elsewhere, not least because other conurbation centres have not shown such marked increases in professional and managerial employment and the associated socio-economic shifts. The residential function of the other conurbation centres is also a much smaller one as the residential component has been more effectively squeezed out over time by commercial and industrial development as indeed it has in the City of London.

REFERENCES

Abu-Lughod, J. (1960). *In* "Housing Choice and Housing Constraint" (N. N. Foote *et al.*, eds). McGraw Hill, New York.

Alonso, W. (1964). *Land. Econ.* **40**, 231.

Banfield, E. C. (1974). "The Unheavenly City Revisited". Little Brown and Co., Boston.

Berry, B. J. L. (1980). *Trans. Inst. Br. Geogr. N.S.* **5**, 1-28.

Cameron, G. C. and Evans, A. W. (1973). *Reg. Stud.* **7**, 47-55.

Chambers, P. A. (1974). "The Process of Gentrification in Inner London". Unpublished M.Phil. thesis, School of Environmental Studies, University of London.

Daly, M. (1971). "Characteristics of 12 Clusters of Wards in Greater London". Greater London Council, Department of Planning and Transportation, Research Report 13.

Daniels, P. W. (1977). *Urban Stud.* **14**, 261-274.

Danson, M. W., Lever, W. F. and Malcolm, J. F. (1980). *Urban Stud.* **17**, 193-210.

de Jouvenal, B. (1967). "The Art of Conjecture". Weidenfeld and Nicolson, London.

Engels, F. (1872). "The Housing Question" (translation, 1935). Martin Lawrence, London.

Evans, A. W. (1973). "The Economics of Residential Location". Macmillan, London.

Fothergill, S. and Gudgin, G. (1978). "Regional Employment Change: A Sub-Regional Explanation". Centre for Environmental Studies, London.

Frayn, M. (1967). "Towards the End of Morning". Collins, London.

Glass, R. (1964). "London: Aspects of Change". Centre for Urban Studies, University of London.

Glass, R. (1973). *In* "London: Urban Patterns, Problems and Policies" (D. Donnison and D. Eversley, eds). Heineman, London.

Gray, R. (1978). "A History of London". Hutchinson, London.

Hall, P. (1966). "The World Cities". Weidenfeld and Nicholson, London.
Hamnett, C. (1973). "Cosmopolitan and Centralists". The Open University Press, Milton Keynes. DT 201, Unit 8.
Hamnett, C. (1974). "Problems of Forecasting Urban Environments". Paper delivered to Inst. Br. Geogr. Urban Stud. Grp. meeting on "The Future of Cities".
Hamnett, C. (1976). *Urban Stud.* **13**, 261-271.
Hamnett, C. (1983). *In* "Geography and the Urban Environment Vol. 6" (D. T. Herbert and R. J. Johnston, eds). Wiley, London.
Hamnett, C. and Randolph, W. (1981a). *Roof.* May/June, 18-24.
Hamnett, C. and Randolph, W. (1981b). *Estates Gazette*, Oct 3rd, 31-35.
Hamnett, C. and Randolph, W. (1982). *The London Journal* **8**, 1, 95-100.
Hamnett, C. and Williams, P. (1979). "Gentrification in London 1961-1971. An Empirical and Theoretical Analysis of Social Change". Centre for Urban and Regional Development Studies, Birmingham. Research Memorandum 71.
Hamnett, C. and Williams, P. (1980). *The London Journal* **6**, 1, 51-66.
Heinemeijer, W. F. (1967). *In* "Urban Core and Inner City" (W. F. Heinemeijer *et al.*, eds). Brill, Leiden.
Hoover, E. M. and Vernon, R. (1959). "The Anatomy of a Metropolis". Harvard University Press, Cambridge, Mass.
Jones, T. P. and McEvoy, D. (1978). *Area* **10**, 162-166.
Ley, D. (1980). "Inner City Revitalization: Contexts, Effects and a Canadian Case Study". Unpublished working paper. Department of Geography, University of British Columbia.
Lomas, G. (1979). *In* "Employment Planning in London Boroughs". London Voluntary Services.
Morrey, C. (1973). "The Changing Population of the London Boroughs". Greater London Council, Department of Planning and Transportation Research Memorandum 413.
Olsson, D. (1976). "The Growth of Victorian London". Batsford, London.
Prince, H. C. (1964). *In* "Greater London" (J. T. Coppock and H. C. Prince, eds). Faber and Faber, London.
Rapkin, C. W. and Grigsby, W. G. (1960). "Residential Renewal in the Urban Core". University of Pennsylvania Press, Philadelphia.
Richards, J. M. (1963). *In* "Human Resources in the Urban Economy" (M. Perlman, ed.). Resources for the Future Inc., Washington D.C.
Schnore, L. (1965). *In* "The Study of Urbanization" (P. M. Hauser and L. F. Schnore, eds). Wiley, New York.
Senior, M. L. (1974). *Envir. Plann.* **6**, 369-409.
Simmons, J. W. (1968). *Geogr. Rev.* **58**, 622-651.
Simpson, M. A. and Lloyd, T. H. (1979). "Middle Class Housing in Britain". David and Charles, Newton Abbot.
Smith, N. (1979). *Amer. Plann. J. Inst.* **45**, 4, 538-548.
Steadman-Jones, G. (1971). "Outcast London". Oxford University Press, Oxford.
Tindall, G. (1971). *New Society* 14 Jan, 17.
Wates, N. (1976). "The Battle for Tolmers Square". Routledge and Kegan Paul, London.
Williams, P. (1976). *Trans. Inst. Br. Geogr. N.S.* **1**, 72-82.
Williams, T., Anderson, J. and Goddard, J. B. (1972). "Living in Central London: A Survey of Housing, Population and Employment". City of Westminster Development Plan Research Report R1.
Zeitz, E. (1979). "Private Urbal Renewal". Lexington Books, Lexington.

NINE

Future traffic problems

A. D. MAY

It would be all too easy, in forecasting the extent of future city-centre traffic problems, to look only at the problem of congestion and to take the view that conditions are unlikely to change significantly. Certainly congestion is the most obvious of city-centre traffic problems, and is one which has been with us for far longer than the motor car. It is interesting, for example, to compare the evaluation of the Victoria line which identified congestion relief as the main benefit (Foster and Beesley, 1963) with the case being made for the first underground railway, over a hundred years earlier, which suggested that congestion would become intolerable within a few years if traffic were not diverted underground. Since then it has frequently been suggested that traffic is likely to "grind to a halt" if action is not taken quickly. Often the suggested remedy is restriction of traffic; as Crowther put it in 1963 in presenting Buchanan's *Traffic in Towns* (Crowther, 1963): "Distasteful though we find the whole idea, we think that some deliberate limitation of the volume of motor traffic in our cities is quite unavoidable". Yet, although little has been done either to restrict traffic or to increase road capacity, traffic has not ground to a halt, and shows no signs of doing so. It could be argued, therefore, that congestion is self regulating and, while undesirable, is a side effect of city-centre activity which has to be tolerated either because it cannot be avoided or because the only possible solutions are themselves less palatable.

This itself is an important issue, because much of the effort in transport planning and management is devoted to relieving congestion. But it would be wrong to think of congestion as the only city-centre traffic problem to be tackled. One of the important developments in the past decade has been the emergence of concern over a far wider range of traffic-related problems. The adverse effects of traffic and new facilities on the environment, the differing conditions experienced by pedestrians, cyclists, bus users and motorists, the growing shortage of energy and the potential impact of poor accessibility on commercial and industrial decline are all issues which the transport planner of the 1960s would scarcely have considered, but which are seen today as fundamental concerns of urban transport policy.

In looking therefore at the issue of future city-centre traffic problems, it is important, first of all, to outline the objectives which might be set for city-centre

THE FUTURE FOR THE CITY CENTRE
ISBN 0 12 206240 X

transport plans, and hence to identify the problems which need to be overcome to enable these objectives to be met. Having done this, this chapter reviews, for each problem in turn, evidence on the seriousness of the problem, past trends and the factors likely to influence future trends. In doing so, it demonstrates the general lack of objective data that are available on many of the problems.

This general conclusion has important implications for the selection of appropriate solutions to current and future problems. It is quite possible that the need to find solutions is either being overstated by particular pressure groups, or understated for lack of evidence of the scale of city-centre traffic problems. It is inevitable that individual solutions will themselves create new problems, whether they are the cost and environmental intrusion of new roads, the restrictions on the individual inherent in traffic restraint techniques or the financial implications of public transport support. The final section of this chapter reviews experience with, and the merits and demerits of, alternative solutions and suggests some appropriate strategies for tackling city-centre traffic problems. Some of the available solutions are strictly outside the terms of reference of this chapter, and are covered more fully in the next chapter.

TRANSPORT POLICY OBJECTIVES

Until the late 1960s the objectives of transport policy could be defined broadly as provision for the efficient and safe movement of vehicles subject to the financial constraints of the transport planning authority's budget. Even these limited objectives raised some conflicts; techniques which reduced the time or cost of vehicle travel were not necessarily conducive to road safety, and finance was rarely available (in the UK at least) for those major highway schemes which were then often seen as the best way of meeting the objectives of efficiency and safety. However, the debates on transport policy of the early 1970s highlighted much more serious shortcomings of these limited objectives. First, their emphasis was on vehicle movement; as it became accepted that vehicle movement was only desirable as a means of providing for the users of vehicles, the emphasis switched to efficient movement of people and freight, and to those vehicles, such as buses, which were more capable of achieving this objective. Secondly, they were only concerned with vehicle users and not with those, such as residents and pedestrians, whose environment was affected by traffic or by the provision of new roads. Thirdly, the desire for faster vehicle movement did not seem necessarily to accord with the increasingly apparent need for energy conservation. Finally, while transport plans were clearly based on an understanding of the effects of land-use planning on transport demand, they did not seem to consider the complementary impact of transport plans on land use and in particular their possible encouragement of decentralization and of decline in city centres' commercial and industrial activity.

These wider considerations have helped identify a longer list of urban transport policy objectives, which can be outlined briefly as follows:

(a) *Efficiency:* ensuring that person and freight journeys can be made as quickly and cheaply as possible, in terms both of the costs to the user and of the provision, operation and maintenance of transport facilities.
(b) *Resource conservation:* conserving those resources, and in particular energy, which are used in the provision, operation, maintenance and use of the transport system, and which are in particularly short supply.
(c) *Finance conservation:* limiting the demands of transport policy on the budgets of the authorities responsible.
(d) *Environmental protection:* minimizing the impact of transport facilities and their use on both users, including pedestrians, and non-users such as residents and city-centre employees.
(e) *Safety:* reducing the loss of life, injury and damage to property resulting from use of transport facilities.
(f) *Accessibility:* improving the accessibility to facilities required by individuals and by business and industry and hence reinforcing the land-use plans of the city centre.
(g) *Equity:* endeavouring not to worsen any of the above factors for any group of people and, ideally, ensuring that benefits are either equally distributed or made available particularly to those with special needs.

Several points are worth noting on this longer list of objectives. First, they will not be considered equally important by different local authorities or, for that matter, by local and central government. One authority may well see transport as a social service and place particular emphasis on the equity objective, while another may consider that the use of transport policy to revitalize industry has the highest priority. Equally, while local government may pay little attention to energy conservation (from which they are unlikely to draw great benefit), it would be surprising if national government did not afford that particular objective higher priority. Thus even if conditions are apparently similar in separate city centres, the perceived seriousness of traffic problems may differ.

Secondly, attitudes to different objectives are not necessarily stable with time. It may well be, for instance, that concern for protection of the environment is receiving less emphasis as attention becomes more concentrated on the problems of commercial and industrial decline. As a result it is important to differentiate between trends in objective measures of particular problems, such as congestion and environmental intrusion, and trends in attitudes to those problems.

Thirdly, it is important to note that many of these objectives are in conflict; it is difficult, for example, to reduce environmental intrusion without at the same time reducing accessibility. Thus any solution inevitably involves a compromise between the problems which it solves and those new ones which it produces. The resolution of these conflicts is the key to successful urban transport planning.

TYPES OF CITY-CENTRE TRAFFIC PROBLEM

Each of these broad objectives serves to identify a number of specific problems on which it will be useful to have some information. Under the heading of efficiency a key problem is the time lost through congestion, but this is by no means the only problem to be considered. Time is also lost through unreliable travel conditions, which either require an unduly early start or result in late arrival. Similarly, a shortage of parking space can lead to time spent searching for one. More fundamentally, inefficiency arises through the peaking in demand for transport facilities, which both results in additional travel time and cost and requires additional capacity.

These problems in turn highlight a waste of resources, whether in terms of provision of road space, vehicles and manpower which are underused for much of the day or in fuel wasted in stopping and starting, travelling at sub-optimal speeds or using less energy efficient modes. Shortage of such resources represents a further set of problems; apart from the occasional shortages of petrol, which have not so far been serious in the UK, but have encouraged a new interest in contingency planning in the USA (Salvucci, 1980), the main shortages are of manpower. Even at a time of high unemployment, certain authorities find it difficult to recruit for relatively unattractive jobs in the public transport industry or as traffic wardens; this can lead to continuing problems of unreliability on certain services and to the under-enforcement of traffic management measures.

Financial problems are most apparent in the constraints which they impose on new investment and in the operating losses made by public transport undertakings. Other, apparently less serious problems arise, however, in the operation of on-street parking, whose revenue was expected to contribute to other transport expenditure, but often fails even to meet the costs of administration and enforcement.

Under the environmental heading, the main problems caused by traffic are noise, atmospheric pollution, visual intrusion, vibration, delay and danger for pedestrians and the resulting severing effect on communities and city-centre activities. In addition to introducing these problems into new areas, new transport facilities also require scarce urban land and impose blight on existing land uses.

Road accidents themselves are of course one of the most serious of traffic problems. It is worth noting that, in city centres particularly, it is not simply the cost of damage caused and the suffering to those involved which are of concern to the community, but also the requirements placed on the emergency services and the resulting disruption to traffic circulation. It is worth considering the issue of danger, included above, separately from accidents, because a heightened sense of danger may help reduce accidents while at the same time restricting use of the location concerned.

Many of the sources of inefficiency outlined earlier in this section also result in reduced accessibility, with the key issue here being the distribution of such effects. It may well be that a traffic management scheme, for instance, results in increased efficiency by easing movement through a city centre, while making accessibility locally more difficult by restricting frontage access or by imposing indirect routes on local servicing traffic. Similarly, increased fares or parking charges may be seen as reducing accessibility in the broadest sense.

More generally, many of the problems outlined above will affect some individuals or activities more severely than others. Their differing effects on different groups of user (and non-user) need to be carefully considered. Several groups of user have particular needs and are thus particularly sensitive to traffic problems; perhaps the most obvious groups being the disabled, and delivery and servicing traffic.

THE SERIOUSNESS OF CITY-CENTRE TRAFFIC PROBLEMS

The first point to note in reviewing the seriousness of, and trends in, traffic problems in city centres is the general lack of objective evidence. Problems are identified and solutions determined much more frequently on the basis of individual complaints or the actions of pressure groups than from careful monitoring and measurement of traffic conditions. As a result little is to be gained from an itemized review of past and future trends in each of the identified problem areas. Instead, the following paragraphs cover examples from each of the main policy objectives.

Efficiency

The lack of objective data is particularly evident in the assessment of trends in congestion, and is particularly surprising, because travel time savings traditionally form the major element in the justification of transport investment. Congestion itself is hard to define, and attempts to estimate the costs to the community of extra time and operating costs resulting from congestion pose difficulties in determining the base against which congested conditions are compared. Estimates made in 1965 suggested that congestion costs in the UK then amounted to £300–£600 million per annum, but it has since been argued (Department of the Environment, 1976a) that these estimates were unduly high, because they made unrealistic assumptions about the minimum travel times which could be achieved in complex urban networks. On the other hand, however, such estimates tend to consider only the direct costs of time lost and extra fuel and wear and tear; they ignore the extra costs involved in allowing for unreliable conditions, the costs imposed in an attempt to avoid congestion and the frustration caused particularly to those who have no alternative but to travel in congested conditions.

Little evidence is available on trends in congestion, and what there is only looks fairly crudely at trends in average speeds on urban road networks. Table 23 presents the most recent information on speeds in urban areas; it represents the results of a few travel time runs made on selected roads in London, five provincial conurbations and eight towns at roughly three-yearly intervals. These laborious and somewhat superficial surveys are apparently about to be abandoned, other than in London, and little effort has been put into replacing them by a less labour intensive means of obtaining more frequent trend data.

The direction of future trends is by no means clear from this data, and is not helped by an analysis of traffic flow trends. Table 24 presents comparable data for average flows on city-centre roads. Because flows in the larger centres have changed little, it could be argued that congestion, and perhaps lack of parking space, is acting as a constraint on demand. This may imply that even if employment levels in the city centre fall as a result of economic decline, land-use redistribution or technological change, traffic levels will not fall significantly. However, congestion does not appear to be a very stable regulator of traffic flow. In the conurbations, speeds have been rising while flows have remained virtually unchanged, while in the towns both speeds and flows have risen. This suggests that the traffic network, or drivers' use of it, has been becoming more efficient. There are several possible reasons for this, which are outlined below. However, it also suggests that, in the conurbations at least, the improvement has not been sufficient to attract a growth in traffic, and it would be interesting to review the reasons for this. Conversely, in central London, after an initially similar pattern, speeds have been falling while traffic flows have risen. In part this will be the result of external pressures, such as trends in public transport fares and service levels, but it does appear that the decline in performance

TABLE 23

Speeds (km h^{-1}) in central areas of UK towns and cities

	Greater London		Provincial conurbations		Provincial towns	
Year	Peak	Off-peak	Peak	Off-peak	Peak	Off-peak
1967/8	20·3	19·4	14·9	17·6	18·2	19·7
1971	20·6	20·2	17·7	20·2	19·7	23·4
1974	22·7	20·6	N.A.	N.A.	N.A.	N.A.
1976/7	19·7	20·2	20·5	21·4	20·8	24·9
1980	19·4	18·6	N.A.	N.A.	N.A.	N.A.

Sources: Greater London Council (1981); Department of Transport (1978).

TABLE 24

Flows (vehicles h^{-1}) in central areas of UK towns and cities

	Greater London		Provincial conurbations		Provincial towns	
Year	Peak	Off-peak	Peak	Off-peak	Peak	Off-peak
1967/8	1930	1490	1413	1192	1194	988
1971	1919	1514	1489	1207	1383	1074
1974	2046	1594	N.A.	N.A.	N.A.	N.A.
1976/7	N.A.	1610	1485	1151	1572	1173

Sources: London, unpublished sources; others, Department of Transport (1978).

is not solely due to increased traffic, but also to a significant deterioration in compliance with parking controls. It is difficult to draw any firm conclusions from this evidence, but it does appear that any changes in traffic flows will be much more gradual in the city centre than elsewhere, unless steps are taken specifically to reduce them, and that congestion levels are likely to remain fairly similar unless a breakdown occurs in the increasingly complex management of our road systems.

This analysis has, of course, only looked at one aspect of efficiency; other time losses in the transport system may well be as important, but here again evidence is slight. Only a few public transport undertakings attempt to monitor passenger waiting times, there are scarcely any regular surveys of journey time reliability by either public or private transport (although London Transport has recently begun to remedy this omission), and there are no surveys of the time taken to find a parking space. Yet such surveys as there have been indicate that waiting time can add perhaps 50 per cent to the average time spent on the bus, unreliability a similar amount, and that finding a parking space in congested areas can add a third to average car journey times.

Resource conservation

Little information is available on energy consumption in city centres, but estimates suggest that 54 per cent of fuel consumption by cars is on urban roads (Leach, 1979). Taking slightly lower figures for goods vehicles produces an overall estimate of perhaps 50 per cent of all fuel consumption in transport, and 12·5 per cent of all UK oil consumption taking place on urban roads. While much of this consumption occurs outside city centres, it is probably in the city centres that most can be done to reduce fuel consumption by improving the operation of the road system and encouraging the use of more efficient modes. As examples, recent estimates for Liverpool suggest that optimizing city-centre traffic signal settings can reduce fuel consumption by 5 per cent (Ferreira, 1981), while earlier very approximate calculations for London suggest that a 10 per cent switch of car travel to bus could reduce fuel consumption there by 8 per cent (Goodwin, 1974). Other than the cost to users, already considered under the efficiency heading above, the main cost of excessive fuel consumption is to the nation's economy. While city-centre fuel consumption seems unlikely to grow significantly in the near future, consumption of energy in transport generally is, along with pressure for conservation (Advisory Council on Energy Conservation, 1979).

While problems of staff shortages in public transport are not strictly traffic problems, those in enforcement are. Here London's problems are far more severe than elsewhere. While current estimates (Metropolitan Police, 1981) suggest that a complement of at least 4000 traffic wardens is needed to provide effective enforcement of traffic management, and particularly parking regulations, the number employed has fallen from a peak of 2000 to 1000 in 1980 and 1200 in 1981. The effects of this can be seen in Table 25, which demonstrates the growth of violation rates for on-street parking controls in central London. While precise

TABLE 25

Trends in violation rates for on-street parking controls in London

	Percentage of parkers offending		
Year	1966/7	1970	1978
Meter feeding	2	11	16
Paid for period exceeded	8	12	16
All meter offences	10	23	32
Non-meter offences	39	42	N.A.
All offences	25	36	N.A.

Sources: 1966/7 and 1970, Yates (1970); 1978, Carr (1979).

figures for non-meter offences in 1978 are not available, it is estimated that in that year about one in three meter users and two in three yellow line users did so illegally, and that only about one in 15 violators received a fixed penalty notice. While the cost of such violation rates are not wholly clear, it seems probable that they are the main cause of the decline in speeds in central London (Table 23). Future trends in compliance critically depend on future manpower levels, which are restricted primarily by working conditions and wages (and to a lesser extent by Home Office staffing ceilings) and on future decisions on alternative, more draconian enforcement techniques. The recent Green Paper (HMSO, 1981) only offers a very small step in the direction required for improvement.

Environment

Evidence suggests that environmental intrusion from traffic is rarely at a level which imposes direct costs in terms of reduced working efficiency or health hazards (Burt, 1972). There are inevitably some exceptions: traffic noise may adversely affect the performance of schools and hospitals; there is considerable concern over the effects of lead pollution; particularly in city centres, delay and danger to pedestrians may well mean that shops on the "wrong" side of the road lose business. But the main effect of environmental intrusion is clearly the sense of annoyance which it engenders. Table 26, which presents results from the 1972 National Environment Survey for England and Wales as a whole, demonstrates just how widespread annoyance with different factors is. It can be seen that among pedestrians, over two-thirds were bothered by the sense of danger (and delay) while crossing the street (a quarter seriously so) and a half by noise and pollution. Because these figures include rural as well as urban areas, it seems likely that the figures for city centres are much higher. While no information is available for employees, the fact that half the residents were bothered by noise at home suggests that levels of annoyance with noise among city-centre employees may well be at least as high.

The difficulty with interpretation of these data is that while the survey also gives some indication of the traffic levels which produced these responses, it gives us no

TABLE 26

Reaction to environmental problems

	% Bothered	% Seriously bothered
Pedestrian changes	69	27
Noise in streets	54	16
Noise at home	49	9
Fumes in street	47	23
Dust and dirt	36	15
Vibration	27	8
Parking	21	12
Fumes at home	7	3

Source: National Environmental Survey 1972 (Morton-Williams *et al.*, 1978).
Sample: 5686 adults from a stratified sample of households in England.

guidance on how much action it would have been worth taking to allay the respondents' concern. Further, because no repeat survey has been conducted and there are no regular surveys of noise, pollution or pedestrian delay levels, we have no guide as to whether conditions, or percentages bothered by those conditions, have changed since 1972, or whether the same traffic conditions would generate more or less concern now. As Armitage (1980) notes, "This is not good enough."

Future trends in environmental intrusion, in the absence of positive action to achieve reductions, are closely linked to trends in traffic flows and on the above analysis these seem unlikely to change significantly. Certainly, given the relationship between traffic flow and level of intrusion it is unlikely that there will be any perceptible change in either noise or pollution levels as a result of changes in flow. Changes in vehicles themselves may, however, have more effect. In the short term the reduction of the lead content of petrol, while not affecting the perception of pollution, will reduce one of the main health hazards. In the longer term perceptible reductions in noise level should result from the current attempts to improve individual vehicle noise standards. However, it will be some time before the proportion of "quiet" vehicles in the vehicle fleet is sufficient to achieve this (Nelson and Fanstone, 1974).

Safety

Road accidents are the one area in which detailed statistics are regularly recorded, and for which comprehensive estimates are made of costs. Even so, the main national source of statistics (Department of Transport, 1980) does not provide separate information for city centres. In 1978, 76 per cent of all injury accidents occurred in built-up areas, although because accident severity tends to be lower in urban areas, these included only 57 per cent of fatal accidents. Estimates suggest that the cost of urban road accidents, including direct cost and an allowance for pain and suffering, amounted to £715 million in 1978. City-centre accidents may well, allowing for higher traffic flows and accident rates, account for around 10 per cent of these accidents and accident costs.

Since the decline from a peak in 1965, there has been a variation of no more than ±5 per cent in the number of built-up area accidents from year to year, and there is little sign that numbers will vary significantly in the future. The main changes have been in pedestrian casualties, which have fallen by 16 per cent since 1972, and in motor cycle accidents, which have increased by 60 per cent in the same period. However, because the former are mainly reductions in child pedestrian accidents and the latter are likely to be distributed throughout urban areas, it seems unlikely that city-centre accident trends are significantly different from those for urban areas as a whole.

Accessibility

Because even trends in average measures of travel time and cost are hard to find, data on changes in accessibility to particular types of activity or for particular types of journey are even less readily available, although some detailed studies have demonstrated, for example, the effects of fares on the relative accessibility of bus and car users to different types of facility (Headicar *et al.*, 1979). Even if significant changes in accessibility to city-centre activities, as measured by the time and money costs of reaching them by different modes, do occur, the effects on land use and economic activity are by no means certain. It is frequently claimed that these effects are strong: that shopkeepers suffer a severe loss of trade if vehicular access or parking is restricted, that congestion encourages firms to leave the city centre and inner city, and that high fares, particularly in central London, are encouraging employees to leave for jobs elsewhere.

Evidence in support of these claims is, however, noticeably lacking. In part this is a result of the complexity of the relationships to be studied; changes in accessibility are themselves difficult to measure, particularly because what is ideally required is a measure of the change in the relative accessibility of different locations. Resulting changes in travel to a centre will take some time to occur, particularly if they involve changing regular shopping or trading activities and even more so if they involve a change of job; when they do occur it is difficult to be sure that accessibility changes rather than other social or economic influences are the cause. Not all such changes in travel patterns necessarily affect the trading performance of city-centre activities; it is perfectly possible, for instance, for shopping to be concentrated into fewer journeys. Finally, even if trading performance is affected (and such information is rarely divulged), this may not necessarily cause firms to close or move.

What little evidence there is suggests that the effects of accessibility on land use are usually much smaller than is claimed. For instance, it is a commonly held view that congestion problems are a major stimulus to firms to leave city-centre locations. Yet, while interviews with management confirm that transport problems are a

TABLE 27
Inner city firms with transport problems

Location	*Lambeth*	*Bradford*	*Leeds*
No. of firms	39	259	98
Problem		% mentioning problem	
Parking	51	13	50
Loading	20	N.A.	18
Road access	44	17	65
Congestion	N.A.	N.A.	8
Street conditions	N.A.	25	3
Public transport	46	9	27

Source: Patterson and May (1979).

TABLE 28
Firms' reasons for relocation

	Lambeth 11 Firms[a]	*London* 88 Firms[a]	*Hull* 23 Firms[b]
Space	36	57	41
Labour	64	22	N.A.
Buildings	27	30	21
Planning	27	16	16
Transport	*36*	*14*	*5*
Costs	18	15	5

[a] Per cent of firms giving reason indicated.
[b] Per cent of points allocated to reason indicated.
Source: Patterson and May (1979).

source of considerable aggravation for industry (Table 27), they also indicate that they are rarely cited as a reason for leaving an area (Table 28) (Patterson and May, 1979).

Equally, it is common for traders to claim that traffic management measures have resulted in serious reductions in shopping activity and turnover. Because traders are reluctant to supply information on turnover, such claims have rarely been tested, but despite this they have frequently led to the abandonment of the measures concerned. One recent study in York suggests, however, that even sizeable reductions in accessibility may well only produce small and short-lived reductions of trade, and it certainly demonstrates that traders' claims may well be exaggerated. A six-month bridge closure there reduced cross-river capacity by around 25 per cent and generated immediate claims that trade had fallen by up to a quarter as a result. However, as Table 29 indicates, while there did appear to be a significant reduction in trade during the closure period, it amounted only to about 4 per cent, even in the

TABLE 29
Changes in retail sales during a six-month bridge closure in York

	% deviation of achieved from expected sales	
Department stores	+1·1	
All other city-centre shops	-2·4	±2·9[a]
Shops by type:		
Food	-6·0	±5·6[a]
Clothing	+1·4	±5·1[a]
Furniture	+3·2	±5·4[a]
Speciality hard goods	-5·6	±5·4[a]
Shops by location in centre		
Inner core	-4·2	±3·9[a]
Outer ring	+0·3	±4·4[a]
By month after closure		
Month 1	-3·8	±4·2[b]
Month 2	-3·8	±3·5[b]
Month 3	-3·8	±3·3[b]
Month 4	+5·4	±3·8[b]
Month 5	+3·3	±4·6[b]
Month 6	-1·2	±4·4[b]

[a] 95 per cent confidence limits.
[b] 90 per cent confidence limits.
Source: May and Weaver (1981).

core of the centre, and was concentrated in the first three-month period, after which trade apparently returned to normal (May and Weaver, 1981).

It is to be hoped that future studies will cast more light on this emotive subject. One current study promises, for example, to determine the extent to which rail fare increases in London and the South-East have affected job and home locations (Mackett, 1981). For the time being there must remain a serious doubt as to whether even sizeable changes in accessibility are likely to affect city-centre land use and economic activity significantly. It seems much more likely that other factors will motivate the growth or decline of the city centre, and that transport policies will need to respond to the resulting changes in demand for travel.

However, even if changes in accessibility or environmental conditions do not significantly affect land use, they may well adversely affect individuals. Detailed accessibility analysis has been used, for instance, to demonstrate the significant decline in accessibility for bus users which recent trends in public transport policy have produced (Headicar, 1980). If the city centre is to remain a location accessible to all, and with facilities which are attractive to all, then trends in both accessibility and environmental conditions for different groups of user need to be carefully monitored.

Several conclusions can be drawn from this analysis of the current and future traffic problems of city centres. First, our knowledge of the scale and severity of current problems is inadequate. As a result many transport policy decisions are based on the partial and perhaps exaggerated claims of complainants or of those who fear that they will be adversely affected. Not only may unnecessary decisions be taken as a result, but some worthwhile solutions to city-centre problems may not be pursued for lack of evidence of the need for them. Secondly, it seems that the most serious problems are likely to be those of inefficient use of the transport system, the environmental consequences of such use, and the inequities to which these give rise. There seems little evidence that the nature of city centres is changing much as a result of these problems, but it may well be that the types of people who use city centres will change. Finally, it seems unlikely that the scale of these problems will vary significantly in the immediate future unless positive steps are taken to reduce them. This conclusion prompts a review of possible solutions.

ALTERNATIVE SOLUTIONS TO CITY-CENTRE PROBLEMS

With the decline in urban road building, most activity in the last decade has been in the development of measures for managing the road system more effectively to reduce the problems described above. These measures have taken broadly two forms. The first is the introduction of traffic management measures which try to cater broadly for the same numbers of people travelling by the same modes at the same times, even if they involve some change in route taken. The second is the development of a new range of measures designed to reduce problems by encouraging changes in mode, timing of the journey, destination, or even in the total number of journeys made. This group of measures can usefully be termed transport management.

The 1970s (and to some extent the 1960s) have been a particularly innovatory period during which a wide range of new techniques has been proposed and in many cases implemented. In the field of traffic management, mini-roundabouts and centrally controlled traffic signals have been introduced to increase capacity, access and bottleneck controls to increase system throughput, bus and lorry lanes to enable these vehicles to overtake queues of cars, and other devices to give buses priority at traffic signals and entry control points. Environmental traffic management measures have included the closure of streets for pedestrian use, traffic cells and mazes which protect access while forcing through traffic to take an alternative route, and area-wide restrictions on heavy lorry movement. Transport management measures have included fares subsidies and new forms of bus service designed to attract car users to the bus, car sharing schemes to encourage more efficient use of cars, flexible and staggered working hours to reduce peak-period demands, and a range of restraint measures using parking controls, time penalties and fiscal and regulatory measures to reduce peak-period car use. It is not possible to review the potential of each of these in detail, but the following comments suggest the ways in which some of the more promising measures might develop.

It would appear that it is the application of traffic management measures which has been primarily responsible for the improved performance of city-centre road systems suggested by Tables 23 and 24. The most important innovation here has been the development of centrally controlled traffic signal systems (urban traffic control, or u.t.c.). Experience with these suggests that they are able to increase network capacity by up to 10 per cent, or to reduce travel times by up to 15 per cent for the same volume of traffic. Accident savings of up to 15 per cent have also been achieved, and the flexibility of control has been used to give additional weighting to the movement of buses (Robertson, 1976). The main limitation with the application of such traffic management measures is that much that could be done has already been done; u.t.c. systems are, for instance, already in operation in 15 cities in the UK, and the emphasis is now on their application to the larger town centres (Phillips, 1981). The main promise for future development is in the introduction of new and potentially more efficient methodologies for optimizing the performance of u.t.c. systems, and in the control of the routes which drivers take through the road system to increase efficiency still further. The potential for these approaches is still being assessed, but it may be that a further increase in capacity of up to 10 per cent can be achieved.

Unfortunately, while such techniques are tending to increase the efficiency with which the road system is used, environmental traffic management measures tend to do the reverse, restricting the extent to which the road system is available for moving traffic. There is plenty of evidence that effective environmental traffic management measures are available. Traffic cell systems have been used extensively on the Continent (Elmberg, 1972) and to a smaller extent in the UK in Nottingham and Derby (Department of the Environment, 1976b). Pedestrian streets and related measures, too, are in widespread use (OECD, 1975). The main limitation on their application on a larger scale is the lack of alternative road space onto which to divert the traffic. It seems unlikely that further traffic management measures will produce sufficient spare capacity to enable much environmental management to be achieved without at the same time seriously increasing congestion.

The only alternative, if congestion and environmental intrusion are to be reduced, is to find some way of reducing city-centre traffic. Considerable faith has been placed on the ability of improvements to other modes to encourage car users to change their habits. Such measures are dealt with in the next chapter, but it is worth noting that attempts to attract car users to use buses have generally had little effect (Webster *et al.*, 1980) while more recent interest in car sharing has been similarly ineffective (Bonsall, 1980). One alternative form of incentive, that of attracting peak-period car and bus users to change the time at which they travel, perhaps offers more promise, but little is yet known about the detailed effects of peak-spreading techniques, or the factors most likely to induce an employer to change his working arrangements (May *et al.*, 1981).

If inducements to change are ineffective, then restrictions on car use are the only alternative approach available. A period of considerable interest in traffic restraint techniques in the mid-1970s demonstrated that there are methods available which can reduce car use; the most notable being the area licensing scheme in Singapore in which a charge of 60p per day to enter the city centre in the morning peak reduced traffic entering by 44 per cent (Watson and Holland, 1978). Equally it demonstrated that other techniques, such as Nottingham's zones and collar experiment, in which delays were imposed on car users, were unlikely to be effective (Vincent and Layfield, 1977) and that the effectiveness of parking control as a restraint method was severely limited by the inability to control spaces in private ownership (May, 1975). However, although we now know how to reduce car traffic, we have shown little sign of being prepared to do so. The main reasons for this reluctance seem to be lingering doubts as to whether measures proven elsewhere would be effective in the UK, resistance to limitations on drivers' freedom to use the road and, perhaps most important, concern that such restrictions would adversely affect the economic activity of the city centre (May, 1981). It would appear that city-centre traffic problems are not as yet viewed as being serious enough to justify the risks which traffic restraint involves.

In summary, then, it appears that, on the one hand, city-centre traffic problems are unlikely to get significantly worse in the near future, while on the other hand the only techniques likely significantly to reduce them are not being introduced because the problems are not considered serious enough. Perhaps more careful monitoring of city-centre traffic problems will demonstrate that they give rise to higher cost than has been realized and it may be that further analysis will demonstrate that the risks involved in introducing traffic restraint are limited. In the absence of these developments, however, it seems unlikely that any effective initiatives will be taken to reduce city-centre traffic problems in the foreseeable future.

REFERENCES

Advisory Council on Energy Conservation (1979). "Report to the Secretary of State for Energy". Energy Paper 40. HMSO, London.

Armitage, Sir A. (1980). "Report of the Inquiry into Lorries, People and the Environment". HMSO, London.

Bonsall, P. W. (1980). "Car Sharing in the UK: Recent Developments, a Realistic Appraisal of Impacts and Reappraisal of Policy Priorities". Proc. PTRC Summer Annual Meeting, Warwick.

Burt, M. E. (1972). "Roads and the Environment". LR 441. Transport and Road Research Laboratory, Crowthorne.

Carr, R. *et al.* (1979). "The Central London Parking and Car Usage Survey". Greater London Council, London.

Crowther, G. (Baron Crowther of Headingly) (1963). "Traffic in Towns". HMSO, London.

Department of the Environment (1976a). "Transport Policy: a Consultation Document", Vol. 2, HMSO, London.

Department of the Environment (1976b). "Traffic Management with Bus Priorities in the Central Area". Bus Demonstration Project Summary Report 9. DoE, London.

Department of Transport (1978). "Urban Congestion Study, 1976: Interim Report". Traffic Advisory Unit. DTp, London.

Department of Transport (1980). "Road accidents, GB, 1978". HMSO, London.

Elmberg, C. M. (1972). *Transportation* **1** (1) 1-27.

Ferreira, L. (1981). "The Role of Comprehensive Traffic Management in Energy Conservation". Proc. PTRC Summer Annual Meeting, Warwick.

Foster, C. D. and Beesley M. E. (1963). *J.R.S.S.* Vol. **126A**.

Goodwin, P. B. (1974). "The Scope for Saving Fuel by a Car to Bus Transfer". Greater London Council (unpublished note).

Greater London Council (1981). "Traffic Monitoring Review". Statistical series No. 4. GLC, London.

Headicar, P. G. *et al.* (1979). *Traff. Engng. Control* **20** (1), 27-31.

Headicar, P. G. (1980). Unpublished note.

HMSO (1981). "Report of the Inter-Departmental Working Party on Road Traffic Law". HMSO, London.

Leach, G. (1979). "A Low Energy Strategy for the UK". International Institute for the Environment and Development, London.

Mackett, R. L. (1981). *In* "Strategic Planning in a Dynamic Society" (H. Voogd, ed.), pp.69-70. Delftse Uitgevers Maatschappij, Delft.

May, A. D. (1975). *Traff. Enging. Control* **16,** (5), 227-229.

May, A. D. (1981). "How Far Can We Go with Traffic Restraint?" Proc. Public Works Congress, Birmingham.

May, A. D. and Weaver, P. M. (1981). *Traff. Eng. Control* **22** (4), 204-207.

May, A. D., Montgomery, F. O. and Wheatley, M. D. (1981). "Work Journey Rescheduling: Literature Review and Study Strategy". Institute for Transport Studies, Leeds (to be published).

Metropolitan Police (1981). "Evidence before the House of Commons Transport Committee 8.4.81". HMSO, London.

Morton Williams, J. *et al.* (1978). "Road Traffic and the Environment". Social and Community Planning and Research, London.

Nelson, P. M. and Fanstone, J. (1974). "Estimates of the Reduction of Traffic Noise following the Introduction of Quieter Vehicles". LR 624. Transport and Road Research Laboratory, Crowthorne.

OECD (1978). Results of a questionnaire survey on pedestrian zones. Environment Directorate, Organisation for Economic Cooperation and Development, Paris (unpublished).

Patterson, N. S. and May A. D. (1979). "The Impact of Transport Problems on Inner City Firms: A Review". WP. 112. Institute for Transport Studies, Leeds.

Phillips, J. (1981). *Traff. Enging. Control* **22** (1), 4-7.

Robertson, D. I. (1976). "Urban Traffic Control Systems—Present and Potential". Transport and Road Research Laboratory, Crowthorne.

Salvucci, F. *et al.* (1980). "Transportation Energy Contingency Strategies: Transit, Paratransit and Ridesharing". US Department of Transportation, Washington, D.C.

Vincent, R. A. and Layfield, R. E. (1977). "Nottingham Zones and Collar Study—Overall Assessment". LR. 805. Transport and Road Research Laboratory, Crowthorne.

Watson, P. L. and Holland, E. P. (1978). "Relieving Traffic Congestion: the Singapore Area License Scheme". World Bank Staff Paper 281. The World Bank, Washington, D.C.

Webster, F. V. *et al.* (1980). "The Demand for Public Transport". Transport and Road Research Laboratory, Crowthorne.

Yates, L. B. and Hewing R. B. (1970). "Parking Offences and Parking Tickets". RM. 233. Greater London Council, London.

TEN

Does urban public transport have a future?

P. J. HILLS

In exploring the background to this chapter, the full extent of the long-term decline in the use of public transport services in urban areas has become clear and the seriousness of its implication for the future revealed—not just of the services themselves but of the activities and patterns of land uses which they help to sustain. Part of this decline is attributable to the attitudes of planners and policy makers towards public transport, which has assumed that a "balanced" modal split is feasible based upon consumers' choice between competing alternatives of public and private transport. Even the strong intervention of recent years, in the form of increasing revenue support, has left the assumption of the fundamental choice mechanism intact. The continuing decline, despite the intervention, is now blamed on the current economic recession but, generally speaking, the changes which would come about as economic growth is restored are likely to make matters worse for public transport not better. The consequences for existing city centres also should not be underestimated.

Towards the end of the chapter, suggestions are put forward of a fairly radical kind which, if implemented, could ensure a more limited but specific role for urban public transport. Without a radical policy of this kind, which would seek to "suspend" the competition with private cars, there is every likelihood that the decline in urban public transport will continue. If so, its survival to the end of the century must be gravely in doubt.

THE ROLE OF TRANSPORT IN CITY GROWTH IN THE INDUSTRIALIZED WORLD

Before embarking on an analysis of the role which public transport might play in the future of city centres in the "developed" industrial countries, it is important to consider the nature of the growth of those cities and of the forces and influences which have shaped them. Mindful that preceding chapters of this volume will have been much concerned with these forces and the way in which cities are likely to evolve in future, only a brief outline is appropriate here.

THE FUTURE FOR THE CITY CENTRE
ISBN 0 12 206240 X

Because in the study of human settlement and patterns of human activity, we are dealing with a highly complex system of economic and social interaction, interpretations of significant events which have shaped the growth and development of cities are necessarily partial and speculative. Testimony to this is the enormous literature on population, migration, demography and planning, little of which can be said to be definitive and yet which provides the only real source of inspiration for our efforts to plan for the future of our cities.

Transport studies, despite their apparent sophistication and frequent resort to mathematical models, share a common heritage with all other aspects of planning rooted as they are in the observing and codifying of human behaviour. Travel behaviour is manifest as a myriad of individual decisions which, taken together in some appropriate way, amounts to what we call "transport need" or "travel demand". The prediction of these needs and demands (indeed, the distinction—if one is to be made—between them) is the source of many inherent difficulties in tackling the subject in a reasoned and scientific way. These difficulties are compounded by our limited understanding of the nature of individual and group decision-taking, especially in the face of future uncertainties and shifting constraints.

Our predominant concern (obsession, almost) with the supply side of transport in the past has misled us into planning specific solutions to presumed and predetermined transport problems (Hills, 1974). Whilst this approach may be entirely appropriate at a detailed implementation level and certainly in the day-to-day management decisions of a transport undertaking, it can create severe distortions and misallocation of resources if it is applied to the long-term planning of human settlements. This may be self-evident to those engaged in planning and forecasting in other aspects of human affairs but, sadly, it has only dawned rather recently on those concerned with transport. Thus, the history of industrial growth and the in-migration of population to form dense, compact cities may be ascribed to economies of scale, to specialization in the division of labour, to the harnessing of power for production and so on but, without the accessibility—to materials, labour and markets—which transport could provide, none of this growth and development would have been possible.

The impact of transport—essentially public transport, up until 30 years ago—on activities, as the determinant of accessibility which enables them to flourish, was as important as the provision of transport to meet the demands for it, arising out of the activities themselves. Unfortunately, the basis of this interaction (between accessibility and economic activity) which has served as a plausible historical explanation for the growth and development of cities hitherto is now being undermined by two profound technological changes. One, that we are familiar with in the industrialized world, is the onset of mass ownership of private transport; the other, whose effects we can barely discern as yet, is the mass deployment and use of telecommunications equipment.

Each, in a different way, has altered the concept of accessibility. The private car, by abolishing the constraints of time, route and frequency, destination and mode of

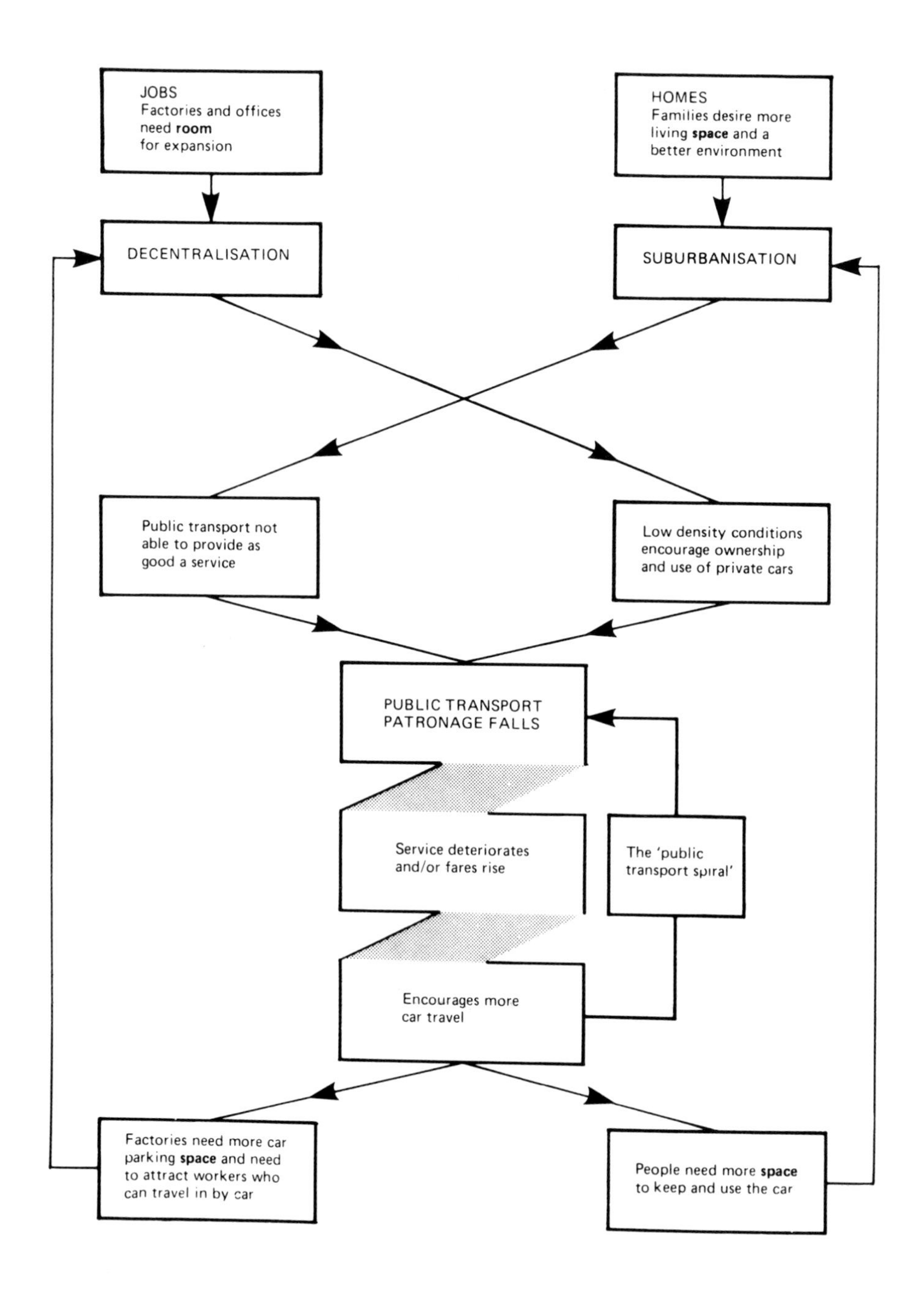

Figure 30. Interactions between decentralization of workplaces and sub-urbanization and public transport use. (Source: TRRL, 1980.)

payment inherent in conventional scheduled services of public transport, has added many degrees of freedom to an individual's perception of accessibility. Misguidely, we have assumed that decisions between public and private transport use continue to be governed by some kind of competitive discrete-choice model (Hensher and Stopher, 1979), which converts these relative freedoms into generalized costs attributable to the alternative modes of transport available. Recent research (e.g. Gwilliam and Banister, 1977) suggests that the opportunities opened up through car ownership are perceived and valued in a quite different way to those previously attainable with public transport. It is certainly very hard to explain the continuing shifts away from the public transport and the increasing outward migration of commuters to expanding suburbs (Fig. 30) in terms of travel time and cost differences alone. Thus accessibility, *unless it can be measured in a way which reflects individuals' perceptions of the opportunities that are open to them*, is no longer an adequate predictor of travel demand let alone of location decisions.

Telecommunications will alter the concept of accessibility more radically than this. Both the domestic and the commercial tele-terminal will remove the constraints on information which have limited the scope of travel choices up to now. Mistakenly (in my view) we are already assuming that telecommunications will *substitute* for travel and yet the long-term evidence from the one device already in mass ownership (the telephone) suggests, on balance, that the reverse is more likely. If we were to compare the trips made by households possessing telephones with those of a similar kind without, we would probably find that, for every trip obviated by use of the telephone, two or three more are generated. Certainly, comparing businesses in a similar way, one would expect that the better firms are tapped into the communication network, the more travel they generate (O'Cinneide, 1980). To argue that they would do more business as a result is merely to convert an accessibility effect into an income effect—probably with a consequent loss of understanding as to what actually stimulates the demand for travel.

The need to recognize the potency of these two technological challenges, not just to the patterns of activity themselves but to the way in which we try to plan for them, has been considered at length elsewhere (Hills, 1974). It is sufficient for our purpose here to consider whether (and if so how) to intervene in the process of change now under way which will shape the future of our cities and, rather especially, their central areas.

THE DEMANDS FOR TRAVEL IN A TECHNOLOGICAL CITY

Over the ten years from the time of the publication of the Buchanan Report (1963), each of the major towns and cities in Britain embarked on at least one transportation study. Almost without exception, the early ones were based upon previous experience in US cities (notably Chicago and Detroit) and adopted similar objectives. They involved the collection of huge inventories of data on the patterns of trip-making by mode, purpose, time of day, etc., with little or no information on motives, perceptions or prevailing constraints on choice. The matrices produced, of origin-to-destination trips for the various modes of transport, were no doubt an adequate reflection of the travel demands actually experienced on the day or week of the surveys themselves, but heroic assumptions had then to be made as to their validity as a base for forecasting. The determinants of forecast growth—with the optimism of that time, every forecast implied a growth!—were mainly related to land use and, above all, to car ownership. The transportation planning process was seen as a recursive five-stage sequence whereby land-use "inputs" could be translated into travel demand as an output; supporting the contention of Buchanan and many others that "traffic is a function of land use" (Buchanan *et al.*, 1963).

To the extent that the provision of the new roads and car parks that would be needed to accommodate all this future traffic implied a cost, it was supposed to be borne cheerfully as part of the cost of progress. Buchanan (*ibid.*) argued that if the community can afford thousands of millions of pounds each year in the purchase of new cars and lorries, then it can surely afford a few hundreds of millions of pounds each year in their decent accommodation (revealing his scant regard for the niceties of economic theory!). Although not a sufficient basis to justify any particular investment in urban transport, global calculations of this kind can be of value in keeping public investment in perspective. For example, the capital cost of the Tyneside "Metro" over the six years of its construction—likely to be about £280 millions at out-turn prices—is equal to the amount expended in this country *every three weeks* on the purchase of new cars and trucks. Again, the emphasis which Buchanan placed upon the effects of traffic on the urban environment predated its emergence as a public concern in the late 1960s: unfortunately, however, those traffic management measures purposely designed to protect the environment were not seen as a positive contribution to traffic restraint but instead as a further public cost of development. Apart from the pioneering efforts (largely ignored) of the road-use pricing adherents (Smeed Committee, 1964), very little thought was given in those days to questions of pricing and subsidies in the regulation of demands for transport. Transport proposals were almost invariably supply orientated.

Another significant weakness of the transportation plans of the late 1960s and early 1970s stems from their assumption that burgeoning car ownership inevitably leads to irresistable and irrepressible demands for road space and concerns the "residual" role which they often assigned to public transport. Buses (it was assumed) were and would always be needed to provide a public service for those not fortunate enough to own a car and, as a second best, for those who were but temporarily deprived of its use. Even with "saturation" car ownership (0·45-0·50 cars per head) it was acknowledged that a majority of people at any one time would still be dependent on public transport and, to the extent that this could not be provided "at an economic price", subsidies would be necessary—again at public cost. Although now (through circumstance) the intricacies of public sector finance are better understood, there is still widespread confusion between the economic value of the resource cost of public investment and the monetary costs involved in financing it. As a result, the major switch over recent years from capital investment in urban roads to the wholesale subsidy of public transport has been undertaken with little regard for its resource implications. Furthermore, the original assumption that such a switch would "save public money" is probably ceasing to be true, because revenue support for public transport (Table 30) in the major urban areas of England and Wales exceeded £140 millions in 1980–1981 (representing one-sixth of all public expenditure on transport for that year).

Many of the shortcomings, both conceptual and methodological, of the early transportation studies (and of the highway and transport plans to which they gave rise) have been remedied in subsequent studies. Perhaps the best example in recent years has been the study (Wytconsult, 1977) of West Yorkshire which explored peoples' satisfaction (or otherwise) with the transport services available to them, their attitudes towards car-use, accessibility by public transport and the residential environment. Elsewhere, notably in Sweden, interesting in-depth studies have been undertaken to measure consumers' satisfaction and preferences using attitude-scaling techniques, as indicated in Table 31. These studies reveal wide differences in attitude between car owners and non-car owners, and between inner city and suburban dwellers, in relation to the public transport services they expect and will accept. It is clear that many qualities other than low fares are regarded as important by would-be bus travellers.

TABLE 30

Revenue-support in relation to transport expenditure: English and Welsh conurbations (1980–1981)

	Population mid-1979 (millions)	1980–81 Revenue-support (M£)	1980–81 All transport expenditure (M£)	1980–81 Revenue-support per head (pence)	1980–81 Revenue support as % all transport expenditure
Greater London	6·918	48·38	232·39	699·3	20·8
Greater Manchester	2·664	20·64	52·81	774·8	39·1
Merseyside	1·546	19·30	40·70	1248·4	47·4
Tyne & Wear	1·165	13·70	31·77	1175·9	43·1
West Midlands	2·712	9·80	30·53	361·4	32·1
South Yorkshire	1·304	12·00	48·32	920·2	24·8
West Yorkshire	2·068	14·49	47·46	700·7	30·5
Avon	0·922	1·25	13·26	135·6	9·4
Cleveland	0·508	1·03	11·61	202·8	8·9
Humberside	0·845	0·61	11·65	72·2	5·3
Mid-Glamorgan	0·538	1·10	11·63	204·5	9·5
Totals	21·190	142·30	532·13	671·5	26·7

Sources: Transport Statistics for Great Britain (1980); Warburton (1981).

TABLE 31
Desirability of improvements in public transport

Improvements sought[a]	Ranking by all public transport users				Ranking by car-owning commuters using public transport				Ranking by commuters using cars			
	Residential location[b]				Residential location[b]				Residential location[b]			
	All	C	I	S	All	C	I	S	All	C	I	S
Bus shelters	1	1	3	1	1	4	3	1	4	4	6	1
Regularity	10	5	10	8	9	1	10	9	9	9	10	9
Chance of obtaining seat	6	6	5	5	6	7	5	5	6	7	5	7
No crowding	5	4	4	6	5	5	6	6	5	6	4	8
Journey speed	4	7	6	4	3	3	2	3	1	2	1	2
No transfers	3	2	1	3	4	2	7	4	2	3	2	4
Fewer stairs and escalators	8	9	8	10	10	10	9	10	10	10	9	5
Nearness to bus stop	9	10	9	7	8	8	8	8	7	8	8	6
Service frequency	2	3	2	2	2	6	1	2	3	1	3	3
Comfort (better heating and ventilation)	7	8	7	9	7	9	4	7	8	5	7	10

[a] The suggested improvements were ranked in order of importance with rank 1 as the most important and rank 10, the least so.
[b] C = central area; I = inner area excluding the central area; S = suburban areas.
Source: Stockholm Area Transport Study (1971).

Despite the periodic hails of criticism which the early transportation studies have received (for example, Independent Commission on Transport, 1974), they did provide a wealth of data on patterns of trip-making. Although much of these data "perished", some analysis has been done to improve our understanding of the role which public transport plays now and of the trends which are apparent. Mogridge (1980), for example, has compared London and Paris data to reveal the spatial variations in modal split for "home-based" and "non-home-based" trips (Fig. 31). These reveal the very small role played by cars within 5 km of the centres and, for home-based trips, the substantial proportion (in the range 20–40 per cent) which involve walking the whole way within the inner core of the city.

Even in cities as large as London, the majority of all trips are now undertaken by car but the overwhelming preponderance of these are in the suburbs (Table 32). The Greater London Transportation Study (1973) reveals that three-quarters of all trips occur wholly within the suburbs (5–20 km radius) and of these two-thirds are by car. Another surprising aspect is the very short average trip-length, by car and by bus in the suburbs, less than 5 km. Only on radial journeys by train do average trip-lengths exceed 10 km (Table 33). In terms of journey purposes, only a third of all trips are to and from work in London, 10 per cent to and from school, the rest being for other-than-work purposes. Buses and trains in London carry 50 per cent of all work journeys (but up to 80 per cent of those in central London). Surprisingly, public transport now accounts for only a quarter of school journeys; this suggests that, as soon as a household acquires a car (and a further 2000 do so in the UK each week), the likelihood is that its children desert the bus in favour of the car.

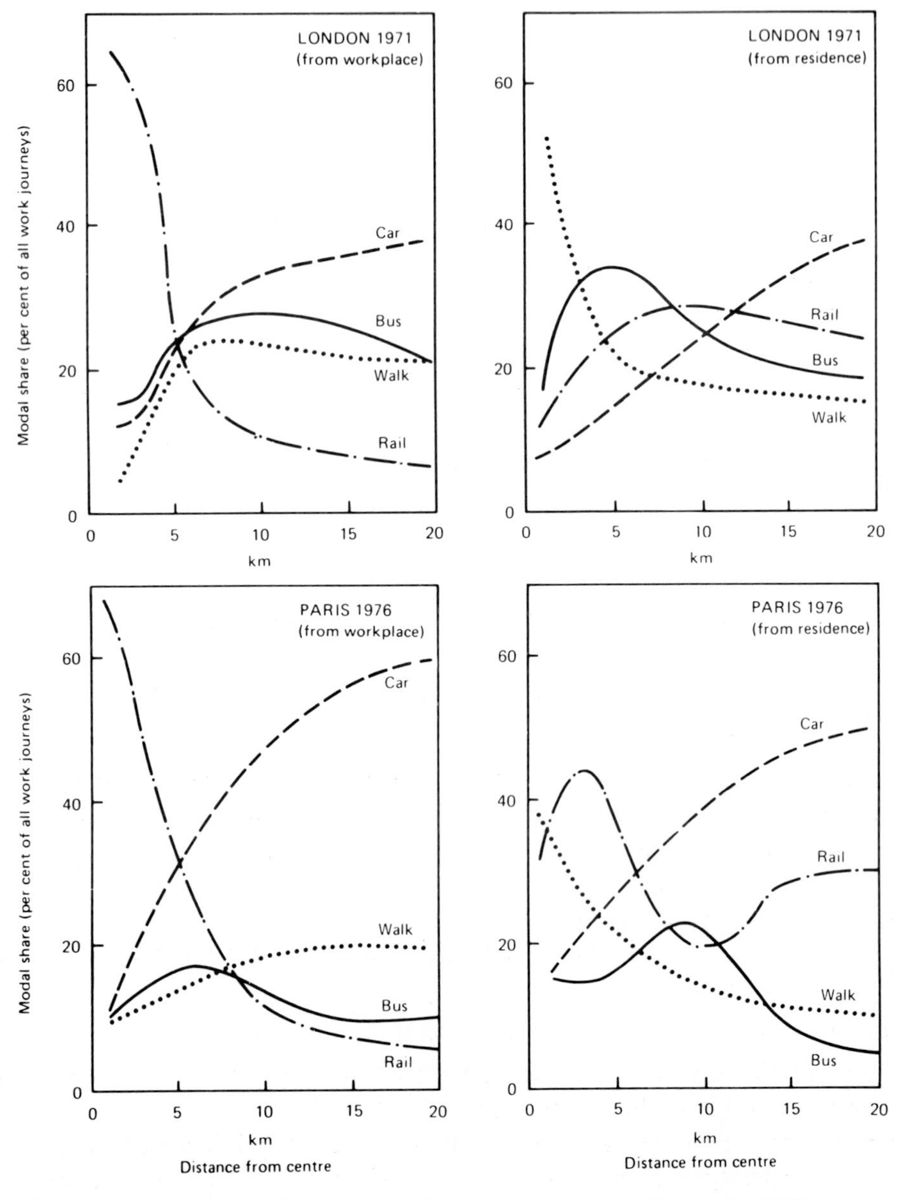

Figure 31. The spatial variation of modal split in London and Paris. (Source: Mogridge, 1980).

TABLE 32
Trip patterns in Greater London (1978)

Trips (M/annum)	Car and taxi	Bus	LT Rail	BR Rail	Total
Central	68 (11%): 101 (17%)[a]	162 (27%)	273 (45%)	1 (0%)	605 (100%)
Radial	153 (23%)	174 (26%)	182 (27%)	158 (24%)	667 (100%)
Suburban	2519 (67%)	1036 (28%)	105 (3%)	74 (2%)	3734 (100%)
Total	2841 (56%)	1372 (27%)	560 (11%)	233 (5%)	5006 (100%)

[a] Car and taxi markets respectively—an approximate allocation for trips within the central area, only, otherwise combined.

TABLE 33
Average journey lengths of trips in Greater London (1978)

Distance in miles	Car and taxi	Bus	LT Rail	BR Rail	Total
Central	2·7 : 1·7[a]	1·5	2·2	—	2·0
Radial	7·0	3·0	7·9	9·9	6·9
Suburban	3·1	2·0	4·8	4·8	2·8
Total	3·2	2·0	4·5	8·0	3·3

[a] As for Table 32.
Source: Wagon (1978).

THE CRUCIAL YEARS FOR URBAN PUBLIC TRANSPORT

Looking at the trends in London over the years 1972–1978 (Wagon, 1978), significant changes are occurring for the public transport market:

(a) the population and employment of the inner areas continue to decline;
(b) the proportion of non-car-owning households continues to fall and their composition changes;
(c) the proportion of car trips to the central area is falling but taxi trips within the central area are rising; and
(d) the fall in train trips is substantial and continuing, on radial corridors as well as in suburban areas.

This last trend is accounted for almost entirely by the population and employment changes and car-ownership growth; the effects of real fare increases have been very slight (Tables 34 and 35).

Outside London, in the major conurbations, similar though less dramatic changes have been occurring. Passengers and passenger-kilometres are falling steadily (South Yorkshire and Tyne and Wear are exceptions to this). The decline is mainly in the

TABLE 34

Percentage change in passenger-miles (expressed as percentages of total passenger-miles for each mode in 1972) in Greater London (1972–1978) due to various causes

Cause	Effect on total pm's		
	Bus (%)	LT Rail (%)	BR (%)
(a) Population changes (b) Employment changes (c) Car ownership changes	-10	-11	-8
(d) Changes in fares level	-1	-2	-1
(e) Changes in fares relativities	+11	-7	-1
(f) Tourism	+1	+3	0
(g) Free travel for OAPs	+4	-2	-1
Total	+4	-19	-16

TABLE 35

Percentage change in trips in Greater London (1972–1978)

Trips	Car and taxi (%)	Bus (%)	LT Rail (%)	BR Rail (%)	Total (%)
Central	-3·0: +25·2	+4·7	-0·9	—	+4·5
Radial	-2·0	+3·3	-19·6	-14·5	-9·2
Suburban	-0·4	-4·5	-25·2	-18·7	-2·8
Total	+0·5	-2·4	-11·6	-16·3	-5·5

Source: Wagon (1978).

longer, suburban bus journeys associated with other-than-work journey purposes. In the provincial cities, it seems, there is a closer relationship between patronage decline and real fares increases (Fig. 32). Work journeys are, of course, generally shorter in these cities and a higher proportion of them are to the city centres.

Passenger Transport Executives (PTEs) and other operators have responded to this challenge and recent efforts to "market" public transport services on a marginal cost pricing and concessionary fare basis have been remarkably successful. Unfortunately, the gains are confined almost entirely to already-captive travellers, for example children in non-car-owning households and old aged pensioners, and do not extend to financially independent car-owning adults. In the face of every effort and despite the concessions, overall patronage by adults for all PTE services has declined by 27 per cent in the last six years. This is a situation with serious implications for the future of urban public transport as it is presently organized and operated. London Transport's recent move to a flat-fare system covering all the outer suburbs is a bold attempt to stem the loss of bus patronage in these areas. But, as car ownership continues to rise and the social/demographic shifts in the population dependent upon public transport accelerate, the present economic base

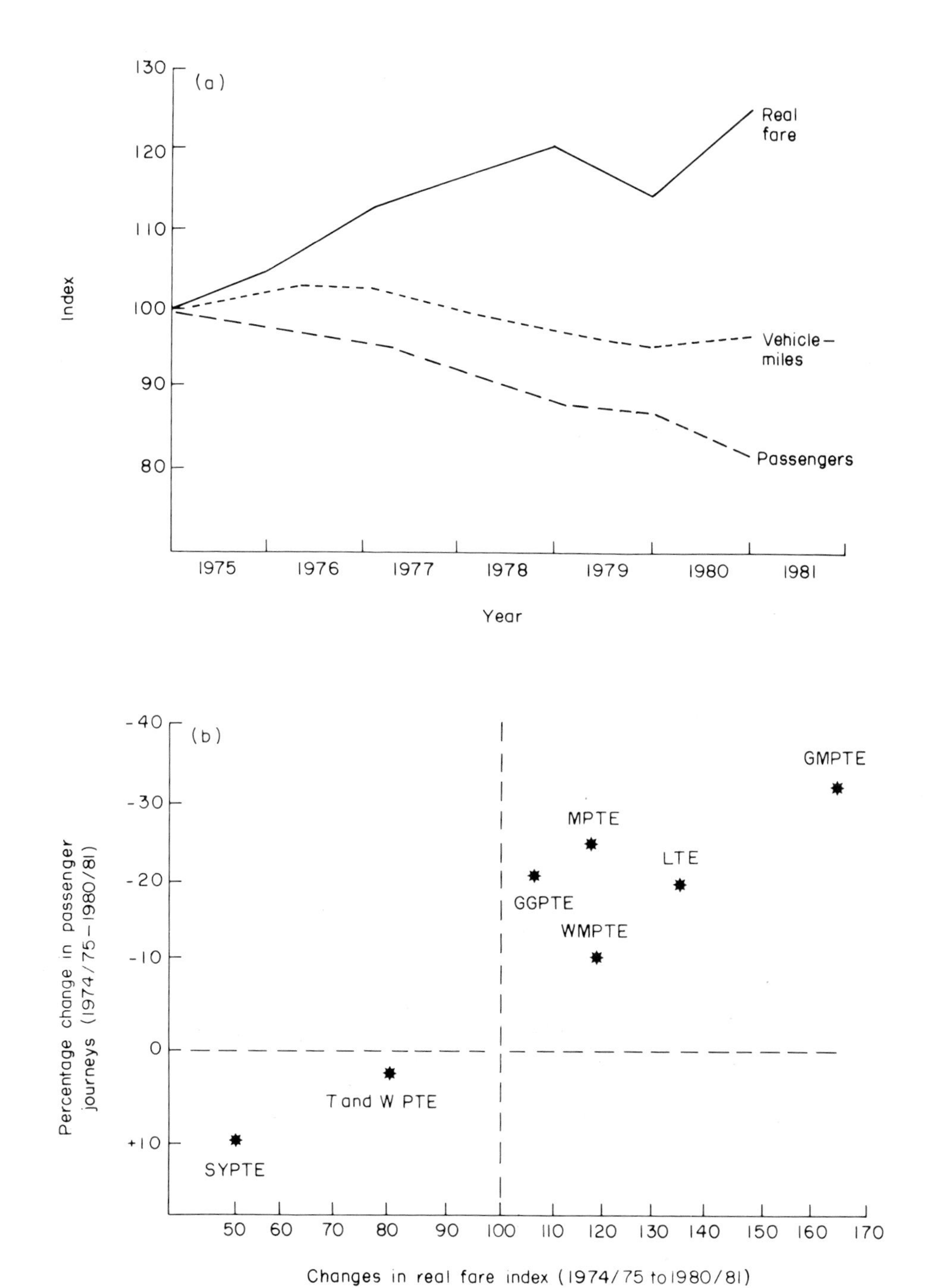

Figure 32. (a) Changes in index values for all PTEs of fares, patronage and vehicle mileage (1975-1980).
(b) Percentage changes in passenger journeys and Real Fare Index (LTE and other PTE).

Figure 33. Trends in car ownership and bus travel in Great Britain. (Source: Jones and Tanner, 1979).

of urban public transport is steadily being undermined (Fig. 33). These effects are compounded by the rising real cost of maintaining the full network and range of public transport services and the very limited scope (by the nature of these services) for further improvements in labour productivity.

In speculating on the likely date of collapse of the urban public transport market, it would be misleading to extrapolate from the trends identified by the Transport and Road Research Laboratory (Jones and Tanner, 1979) which show an overall loss of 50 per cent of the market during the last 20 years. The loss of the other 50 per cent could be even more rapid unless total collapse can be averted by the progressive withdrawal and abandonment of less viable services and the retrenchment and continued support of those relatively easier to defend. In the rather antiseptic prose of Jones and Tanner (1979), "About half to two thirds of the geographical variation in public transport provision appears to be attributable to variations in car-ownership, the remainder being due to direct effects of other factors such as incomes and (residential) densities". Again ". . . high levels of car-ownership are associated with low levels of public transport (use): this is true on an area basis (countries, cities in UK and states of the USA), at a (disaggregate) household level and in time series (analysis)".

To predict the effective demise of urban public transport in this country by the end of this century is neither to exaggerate nor to be alarmist. On the face of it, the present decline is part of a steady long-term trend of diminishing market share. Withdrawal of scheduled services is already a reality in many rural areas (Warburton, 1981): outer suburban and inter-town services may well be next. Aware of the extent and persistence of the downward trend, operators speak of a "levelling out" in the near future, as if it were somehow pre-ordained. More detached judgement suggests that those pressures which are causing the decline (decentralization of activities, drifts of population to the suburbs and smaller towns, lowering of densities, spiralling car ownership, increasing real costs of labour, etc.) are likely to intensify rather than diminish, especially during an emergence from economic recession. It is hard to see, in the natural order of things, where are the sources of any countervailing pressures.

CAN SUBSIDIES COME TO THE RESCUE?

Evidence can be offered to support the case for specific subsidies to stem the tide but they are unlikely to be the salvation in the long term, particularly in view of their possible adverse effect on productivity (Fig. 34). Experience in South Yorkshire shows that, despite fare levels that are only one-third of the average (14·8 p per mile) for all PTEs and scarcely a quarter of the most expensive (Greater Manchester @ 20·9 p per mile), South Yorkshire's PTE have achieved less than a 10 per cent increase in ridership over the last six years of their cheap fares policy. Their annual fare-box revenue in 1980–1981 was £20 million less than that of Merseyside PTE, who ran the same total vehicle-km (60 million) in that year and almost the same number of passenger-km (just over 1000 million). The flaw lies in the assumption that price is the prime determinant of demand for bus service. And yet, many PTEs are set to follow the lead given by the GLC (*Transport*, 1981) in drastic fare-cutting policies. Without equally radical reshaping of routes and schedules, the experience is likely to be a costly one. London Transport is already finding from long-term research into consumer preferences and attitudes that, as incomes rise and the additional freedoms of car ownership are acquired, price diminishes in importance as an attribute—to the point where "fare-free" public

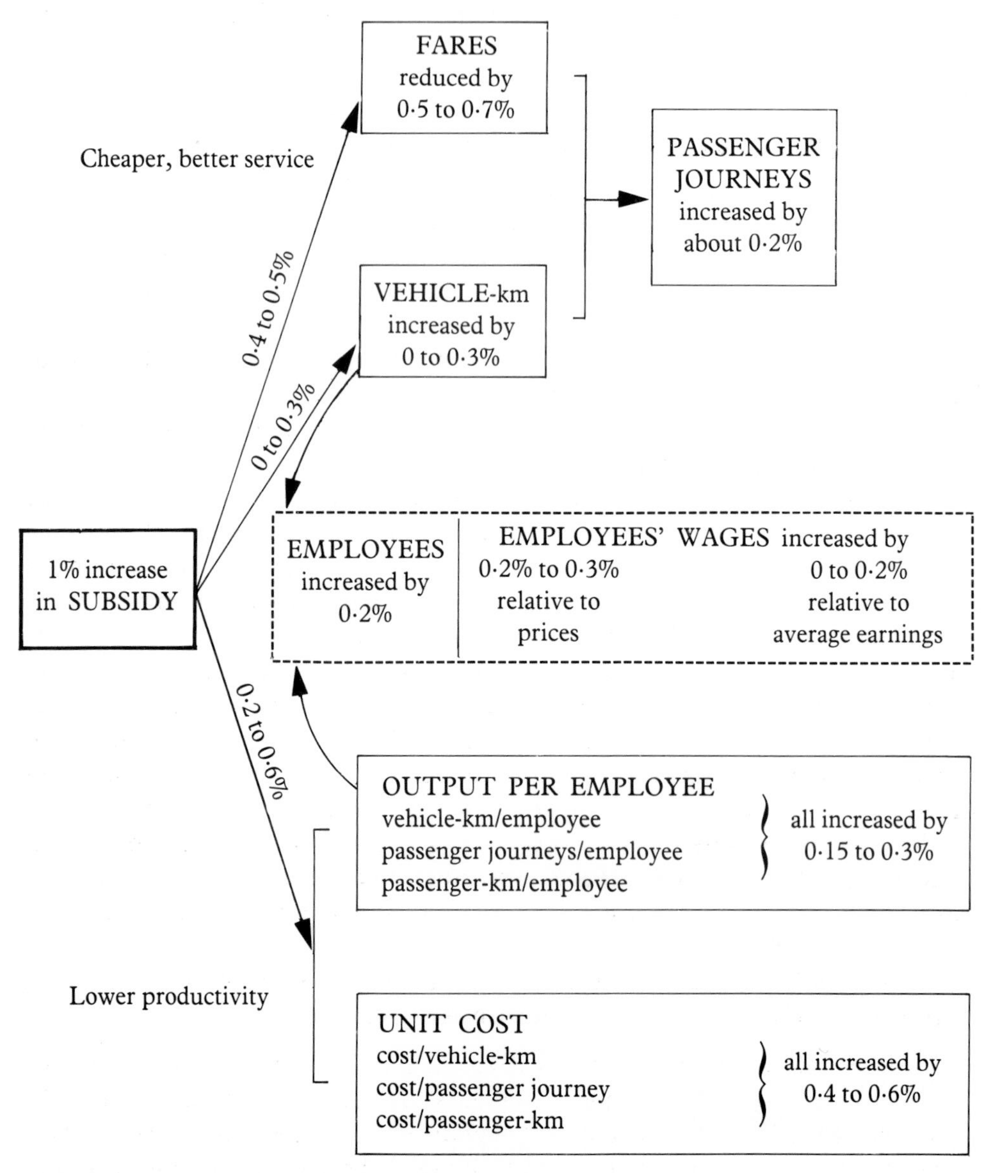

Figure 34. Illustration of the most likely effects of changes in transport subsidy. (Source: TRRL, 1980).

transport, too, would be rejected in favour of a more comfortable and convenient mode by all those who were not captive to it.

Fresh evidence on the key role likely to be played by future economic growth in the further undermining of bus patronage is presented by Oldfield *et al.* (1981), who make long-term predictions of the use of stage-carriage buses in Britain from now to the end of the century. A number of different scenarios are tested using two discrete forms of a prediction model; one, called a "traveller-type" model, which categorizes trips by purpose and type of person; and the other, called an "area-type" model, which combines all types of trip but deals separately with different types of operating area. The performance of the model appears to be reasonably good, judging by its ability to "explain" the long-term downward trend by means of back-projection to the 1950s, using 1977 as the calibration year.

The effectiveness of subsidies, explored with this model, is seen to be offset strongly by the consequences of real income growth. Thus, in order to keep patronage constant, it is estimated that subsidies in real terms would have to increase at about 3 per cent per annum, if economic growth were 1 per cent per annum; but they would have to increase at 8·5 per cent per annum, if economic growth were a mere 2 per cent per annum. The corresponding amounts of total subsidy would rise from the present £400 million (at 1974 prices) to £640 million or £2000 million respectively by the year 2000 A.D.

In detail, the effects of various changes in the patterns of subsidy are shown in Table 36 which summarizes the output from the "traveller-type" model.

It is interesting to note the reference to 2 per cent per annum as "high" economic growth, because this figure may be regularly exceeded in the years of economic resurgence following the end of the current recession. Some light is shed, too, on the relative insensitivity of fuel prices as a means of sustaining bus use. For, if subsidies were to be held constant (1979 prices), it would require fuel prices to be 3·5 times higher in real terms by the end of the century (assuming a "low" economic growth) to maintain present levels of bus patronage. With so-called "high" economic growth, fuel prices would have to be sky-high at levels of 10-15 times more than now (in real terms). The fact is that the output of the model is far more sensitive to small changes in economic growth than to changes in either fuel prices or subsidies. To the extent that it reflects the real world in the next few years, it provides the best evidence available in support of the case being presented here, and it must raise severe doubts about the future of bus services in the form in which they are currently operated.

The relationship between income levels and the future of urban public transport (Figs 35 and 36) is, therefore crucial for six main reasons:

(1) Urban public transport services have relied hitherto upon captive travellers who, lacking a private transport alternative, are denied an adequate basis for comparison. The captive market is dwindling (in several North American cities, old age pensioners now constitute the majority of bus users in both passenger and passenger-km terms).

TABLE 36

Estimated changes in patronage levels in the year 2000 using the traveller-type model

Subsidization policy	Percentage change in bus patronage from 1979 to 2000 for growth rate of economy of: 1 per cent per annum "low" growth	2 per cent per annum "high" growth
Constant subsidy		
M£350 at 1979 prices	-9	-42
with free travel for OAPs	-2	-34
with no concessions for OAPs	-13	-45
with improved concessions for school children	-6	-37
with no concessions for school children	-12	-46
No subsidy		
but retention of OAP and school children concessions	-22	-51
and no concessions for OAPs or school children	-32	-61

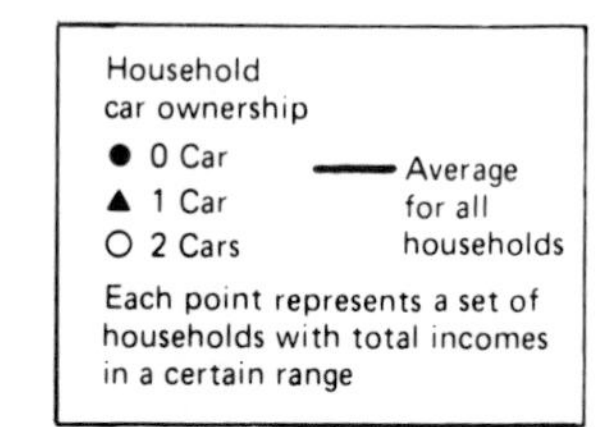

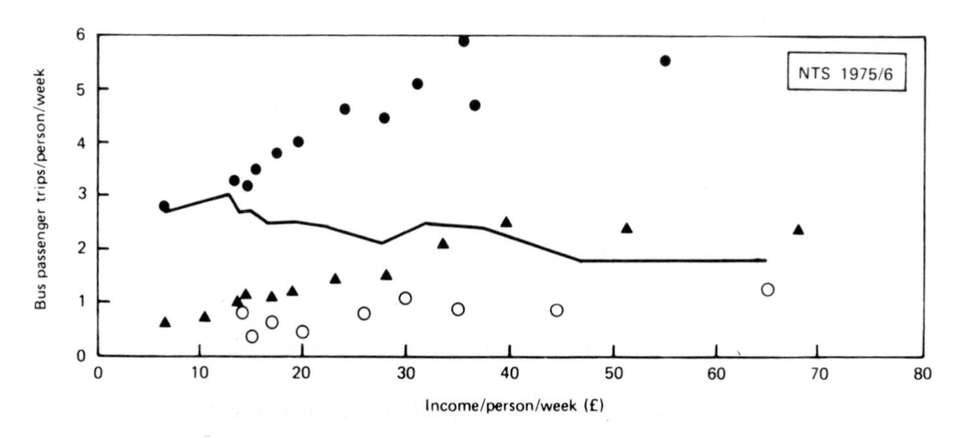

Figure 35. Effect of income on trip-making by bus. (Source: National Travel Survey, 1975-1976).

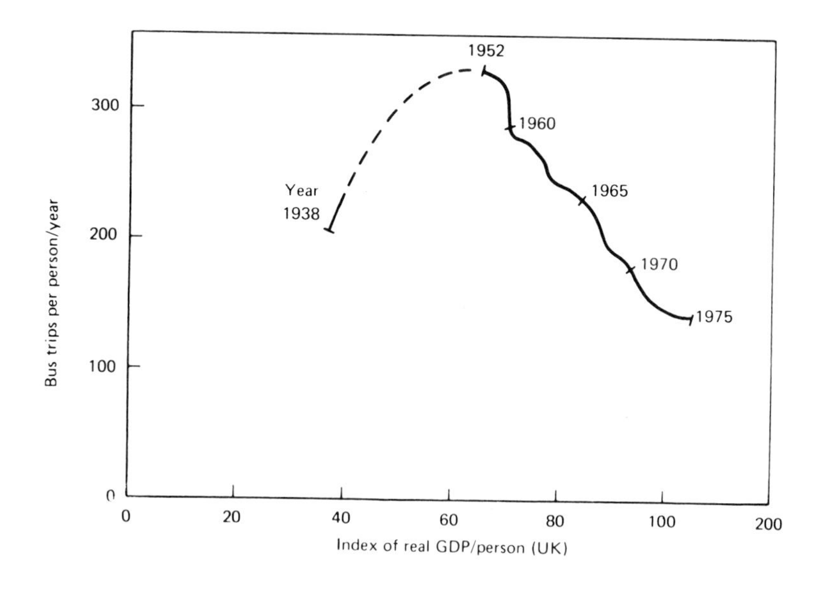

Figure 36. Effect of national wealth on bus trip-making. (Source: Webster, 1977.)

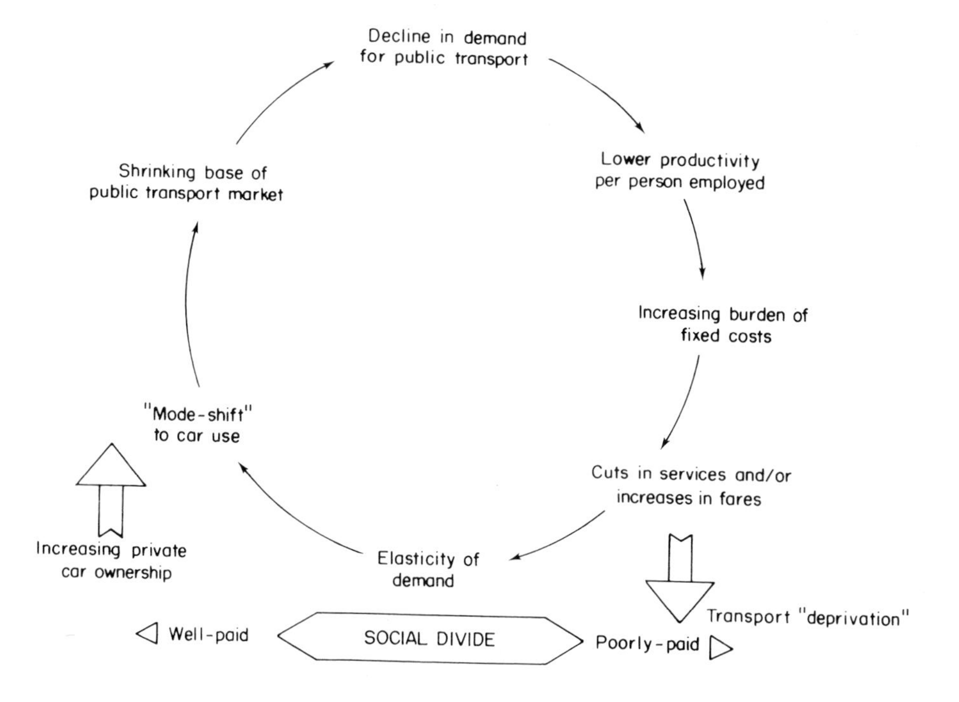

Figure 37. The "vicious spiral" of decline in public transport.

(2) Almost by definition, captive bus travellers have lower than average incomes. This tends to reinforce the public service obligation, denies transport operators the freedom to exploit such market opportunities as might arise and almost guarantees political involvement in the decisions regarding fares policy and service changes.

(3) As car ownership passes through the 0·3 cars per head figure or thereabouts, the majority of cars purchased will be as second or subsequent cars in already car-owning households. This will raise average car availability in such households throughout the day and the biggest impact will be felt on suburban bus services for non-work journey purposes.

(4) The consequences of the so-called "vicious spiral" of decline in public transport are socially divisive and tend to reinforce similar spatial trends in housing, education and employment (Fig. 37). The shift in employment opportunities away from central and inner areas of cities is not unrelated to public transport's decline in these areas, although the causal nature of the relationship is often exaggerated (Hedges and Hopkin, 1981).

(5) Certainly, as the economy in Britain expands again to sustain real income-growth, redevelopment will be concentrated in larger units in the more peripheral areas most accessible and easily served by private road transport. The fall in average densities by about one-third over the last 50 years (TRRL, 1980) can be closely correlated to the growth of real incomes.

(6) As disposable incomes grow, tastes and preferences change and expectations tend to rise. As far as public transport is concerned, its image is increasingly a "welfare" one. To strive to offer the same range of qualities of service that private cars provide, but within tightening financial limits and with a declining economic base, may present an impossible task to PTEs and other operators.

DOES URBAN PUBLIC TRANSPORT HAVE A FUTURE?

We could conclude that, in the interests of conserving urban public transport—and city centres, come to that—we should restrain the growth of real income! It is quite clear, however, that the dominant aim of national economic policy, pursued for years by governments of every persuasion, is to boost productivity, enhance production and generate affluence in our society. They even point to car production as the "barometer" of economic performance!

Some would contend that the pursuit of economic growth will inevitably be frustrated by an ultimate oil crisis and that transport, as a prime user of crude-oil products, will be hit first. Space does not permit full-scale discussion here of the long-term effects of OPEC-induced oil crises. Suffice it to say that transport is not the only user of crude-oil products and, in fact, it accounts for only a quarter of total consumption; the others ranging from domestic space-heating to detergents, fertilizers and paints. In practice, transport, precisely because it is a prime user, could sustain higher price-rises (if oil became really scarce) than secondary users, like domestic and industrial boilers, for which substitute fuels are available. All the scenario-building to date (for example, the WAES report, 1978, and Bly and Webster, 1980) suggests that petrol prices would have to rise very greatly in real terms before it significantly influenced either modal split or car ownership itself. At present, fuel accounts for less than one-eighth of the average operating cost of a bus compared to more than five-eighths for labour.

If our experiences since 1973–1974 are representative of the periodic oil crises we may expect in future, the adjustments required in the transport sector are not very profound or radical, particularly in view of the efficiency gains likely with new engine designs and the possibilities emerging for fuel synthesis and energy conversion in the long term. If, on the other hand, a future crisis is going to be more precipitate, finding the fuel for private cars or buses will be amongst the least of our worries!

To return to the theme, what—in the face of an apparently inevitable decline of urban public transport—can be done to halt the trend and to what extent could policies on the future of the city centre assist in this? These questions can be answered with a number of practical suggestions as to the direction which transportation and planning policies should take in the next few years. All of them are predicated on the assumption that the unplanned "minimum intervention" outcome is undesirable—in terms of its impact on energy, economy, equity and environment. That is to say, it is the author's belief (and one clearly shared by Sir Wilfred Burns) that high-density, compact city centres have virtues which we should endeavour to protect and enhance by the intervention of planning measures; and it can be contended that, in an age of mass car ownership, only vigorous traffic restraint and selective discrimination in favour of appropriate forms of public transport can enable city centres to survive.

The important steps in what might be called a "manifesto" for urban public transport provision in support of that aim are, as follows:

(a) to identify those transport functions (or market segments) for which public transport is best fitted or which it can best hope to serve, by carrying out an urban equivalent of the National Bus Company's viable network (MAP) exercise. That is, to determine the costs and revenues of services on a route-by-route basis and forecast elasticities of demand for each (Fig. 38).

(b) to use these analyses to direct resources towards those services most capable of resisting the forces of decline and allowing the remainder (if necessary) to wither away.

(c) to abandon, in the selected market segments, the concept of a balanced modal split (i.e. suspend the rules of competition with private transport). In the case of radial routes to city centres, particularly for work journeys, this implies severe restraints on long-term parking in city centres and well-timed restrictions on entry to the central area by car.

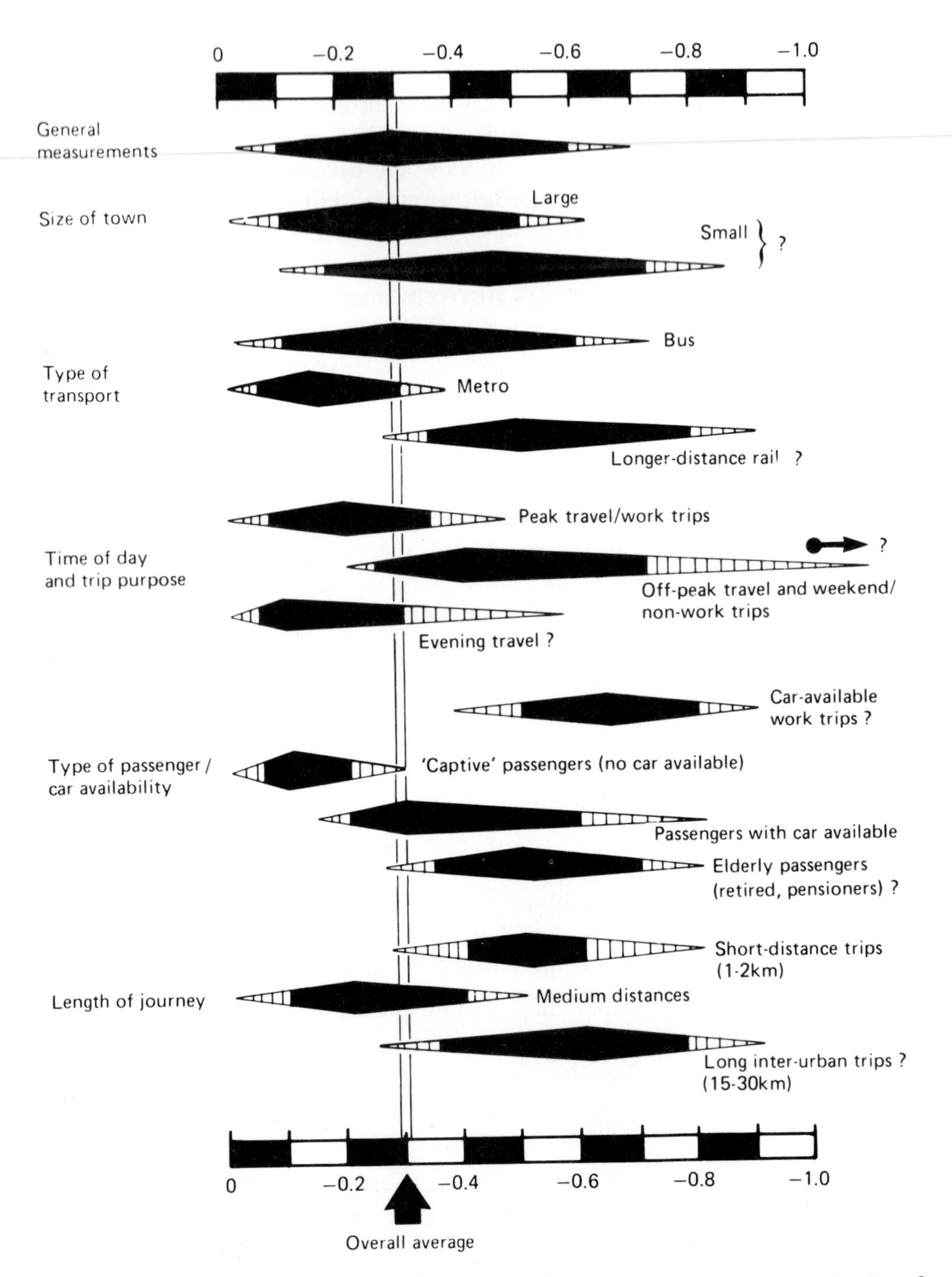

Figure 38. Fares elasticities for different travel characteristics. (Source: TRRL, 1980.) Note: In view of the wide variability of measured elasticities, this representation in different categories is necessarily very approximate. The solid black areas indicate the most likely range of values, while the shading on the ends indicates that values may exist well outside this range. A question mark indicates that the conclusions are somewhat speculative.

(d) to determine, in the failing/undefended market segments (for example, suburban off-peak services serving largely social recreational journeys), the extent and value of the public service obligation which the scheduled bus service currently provides, so as to set a limit on the size of subsidy. Thereafter, within the limits for each service a social "contract" should be negotiated and agreement reached with that operator (public or private) who can offer the best service for the resources available. In my view, there is enormous scope in co-ordinating the "informal" voluntary sector, which provides a host of different transport services (ambulances, minibuses, shared-taxis, etc.) in suburban areas.

(e) to concentrate public investment in urban transport on projects which either enhance productivity (automatic fare-collection (AFC), passenger information systems, route-control and vehicle-detection, etc.) or promote the image of public transport (new Metros, purpose-designed interchanges, etc.).

(f) to discriminate heavily and consistently in favour of public transport in central areas (bus-only streets, linking traffic "cells", extensive traffic restraint measures coupled with area-wide pedestrianization, progressive restrictions on private non-residential parking, etc.).

(g) to experiment in larger cities with an "intermediate" (shared-hire) taxi system which could operate on a two-tier tariff. In periods of slack demand, it would operate as a normal taxi at a high tariff (on exclusive hire), whereas, at other times and according to demand, it would operate at a lower tariff on a "hail-a-ride" (or shared-hire) basis, with other passengers being picked up and set down at intermediate destinations, according to the route displayed on the vehicle for that trip.

Although this is an intriguing idea in principle, experience suggests that it could well founder in practice on the reaction of either taxi interests or public transport workers or both. Perhaps, if the Unions, the taxi companies and the PTEs could work out a joint system that offered scope overall for additional employment there would be some hope for its success.

In conclusion, one must acknowledge that many of these ideas have been tried out in small ways already by operators of public transport in many parts of the world. Mostly, being in wealthier countries than ours, they have failed in the end to survive the twin onslaughts of "saturation" car ownership and low-density suburbanization. The notable exceptions (one or two American cities, most Scandinavian and some West German cities) are those where these innovations have been most ruthlessly deployed during the crucial years. From the preceding review of the prospects for public transport in Britain, it would seem that the crucial years are very near at hand, and so too to a large extent for the future of our city centres.

The answer to the question, "Does urban public transport have a future?" depends, therefore, on whether we as a community see any value in retaining it. As things stand, we seem unable to halt its decline which is rooted in its inherent inability to compete with private transport. Unless and until we can reshape our urban transport policies to take account of this reality, we could witness the disappearance of urban bus transport before the year 2000 A.D.

REFERENCES

Bly, P. and Webster, F. V. (1980). "Changing the Cost of Travel". Paper D35. World Conference on Transport Research, London.

Buchanan, C. B. *et al.* (1963). "Traffic in Towns". HMSO, London.

Greater London Transportation Study (1973). GLC, London.

Gwilliam, K. M. and Banister, D. (1977). *Transportation* **6** (4), 345-363.

Hedges, B. and Hopkin, J. M. (1981). "Transport and the Search for Work: a Study in Greater Manchester". Supplementary Report 639. Transport and Road Research Laboratory, Crowthorne.

Hensher, D. A. and Stopher, P. R. (1979). "Behavioural Travel Modelling". Croom Helm, London.

Hills, P. J. (1974). *In* "Urban Planning Problems" (G. Cherry, ed.), pp.154-184. Leonard Hill, London.

Independent Comission on Transport (1974). "Changing Directions". Coronet Books, London.

Jones, S. R. and Tanner, J. C. (1979). "Car-ownership and Public-Transport". Supplementary Report 464. Transport and Road Research Laboratory, Crowthorne.

Mogridge, M. J. H. (1980). "Analyse des Caracteristiques des Placements et de Leur Relation à la Structure Urbaine: Une Comparaison entre Paris et Londres". L'Institut de Recherche des Transport, Arcueil Cedex.

O'Cinneide, D. (1980). "The Use of Telecommunications to Save Energy". Paper to UTSG Conference, University of Newcastle upon Tyne.

Oldfield, R. H., Bly, P. H. and Webster, F. V. (1981). "Predicting the Use of Stage-Service Buses in Great Britain". Report LR 1000. Transport and Road Research Laboratory, Crowthorne.

Smeed Committee (1964). "Road Pricing: the Economic and Technical Possibilities". HMSO, London.

Stockholm Area Transportation Study (1971). TU 71 Survey, Stockholm City Council.

Transport (1981). Editorial Vol. 2, no. 4, July/August, p.3.

TRRL (1980). "The Demand for Public Transport". Report of International Collaborative Study. Transport and Road Research Laboratory, Crowthorne.

WAES Report (1978). World Alternative Energy Sources, UNO.

Wagon, D. (1978). "London's Changing Transport Markets (1972-84)". LTE Planning Research Office (unpublished).

Warburton, S. (1981). "Needs and Provisions of Rural Public Transport". Transport Operations Research Group, Research Report (forthcoming), University of Newcastle upon Tyne.

Webster, F. V. (1977). "Urban Passenger-Transport: Some Trends and Prospects". Report LR 771. Transport and Road Research Laboratory, Crowthorne.

Wytconsult, P. (1977). Reports on transportation studies for West Yorkshire, W. Yorks Metropolitan County Council, Wakefield.

PART THREE

Case studies

ELEVEN

Commercial pressures in central Paris

M. BATEMAN and D. BURTENSHAW

Paris n'est pas une ville, c'est le monde—Francois I.

There is little evidence to suggest that there has been any fundamental change of attitude towards the Paris of the twentieth century from that of the sixteenth. The centre of a highly centralized state, it has had many pressures brought to bear upon it and its urban fabric. Commercial, political and administrative pressures combine to affect the development of the centre of the city, perhaps more so than in any other city in Western Europe. In this brief study of central Paris, many of these pressures are discussed together with the reasons for their existence and their effects. A detailed case study of the development of one central site is presented as an example of the manner in which the various pressures are exerted. Finally, an attempt is made to look to the future pressures in the centre of the city, although recent political change combined with economic uncertainty makes such prediction difficult.

Central Paris has been changing rapidly during the past 20 years. Functional change has been particularly apparent as the employment structure has become increasingly dominated by the tertiary and quaternary sectors. In contrast, more traditional functions, particularly those of small-scale artisan industry have declined, in some cases in a quite dramatic fashion. A further change has been that of a declining residential population, threatening to rob Paris of its one quality so envied by other world cities, that of a vibrant, cosmopolitan, living core with a varied residential population and its associated services, rather than a dead commercial heart dominated by offices used for a small part of the day. The city is the centre of one of the most centralized states in Europe and this role has required that certain functions, particularly offices, grow not only to maintain this national pre-eminence but also to establish and maintain a growing international position. These changes have been reflected in commercial pressures, seeking to satisfy the demands for space and for new functions, whilst endeavouring to replace the buildings in less than optimum use with new ones which will be more profitable, and this inevitably means growth in the office sector.

The example of Paris demonstrates how these commercial pressures, themselves the magnification of the same pressures felt in many smaller cities, have arisen and

THE FUTURE FOR THE CITY CENTRE
ISBN 0 12 206240 X

how they have been channelled in the plans for the centre. It is possible that lessons can be learnt from the experience of Paris to be applied not only in the handful of comparable world cities, but also in cities of more modest proportions which have encountered the same type of problems but on a diminished scale.

Central Paris, for the purpose of this discussion, is the twenty arrondissements of the *Ville de Paris*, and this discussion concerns the development and planning of this part of Paris. Paris *intra-muros* is a term which refers to its historic morphology, although it is best defined today as being encompassed by the Boulevard Périphérique. It is a separate *département* with its own *Schéma Directeur* which was approved in 1977. The planning of Paris is complicated by the fact that it is an integral part of a region, *la Région de L'Ile de France*, which covers the entire metropolitan area, including the five new towns. It too has its own *Schéma Directeur* which was originally published in 1965 and last modified in 1980. Until recently Paris was directly under the authority of a Prefect and through him to the Prime Minister, with the city council being unable to play an effective role (Castells, 1977). However, since the reform of the local government structure, the newly created Mayor of Paris has become a major political force, often in conflict with the national political will in the person of the President, with reference to planning issues. There are, therefore, a number of stages and a number of different actors and any understanding of planning pressures and conflicts in the city is dependent on appreciating the multiple levels of involvement and intervention.

THE FUNCTIONAL CHARACTER OF CENTRAL PARIS

Central Paris has long been considered to be divided into an eastern part dominated by industry and lower income housing, *Paris populaire*, and a western part containing the main business and commercial quarters together with the diplomatic quarter and high-income residential areas. Although this is something of an over-generalization, it none the less serves as a general background against which to consider commercial pressures. A major concern has been the increasing westward movement of the major commercial heart of the city and of its more wealthy residents. Meanwhile, the east has often been transformed by large-scale redevelopment such as that at Belleville, displacing industry and low-income residents in order to provide middle-class housing (Burtenshaw *et al.*, 1981).

As Fig. 39 shows, the essential functions of commerce and administration occupy distinct zones in the centre. The 8th and 9th arrondissements traditionally housed the business quarter, whilst central government administration and diplomatic activities were to be found mainly in the 7th arrondissement, which has changed less in character, and in parts of the 16th. Recent developments, however, have changed the location of the business quarter somewhat, with its expansion westwards to neighbouring parts of the 16th and 17th arrondissements, especially the Avenue de la Grand Armée towards Porte Maillot. Other business foci such as the 15th centering on Montparnasse are now well established. Retailing is somewhat more

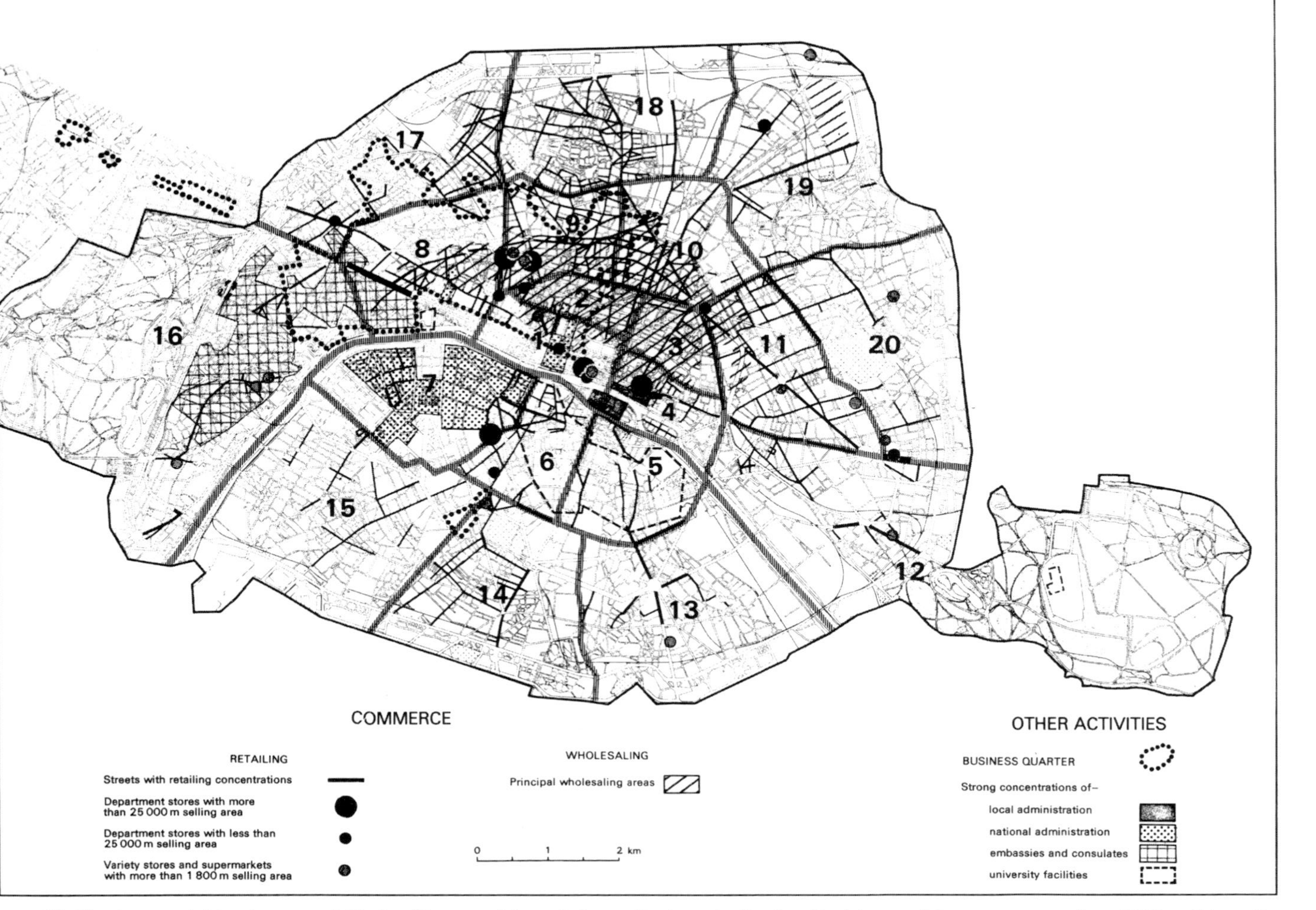

Figure 39. Tertiary activities in central Paris. (Source: Adapted from *Paris et la Region Parisienne, Atlas pour tous, sheet XIV, editions Berger Leurault, Paris,* 1972.)

dispersed and takes the form of more linear concentrations (as shown in Fig. 39), with popular retailing in Boulevard Haussmann closely intermingled with the cores of the business quarter. Other areas are more physically separate, such as the Rue de Rivoli and the fashionable tourist retailing zones of Champs Elysées or the more exclusive Rue Faubourg St. Honoré and Avenue George V. Elsewhere in the city are to be found distinctive zones such as the *Quartier Latin*, with its educational specialization together with publishing activities often associated with university quarters, whilst closer to the river it becomes part of the by now well recognized central tourist district of the city. Intermingled with these uses are some of the world's major tourist attractions, each of which increases pressure on the surrounding area for coach parking, cafes and souvenir shops.

RECENT CHANGES IN CENTRAL PARIS

Certain changes have taken place which have brought new pressures to the city. A change regarded with particular concern has been the fall in the residential population of Paris. Between 1954 and 1975, Paris lost nearly 20 per cent of its population, falling from 2·85 million to 2·3 million, which was approximately the level of the population in the city in 1886. Population loss has been a continuing phenomenon and is part of a more general demographic adjustment in the wider Paris region which has produced an outward movement of population. Simply then, Paris had a smaller share (23·3 per cent) of the regional population of 9 885 000 in 1975 than it had in 1954 when its share was 38·9 per cent of 7 317 000 (APUR, 1980). Whilst the precise nature of this change need not concern us unduly here, it should be noted that the population has been ageing, becoming more middle-class and, critically, its regional redistribution has led to a considerable increase in the intensity of the journey-to-work problem focused on central Paris.

Two major aspects of the redistribution of the middle-class population that need concern us here have repercussions in terms of planning problems. First, there has been a steady gentrification of areas such as Ile St. Louis and the Marais aided by building renovation policies which are seen by Castells (1977) as tools of a middle-class reconquest of the city. Secondly, the middle-class dominance in the west of the city has been strengthened both by internal movement and by the immigration of a large, international, middle-class labour force seeking desirable addresses during their tour of duty in Paris.

At first sight, it would appear that employment has changed little, thus suggesting the journey-to-work problem has not increased greatly. Certainly the absolute number of persons employed has changed little and has indeed stabilized at around the two million mark. Indeed, there was a slight fall of 4 per cent between 1954 and 1975. The development of the wider region of the Ile de France, including its new town and suburban growth centres, has ensured that whilst 55 per cent of the jobs in the region were in Paris in 1954, by 1975 this figure had dropped to 41 per cent. But these figures conceal some very significant changes which have ushered in new commercial pressures. First, demographic changes have meant that the number of non-active residents has increased, leading to an increase in job ratios (i.e. number of jobs/employed resident) from 1·32 in 1962, to 1·47 in 1968 and to 1·59 by 1975. Secondly, and more fundamentally, the economy of Paris has been restructured to produce an employment balance which is far less varied than before and which is heavily dependent on the tertiary sector. Industrial jobs have been lost at a rapid rate, in much the same way as inner city jobs have been lost in Britain (see Dennis, 1978). The loss in Paris was 12 000 per annum between 1968 and 1975. Some examples serve to illustrate this decline. Metal-working with 120 000 employees in 1975 suffered a loss of 21 per cent of its workers between 1968 and 1975. The clothing industry, which was still well represented with 50 000 employees in 1975, lost 18 per cent in the same period. The economic situation and technological innovations meant that printing and publishing lost 22 per cent of its jobs in this period, leaving 7500 employed in 1975 (APUR, 1980). This list is not exhaustive and indeed many more traditional Parisian industries have declined. It has meant that a city which was multi-functional previously has become more and more mono-functional, losing in the process much of its unique atmosphere and character.

The counterbalance has been provided by growth in the service sector with some 29 per cent of the employment in Paris being in the public sector, a figure in excess of 500 000 with a growth rate of 19 per cent in the period 1968–1975. On the whole, the rate of growth is showing signs of slowing down. The growth in the tertiary salaried sector in the Ile de France region was 2·53 per cent per annum between 1968 and 1975 compared with 2·89 per cent in France as a whole and this had declined to 1·83 per cent between 1975 and 1978 compared with 2·3 per cent in France. In 1979 the growth in tertiary employment in the Ile de France was 1·1 per cent compared with a national growth of 2·5 per cent. As in other major European centres such as Brussels and Frankfurt, the financial institutions were among the strongest growth areas in the 1960s and 1970s, with 5 per cent growth in employment in these sectors in Paris between 1962 and 1968 and a massive 29 per cent increase between 1968 and 1975. This growth has been especially strong in the banking sector which by 1975 employed 115 000 workers. On the other hand, insurance has shown a great predisposition to move out to new regional locations such as new towns, which is reflected in somewhat lower growth figures in Paris itself. These trends have particularly affected the 9th arrondissement, still a major office area in spite of the loss of relocating insurance companies, and the 8th arrondissement, where the growth in banking at the expense of general commerce has been especially strong.

What has been most notable in recent years has been the growth of the quaternary sector. In 1979 alone there were 9000 extra jobs in this sector. Quaternary employment has concentrated in areas of relatively low office rents, especially the 12th and 13th arrondissements. Another employment trend that complements those already noted is that while male employment in the Ile de France is falling slightly (a decrease of 0·76 per cent in 1979), female employment is rising slowly (an increase of 0·6 per cent in 1979).

Functional change has been highly significant in the past 15 years. Tertiary employment which accounted for 50 per cent of all jobs in the Ile de France in 1968 had taken a 64 per cent share of jobs in 1978, whilst in the centre of Paris the tertiary sector took 78 per cent of all employment. It is never easy to decide whether the provision of offices provoked functional change or vice versa, but it is fair to assume that once the ball began rolling then the demand for new office space was a strong one which property interests did not endeavour to stop.

The growth in office building activity was dramatic in the 1960s and 1970s, bringing a degree of control by the mid-1970s. Thus a total of 1·7 million m^2 of office space was covered by construction permits during the period 1969–1974, but the annual amount rose from 325 000 m^2 in 1969 to a peak of 482 000 m^2 in 1971 and then declined, so that by 1976 the permits granted covered only 37 000 m^2. The major office schemes which were constructed between 1971 and 1977 are shown in Fig 40. It will be seen that pressure for office development has been especially strong in the 8th arrondissement and its immediate environs, notably the Avenue de la Grand Armée, and beyond the ville towards the La Défense office complex in Nanterre. Between 1962 and 1972, 365 000 m^2 of offices were constructed in the 8th arrondissement, 385 000 m^2 in the 15th including Montparnasse, 271 000 m^2 in the 13th including the Italie sector, and finally 217 000 m^2 in the 12th including the Ilots de Rapée-Gare de Lyon development. But further pressures exist for more office space despite controls and the downturn in demand which came with economic recession.

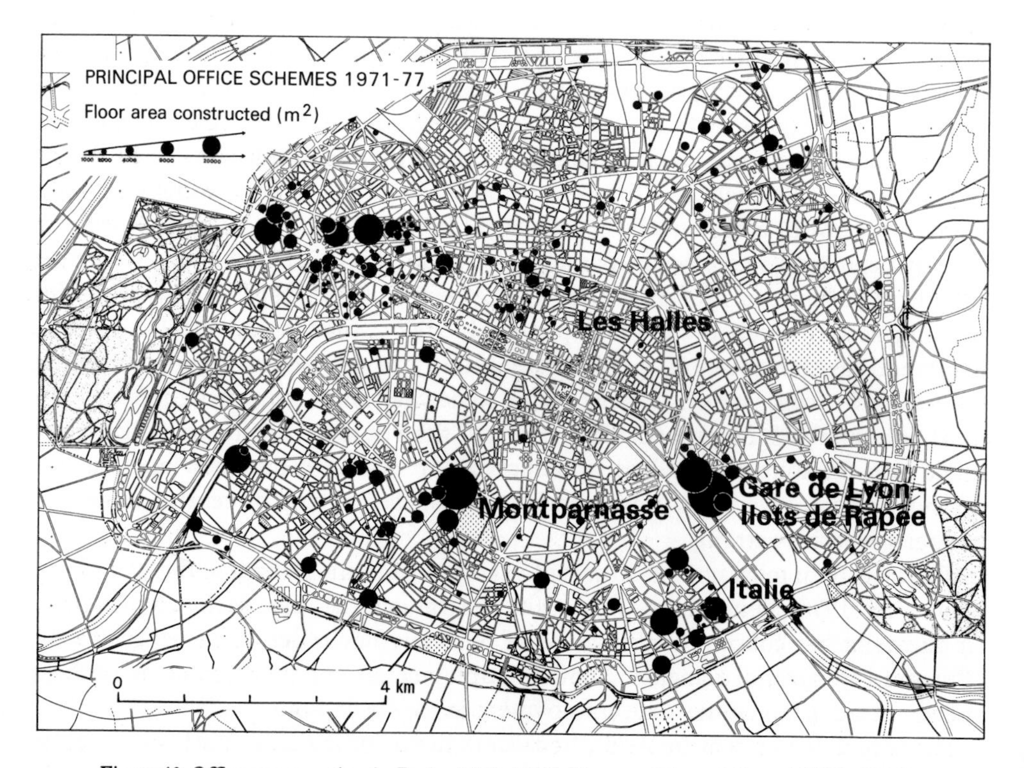

Figure 40. Office construction in Paris, 1971-1977. (Source: Adapted from APUR, 1980).

There are only 13 m^2 of office floor space per employee in Paris, compared to figures of 18 in London and 20 in New York. There is a reasonable expectation therefore that, even if there were to be no demand to house an increase in the number of office workers, the demand is present to replace existing offices with more modern and spacious premises.

Much of this pressure comes from Paris' role as an international centre which is a constant political pressure that was confirmed by a report published in 1973 (Documentation Française, 1973). The proposals were to make the city what was termed "geocentric" by the year 2000. To do this, improvements in the infrastructure for marketing, information and financial planning were proposed, together with promoting the city as a centre for multinational organizations linked both to the Third World and the Eastern Bloc. At the same time, it was proposed to improve the legal, educational and health infrastructure to cater for the demands of the international quality labour market. Paris' role as a seed-bed or nursery for new ideas in all fields was also stressed. Already the computerized telephone system has improved international telecommunications, so that Paris is a more attractive location than other world cities for companies who value efficient telecommunications.

The objectives of the 1977 *Schéma Directeur d'Aménagement et d'Urbanisme de la Ville de Paris (SDAU)* firmly recognized the problems implicit in this growing tertiary dominance of central Paris (APUR, 1980). Amongst them were the stated aims to defend the residential function of Paris, to limit employment growth and to combat the increasing structural imbalance, whilst at the same time preventing a too marked geographical split between the various functions of the city. The question of controlling tertiary employment in the centre is a vexed one, for whilst it is generally agreed that a policy of deconcentration from the centre to the periphery is desirable, not least because of its assistance to the public transport system, Paris needs to retain its status. It is this element, the quality of the city, which permeates many problems of the city centre; there is no desire to decant the headquarters of international companies. There is a feeling that planning should reflect Paris as the head of a major state, and it manifests itself in widespread interest in areas such as the Les Halles site when they become available. Thus, in the case of tertiary employment, the role of Paris as a financial and economic centre, much cherished by the former President Giscard d'Estaing since his position as Minister of Finance, must be preserved. There is, therefore, no question of a standstill in office development. Indeed, it is recognized that modernization is essential and, in most cases, a moderate growth is foreseen. Essentially the increasing obsolescence of offices in central Paris means that new offices have to be provided to replace old and inadequate premises, although as Fig. 41 shows, in the most congested area a policy is now being pursued to allow modernization without an increase in employment. At the same time and in keeping with the stated objectives summarized above, offices are now allowed to take the place of residential functions anywhere in Paris and so further promote the demographic decline of the centre.

The way in which this demand is to be met in the future is to establish new poles of office concentration, particularly in the eastern part of the centre and at certain principal transport interchanges. Thus new office centres have emerged and will be strengthened in the Seine Sud-Est sector, including the station areas of Gare de Lyon and Gare d'Austerlitz. A further area of growth has occurred at the junction of the eastern autoroute from Charles de Gaulle Airport with the Boulevard Périphérique just outside the *ville.* This policy will also help to reduce the geographical segregation of functions in terms of the increasing east-west division of the centre. In establishing such new growth poles, it has been necessary to overcome the traditional image of the eastern part of the city, although rent levels still reflect the differentiation between the fashionable west and the less popular east.

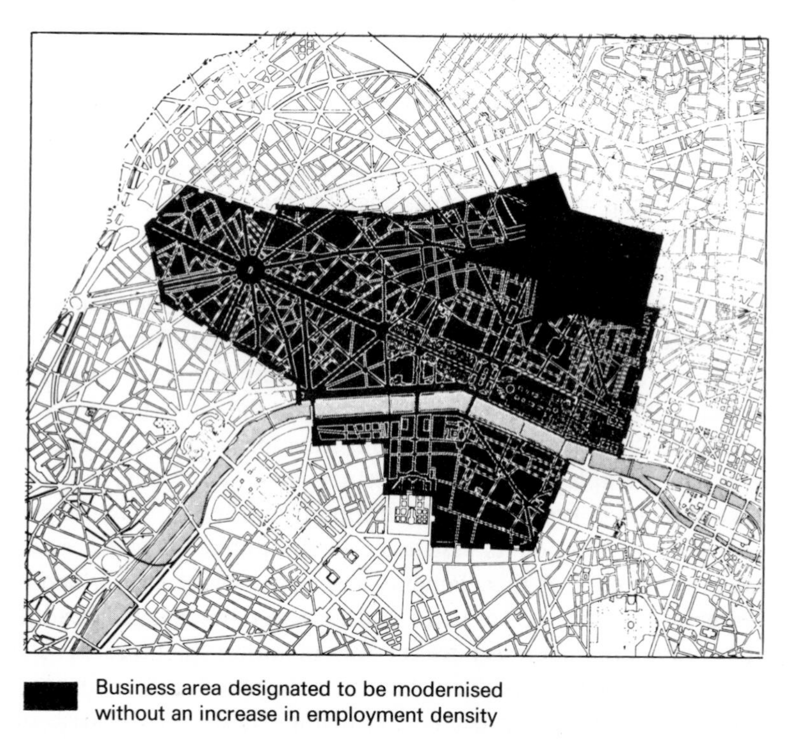

Figure 41. Office-building policy in the principal business quarter of central Paris. (Source: APUR, 1980.)

In the retailing field, central Paris presents a problematical case. There have been a number of new developments in the last ten years which have taken the form of covered shopping malls of various types, but the lead in retailing innovations has been taken very much in the suburbs rather than the centre. The creation of some ten regional shopping centres in suburban locations have taken chain and department store retailing out to the previously impoverished suburbs on a scale unparallelled in Western Europe. Yet far from attempting to counter or respond to this, the retailing of central Paris has remained traditional with no real attempts at pedestrianizing shopping areas to create a more attractive environment. The only large-scale pedestrianization schemes are in the traditional tourist area of the Latin Quarter and the emerging tourist area of Beaubourg-Les Halles. Meanwhile the traditional retailing areas remain much as they have been for the past 20 years. It is arguable that the lack of a strong core of retailing giants, willing to push for innovation or experimentation in the centre could explain this. Indeed, the recent financial predicament of some stores such as Le Printemps, somewhat embarrassed in the suburbs with its over-commitment to the new shopping centres resulting in its withdrawal from Créteil, may dictate a policy of caution rather than innovation. Even the latest centre which opened at La Défense in 1981 had problems arising from a reluctance on the part of some major stores to commit themselves to commence trading at an earlier date.

However, when the new sites have become available in central Paris, a degree of experimentation has taken place and retailers, though not the French department stores, have not been slow to move in. The first example was that at Maine-Montparnasse where a retailing complex forms the base for the controversial tower block of offices outside the station. More recently in 1979, the Forum, with 40 000 m^2 of retail floor space, was opened at the Les Halles site. This, however, has formed the focus for debate about what type of retailing is needed in central Paris; whether one should be catering for the rich Parisian or the diminishing local population. On a larger scale, the remainder of the Les Halles site became the focus of heated debate as to its best use. It is worth looking more closely at this example, because it illustrates the commercial and political pressures which can be brought to bear in a major city when a prestige city-centre site becomes available for development.

LES HALLES

It was decided as early as 1960 to move the wholesale marketing function from its congested site in the centre of Paris to a more accessible location to the south at Rungis, on the A6 leading to Orly Airport. This decision marked the end of a trading function on this site which had its origins at the end of the twelfth century. Whilst it could be agreed that by comparison 20 years is no great period of time in which to make a decision on the future of the site, the political disputes which have characterized the debate on its future illustrate many of the problems of planning in a prestigious city-centre site (see Tuppen, 1981).

Whilst the origins of the market may indeed be traced back several centuries, it was the market hall buildings of the nineteenth century which were to be the focus, and perhaps the symbol, of more recent protests over the fate of Les Halles. The great wrought-iron pavilions, designed by Baltard, had been commissioned by Haussmann who himself did so much to re-shape Paris during the mid-nineteenth century. Six pavilions were built between 1854 and 1858, inspired by the architecture of the Gare de l'Est. The remaining pavilions followed later in the nineteenth century, with the last two not completed until 1936. The decision to remove the wholesale marketing function produced a number of key questions to be answered. What was to take the place of the wholesale marketing function on this key site? What was to become of the Baltard pavilions? How was the entire quarter, so intricately tied to the market and its richness of life, to be revitalized once the market had departed? (See Zetter, 1975, for a full analysis of the early debate surrounding the redevelopment of the Les Halles site.)

An early attempt was made to answer some of these questions when in 1963 the *Société d'Études d'Aménagement des Halles (SEAH)* was established. It was charged with carrying out a comprehensive study of the quarter, shown in Fig. 42, including its demographic and social structure, its architecture and its financial structure. Four years later, in 1967, a zone of 35 hectares was designated as the area of redevelopment for Les Halles. This was actually a much larger area than that occupied purely by the former market. In the same year it was decided that a new project should include between 800 000 and 900000 m^2 of new floor space, together with a diversity of functions, and this brief was given to six architects whose designs were eventually produced for public debate. But in 1968 the local authority, the *Conseil de Paris*, refused to make a choice between the six architectural schemes, preferring to debate again the broad planning objectives rather than the architectural details of a specific scheme. Thus a new body, a permanent commission for the Les Halles sector, was created and the *Atelier Parisien d'Urbanisme (APUR)*, the planning authority for the *Ville de Paris*, was charged with producing planning studies. The overall programme was changed to lessen the floor space in order to reduce the amount devoted to offices to make maximum use of the underground area and to conserve the architectural heritage of the locality. This new move was taken largely to assuage press and public criticism of the various projects put forward by the original six architects. The public wanted to preserve much of the old quarter, whilst the planners were pointing to the appalling conditions existing behind the historical façades; 40 per cent of the apartments had only one room, 30 per cent were overcrowded and 32 per cent lacked running water.

Plainly a new approach was required if the plan was to gain public acceptance. In December 1968, *l'APUR* was charged with producing a plan which was approved by the *Conseil de Paris* in July 1969. So, at this stage, when the wholesale markets were actually moved in March 1969, a plan existed based on a number of key elements. These were the building of a métro interchange, including the new express métro (the *RER*), and the new suburban line to Sceaux; a public library of some status; an international centre of commerce; hotels; mixed housing; commercial, sporting, cultural and social activities, and some open space. The use of underground areas was seen as vital if the surface was to be kept free of high density development. Finally, and critically for the success of the scheme, the creation of a Forum with the métro interchange at its core was an integral part of the planning of the Les Halles site—a place of interchange and meeting parallelling the forum of ancient Rome. In December 1969, the *Société Anonyme d'Economie mixte d'Aménagement de Rénovation et de Restauration du Secteur des Halles (SEMAH)* was created. Finally, in what had been an eventful year, President Pompidou decided on the construction of the "Museum of the 20th Century" on the Plateau Beauborg rather than in the parkland at Nanterre. At least that part of the project was to

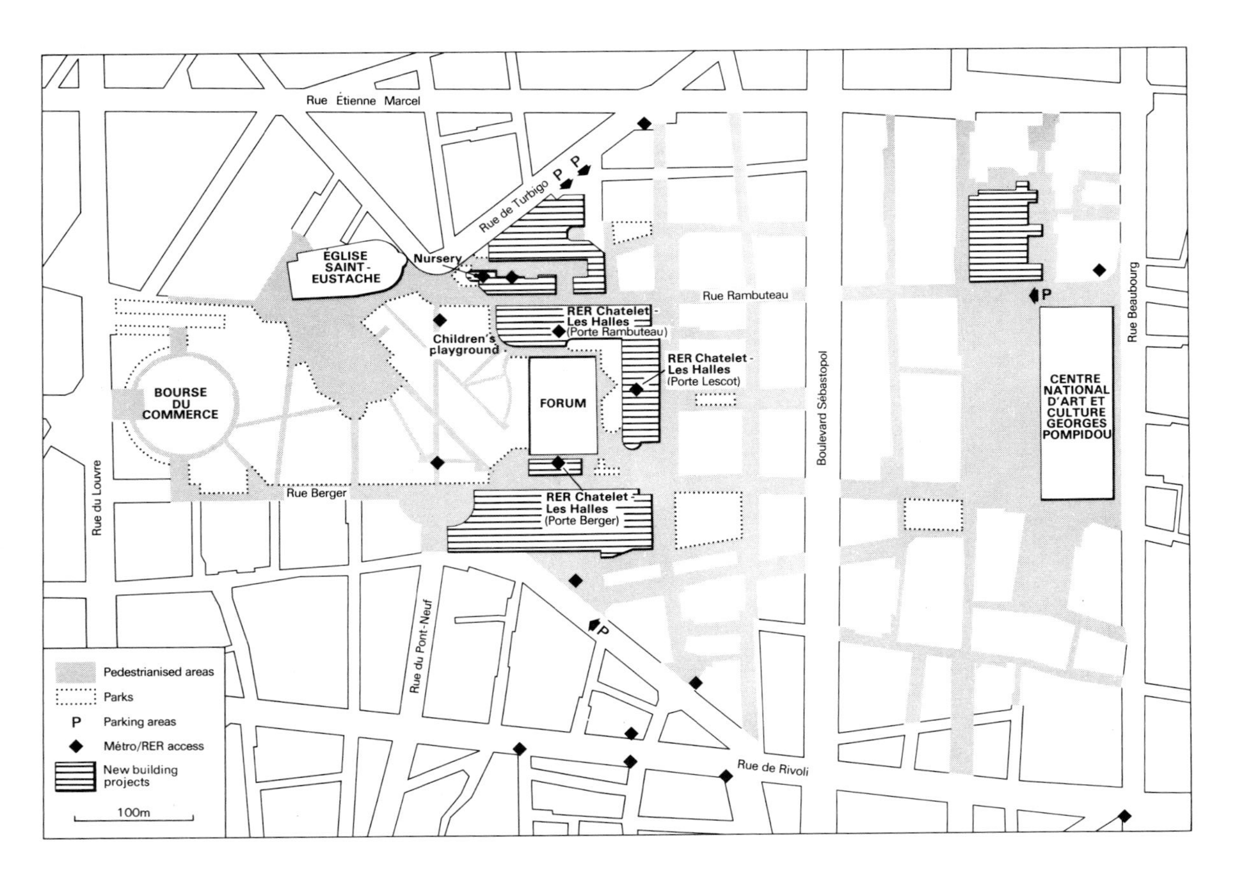

Figure 42. Les Halles—site plan and proposed developments. (Source: SEMAH, 1980.)

proceed according to plan, albeit to a controversial design produced by Piano and Rogers (*SEMAH*, 1980).

By August 1973, *Le Monde* was able to look forward to the commencement of the *Centre Francais de Commerce International (CFCI)*, a development of 93 000 m^2 carefully designed to be part above and part below ground, with landscaped gardens, all with the aim of preserving a sympathetic setting for the church of St. Eustache, which dominates the north-west sector of the site. Work indeed proceeded until one year later when President Giscard d'Estaing decided that the scheme should be abandoned and the area devoted to an extension of the planned open space. The decision was generally welcomed by the French press and public, neither of which was anxious to see the creation of more offices in central Paris, especially on such a prestige site. But the decision obviously led to financial problems for the project as a whole, because the promoters of the scheme had to be compensated. Inevitably the decision led to a reappraisal of the project, leading to the retention of three architects in late 1974 to produce schemes for the site. Amongst these were the controversial Catalan architect, Ricardo Bofil, whose work is now well represented in the Paris region in the new towns of St. Quentin-en-Yvelines and Marne-la-Vallée. The projects of only two of the three were progressed and in April 1975 yet another architect, Emile Ailland, was retained to co-ordinate their work. By November, having made little progress, he resigned. In his place a college of architects, four in all, including Bofil, was constituted and their plans presented in 1976. But it was increasingly plain that there were irrevocable differences between the views of the French public and its elected representatives, the President and the management group, *SEMAH*. The first had always wanted the use of traditional materials and design in any new building and was, in that sense, preservationist in outlook. President Giscard d'Estaing was thought to have more classical tastes, whilst the president of *SEMAH* was talking of an "*architecture de notre temps*". Some progress took place in 1977 with the opening of the *Centre National d'Art et du Culture Georges Pompidou* and the opening of the Châtelet-les Halles métro/*RER* interchange, the latter directly beneath the disputed site. But 1978 saw yet more delays and disputes. First, in August the Minister of State for Culture withdrew his support for an auditorium in one of the projected buildings, which led to a presidential comment that the planning of the site was the responsibility of the city, whilst the state was interested only in the creation of the open space element of the plan, because it had a financial stake in that aspect of it. Then, almost incredibly, the mayor of Paris, M. Jacques Chirac, rejected the design of Bofil for a large building on the northern edge of the site, calling for a building more in keeping with the environment. Once again, the building had actually begun and on this occasion the actual structure had begun to emerge. The final design for the scheme was given approval in 1980 and is shown in Fig. 42. By that time the Forum was open, with 40 000 m^2 of retailing space and 16 000 m^2 of circulation space (*SEMAH*, 1980).

The Forum is a three-level covered shopping centre below ground level but focusing on a sunken square "*La Cratère*". Three-quarters of the retail outlets face on to the covered galleries surrounding the square and receive natural light through the vast windows. Functions have been segregated within the scheme so that clothing and fashion outlets occupy the upper level, furnishing and household goods the second level, and cinemas and restaurants on the lowest level. The warm, centrally-heated centre has attracted a full complement of shops which cater very much for middle-class and tourist tastes. The chic clientèle contrast rather markedly with the semi-permanent population of down-and-outs and the young who have taken advantage of the warmth and the need for the galleries to remain open to provide access to the métro.

The completed Forum and transport interchange also contain 1750 parking places and associated access roads. More car parking places will be provided in the western half of the Les Halles site towards the Bourse. This as yet incomplete section will comprise 40 000 m^2 of public cultural and recreation space, including a swimming pool and gymnasium and 18 000 m^2 of facilities for the Post and Telecommunication Services all lying beneath a 5-hectare area of gardens. Around the gardens 220 *HLM* (social housing) apartments and some offices are being built together with a 240-room hotel.

The eastern half of the scheme beyond Boulevard Sebastopol around the Pompidou Centre has settled into its new role as a centre for cultural life. Street theatre abounds in the square and the seventeenth- and eighteenth-century buildings have been extensively restored to include some *HLM* apartments. The network of 1·7 km of pedestrianized streets is no longer the preserve of the old market cafés, but the ideal site for smart restaurants, fashionable antique shops, art galleries and tourist souvenir emporia. Despite the *HLM* housing, the forecast of increasing urban reconquest of central Paris by the middle-classes aided by state power, made by Castells, are still basically correct. For Castells, Les Halles is a reflection of the values of advanced capitalism within France, striving to make the city the business and economic centre of Europe aided by state power (Castells, 1977).

A number of lessons can be learnt from the experiences of the Les Halles site and its troubled history. Certainly the difficulty of reconciling interests from central government, local government, commerce and the general public is clearly demonstrated. It could be contended that these pressures are not to be found elsewhere, but even in a scaled down form, the Les Halles case points to the need to define responsibility clearly and to have full consultation at an early stage with all parties involved in the planning process. Perhaps it could also be suggested that a very careful appraisal is made of what is of value in a site due for redevelopment, because there are many who even now feel that the Forum with its twentieth-century glass, steel and plastic, can never be compared to the grandeur of the vanished pavilions of Baltard. The comparison with the reawakening of London's Covent Garden after its brief period of transformation is inescapable, because that too was a controversial area for renewal (see, for instance, Christie, 1974). Twenty years of indecision or, worse still, changed decisions demonstrates the intensity of pressures which are brought to bear in major cities such as Paris over key sites such as Les Halles.

The Les Halles controversies also bring into profile the relationship between planner and politician in France. In endeavouring to look forward it seems unlikely that the relationship is likely to change although the 1981 Presidential and General elections, ushering in a government further left than any in France since the Revolution, make predictions hazardous. Pompidou, as president, took the Gaullist path of creating a capital for France with a taste for the monumental. The Centre Georges Pompidou is an appropriate edifice by which to remember his policy, but there were others such as the right-bank expressway, destroying for many the bank of the Seine as a place along which to walk, and the 56 storeys of the Tour Maine-Montparnasse, destroying the intimacy of a formerly harmonious *quartier*. Giscard d'Estaing changed direction by modifying many of the schemes designed prior to his term of office. It was promised that there would be no more point blocks like the Tour Maine-Montparnasse, the massive redevelopment of the Italie sector in the 13th arrondissement was moderated somewhat and plans for a left bank expressway were abandoned. It would be reasonable to assume that the Mitterrand succession will not permit major business interests to call the tune to the extent of despoiling central Paris. Indeed, it is possible that certain policies will be much changed, such as those associated with residential renovation resulting in expulsion of tenants in favour of a middle-class, higher-income population. This disregard for the workers in Paris has led to much of the demographic imbalance outlined earlier and has been seen as a form of exploitation by many writers, notably Castells.

THE FUTURE OF THE CENTRE OF PARIS

It may be that Paris, along with the major cities, will feel an increase in demand for office space at the centre, as international commerce and finance, and international administration increase. It is certainly the type of function that a Frenchman of any political persuasion is unlikely to reject. The growth of the multinational companies and their activities has required offices, so too have the banks in the international finance sector. London, for instance, as the international banking centre of the world, now has offices of 366 foreign banks compared to 73 two decades ago. If this pressure is extended, and as the recession comes to an end, it would be unrealistic to tell a major international company to develop its French or European headquarters in a new town in the suburbs, because the company will probably defect completely to an alternative European city. Thus, despite the policy of deconcentration, there will be a continuing demand for offices at the centre which will have to be met. The only consolation which Paris has in this respect is La Défense, which has attained sufficient status to attract offices from the centre of the city. Once this is complete however, in the mid-1980s, with over 1·5 million m^2 of offices, it is inconceivable that another project of that scale will ever be attempted, either in Paris or any other European city.

In terms of its future, it is reasonable to expect a cautious, reasoned approach. French consumerism of the post-war period may well be tempered by a greater concern with social welfare goals which will be reflected in planning decisions. What is as yet uncertain is the manner and speed of any such change and the way in which it will be manifested in the city centre. One is left with the distinct impression, however, that the slogan adopted by Castells and others, "*le bulldozer ne passera pas*", may be a more realistic prediction during the next 20 years than it was 20 years ago.

REFERENCES

APUR (1980). "Schéma Directeur d'Aménagement et d'Urbanisme de la Ville de Paris". *Paris Project* Numero 19-20, l'Atelier Parisin d'Urbanisme.

Burtenshaw, D., Bateman, M. and Ashworth, G. J. A. (1981). "The City in West Europe". Wiley, London.

Castells, M. (1977). "The Urban Question". Arnold, London.

Christie, I. (1974). *Town Plann. Rev.* **45** (1), 31-62.

Dennis, R. (1978). *Urban Stud.* **15**, 63-73.

Documentation Française (1973). "*Paris Ville Internationale: Roles en Vocations*". Travaux et Recherches de Prospectives Paris.

SEMAH (1980). "10 ans d'Activité aux Halles". *SEMAH*, Paris.

Tuppen, J. (1981). *Town Cntry. Plann.* **50** (5), 137-139.

Zetter, R. (1975). *Town Plann. Rev.* **46** (3), 767-794.

TWELVE

"Ideplan 77" for Copenhagen's city centre

O. KERNDAL-HANSEN

Ever since the so-called finger plan for the Copenhagen region was worked out in the late 1940s centre planning in the region has been based on the principle that commercial and public services should be located as close as possible to where people live. With the politically accepted aim of decentralizing services there has been a very extensive build-up of community-level centres in the suburbs during the last 15-20 years. Together with two regional-level centres these community centres account for about 50-60 per cent of all purchases of shopping goods made by the suburban population.

These developments within the metropolitan area have, of course, reduced the relative importance of the central area of Copenhagen as a retail focus. Although there has been a marked decline in the proportion of total turnover accounted for by shops in the city centre from 24 per cent to 13 per cent, the volume of actual turnover has remained fairly steady due to an increase in the metropolitan population and an economic boom that has meant a rise in the general level of consumption. However, a side effect of the economic boom was an increase in operating costs for the shops and, with a stagnating turnover, a number of the bigger stores in the city centre were forced to close down.

For shopping purposes Copenhagen's central area is still the most important centre in the region as will appear from Table 37, which is based on an extensive consumer survey undertaken in 1976. The question is, however, whether the central area will be able to maintain its position as a highly diversified centre of commercial, cultural, social and educational services in the coming years.

The municipality of Copenhagen has formulated a policy for the development of the city centre based mainly on the following goals:

(1) The cental area should be maintained as the main centre for the greater Copenhagen region and as the dominant economic focus for the whole country.
(2) The most specialized central area functions should be intensified and refined.
(3) A considerable number of dwellings must be maintained in the central area.
(4) Any urban renewal projects in the old district (the former medieval town) must respect the special environmental qualities contained therein.

THE FUTURE FOR THE CITY CENTRE
ISBN 0 12 206240 X

TABLE 37
Share of trade captured by Copenhagen's city centre, 1976

Residential areas	Distance from Copenhagen City	Clothing and textiles bought (%)	Other shopping goods bought (%)
Old, densely populated areas	0-4 km	40-60	25
Outer districts of Copenhagen and adjacent suburbs	4-25 km	35-40	20
Most distant suburbs and the outer region	25-45 km	20-30	5

Can these goals be achieved? And if not, what proposals could be made to improve the possibilities for the city centre retaining or even extending its position as a very diversified and sophisticated centre of private and public services? These questions were put to the Institute for Centre-Planning by the Copenhagen City Centre Association. To answer them, the following paragraphs give a brief account of work undertaken in 1975-1977 by the Institute for Centre-Planning that resulted in the formulation of Ideplan 77 for the central area.

REGIONAL TRENDS

The future for Copenhagen's city centre depends to a very great extent on what will happen in the other parts of the metropolitan region which form the catchment area for its services. The first step in the Institute's work, therefore, was to describe the situation for the city centre if the regional trends with regard to population, employment, the service sector and transportation continue. According to the forecasts the stagnation of the *population* in the region is expected to prevail, so it will still be around 1·75 million by 1990. However, the distribution of the population will change. Urban renewal will be one of the main reasons why the population in the densely populated areas close to the city centre will be reduced. On the other hand, the outer region (25-45 km from the city centre) will have 35 per cent of the population in the region in 1990 compared to 24 per cent in 1975.

As mentioned, the *service sector* in the suburbs has been extended considerably in the past 15-20 years. In this period more than 600 000 m^2 of retail space have been built in community and regional centres in the suburbs, i.e. more than the present 550 000 m^2 of retail space in the city centre. This heavy build-up of the suburban capacity in retailing as well as other services has brought about keen competition between the city centre and the suburban centres.

In the regional structure plan a further three regional centres have been proposed. With the present economic outlook it must be very doubtful whether these centres will ever be established. In the next 10–15 years the increase in suburban retail space is expected to be modest and it will mainly take place in rather small community centres in the new suburban areas in the outer region. Even so the previous and future development in the suburban service sector will cause a deterioration of the retail base of the city centre, at least for that part of retail trade that primarily competes with, and only to a small extent supplements, retail trade in the rest of the region.

A third factor that will change conditions within the city centre is the *regional transport network.* The city centre is still that area in the region that has the best accessibility due to most of the major traffic arteries being directed towards it. However, in the regional plan it is implied that major cross traffic routes should be built-up giving a high degree of accessibility from the suburban residential areas to new industrial and commercial areas, which will thereby become alternative nodes of activity to the city centre.

Fourthly the outward shift in *job opportunities* from the central area to other parts of the region has been considerable. From 1960 to 1975 the number of people employed in the city centre fell from 190 000 to 125 000. This trend is expected to continue.

The consequences for the city centre of all these trends could be very grave: the number of visits made to the city centre are likely to continue to fall; turnover in retailing must be expected to decline. The urban decay which is already to be seen in some parts of the central area may become even more widespread as the relocation and closure of firms leads to a reduced interest in renting premises in the city centre. The conclusion must be that to maintain the city centre as the superior centre in the region it will be necessary to promote initiatives that turn the tide of these unfavourable processes.

TRADITIONAL SOLUTIONS

This section is concerned with a discussion as to whether it is possible to change these regional processes by the use of traditional policies such as developing the retail base, creating more jobs or increasing the number of dwellings in the city centre.

Model 1: more retail space in the city centre

The most important preconditions for a model of a retail-oriented city centre are partly a change of profile towards a higher degree of specialization of the existing retail trade, and partly a large extension of the retail space in the city centre. To enlarge substantially the amount of area devoted to retailing in the city centre would mean revoking much development already in progress and would be in conflict with the goal of the regional plan that services should be located as close as possible to where people live. Moreover, the local plans for the old part of the city centre do not allow for the accommodation of new, expensive retailing activities. Building regulations are very restrictive, for example on the size and scale of new buildings; and in many cases preservation clauses for the existing properties prevent the procurement of any larger adjoining areas for retail purposes. Furthermore, because most of the properties have a relatively short frontage, land assembly could pose severe problems.

Consequently any large extension of the retail area must take place in border areas of the city centre and not just within areas adjacent to the existing core but also at some distance from it because of the presence of physical barriers such as parks and big public institutions. Therefore, there are difficulties in connecting any large retail extensions with the established shopping quarter of the city centre. The greatest effect from a new retail development of say 50 000 m^2 implanted into a border area of the city centre will occur where there are high levels of population such as in the inner city. For consumers in the suburbs, the new development would represent only a small increase of the total retail opportunities available in the city centre (approximately 10 per cent of existing floor space) and as the environmental qualities and the functional composition of the new development would be similar to what is offered in suburban centres anyway, the additional attraction presented to these groups would be relatively little. For trade in the city centre itself, however, a new retail development in a border area would mean more intense competition. It is expected that about half of the turnover in a development of 50 000 m^2 would be taken from the existing retailers in the central area. Such a development would also require some considerable investment in traffic management schemes and while there might be improvements in accessibility to the city centre as a whole, the increase in turnover that might result from this would not be enough to outweigh the reduction in trade caused by new development in the border area.

Model 2: more jobs in the city centre

The underlying goal of this model, involving the creation of more jobs in the city centre, is to maintain and even extend the position of the city centre as the most important centre in the region and the dominant economic focus of the whole country. But is it realistic to think that the number of job opportunities can be increased considerably? The existing workforce in the city centre (about 125 000) is estimated by the Institute to account for about 10 per cent of the retail turnover in the central area. To obtain an increase of a further 10 per cent in retail turnover it would therefore be necessary to create another 125 000 new jobs. The main contribution to new employment, however, will come from the office sector. The floor space required to support this would be about 3 million m^2. The consequences with regard to building and traffic of such an increase in floor space are quite enormous. By comparison, the total amount of floor space that exists at present in the city centre is only 2·3 million m^2. What are the possibilities then of carrying through such a model for creating more jobs in the city centre?

First, the number of people employed in the city centre has been decreasing sharply over the last few years. Only the public sector has expanded. Many of the big firms have moved out and more are on their way. Secondly, various analyses show that the locational requirements of many firms (such as for rational premises and room for expansion) are very difficult or impossible to meet in the city centre. Furthermore the location criteria that many people and especially planners thought were essential for big firms seem to have only secondary or very little importance to the managers themselves (such as good accessibility by public transport and face-to-face contact). Thirdly, the regional plan has as one of its goals an improvement in the supply of jobs closer to where people live. Another goal is to seek to promote a geographical concentration of those firms that move to the suburbs. The new employment areas mentioned earlier are planned to absorb a great number of office jobs. A heavy expansion of office premises in the city centre would not therefore be in accordance with the regional plan. Fourthly, it must be emphasized that the building of extensive new office blocks in the city centre would not be politically realistic because of a general wish to maintain the qualities of the existing environment.

Model 3: more dwellings in the city centre

The purpose of this model is to increase considerably the amount of residential accommodation to ensure a strong, local catchment area for the many service functions in the city centre. The new dwellings would be provided by new buildings, by amalgamating existing small flats and by converting floor space now used for other purposes into a residential function.

Within the city centre and its border areas there are at present some 25 000 flats. The goals of the regional plan as regards housing imply a continued improvement in the standard of these flats through an urban renewal programme. It must be expected therefore that some of the existing flats will disappear in the coming years as a consequence of demolition or amalgamation. As regards the establishment of new flats, the possibilities are limited. A maximum of 3000-4000 flats might be constructed but this would be insufficient to make up for the reduction in population that has already taken place in the city centre during the last five years.

For the number of flats to have an appreciable positive effect on the number of visits made to, and the retail turnover generated within, the city centre, such a large number would be required that a very negative effect on the employment resources of the city centre would result. This is because new flats would take away space from employment uses in these already overcrowded buildings. It is estimated by the Institute that purchases in city-centre shops by households living within the central area and its border areas account for about 15 per cent of total turnover. An increase of 10 per cent in total turnover from households, living within the central area and its border area would require an increase in the number of dwellings of some 15 000, or 60 per cent more than exist at present.

Conclusion

It is evident that as a result of prevailing physical, economic and political conditions none of the more traditional policies can be used to effect a radical change in the prospects for the city centre. Nor is it possible to combine some of these policies, for example, by encouraging a limited increase in the number of jobs together with a modest increase in the number of flats, for jobs and flats compete for a small amount of potential floor space that is itself caused by regulations governing the exploitation of land.

Therefore, the conclusion must be that to solve, or even ease, the basic problems that the city centre has experienced in recent years, it is necessary to seek more radical solutions.

THE BASIS FOR A CHANGE IN THE CITY CENTRE

The formulation of a new and radical policy for the development of Copenhagen's city centre must be based on good information which can allow the identification of both the possibilities and the constraints. The Institute has therefore carried out analyses of: the level of rent paid in the city centre; the number, location, and degree of specialization of its service functions; and the behaviour, perceptions, and attitudes of consumers in the whole region in relation to Copenhagen's city centre. The most important results from these analyses are listed below:

(a) The city centre consists of a number of "part-cities" that direct themselves to different groups of users, characterized by, for example, age, income, interests and life-style.
(b) In recent years there has been a refinement of both shops and tourist-oriented functions in the city centre.
(c) The main part of the city centre has become smaller geographically in recent years.
(d) The rent for retail space is high in the main shopping streets although it varies considerably, but on average it is not higher than in the suburban centres. Rent in the side streets is relatively low.
(e) There is an increase in demand for flats in the city centre caused partly by the high environmental qualities of some quarters.
(f) Due to past policies of decentralization in the region the demand for floor space has been limited. There is no great pressure therefore on the city centre and this has led to only a moderate increase in prices for property and in public appraised value compared with, for example, the suburbs. It has also led to a less intensive use of the land, for example with regard to the height of new buildings.

From the consumer survey of 1500 households within the whole region the following results seemed most important in relation to "Ideplan 77":

(i) The centre is conceived as an attractive and exciting area with a high level of activity.
(ii) There is a very positive attitude towards the pedestrian streets and the quarters with old, well-preserved houses. But the attitude towards areas dominated by modern buildings is mostly negative.
(iii) Most consumers like the small and specialized shops, the museums, the theatres, good restaurants and the department stores. Most dislike the pubs and bars.
(iv) Half of the households in the region only go to the city centre if it is strictly necessary; 60 per cent think that if one has a car it is more obvious to shop in a suburban centre.
(v) There seems to be a decline in the number of visits being made to the city centre.
(vi) However, most people think that it has a more varied assortment of goods and that it is a more exciting place to shop in than in a surburban centre.
(vii) There is a general opinion that the main part of the city centre is too far from transport terminals (underground stations and bus stops) and car parks.
(viii) Seventy-five per cent of car owners think that it is too difficult to find a parking space when visiting the city centre.
(ix) Half of all visits to the city centre area are for shopping.
(x) The time spent in the city centre varies with distance from residential area. People living in the nearby, densely populated areas spend on average 2·5 hours; people from the outer region about four hours. For comparison, the time spent in a suburban community centre is about one hour.
(xi) Visitors to the city centre think it is important that they can move around without being annoyed by traffic.

Judging from the above results and general knowledge regarding the problems of Copenhagen's city centre there seems to be a good basis from which a policy can be formulated.

"IDEPLAN 77"

It must be emphasized very strongly that "Ideplan 77" is not a plan in the usual sense of the word. It is not a detailed description of how to proceed in changing Copenhagen's city centre, nor one which has been tested for realism in the many preconditions of a plan. "Ideplan 77" must only be considered as some ideas to be used in the development of the city centre and needs to be given a physical expression. Therefore, "Ideplan 77" is only among many possible approaches. What is important, however, is that whatever concrete plan in the end is worked out for the city centre it must, in the opinion of the Institute, be based on some fundamental principles that also form the basis of "Ideplan 77". In order that the ideas put forward may be checked to some extent in relation to the possibilities and restrictions of the present physical, economic and functional structures of the city centre a few blocks have been selected in which these aspects have been more thoroughly dealt with.

In this section the fundamental principles of "Ideplan 77" are first described, and then the concrete contents of how it might be applied are demonstrated.

Fundamental principles

1. The future of the city centre must be based primarily on the needs of the population in the region for a city centre

We have today a city centre which has a value for many different interested parties. For the population of the region it functions as a service centre and as a source of employment. For private firms and public institutions it provides an outlet for investment and generating activity. For private and public property owners it secures an economic asset. For people living in the city centre it provides a social setting.

In the analyses it has been ascertained that the relative importance of the city centre has in some respects been falling for a number of years. This trend should be changed but it is then necessary to choose and assign priorities to alternative requirements; to choose the party that seems to have the greatest need for the city centre; to give priority to that policy that will best meet the most important needs of this party.

The party chosen is *the inhabitants of the region* with all the differences between them and with all the different needs that they have. The main task of the city centre is to be the superior centre for service provisions within the region—but not for that part of the service sector that can be or is established close to where people live, in local centres, in community centres or in regional centres. *The city centre should be developed primarily in such a way that it is the area in the region where everything does happen and can happen that does not take place anywhere else in the region—and it should be a better source of these activities than it is today.*

Of course, the city centre will in future contain a very large number of traditional functions and activities like department stores, office and public administration buildings but the weight of new development should be placed on something else. The analyses show that the aim must be to increase the variety, the specialization, the sophistication and the consciousness of—but not necessarily the knowledge of—the scope of services available. The city centre should be the one area in the region where not only commercial activities are found but where there is a combination of commercial, cultural, and other leisure time activities. It should be the place where you have a right just to be—to seek contact with other people or perhaps simply to observe them. This contact is in contrast to the more purposeful, functional service role offered in the rest of the region.

2. The city centre consists—and should consist—of a number of "part-centres"

Today the city centre is not a coherent central area but it consists of a number of "part-centres". By a "part-centre" is meant a geographical part of the city centre, an independent area containing specialized functions and a special clientele.

Experience shows that highly specialized service functions have a tendency to locate close to each other. Examples are streets with antique shops or old books. These functions are in keen competition with each other, but what is more important is that they also supplement each other by their different assortment and services. By locating in the same confined area these service functions obtain an attraction that is greater than would be the sum of their individual attractions if each was located in an isolated position. The area thereby develops its own identity.

Every "part-centre" is dominated by a certain group of people—the young, the old, people with high or people with low incomes. Only to a limited extent can people use other "part-centres" than those to which they feel a natural affinity. This is regarded as a negative effect by many people. Segregation of the population should be avoided. However, it may also be interpreted in a positive sense. It is a fundamental feature of a central area but one not sufficiently developed.

The basic reason for the existence of "part-centres" is that we are different and have different interests. This fact ought to be developed further within the city centre than elsewhere, because this is the superior centre for the whole region. Different groups of people with the same interest should be able to develop their particular interests to the most specialized, varied and composite level possible. This could take place in a number of "part-centres" each providing its own speciality and which through the public planning process could be given the physical and economic support necessary for its achievement. Service functions with special demands for accommodation, or those with an ability to pay a high rent or only low rent, should all fit into each "part-centre". This type of segregation can be accepted, because instead of a separation of people by age groups, income groups etc., it would be possible to make a separation of groups with the same interests, a mutual connection that will often cut across the present forms of social divide.

3. The environment in the city centre should be preserved and developed through an urban renewal programme

In its old buildings, its streets and squares, the city centre clearly has an asset of very high value. The analyses made show that the inhabitants of the region think that these features create environmental qualities of a high standard. Historically and architecturally they are an important heritage for society. But they are also an important basis for the development of the city centre according to the principles mentioned in the last two paragraphs.

In the suburban centres the floor space is adapted to the demands made by the users. They are very functional. A very large part of the floor space in the city centre, however, is not functionally adjusted to modern demands. This could be changed by an urban renewal programme that did not, to any great extent, take preservation values into consideration. The result of such a programme can be seen in many large European cities.

But you could also go about it in another way. You could respect and preserve the mass of buildings as it is and instead let the functions and activities adapt themselves to the given physical frame. Of course, there is a need for restoration and rebuilding. Demolition will also need to take place. Not everything is worthy of preservation. But the urban environment of the city centre should be preserved and developed in accordance with its own conditions. In this way the central area will contain, not the most functional but the most varied floor space in the region. The city centre should not be marked by the planners "fear of conflict", the principle that the various functions and activities such as dwellings, offices, shops and industry should be kept separated and be channelled to distinct areas. On the contrary the city centre should represent as many types of buildings and mixtures of activities as possible. In the future it will still contain primarily "traditional" central area functions. But it should also be possible to develop new and highly specialized functions and activities that both in the form and in their environment will be unique within the region.

4. Utilization and development of the city centre's existing buildings, traffic systems and parking installations

Every endeavour should be made to secure better utilization and returns from existing investment in the city centre. As far as *buildings* are concerned additional floor space should be created mainly by the rebuilding of existing buildings. There is no sign that *private vehicular traffic* will require major motor roads servicing the central area. In the *public transport sector*, the establishment of an underground through the heart of the central area has been discussed during recent years. From a capacity point of view there is in the opinion of the Institute no need for such a subway. Even if it could be afforded it would seem to be unnecessary and undesirable. In general, distances by foot within the central area would be reduced, but only limited areas around the new stations would see an improved accessibility to the detriment of the rest of the central area. Prices of land in areas around the stations would increase steeply, intensifying the creation of blight in the rest of the city centre.

It is far more important, and would be cheaper, to improve the existing underground and bus services. Here the biggest problem is that the terminal points are located on the margins of the central area creating long journey distances by foot to most parts of the city centre. *Parking* problems in the central area are to some extent similar to the public transport problem. There are large car parks on the periphery but they are under-utilized, even in rush hours.

5. A levelling out of economic values in the city centre

Price of land and property as well as rents vary considerably between different parts of the central area. The highest values are, of course, to be found in the main streets but just a short distance away from these some of the lowest values are to be found. In some localities the low values reflect a poor standard of building, something that is very difficult to change; but in other areas they, and the blight conditions with which they are associated, are due to the fact that the land or premises have not been put to a better use. An essential element in a future policy for the city centre must be to exploit these possibilities and make the areas attractive for new activities. The economic consequences of this would be higher values and rents but, carried out in the right way, they will nevertheless be of a level that is substantially lower than in the main streets. There will still be a great variation of rents in the central area.

An important reason for levelling out prices and rents is to see to it that service functions with an ability to pay high values as well as those that can only afford low values will be able to establish themselves in attractive parts of the central area, especially when they are of importance to the regional role of the city centre. A wider distribution of activities in the city centre would lead to a reduction in demand for premises in the most central locations where such premises today are sold or rented out at the highest prices. The effect will be a lowering of prices or rents in these most central locations and altogether a levelling out of values all over the central area.

6. The renewal of the city centre must be controlled and implemented through both public and private efforts

It is not the municipality's responsibility to carry out all aspects of urban renewal in the city centre. Local government must formulate a policy, work out plans for the accomplishment of this policy and ensure control over the realization of the plan. But the realization of the policy will involve a very great number of projects, private as well as public, over a long period of time. It is a jigsaw-puzzle where the total picture will appear in the plan made by the public authorities but where individual pieces must be inserted by many interested parties. In such a plan goals will have to be formulated that will require far stricter control over development than is normal in smaller city centres. In modern suburban centres such tight control is normal, but in these cases it is easier to handle because there is usually only one owner of a centre.

Within the city centre, the various interested parties are only kept together by a mutual interest and a mutual necessity to realize the plan. The role of local government is to work out the overall plan and ensure that it is politically acceptable. It should also contribute to the establishment of agencies which co-ordinate development within and between the "part-centres". How such agencies could perform the control required should be clarified in a detailed city-centre plan.

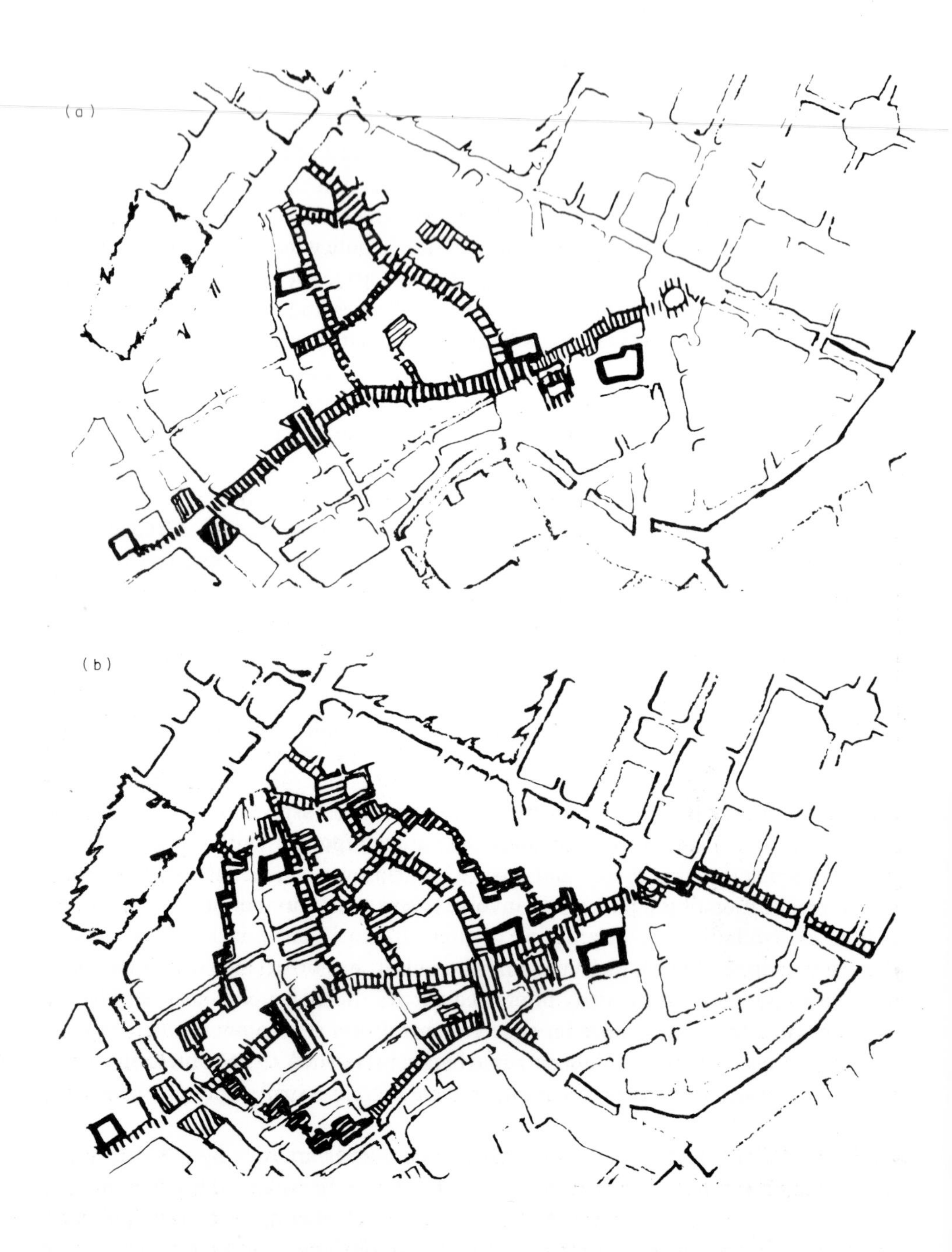

Figure 43. Comparisons of the existing network of pedestrianized streets and proposed pedestrianization in Copenhagen's central area. (Source: Institute of Centre-Planning, 1976).

Contents of "Ideplan 77"

What follows is an example of how the basic principles for a city-centre plan could be combined to create some new possibilities for the central area of Copenhagen.

Recreational areas and lines of communication

One of the main purposes of "Ideplan 77" is to provide good floor space within old buildings and to establish new, attractive lines of communication that will bind the central area together in a new way. The majority of the population in the region feel that streets and squares free of traffic as well as well-conserved, old buildings make the central area more attractive. Because future visitors to the city centre will also live still farther away from it than the bulk of present-day users, they will (according to our analyses) spend more time in the central area. There will, therefore, be a stronger demand for recreational and activity facilities where visitors may just sit and pause.

It is very difficult to introduce such facilities into the existing physical structure of the main streets. However, some realistic possibilities may be found in the middle of adjacent building blocks. By demolishing some of the most unsuitable and outdated back premises it is possible in a number of blocks to create more leisure-based environments. It is desirable that these new areas should be connected with each other to form an alternative, pedestrian network of communication lines through the city centre. In Fig. 43 a comparison is drawn between the existing network of pedestrian streets and the proposed alternative network which, of course, also implies the removal of fences between the individual properties in the blocks. We know from experience that to induce sufficient levels of pedestrian traffic flow it is necessary to direct the pedestrian line towards important targets. Therefore, the proposed lines are drawn through the blocks in such a way that they are directed towards the major transport terminal points. By creating new lines of communication and by opening up the blocks, the backyards and back views of premises will be made accessible to visitors to the city centre (Fig. 44).

In the middle of the blocks new façades along the pedestrian lines and squares could be established. With this it would be possible to create new locations for a number of highly specialized service functions that cannot now locate along the main streets because of the high rents there. But they still require locations along attractive pedestrian ways to be in contact with a sufficient number of potential customers.

A detailed analysis of a single block has shown that, by converting the core of the block through limited demolitions and some rebuilding of existing premises, the rent of the improved floor space will be sufficient to pay for the conversion when the ground floor is rented out for commercial use (for example, for shops) and the other storeys are used for flats. The rent for commercial floor space would be about half of what is demanded in similar premises in the main streets. However, as we have indicated, the conversion of several blocks would create some deflation of the

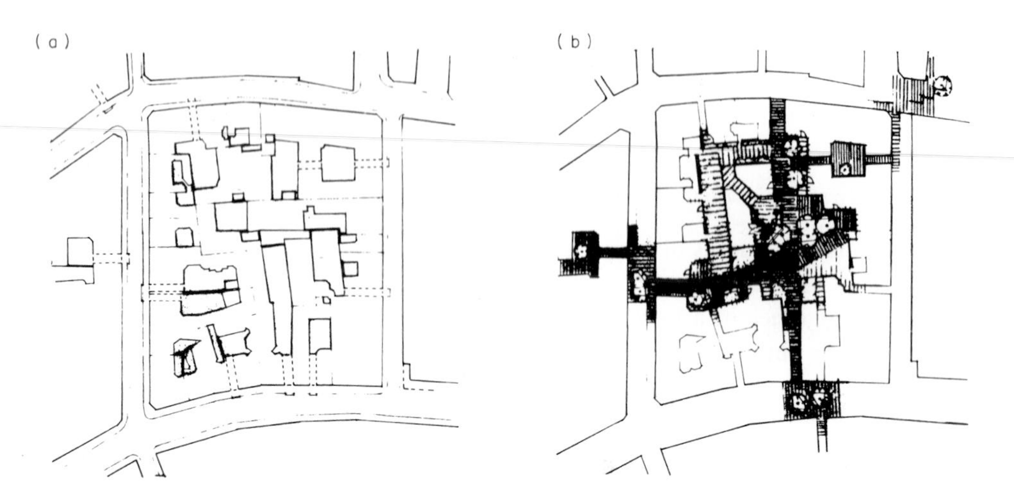

Figure 44. The possibilities for renovation at the street block level in Copenhagen's city centre. (Source: Institute of Centre-Planning, 1976).

rent level in the main streets. The general tendency to even out differences in rent levels would then make it easier for some of the shops in the main streets to carry out their operations even if their turnover may decline to some extent.

Theme-centres

Our analyses have shown that even if shopping is still the most important purpose of a visit to the city centre in Copenhagen, leisure activities such as going to theatres, museums, concerts, cinemas, restaurants, and educational classes are also of importance. Today the main attraction of the central area is still the large supply of shops and commodities. In future, however, the demand for leisure activities will increase considerably. The city centre has the potential to play a significant part as regards these future trends, being the place in the region where leisure time activities in their most varied and sophisticated form may be found. There are already a number of "part-centres" based on a concentration of commercial functions. With an increasing demand for meaningful leisure time activities this specialization must also be extended to non-commercial activities, the basis being the leisure time interests of certain groups of people. It is, therefore, suggested that attractive "part-centres" are created where commercial and non-commercial service functions are integrated physically and where the supply of commodities and various activities are concentrated together around a theme.

By a theme is meant a number of activities that seem to be mutually compatible. Some of the activities, however, might only be able to afford low rents; hence, to ensure a sufficient representation of activities based on a common theme a location in a converted block as mentioned above may be the best solution. Some examples of the various themes we might consider are:

Music-radio-television;
Film-photo-books-theatre;
Art-handicraft-antiquities-museum;
Gourmet-delicacies;
Travelling-vacation-tourism.

Within each theme it would be possible to put together an assortment of outlets that would meet the demand both for commodities and for leisure time activities.

The activities we can contemplate within a theme-centre may be divided into categories according to differences in their characteristics and their need for varying kinds of premises and location. As an example, we can take the theme "Music-radio-television". The broad representation of this theme demands both a supply of retail commodities and leisure time offerings of a more traditional and institutionalized kind as well as possibilities for facilities that will encourage an active and/or spontaneous participation. It involves in general both public and private service functions. The commodity supply might comprise shops selling:

Musical instruments;
Radio and TV sets;
Radio parts;
Records and cassettes;
Books and sheets of music.

The leisure time offerings might be:

Music library (books, records, sheets of music);
Music lessons;
Lessons in the construction of radio installations.

Other activities that could be found in the theme-centre include: concerts; open-air music events; possibilities for musicians to practise together and to get in contact with others; exhibitions; disc recordings; TV recordings on video; information on concerts, interest groups etc.; lectures and discussions.

The list contains only examples and the detailed nature of this is not really important. The essential thing is that with such a theme-centre an area is created within the city centre where the population of the region may find the most varied and specialized range of activities within this theme whether they wish simply to buy commodities, to study or to participate in certain activities themselves. Some of these activities will require normal shop facilities or corresponding forms of premises. A number of activities can function in rooms which they might share in common with other activities; and certain activities can be performed in the streets and in the squares, for example some forms of theatre or musical events. Regardless of the demands for premises, it must be realized that some activities can afford a high rent, others only a low rent and some may be unable to afford any at all. To ensure satisfactory coverage of the theme therefore, each theme-centre will need an organization to co-ordinate its activities and to ensure that desirable non-commercial activities are represented as well as those of an economic kind.

Internal traffic

Many visitors to the city centre find it difficult to park their cars, as we have said. On the other hand, studies have shown that the parking lots on the periphery of the main core are only half filled at peak hours. Part of the explanation for this is that there is insufficient knowledge about the parking opportunities available. It is also true that many car owners find there is too long a walking distance between these car parks and the most important service functions in the central area. Visitors coming to the central area by public transport also think that they have to incur too long a walk from the transport terminal points on the margins of the core and that public transport services within the core itself are poor. As part of "Ideplan 77" it is proposed that a minibus system be established to provide services from the transport terminal points to the most frequented parts of the city.

Other suggestions of "Ideplan 77"

"Ideplan 77" also describes how the central area may be linked up in a better way with the public parks that border it (Fig. 45). Likewise "Ideplan" puts forward some ideas on how to create a more attractive environment along the canals and the harbour front.

Execution of "Ideplan 77"

It has already been mentioned that the practicality of some of these ideas has been tested by analyses of a few blocks in the central area. To implement the "plan" according to the basic principles which have been enunciated, however, some fundamental conditions must initially be fulfilled. First of all, the municipality of Copenhagen must work out a plan for the central area as a whole within which the proposed urban renewal can take place. Furthermore, an organization must be established in order that the suggestions about theme-centres can be co-ordinated and worked out sensitively. One of the major hurdles, too, will be getting cooperation between the property owners in the blocks which are going to be converted.

So far very few of the ideas put forward in "Ideplan 77" have been implemented. The Copenhagen City Centre Association has just filed an application for a permit to run a minibus service and the Association is very actively promoting the central area as a centre for shopping as well as for cultural and other leisure time activities. However, no city-centre plan has been worked out and no blocks have been converted into theme-centres. In many ways the suggestions contained in "Ideplan 77" are so radical and the inertia confronting the initial phase of such proposals are so overwhelming that only by a big and concerted effort by public authorities, private investors and other organizations can the ideas be got off the ground. Whether the necessary will and enthusiasm can be found still remains to be seen.

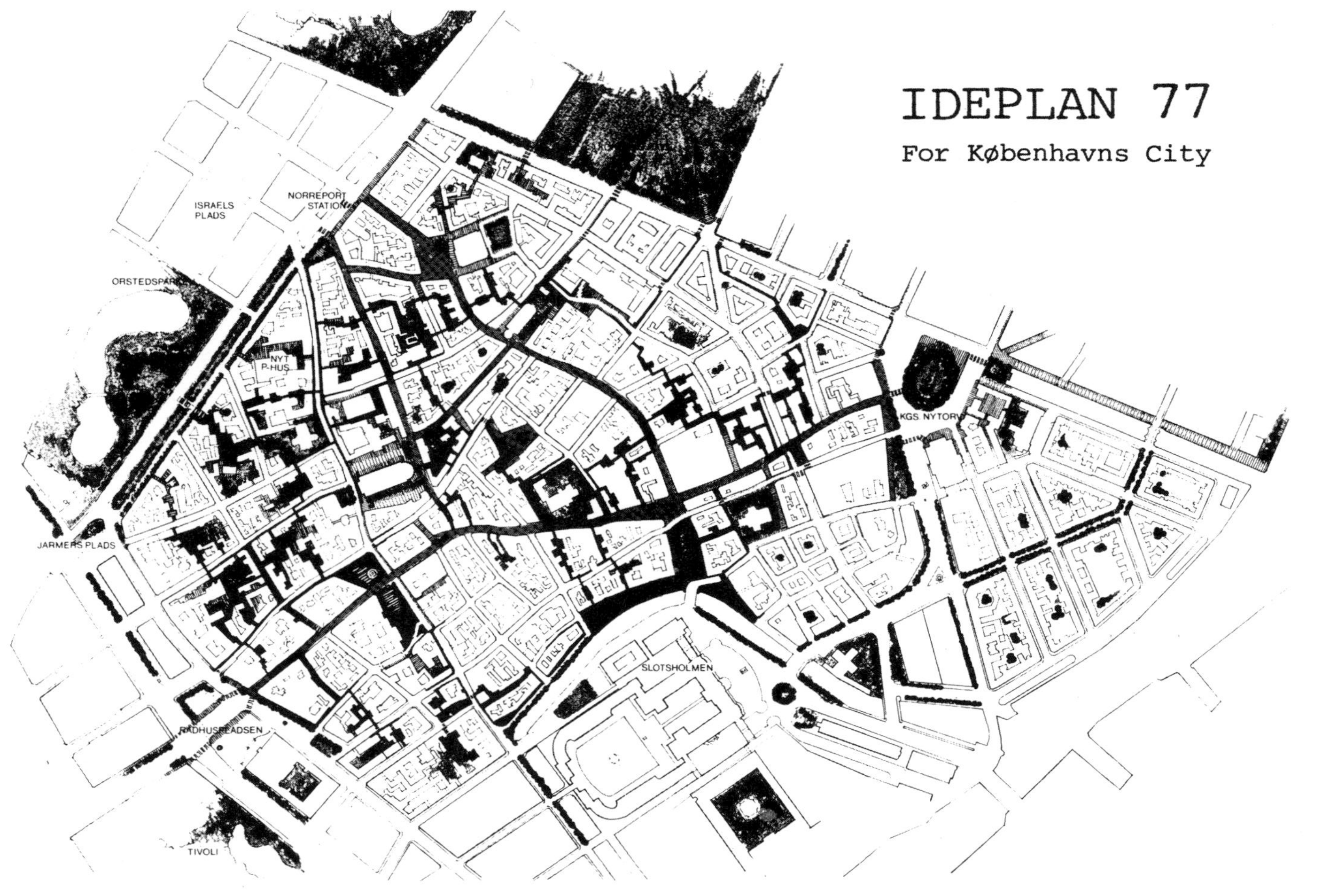

Figure 45. The general proposals for renovation and pedestrianization within Ideplan 77. (Source: Institute of Centre-Planning, 1976.)

IS "IDEPLAN 77" APPLICABLE TO OTHER CITY CENTRES?

There are some special circumstances that may make it easier to implement "Ideplan 77" in Copenhagen than in other city centres around the world. First, retail and commercial planning in the Copenhagen region has been aimed at a decentralization of the service sector, which, by reducing the pressure for space in the central area, has caused a lowering of rents and property prices below that found in other city centres. Secondly, local taxes on land and property are lower than are found elsewhere. Thirdly, Copenhagen's city centre has not hitherto been radically changed. The built-form is still dominated by rather small old buildings and the interiors of many blocks remain quite spacious. Fourthly, rent levels differ very much between the main streets and other parts of the city centre. Rents are especially low in the interiors of street blocks because the premises there are in general being used only extensively. Whether the ideas of "Ideplan 77" can be applied in other city centres depends, therefore, to a large extent on how far these circumstances might be paralleled.

REFERENCES

Egnsplanrådet (1971). "Regionplanlaegning 1970-1985". Forudsaetninger, Copenhagen.

Egnsplanrådet (1974). "Regionplan 1973 for Hovestadsregionen—Hovedstruktur og Byvaekst" Copenhagen.

Gruen, V. (1965). "The Heart of our Cities". Thames and Hudson, New York.

Heinemann, H. E. (1970). "Rum för Kulturen". Föreningarna Nordens Förbund, Stockholm.

Hovedstadsrådet (1978). "Regionplanens l.etape". Copenhagen.

Institute of Centre-Planning (1976). "Hvad med City?" Copenhagen.

Institute of Centre-Planning (1977). "Hvad med City? Interviewundersøgelse". Copenhagen.

Institute of Centre-Planning (1977). "Idéplan 77 for City". Copenhagen.

Matthiessen, C. W. (1975). *Kulturgeografiske Skrifter Bind* **10**.

Stadsingeniørens Direktorat (1967). "Amager og Generalplanen". Copenhagen.

THIRTEEN

Transport for central London

M. FOULKES

The central area of London has always held the key role in London's economic strength and expansion. Its size has changed—its growth parallelling and priming the growth of London itself. Its mix of activities has changed, reflecting its changing role as the national and world economic developed. We see it now at a time when its growth has stopped and arguably it is in decline. It is an appropriate moment to look at the role and importance of the central area for London and the nation as a whole and the mechanisms that have created and are creating a mixture of growth and decline. We can also look at the way in which changing policy has used these mechanisms knowingly or unknowingly over the years and what the options are that lie before the new administration at the Greater London Council (GLC).

Why is it that a transport planner has the temerity to broach this subject? Quite simply because transport and trade have been the most decisive factors in London's growth. Because we believe that transport will continue to both affect and be affected by the development of the central area, we are undertaking substantial transport-based researches which indicate some trends likely to be critical to its future. This chapter therefore possibly takes a partial view but one that is informed.

We find ourselves at a time of great change, much of it adverse. We need therefore to look to the fundamental mechanisms that make the city centre viable if we are to understand whether and how the change can be guided. No apology is made for going back to these basics as a starting point. Transport is a critical element in the functioning of town centres and is often a significant factor in the environment. Transport policies and programmes are therefore closely related to the functional and physical development of the centre and the surrounding city.

In as much as planning is or is intended to be a decisive influence on this development, it has been a central tenet of the planning profession that there should be an integrated approach to transport and urban planning. There has also been an implicit belief that, though both could be seen as a means to an end, nevertheless transport was more of a "means" whilst urban planning was more of an "end". For this reason transport policies should follow and reflect the planning decision. Though historically exactly the opposite was true, the balance has shifted steadily over the years to a point where urban function is normally decisive for transport rather than the other way round.

THE FUTURE FOR THE CITY CENTRE
ISBN 0 12 206240 X

In the completely ordered world the logic of this would be unassailable. However, in the confusion of reality planners have considerable difficulty in determining what people want and then in simplifying it to match the rather clumsy planning mechanism. Not surprisingly, people's behaviour frequently fails to mirror the planner's simple and, at the time of fruition, outdated expectations. Transport policies may thus come to have a different relationship to planning—with their role being one of providing flexibility and allowing people to make the best of what fate the planner has given them! They might create new matchings of chosen job, home, education and leisure, even though these may be dispersed in a way that the planner has not foreseen or possibly even disapproves of.

Making the best of what you have is critical to the success of society and is the dominant underlying philosophy for most people. This is not to deny the need for us to make the best possible decisions and to plan the improvement of our infrastructure but rather to suggest humility in recognizing that such decisions will not be totally right in a "definitive" sense; nor, will they be totally wrong.

Thus, in spite of scepticism, it is reasonable and right to expect that London's transport policy would reflect a number of considerations:

(a) the role of transport in the development of London;
(b) the present role of the central area;
(c) the planning intentions;
(d) the scale of the transport network and the present level of and trends in usage including the attitudes of Londoners which underlie the changes.

In that this chapter is intended as a case study, it covers all these aspects in order to demonstrate how the transport decisions relate to the wider functional and planning considerations.

First, however, it is necessary to define the central area of London. For the purposes of this chapter, there seems no reason to depart from the standard definition as used in the GLC surveys and in the Census (Fig. 46). It extends some 26 km^2 and includes primarily the City and the West End. It has a residential population of 200 000 (1975) and employment of a million. The housing ranges from that of Victorian charitable trusts such as the Peabody Mansions, through various types of council housing to the most elegant of housing, including several palaces. It lies primarily to the north of the river because development initially reflected the existence of Westminster and the City on the north side, but there is also a significant element to the south, as is shown in Fig. 46.

That is the city centre as it is today, situated at the centre of the Greater London conurbation which covers some 1600 km^2 and has a population of some 7·0 million and employment of around 3·4 million in 1980. It is the result of some 2000 years' growth, yet it is important to recall that only 200 years ago London was itself roughly the size of the present central area.

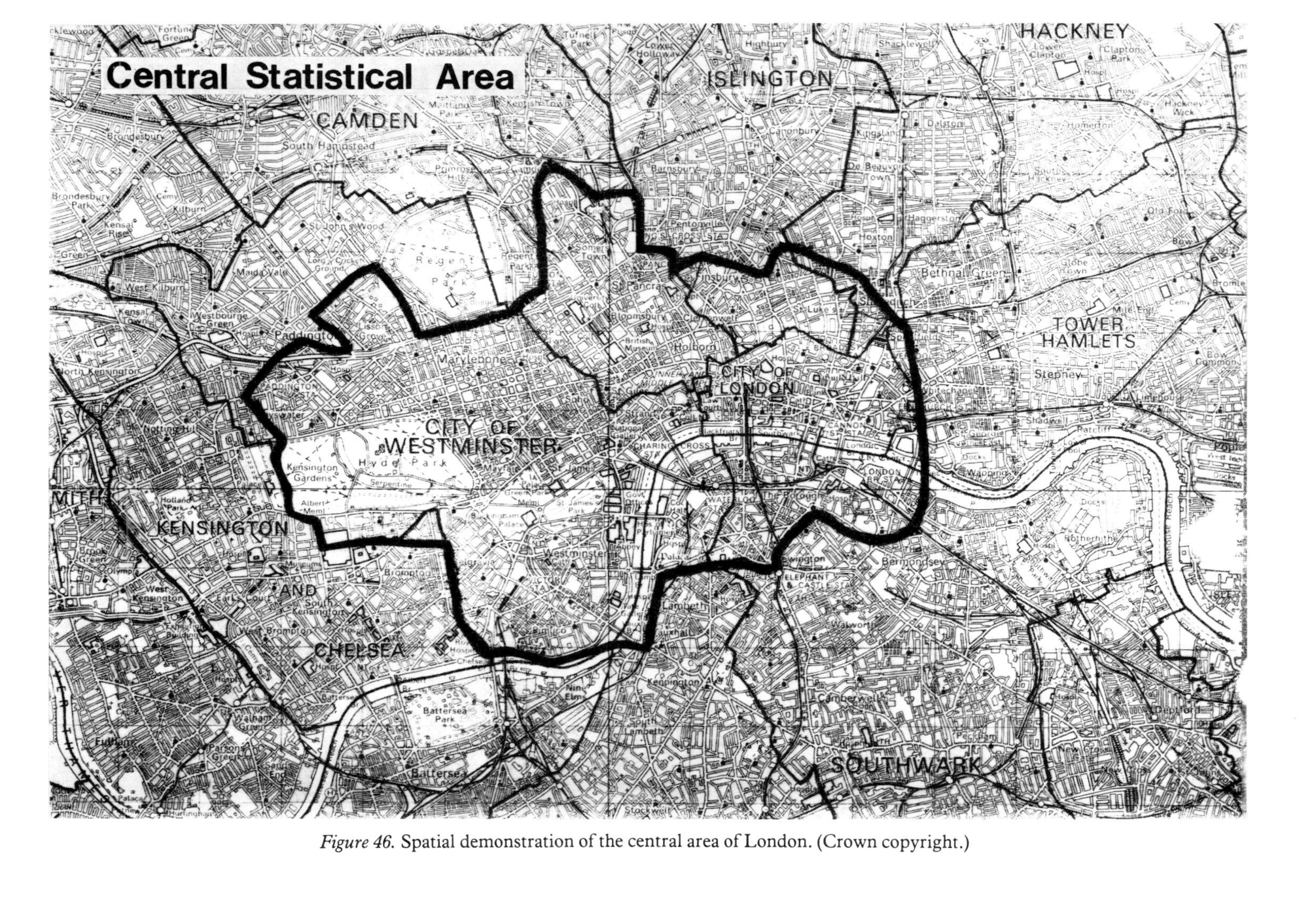

Figure 46. Spatial demonstration of the central area of London. (Crown copyright.)

THE GROWTH OF LONDON AND THE CENTRAL AREA

Key location

London's growth has always related to its being a focal point for transport—offering trade and transport access up the Thames as well as a river fording point. Thus its accessibility attracted specialized activities which could serve a larger area. The impact of such a nucleus of activity was magnified by the need of people engaged within it to have the normal services of builders, weavers and food providers, in a range which increased continually as society became more sophisticated. By its nature the city tends to be in the vanguard of development of both nucleus and supporting services and activities. The availability of the most advanced techniques itself gives the city added attractions.

Changing scale

With growth there arises a distinction between the centre with its key activities and the more general development surrounding it. The central area has therefore traditionally been the home of either specialized or new and developing activities which locate there because of relatively good access to a wider market and to business and other contracts. With growth of demand both from an increased standard of living and a growing national population, activities and services originally focused in the city centre will be dispersed more widely.

Over the centuries we have seen these factors augmented by changes in accessibility, with roads ranging from Roman to turnpike to motorways; with canals and navigations for freight; railways since the 1830s; the internal-combustion-engined bus and car in this century, and most recently, in air transport and telecommunications. These have had profound effects on the scale of the central area and London as a whole. For industrial and service activities, they have changed the balance of locational advantage. All except car and lorry and larger ships have encouraged growth in the city's accessibility and in the type of activities that would need to locate there.

Until the 1960s, the shift towards service and office activities outweighed the dispersing effects of the car, lorry and telecommunications, so that central London continued to grow in employment and effectively in size as well.

In other countries city-centre growth is still continuing often because the city is allowed to grow by continually expanding and accommodating lower density development on the periphery. Here the firm or individual is required to pay a minimum premium in price or conditions for the possible marginal benefit of proximity to the city. Though they only make a marginal use of the central area, it is nevertheless an additional supportive demand. Another factor is that in other countries more rapid growth in standard of living and innovation may also reinforce their city centre, more than is the case for London.

Changing activities

The activities within the central area have also changed, partly reflecting the decline and disappearance of earlier activities which are no longer required or do not now require a city-centre location. There has also been a change in that overall growth in the activities that must be in the city centre causes the central area to grow and displace other activities such as residential and industrial activity. If we look at the size and population of London as it developed over the years and the changing pattern of activities in the central area, the trends described above are well illustrated.

It is important to recognize these very simple facts that have underlain the growth of London and its central area because there has not been continuous growth. Its economic health has always depended on its attractiveness to certain changing markets. It has no automatic destiny of growth or success.

THE ROLE OF THE CENTRAL AREA TODAY

The role now is to provide leisure and business services for London, the south-east region, the nation and internationally. This appears in many forms, some of the most important of which are: banking, insurance, broking; head offices; government; specialized retailing; tourist hotels, restaurants, entertainments. Its resident population is small at 200 000 and the secondary support services are primarily related to serving people coming to the area to use or work in the above types of activity. The support services are therefore largely paid for by these special activities and their customers.

Economic aspects

The central area activities attract a substantial international and national income into London and it is this that in financial terms fuels and drives much of London's economy and the national economy in the case of London's international income. That input is essential to setting in motion a whole sequence of demands and employment of great complexity and significance. Perhaps the equivalent of 200 000 jobs are employed in attracting international income of some £3000 million and possibly 200 000 jobs are employed in attracting national non-London income. In turn the demands of these employees and their families for services and supplies provides employment for hundreds of hundreds of workers in London and elsewhere.

The element based on the attraction of national wealth clearly involves only a geographical redistribution, but the international wealth element is a national gain. In as much as these activities could not be successfully pursued in more dispersed locations, they are central London's contribution to the national economic well-being. The international income probably results in employment approaching one million people in the country. I mention these figures to give a feel of the order of magnitude. To define them exactly is an endless and fruitless labour.

There are doubts often expressed (mainly by non-Londoners) as to how far it is true that activities can only be successful in central London—but in most cases the high cost of space, rates and support services means that firms do seriously weigh the additional benefits against costs, though the balancing factors will vary considerably. Thus London's central area is a major and unique asset and it would seem sensible to exploit it for the national good particularly as the national non-oil economy is not only weak now but shows signs of remaining structurally weak after the end of the world recession.

That is a view reinforced by the fact that the central area of London itself can no longer rely on economic growth. Even to sustain the existing level of activity represents a major challenge which requires a careful examination of the various elements, their needs and the ways in which London can ensure that they are met sufficiently well to retain existing and attract new activities.

Banking, insurance, broking

Clearly these are key activities involving participation in the market, personal contacts with other interests and customers and international links. They require office space within closely specified locations and good communication; costs are not usually a critical issue. The close interaction was well illustrated by the fact that in the mid-1960s 50 per cent of business trips to and from national and international offices in the City were on foot. It is a different situation when we look at the more routine activities which were initially located in central London because of the benefits of a single office able to contain all of the business and because of the availability of an ample labour supply. Now high rents and rates, problems of access by car, and in some cases the expense and inconvenience of travel to work can lead to activities moving out. Large offices predominate in this major sector of banking and insurance; the establishments with over 250 employees accounted for 50 per cent of employees in the early 1970s and this implies particular vulnerability to support activities moving out.

Central Government

London has been the traditional focus for central government offices. This has reflected the original desire for proximity to Parliament plus the desire of management to be in London and the much better accessibility it affords. Some of these factors have become less significant for the main bulk of work and large elements have been moved out of London. Further substantial moves would be quite feasible operationally but have been resisted by staff. Of all the elements of central area activity, this is one which can be moved with least risk of harm to the national economy. Such relocation could be to Docklands or to other parts of the country needing injections of new prosperity. They would probably in large measure take their workers with them initially. Previous dispersal was perhaps facilitated by the concurrent expansion of the Civil Service.

Central services

These cover a very wide range of specialized shops, showrooms, advisory services, publishing, newspapers. These all draw special advantages from being at a focal point of demand and accessibility. However, high costs and operating difficulties, coupled with employees' pressure in favour of relocating outside the central area, has led to some relocation of this type of activity even outside London. Examples include the move of consultants out to the suburbs, the opening of substantial department stores in suburban centres, the exhibition centre at Birmingham and the shift of newspaper presses into Docklands.

Head offices

The choice of the central area in the past reflected some of the factors referred to in the previous sections. It also, as with those elements, was influenced by prestige and political links. In these more volatile times, cutting costs means more and London is losing parts or the whole of the head offices of firms which are feeling financial pressures. The strength of central London's attraction has been strongest for large companies with 70 per cent of the top 100 industrial companies but only 36 per cent of the top 1000 being located there. The large head offices are, on the other hand, again those most likely to decant part of their staff.

Tourism

This is an industry in which central London's concentration of historical interest and entertainment coupled with good accessibility has made it pre-eminent. It has partly been eroded by the high cost of London accentuated by the high value of sterling and also by the fact that London's current tourist capacity has been saturated in recent peak seasons with adverse effect. In general, however, it is unlikely to be seriously undermined by marketing of other areas. Some 60 per cent of overseas visitors come by air, emphasizing the support of airport location to London's dominance.

The residents

Despite the critical importance of central London's economic activities, we must recognize that London's success also depends on its ability to offer people a satisfying life which will attract them to live in London. It is the residents' contribution financially through their spending and socially through their communal activities that makes London work.

The central area makes a modest contribution in its own resident population which has steadily fallen to its present level of about 200 000 but its employment and social activities make an immense contribution by attracting people to live in other parts of the city. Thus 80 per cent of those who work in the central area live within London. In turn their living in London becomes a reason for firms locating there. Once that cycle is weakened and large numbers of employees live or would like to live outside London, then many firms are likely to move some, if not all, of their activity out.

The central area's role as a cultural and leisure centre does have a significant effect in influencing young or single workers to live in London; for families the central area's contribution to London's attractions is almost entirely in the availability of jobs. It is perhaps worth looking very briefly at how the central area's workers homes are distributed amongst different areas of London. Inner London supplies some 40 per cent of central area workers; for example, in Tower Hamlets to the east of London, 24 per cent of the resident workers commute to the central area. There are other areas with a less clearly-defined traditional economic life of their own which are more closely associated with the central area. This is often also influenced by the fact that property, though old, is often of a higher quality and lends itself to rehabilitation. Thus in Kensington and Chelsea we find 44 per cent of resident workers commuting to the central area. When we come to look at the type of jobs they do and how this relates to the total employment pattern (Table 38), it becomes clear that the central area is very important now but could be equally important for future generations.

TABLE 38

Percentage split of residents' employment for four boroughs—1971

	Borough of residence			
	Lewisham	Tower Hamlets	Barnet	Croydon
1 Central area office	15	12	20	15
2 Central area service	11	12	10	5
3 Manufacturing industry in borough[a]	7	16	7	12
4 Office employment in borough	15	7	15	15
5 Other employment in borough	8	29	20	18
6 Office employment in other boroughs	10	4	11	10
7 Other employment—outside borough including 8	34	21	17	15
8 Manufacturing—outside borough[a]	12	11	8	5

[a] Manufacturing category applies only to operatives—the total employment could be 50 per cent higher if office workers are included.

TRANSPORT'S ROLE

Although transport is a means to a wider end (except for the dedicated railway and bus enthusiast), it is also the case that its availability and the standard that can be provided has been particularly decisive for London's development and will probably continue to be so.

International and national services

International services are important to the city and its international role. Thus Heathrow, Gatwick and the third airport, when and if it appears, are important together with rapid links between the airports and the city centre. The Channel Tunnel would be another important addition, though less critical. London's airports now handle some 39 million passengers a year including 13·7 million foreigners and 11·5 million UK residents bound for or starting from London. The Channel Tunnel would carry some 6·2 million passengers in 1990 which it is estimated would include: 2·8 million foreigners coming to London and 3·4 million UK residents going to Europe. The national links by rail and by road are another critical element in London's role bringing 10 million non-commuters to central London from outside the GLC in 1971, 7 million of whom came by rail.

Commuting

On a far greater scale are the daily flows of workers to London and the transport system necessary to carry them. According to the 1980 figures for the peak period, this movement is split by mode as follows: British Rail, 412 000; LT Underground, 323 000; LT Bus, 103 000; Car, 184 000.

Whereas commuting to central London makes up 15 per cent of all passenger trips in London, its importance varies between the different modes, being highest for British Rail (55 per cent) and LT Underground (45 per cent) and below average for LT Bus (10 per cent) and car (3 per cent).

The system that carries these loads is very large. Thus British Rail has 770 km of route in London and London Transport Underground 390 km (Fig. 47), while they operate 297 and 279 stations respectively. This great density of rail service largely reflects the tremendous and unrealistic intensity of competition of the last century between railway companies. As a result 94 per cent of Londoners live within a mile of a station. The underground predominantly relates to the GLC area, whilst nearly half of British Rail commuters are drawn from beyond the GLC. The bus network is denser but is less orientated towards the central area and in fact very few routes serving the central area penetrate deeply into the suburbs (Fig. 48).

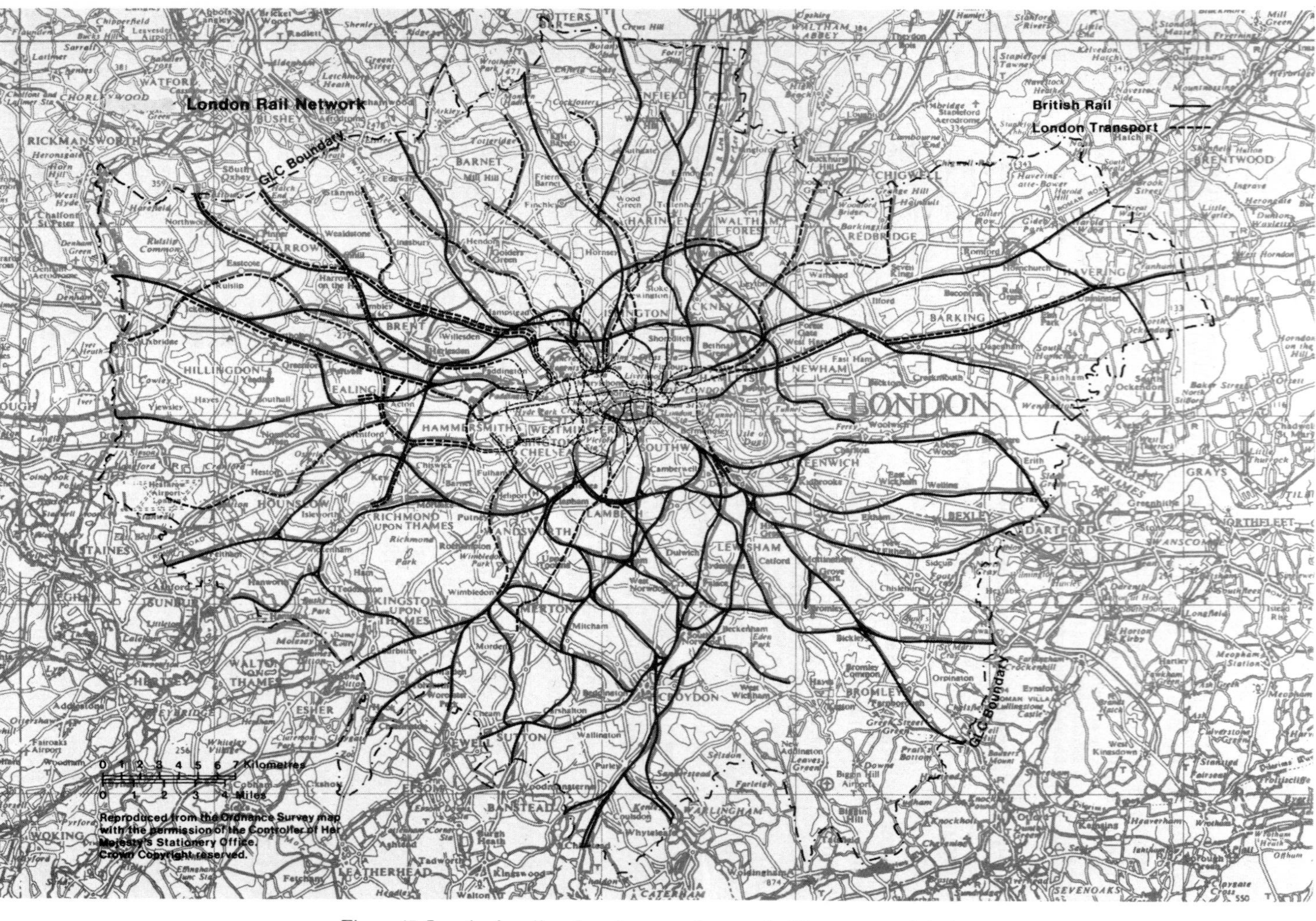

Figure 47. London's rail and underground network. (Crown copyright.)

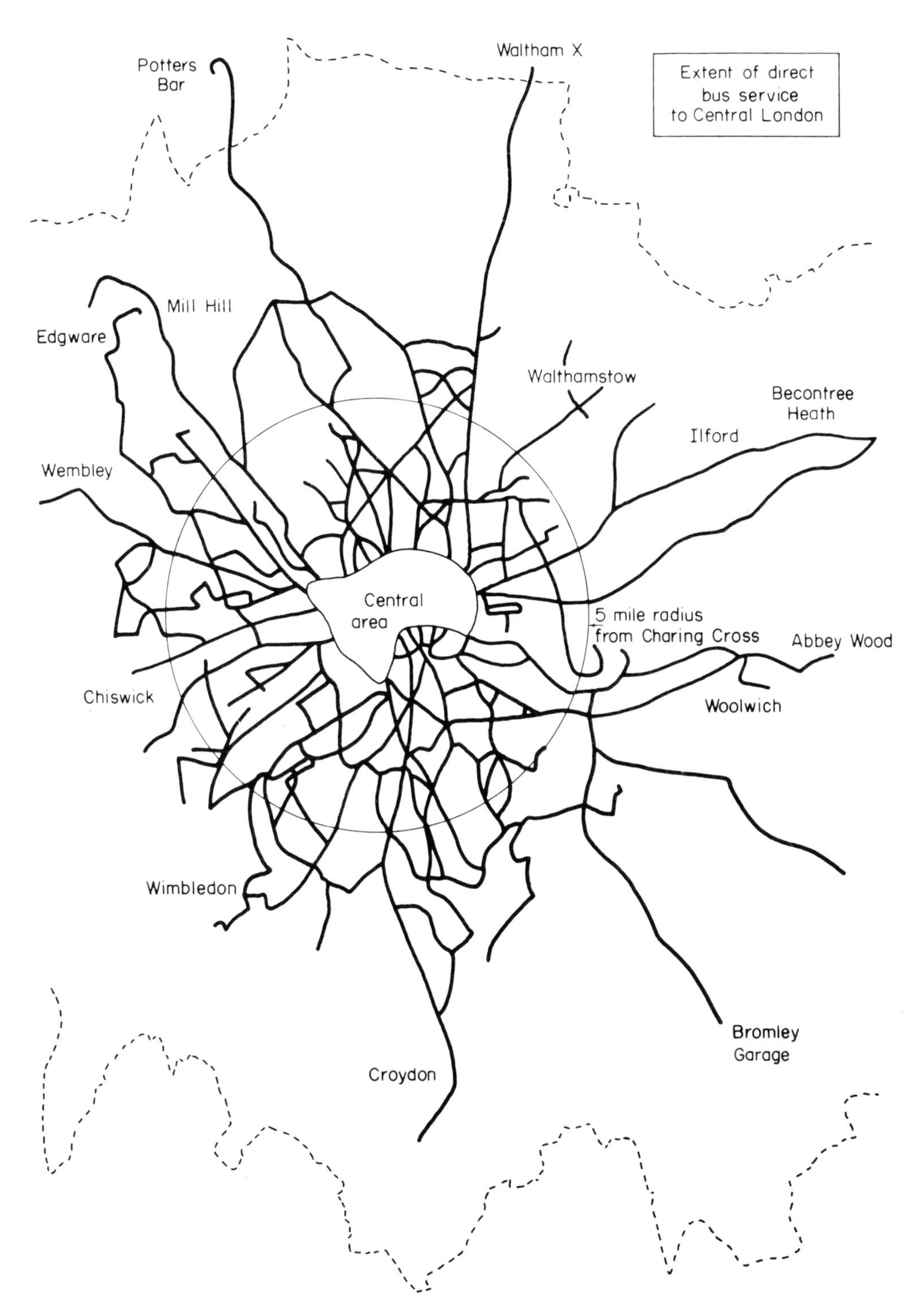

Figure 48. Central London's bus network into Inner and Outer London.

British Rail's fares taper with distance and offer very substantial discounts for season tickets. The Underground offers similar discounts but on a less advantageous scale. All the systems run at a substantial deficit met from local and national taxes. London Transport in 1980 received nearly 30 per cent subsidy for operating costs in 1980, but with the "Fair's Fare" reductions it would have been around 45 per cent in 1982.

THE LONDONERS' VIEW

Great changes are now in motion with cities losing some of their traditional attractions for firms and residents, both because of increased costs and social stress but also because other areas are now more accessible. At the same time social attitudes to life-style are also changing as is the structure of job availability and pay structures. It is necessary therefore to stay in very close contact with these changing attitudes and to understand the process of change that is underway. This is not to suggest that a city is a "consumer product" that can be redesigned overnight to match changing "market" attitudes. Indeed, it can be argued that if attitudes are changing rapidly one does not want to invest heavily in changing the fabric because one will have all the visual and operational havoc with a high probability of making a large-scale mistake.

What it does suggest is that we should pay great attention to how the existing fabric can be used to match changing needs. In this, transport is one critical factor; maintaining an adequate supply in terms of quantity and range of choice of homes and work buildings is another. This remains true whether public or private ownership is the preferred form of tenure.

At the GLC we have therefore been establishing surveys of attitudes to job and home location, and particularly the reasons underlying recent or likely future change. The answers of people working in central London are those relevant to this chapter—and some of the preliminary results are indicated below.

Residents

The selection of the central area as a work location is primarily related to availability of style of work and higher pay. For younger people, the social excitement of the central area is also a factor. If jobs were available locally, then a significant number, particularly of women, would prefer to work locally.

The home location choice is strongly influenced by house prices, fares and by environment. People who may well look to living close to the central area in their early twenties are tending to move outwards, often choosing the outer suburbs as a compromise relating to environment, fares and house prices; to live further out is considered to involve much higher fares and little compensation in house prices—the opposite of the situation only 20 years ago. To live closer in is seen as involving higher housing costs and poorer environment. A significant proportion of those deciding to live in London would prefer to live outside of London if the costs could be afforded.

Firms

The surveys of firms indicate that most firms are seriously reappraising whether they need to be in central London and, if so, whether they must have all their activities there. The factors influencing them are high rents (particularly impacting at lease renewal), high rates and other overheads, and workers attitudes to cost and inconvenience of travelling to work. The outflow which has been very substantial has been primarily to London suburban town centres and the rest of the South-East, though some have relocated further. The outflow has been balanced in part by the inflow of foreign banks and similar specialized commercial activities. Recession has heightened pressures for some, a situation which could well be sustained.

PAST POLICIES

In the past it has been generally accepted that central London offered unique opportunities and that these should be realized by increasingly intensive developments and use over an expanding area. Thus over the centuries the area between Westminster and the City became infilled, originally with large estates which in due course were largely redeveloped for denser housing. The river bank marshes were filled to create opportunities for lower-income housing. Many of the industries and trades have steadily been pushed out to adjacent areas by economic and social pressures. In this century housing has been displaced by offices, shops and more recently hotels. The structure therefore reflects the early existence of the two focal points of the City and Westminster and, to a more modest extent, the existence of large estates which controlled development patterns.

Physical disasters have created opportunity for radical reshaping. The Fire of London created one, the Second World War another. In fact, on both occasions radical change was espoused, but was ultimately considered impractical or undesirable. There have been initiatives in driving individual roads through, but these have had little effect on the pattern of development. The driving of the Underground greatly increased capacity and accessibility, but has tended to reflect rather than create a pattern of development. Development initiatives have tended to relate to individual sites.

Thus, until the 1940s, there was little true comprehensive planning policy, though some individual decisions had relatively widespread implications. Those that are particularly striking are: the planning of the major estates; the retention of the Royal Parks; and the decision to stop the main railways on the perimeter of the central area. Within the framework of these guiding forces, development took place very much as a reflection of market forces.

The 1940s saw the emergence of planning in London. Perhaps most critical to central-area transport planning was the issue of office employment and this happened to be the area in which planning policy was most clearly focused. It is perhaps appropriate to look briefly at the development of planning policy in this field as well as transport.

Planning policy for offices

The 1939–1945 War reduced the central area's office supply by about 10 per cent to some 7·2 million m^2 and immediately after the war the climate was not encouraging to office growth. There were 100 per cent development charges instituted by the 1947 Town and Country Planning Act. The Abercrombie Plan of 1944 suggested that some offices might well be expected to move out to the suburbs or beyond. The City of London Plan for 1944 proposed a return to pre-war levels of activity, but this was rejected by the Government and the Holden-Halford Plan of 1947 looked to a 6 per cent reduction in activity compared with 1939. The London Development Plan of 1951 looked to decentralizing industry and commerce in correspondence with the reduction of population, so as to reduce travel to work and facilitate the reconstruction of the inner congested boroughs. Employment zones were reduced but the area zoned for offices in central London was increased.

In 1952 central government removed the development charge, eased development and increased the compensation involved for revocation of planning permission. As a result planning permission for over 2·5 million m^2 of offices was given by 1955. In 1956 the government raised the bank rate and it also became more difficult to make rights issues. As a result insurance companies began to dominate financing. The pace of growth raised further concern about congestion and the London Plan (finally approved in 1955) zoned less space for offices. In the later 1950s the London County Council was actively encouraging offices to decentralize to selected locations in inner London including Hammersmith, Archway, Notting Hill Gate and Elephant and Castle, all with good transport links to the central area. The areas just outside the County of London joined in with some gusto, with Middlesex giving approval for 1·6 million m^2 between 1955 and 1964, and with Croydon gaining some 0·3 million m^2 over a similar period. This seemed to result in growth in the suburbs as well as the central area rather than the shift expected and as a result the level of planning permissions around London then fell.

In general, governments placed their faith in land-use planning and voluntary action, but this did not in the event prove very effective. The restriction on land use had been largely vitiated by the allowance of a 10 per cent increase in cube of buildings on redevelopment. In 1963 central government took stronger measures; the 10 per cent cube changing to 10 per cent area increase in the 1962–1963 Town and Country Planning Acts. Government office dispersal was speeded up and the Location of Offices Bureau (LOB) was set up in April 1964 to encourage relocation. In 1964 the South East Study accepted increased employment in the central area. The shift of one million people out of London was favoured, but the study recognized that 40 per cent of workers moving would commute back. In November 1964 the Government took powers to bring office development to a virtual standstill within a 40 mile radius of London. Office Development Permits (ODPs) were introduced and there was no appeal or compensation in the event of refusal. Applicants had to produce named occupiers at the outset. The pressure of demand eased by 1965. Though initially applying to a 40 mile radius area, ODPs were extended to the whole region in 1966.

In 1965 the newly created Greater London Council, covering 1600 km^2 and embracing the old London County Council's 310 km^2, favoured moving offices out of London and the south-east region. The subsequent ten years of work on the Greater London Development Plan, eventually published in modified form in 1976, resulted in a general favouring of office development in the outer suburbs, but no very specific view on the central area.

Since then, the development of local plans for the City and Westminster has pointed to a restraining policy on office development. There has been a steady easing of Government controls, with the ODP system and the LOB being abolished in 1979, moves welcomed by the GLC at the time.

The Labour-controlled GLC elected in 1981 is relatively less sympathetic to offices and, in particular, is opposed to expansion of the central area further south of the River, in order to protect local housing and employment there. This decision was taken against the background of a very substantial amount of outstanding office permissions which it was felt would meet the central area demand for a number of years.

Transport policy

This was developed by the various bodies with direct responsibility for different transport components. For the central area this has primarily been British Rail, London Transport, the LCC and then the GLC, with varying levels of central government interest. It is probably fair to say that the initial reaction in any of these fields has been to try to meet growing demand and in each case this has proved very difficult.

In the case of roads, various road improvements were proposed and progressed over the years, but they could not match the rapid growth of road traffic. Traffic management was then employed to increase the capacity of the existing system. At the same time, it was increasingly recognized that it was a losing battle and so measures were introduced to restrain traffic by limiting new private parking provision and by controlling on-street and public car parking. Interestingly, more dramatic restraints have been under discussion technically for over a decade, but none have been considered acceptable.

The GLDP made general statements on the need to provide balanced transport facilities, but its major specific proposal related to a new network of roads. The one most relevant to the central area was Ringway One (alias the Motorway Box), the equivalent of the Boulevard Périphérique in Paris. This proposal was dropped along with all the new orbital routes and the final approved plan limited itself to restating the traffic problems. To many this seemed scant progress after ten years' effort on all sides. With the abandonment of the one major proposal, the final GLDP must be regarded as rather general. It is thought by some to mark a retraction from strategic planning in London; a process which was reinforced by the lack of public funding or development pressure necessary for creating major change.

Railway planning has been the subject of various policy reviews over the years. Self-interest initially encouraged the surface and Underground railways to cooperate, a relationship formalized when both were nationalized and placed in the BTC. The passing of London Transport to the GLC in 1970, whilst British Rail remained under Government control, raised no major problems and a joint review was undertaken in 1973 to produce the London Rail Plan advocating an array of improvements, but also recognizing that commuting demand was likely to decline. Though those close to the situation have been conscious of missed opportunities, in reality much has been achieved in terms of increasing capacity of the system to meet the problems of gross overcrowding that arose in the early 1960s and led in part to the office ban. Now the problem is less likely to be one of overloading but rather of how to finance the services and achieve greater integration of fares.

Bus services have generally suffered from serious unreliability. This has been due mainly to traffic congestion and staff shortages, but has been compounded by other factors. Costs have risen and the fares have tended to rise faster than inflation. In the case of the central area these problems have been coupled with an improving rail alternative and the decline of commuting from the inner city to the central area, all leading to a very substantial fall in bus traffic to and within the central area.

A TIME OF CHALLENGE

Planning had tended to see the central area as a place with inevitable growth, so that its prime role was to contain that growth. Now it is clear that as a result of various policies, an inability to meet the customers' needs and changes in the needs themselves, central London is in decline. Though some might view that as a desirable result in planning terms, in isolation it could potentially weaken the future prosperity of Londoners as a whole.

The challenge is how do we respond to this situation. Is it by trying to develop new areas for tourism and offices? There are certainly areas in or adjacent to the central area which could move in this way and which have adequate accessibility. Alternatively, we could seek to promote a satellite centre as has happened in Tokyo and Paris; there are locations where this is physically feasible. If none of these are acceptable, then it would be logical to move out those activities which cannot be lost to the national economy by relocation, such as the Civil Service. This would hurt the London economy, but it would be far better for the country if this then left the central area clear in its desire to attract other international and specialized national activities which may only flourish in London. Central London could potentially attract a new generation of manufacturing and service industry of high technological input, with widespread markets and very lightweight processing which can be carried out in multistorey buildings with high density employment.

The GLC's new administration (1981) has still to make up its mind on many of these issues. Almost certainly its priorities lie with the well-being of the poorer inner city residents whose well-being many feel has been disregarded or whose needs have been defined in an inflexible doctrinaire way which is out of keeping with personal and economic reality. At present the indications are that the expansion of the central area into the inner city will not be looked on favourably because it will result in direct loss of land and because rising land values will undermine locally-based activities. The planning authority's attitude is almost inevitably ambivalent in recognizing the benefits and faults of a city centre.

It is against this background that I would define the more specific challenges for transport as: first, to help the central area work smoothly; secondly, to reinforce whatever planning policy may be adopted—whether it be to attract new activities, general growth, a satellite centre, etc.; thirdly, to provide resilence to changing circumstances and public attitudes; and finally, to do all this as effectively and as economically as possible—particularly having regard for the present trend of decline in total demand.

TRANSPORT POLICY

Railways

First, public transport continues to receive a high priority. The objectives are to give reasonable comfort and reliability of service for commuters. This has led to investment in signalling, electrification, new rolling stock, increased penetration of the central area by suburban lines and some additions to the Underground. This would represent the continuing intention as far as funds can be found, except that it is less likely that major new Underground links will be added because of their high cost and the falling total demand. The electrification of suburban lines has created new opportunities for the services to penetrate the central area using existing tunnels; for instance, Great Northern and Midland services into Moorgate.

The major opportunity for a new line is in the east river corridor where the industry is largely run down and the housing and environment is decayed. Here the accessibility to the central area has been poor because employment was localized particularly round the docks and the meandering river has formed a barrier. Such a new link would encourage commercial redevelopment and would make the central area much more accessible, thus helping to ensure an adequate job supply for succeeding generations of residents. This was to be the role of the Jubilee Line at a currently estimated cost of around £30 million per mile. New lower cost options such as an LRT or extending the existing East London line underground (partly built by Brunel Senior), are being assessed. The economic case for the Jubilee Line was weakened in Government's view by the desire for development of the corridor to be orientated towards local industrial employment rather than attracting city-centre type activities and being closely linked to central area employment.

Financing a new line in London now seems impossible, partly because the level of economic activity in central London is declining, but in fact much more because central government policy on transport spending has steadily declined over the years without allowing any compensatory expansion of the local tax base.

Buses

These have had a declining role in London but even more particularly in the central area. This has reflected their unreliability due to traffic conditions and staff shortages which are particularly adverse in the central and inner areas. This has led to a trend towards using the Underground and, when coupled with increasing prosperity, it has also led to increased use of taxis. Both these trends have been particularly true for tourism. The distribution of bus routes and the speed and reliability of operation has meant that they are used in the central area for short rather than long trips.

The GLC is now pursuing bus priorities of various types and LT have taken steps to alleviate staff shortages by steadily moving bases for bus operations outwards to take advantage of the better staffing situation in outer London. The first priority is now reliability of operation rather than sophistication of design. It could be that difficulty in pursuing car restraint and the narrowness of London's roads precluding continuous bus priorities will lead to adoption of more bus/taxi roads like Oxford Street. Traffic conditions would worsen on adjacent roads and the bus operations might have to be concentrated on the priority routes. Such routes would obviously be at a lower density than at present and there would have to be an attempt to locate them where there is not an Underground link. This could reduce the overlap of systems and shift more traffic from bus to Underground.

In the past the expectation of other solutions has reduced the incentive for a basic restructuring of the use of central London's roadspace. Now I think we can say with some confidence that it is possibly the only long-term proposition.

Fares and marketing

In a situation where fabric and infrastructure change little in the short term, fares and marketing policy constitute the primary way of meeting changing needs and challenges and may also be the key factor in reducing operating costs. In relation to the central area the main objectives would include the following: making travel to the central area easier, with particular priority given to work trips and to facilitating access from inner London; assuring the fullest utilization of the services provided by encouraging optional trips where capacity exists; and reducing the unit costs of public transport to allow greater provision of services or saving of taxes. The achievement of these objectives would involve lowering the fares particularly for inner London, simplifying ticketing and particularly through-ticketing to make the system more accessible, making optional travel very cheap, and concentrating concessions primarily on those who live in London.

Such a simplification also offers the longer-term opportunity of increased productivity, though views on how this potential should be pursued vary. If the commitment is to use it to increase services and customer satisfaction without reducing staffing, then it has different implications. More immediately such measures are likely to reduce revenue and increase the need for generating the revenue from an alternative source.

It was this type of policy which was introduced by the GLC in autumn 1981. At the time the scheme was intended only as a first step towards a zonal fares system, with a general reduction and avoidance of a major increase in minimum fares. The buses were put on a concentric zonal fares system, but only the central area of the Underground was split into compatible zones. The overall reduction in revenue was 25 per cent, giving an average fares reduction of 32 per cent. For central London the main effects were a substantial reduction in the cost of travel to and from it and an even greater simplification and reduction in cost of travelling within it.

Approaches were made by the GLC to fund British Rail to adopt similar fares, but the government intervened to prevent this. Had this been possible the way would have been open for integration of the London Transport and British Rail fares systems. Instead, because British Rail was forced to increase its fares in November 1981 in order to match its financial constraints, the gap between the two fare systems was widened. Common sense should have made this a temporary aberration.

The final steps are not decided. The whole policy was seriously undermined by the ruling of the courts and House of Lords that the cheaper fares involved were illegal and by the ensuing fares increase. Previously, the next logical step would have been the adoption of a zonal system for Underground and British Rail with more zones than for buses. This could be used for season tickets and single tickets on the basis of being valid for all modes. However, if rail fares were higher than bus fares, this would mean that, though a rail ticket could be valid for bus use, a bus ticket would not be valid for rail use. Though in many ways the adoption of a completely common bus and rail fare scale would be most logical, this would involve a further large drop in revenue. The intermediate stage would probably have involved a substantial move towards the Carte Orange type of system adopted in Paris.

The short-term increase in travel was expected to have been some 8 per cent, mainly in optional travel. The longer-term effect of fares initiatives, however, coupled with planning and development initiatives, could not only be modal change and generation of optional trips but some modest change of job/home distribution.

Roads

The possibility of substantially alleviating traffic congestion (Figs 49 and 50) in central London by road construction is now generally dismissed. Though a ring

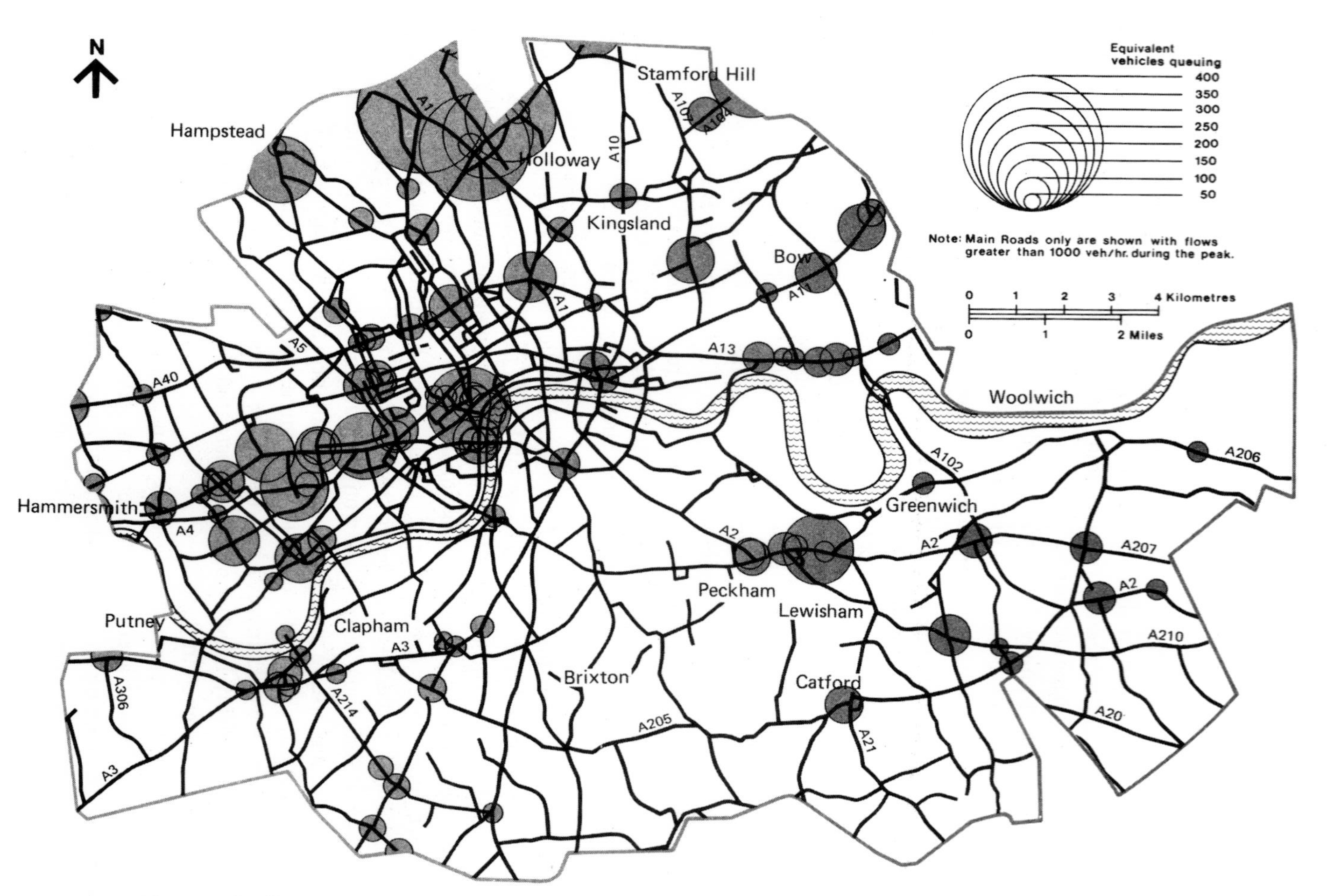

Figure 49. Traffic delays in central and inner London, morning peak times (1977-1979). (Source: GLC, 1981.)

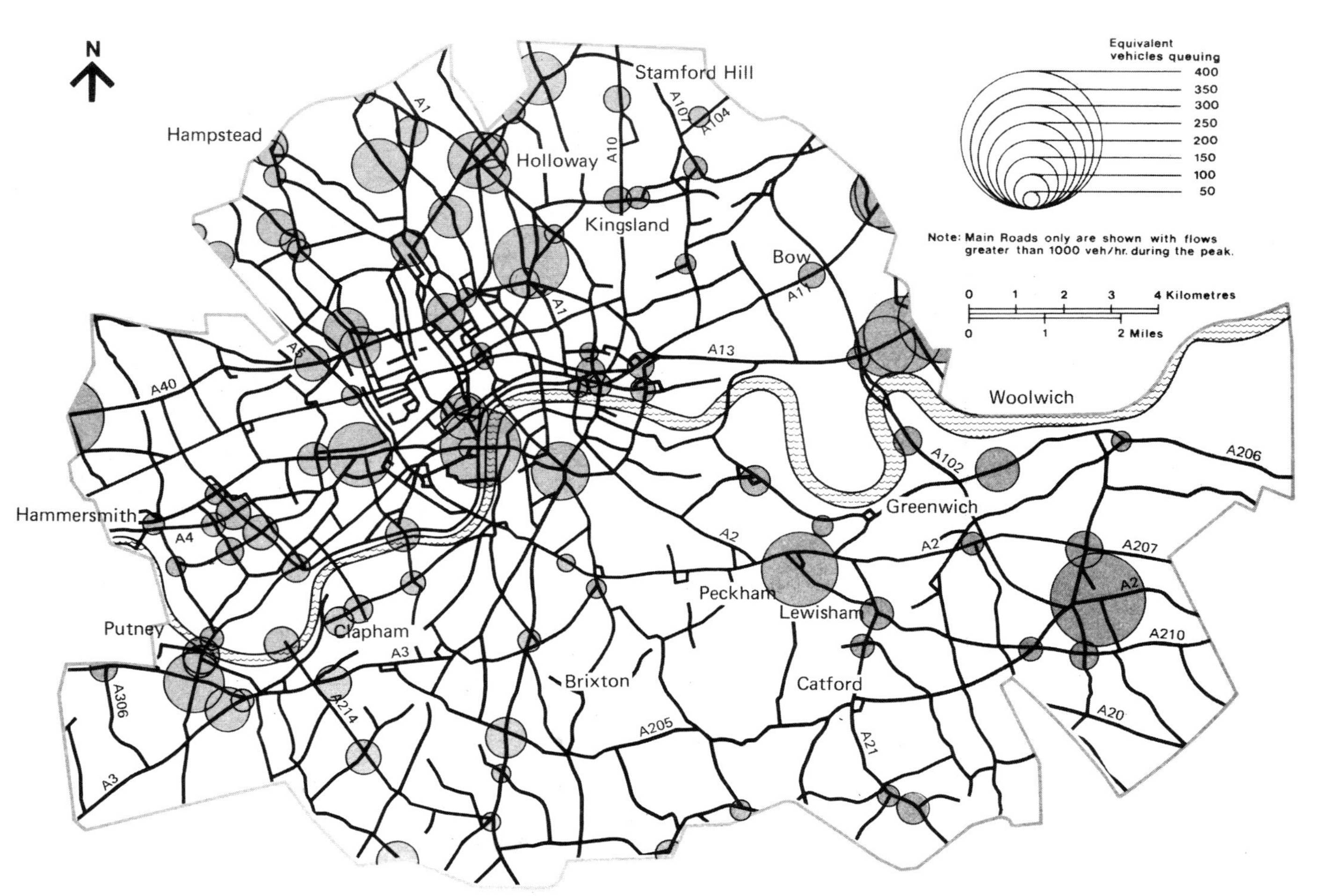

Figure 50. Traffic delays in central and inner London, afternoon peak times (1977-1979). (Source: GLC, 1981.)

route round the centre may be improved, it will be of relatively modest standard. Much attention has therefore been directed to an alternative solution, that of reducing the volume of traffic destined for central London and preventing additional through-traffic being attracted by improved conditions. The main possibilities are parking control in various forms, permit or licence control for entry into the central area or use of physical bottlenecks with bus priorities to limit the traffic flows entering.

Parking control is the easiest and most accepted initial approach and all on-street parking spaces in the central area are controlled, but there are many problems at present. First, there is the problem that the parking supply is inadequately priced and therefore always overdemanded. Someone who arrives in a car and can find no free parking space is under heavy pressure to park illegally. There is also a problem in enforcing control because of difficulties in processing fines. Even if that difficulty is overcome, the warden force is now nearly two-thirds down on its requirements and the fines may be too low to be an effective deterrent. It demonstrates the difficulties and high costs of intensively managing an urban situation, as well as highlighting the risks of creating a system which, though based on market pricing, is nevertheless subject to intervention.

Nobody expects control of public car parking to be sufficient to contain traffic congestion. Indeed, if public parking was entirely eliminated there could still be congestion from those using private parking, from through-traffic and from the increasingly larger taxi fleet. Though it may be overstated, there could be unacceptable damage to the central area's function if all car access was banned, whether we consider salesmen, theatre-goers, people working unsocial hours, or rich tourists.

It is therefore necessary to consider restraint on private parking and on through-traffic, but this raises problems. The control of private parking is a retrospective intervention and is only accepted if it is financially attractive to the owner. Moreover, the planning authorities may well be embarrassed, because the parking was probably provided originally at their behest when the first priority was felt to be accommodating the growing demand for parking off the roads. The attack on through-traffic, other than by enticement to a bypass, is fraught with practical problems ranging from the difficulty of implementing and enforcing a permit scheme to the effects of heavy traffic flow on perimeter routes which are already recognized in several cases as being totally unsuitable as major traffic routes. If we have failed so far to enforce parking controls there must also be some doubts about enforcing something more demanding.

Though we have come to consider parking control as a traffic restraint measure it was originally a way of managing the parking supply in an orderly manner—to ensure that both kerbside loading and unloading space and car parking was available. The collapse of parking control has produced a situation where deliveries are becoming very difficult.

The environment

Though the central area is a core of intensive activity it does have parks, temples and squares that provide havens of peace. There is nevertheless a desire to reduce the environmental intrusion of traffic. Unfortunately, actually to extract traffic from some sensitive areas requires a road capacity on alternative routes which is just not available. In other cases the traffic is mainly servicing residents and firms in the streets concerned. Removal of through-traffic or a reduction in terminating traffic would make some progress, but the problems in achieving this have already been referred to.

It may well be that improvement in terms of pedestrianization will depend on arbitrary initiatives in specific locations. The pursuit of pedestrianization in areas that are less busy might well attract specialist shopping to those areas. This would be an interesting reaction to the problem that major shopping is along the key traffic routes which therefore cannot be freed of traffic. Covent Garden offers one rather special example of this, so it will be interesting to see how strong a market its shopping element can attract.

Other opportunities may lie in excluding specific types of vehicle. Lorries are the most obvious candidate and already those over 40 feet in length which do not need access are excluded. The GLC has examined more drastic restrictions such as excluding through vehicles over 16 tons GVW (Gross Vehicle Weight) and excluding all vehicles over 16 tons GVW. Forces working against such restrictions are increased costs and difficulties for activities in the central area or objection to the increased loading on the perimeter routes of through traffic. With a stronger economy or increased perimeter road capacity, these side effects would become more acceptable. The balance of judgement itself may change and the environment be given even greater importance, as intended by the GLC administration elected in 1981.

Transport terminals

London's unique ability to offer good access, inherited from the days before the car, has been eroded, but the city has retained a powerful advantage in being the most logical location for access to long-distance passenger transport. Thus we see continued expansion of airport throughput at Gatwick with the proposed Terminal 2, Heathrow and Terminal 4 and the proposals for a third airport resurrected in 1981. The first two have, and a third airport would have, powerful transport links into central London.

The Channel Tunnel project is making slow but steady progress and again a central terminal could be provided, though it is likely to be on the periphery of the central area, with Waterloo now seen as BR's favoured location. There is a proposal for a tunnel link for through-operations between Victoria and Euston or Kings Cross primarily for inter-city trains to speed through journeys. British Rail consider the resulting benefits and increased revenue could possibly justify the cost of some £330 million. From London's point of view it has rather limited attractions, because it primarily takes people through London and also partly duplicates an existing Underground link.

Coach terminals are expected to have an expanding market. Now that the Victoria Coach Station is fully occupied, a site at Kings Cross is being pursued for a second permanent terminal; particularly because Kings Cross coach station has been displaced temporarily by redevelopment. The main rail terminals are steadily being refurbished or in some cases redeveloped, but the achievement of the latter depends on financing from associated office development. Achieving the acceptance of such proposals has often posed difficult and lengthy problems.

Transport terminals no longer have the same strong power to attract development to a city that they did, for example, when railways were the only significant means of longer distance travel. Thus whilst industry is now influenced by the availability of a major airport in much the same way that it used to be influenced by the availability of a port, it is now often adequate for the airport to be within 50 or 100 miles. Nevertheless, terminals still help concentrate development in the centre because all rail and air services are accessible only from there. For this reason the GLC continues a supportive policy even though terminals bring their own problems.

CONCLUSION

The market trends and, to some extent, the creation of the Green Belt have meant that London's central area no longer experiences an automatic pressure for growth. The ambivalence of planning policy between a desire to encourage the central area economy and a wish to reduce the level of activity has meant a fluctuation of policy, but this has had limited effect on the scale of physical development, because during periods of encouragement a large reservoir of planning permissions has been built up to tide development over the periods of restraint. One major result, however, has been the absence of a coherent and confident initiative to promote and attract activity to the central area. Financial gain has sustained a pressure from developers and landowners to achieve development, particularly of offices and hotels, but this has usually been an unconcerted process, except where a single owner had a large holding.

Railways have expanded to meet the challenge and this has been possible because it did not involve intruding on non-transport land ownership on any large scale. Now the weakening economy and declining scale of demand and increasing unit costs of public transport leave an increasing financial problem.

The solution of the traffic congestion problems requires at least some intrusion on the fabric and land ownership to widen orbital roads or tighter control of use of existing parking. It may well be necessary to go beyond this, but such steps encounter great reticence on all sides. So far the main successes have been in management of the traffic.

One critical question in relation to London's central area is simple; do we want to encourage economic growth and, if so, how and where are we prepared to encourage it or do we want to positively diminish the scale of the central area? In reality there is no simple right answer however much that might suit the transport planner. However, it is conceivable that decline could become so substantial that there will be a concerted and undisputed effort to encourage growth to try and stem the tide.

In transport terms the policies may have to be compatible with all these possibilities and would therefore include:

(a) no major overall increase of public transport or road capacity, though certain very specific schemes may be justified including international travel terminals;
(b) a concerted effort to contain costs and a recognition that some rationalization of the system may be sensible if demand declines on some routes;
(c) even greater initiatives in making the public transport system easy and attractive to use, for instance by simplification and, if necessary, by lowering fares and funding by an alternative means;
(d) a search for a practical approach to controlling road traffic which is readily accepted by the public and less demanding of manpower and court time.

The options and opportunities thus do not seem to rest primarily with grand constructions, but this is a disappointment more to the engineer and planner. It is good news for a public that feels it spends too much of life weaving between scaffolding and temporary hoardings and may also be welcomed by those who have to look at the ever-increasing on-going burden of maintaining as well as operating an ever-expanding infrastructure.

The main opportunities lie in the management of the system. This requires skill and a close understanding of the public at large. Above all, it requires a will on the part of the public and the various authorities, and particularly the need for a consensus approach to transport. Given that transport in London has featured so often as a prime political issue over the last decade, this may seem optimistic. It can only be hoped, however, that out of debate comes a new understanding and consensus embracing the public and forming the basis on which to pursue positive policies that realize the full potential of the central area. Even if that proves too optimistic the central area will survive by its own momentum, but probably only in a contracting form beset by the frustrations that come from a lack of communal purpose and commitment.

The situation described for London is not untypical of most large cities, though the problems and attitudes may develop in a different form or sequence. The past record indicates that in each case they seem to survive emerging from their afflictions adjusted and strengthened, but more recently many new forces seem to be at work. It is their ability to absorb such changes that is their abiding hope.

The author wishes it to be known that any views expressed are purely personal and not necessarily those of the Greater London Council. The Greater London Council and others have taken decisions on many of the issues referred to in this chapter. An effective review of these is provided by GLC (1982).

REFERENCES

Barker, T. C. and Robbins, M. (1963). "A History of London Transport". George Allen and Unwin, London.

Daniels, P. (1975). "Office Location: an Urban and Regional Study". Bell, London.

GLC (1976a). "Approved Greater London Development Plan". London.

GLC (1976b). "Transport and the London Economy". Internal Paper, London.

GLC (1976c). "Travel to Work by Borough, Employment and Mode—Analysis of 1971 Census Data". London.

GLC (1977). "London as a Location for the Head Offices of Manufacturing Industry". Internal Paper, London.

GLC (1979). "Some Aspects of London's Economy". Internal Paper, London.

GLC (1980). "Summary of the History of London Office Policy 1939-1979". Internal Paper, London.

GLC (1981a). "A Socialist Policy for the G.L.C.". London.

GLC (1981b). "Evidence to the House of Commons Transport Committee, 4 October, 1981". London.

GLC (1981c). "G.L.C. Transport Policy and Programme. 1982-1984". London.

GLC (1982). "Transport in London. The Medium Term Plan" and "Transport Policies and Programme. 1983-1985". London.

GLC (forthcoming). "Survey of Factors Influencing Central London Office Employers Locational Choice". London.

GLC (forthcoming). "Survey of Factors Influencing Central Area Office Workers Choice of Job and Home Location". London.

GLC and DoE (1974). "London Rail Study". London.

Manners, G. and Morris, D. (1981). "Does London Need an Office Policy?". Centre for Environmental Studies, Conference Paper, London.

FOURTEEN

The local plan for the city centre of Newcastle

R. M. ANGELL

It is fortunate timing that the draft proposals for the Newcastle City Centre Local Plan 1981 have been published only just before a conference on this theme in this city.

This chapter is concerned with the thinking that went into the preparation of this Plan and the main proposals of the Plan itself. Some reference will also be made to the 1961 Plan, as it will be called here, prepared under the guidance of Sir Wilfred Burns. This will give us a greater appreciation of how the form and structure of the more modern parts of the present city came about.

THE REGIONAL SETTING

The city centre's functions can be grouped together under four broad headings: business, shopping, further education and public administration. In each of these cases the city centre acts as the regional capital. It is the focus for business, professional and commercial activities so essential to the smooth working of industry throughout the region: it is the region's dominant shopping focus offering a very wide range of goods for sale. The University and Polytechnic, together with the Royal Victoria Infirmary in its role as a teaching hospital, are grouped close together within the city centre itself. The headquarters of two local authorities, Newcastle and Tyne & Wear, together with the regional offices of central government make the city centre a regional centre for public administration.

All these activities are contained within a relatively small and compact physical framework which has grown and adapted to new circumstances since Roman times. Successive ages have developed what is now the city centre in response to their needs. Today the city centre contains buildings and patterns of development of great architectural and historic importance.

The city centre is also the principal focus of the region's transport network. The rail network and the principal road network made it readily accessible from points outside the region. It is also the most important focus within the conurbation in terms of trips by public transport. Activity, accessibility and physical fabric are

THE FUTURE FOR THE CITY CENTRE
ISBN 0 12 206240 X

therefore bound up together in producing the present characteristics of the city centre.

THE 1961 PLAN

Within six months of the formulation of the new City Planning Department in November 1960, Wilfred Burns and his team produced a document entitled "Central Redevelopment, First Report". This was essentially a scene-setting document for a series of redevelopment proposals and the forerunner of recommendations regarding several Comprehensive Redevelopment Areas. At that time there was no statutory framework for a document of this nature. It was, however, a clear statement of general intentions (rather than specific proposals) backed by a strong political commitment. As the document itself states, "The process of redevelopment will be one almost of central area revolution rather than evolution"—and so it was.

There were three main intentions behind this 1961 plan (Fig. 51). First was the redevelopment of areas of decayed nineteenth-century buildings. This entailed keeping the best of the old development but integrating the new into the city centre in a way which would give continuity. By such redevelopment and improvement the status of Newcastle as the regional centre for the North would be confirmed. This eventually resulted in the redevelopment and expansion of the regional shopping facilities at Eldon Square and the Newgate Shopping Centre—a new library and shopping complex at Princess Square and an expansion of office development in the Quayside (Pilgrim Street/All Saints Area) and Gallowgate.

The second intention was to deal with the increasing traffic problem by putting forward radical solutions to stem the deterioration in conditions and allow convenience to be restored to all central area users. A hierarchy of roads was proposed to serve different needs with an ambitious programme of central urban motorways. Of the motorway proposals, only one out of the four proposed was constructed (i.e. the Central Motorway East). However, several new and vital lower order roads were constructed. Considerable additional parking space was proposed and several new car parks were built. Separation of pedestrians from vehicles, particularly in shopping streets, was also a firm intention of the Plan and this was partially realized by the construction of many footpaths, footbridges and pedestrian areas for shopping.

Finally, and the need for brevity precludes elaboration of many other interesting facets of the 1961 Plan, the Plan safeguarded the future expansion of the University, Polytechnic and numerous public buildings. It also put forward the intention to provide additional residential, hostel and hotel accommodation. Over the last 20 years much of this provision has been realized.

In summary, many of the intentions in this 1961 Plan were translated into solid achievement on the ground. Some, however, became uneconomic and unacceptable, such as the full urban motorway system. Other intentions, for example provision of

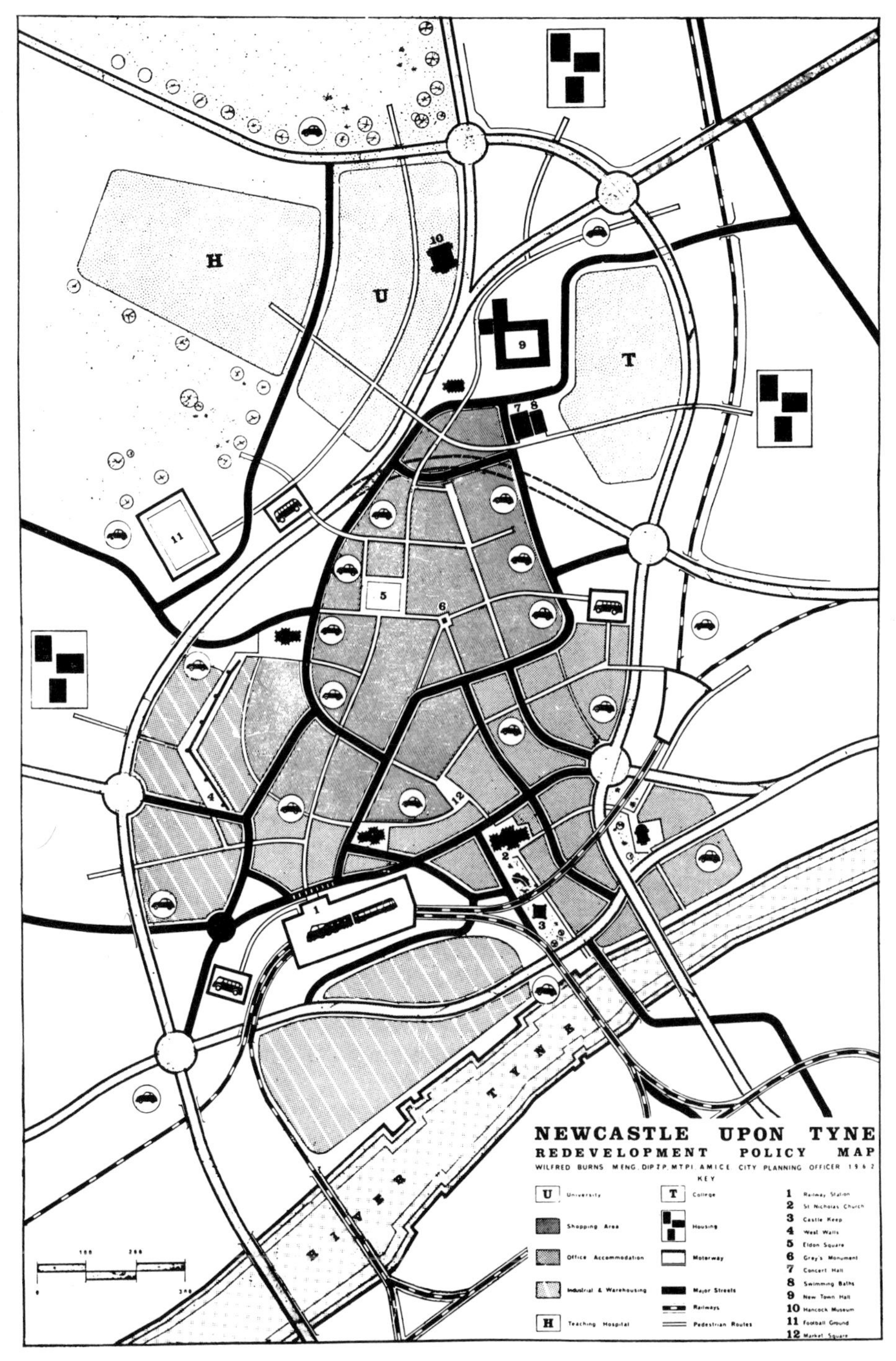

Figure 51. Central area redevelopment plan map, Newcastle upon Tyne, 1961. (Source: Newcastle upon Tyne City Council, 1961.)

better pedestrian facilities for shoppers, rejuvenation of the Quayside, are valid more than ever today and form important proposals in the 1981 Plan.

THE 1981 PLAN

In contrast to the 1961 Plan, the style and format for the current Local Plan has been dictated to a large extent by legislation. The document, which was by summer 1981 in a format for submission to the Secretary of State, is the product of five years of research, analysis, public participation and political decision-making by Newcastle City Council in association with Tyne & Wear County Council. There is no doubt that the two-tier system of government considerably lengthened the period of plan preparation, because many of the proposals stimulated much argument which could have been far more quickly resolved given the county borough conditions of the 1961 Plan.

The preparation of the Plan took particular notice of Section 12 (a) and (b) of the 1971 Act which relates to giving adequate publicity to both survey material and proposals. The Council, however, decided that, given the importance of the central area, the change in circumstances since the 1961 Plan and the complexity of contemporary problems, it would exceed these requirements and provide an additional stage of public participation on alternative choices regarding the formulation of policies. This, of course, lengthened the preparation period but in my view this additional stage proved well worthwhile and indeed almost essential.

Public participation

There were three stages involved in the public participation exercise, which can be termed Position and Issues, the Alternatives, and the Proposals. The following account does not go into the various problems of public participation in an area like the city centre, but simply looks at the methods and results.

Position and issues

A leaflet entitled "Where Do We Go From Here" was prepared for general issue and to go alongside various questionnaires: and a "Public Discussion Paper" was written for interest groups and individuals wanting more information.

Approaches were made to different groups of city-centre users—residents, employees and shopkeepers, by way of questionnaires which posed general and open-ended questions. Employers were also asked to set down what they saw as being the good and bad points of the city centre as a place to work. A postcard questionnaire was used with the leaflet in approaching the general public, and those receiving the "Public Discussion Paper" were asked to set down their views in a letter. This approach was adopted in order to gain the benefit of receiving different viewpoints, both about the city centre as it is now and about priorities for the future.

In terms of success in drawing a response, the exercise resulted in 607 replies to the leaflets made available at public counters in the city centre: 78 replies to the questionnaire sent to a sample of employees working in the city centre, 73 detailed letter replies to the "Public Discussion Paper", 24 replies to a questionnaire sent to a sample of city-centre residents and 118 replies to a shopkeepers questionnaire. In addition, ten meetings were held with the representatives of 39 interest groups, and a public meeting was attended by about 200 people.

The degree of interest shown and the response received was encouraging. Whilst it cannot be said that the results of the exercise constituted "representative public opinion", they did give some indication of the topics which concern particular central area users. The exercise provided a guide to opinion which was important at this early stage in the preparation of the plan. The results were incorporated into a document entitled "Report of Findings" which also dealt at some length with the plan's technical considerations.

The alternatives

This was the most important stage, not just to clarify the public's views but also those of both the professional planners and members of the two Councils.

"Choices for the Future" was prepared as the main document in this round of public participation drawing together in a considerable degree of detail a series of choices and opportunities for the future development of the city centre on a topic-by-topic and area-by-area basis. It was intended that the document should be both informative and also stimulate a response, and as such was arranged with a page of text, a map and a tear-off reply sheet for each topic and area. The reply sheet summarized the choices and opportunities available, and contained boxes to be ticked for preferred choices and space available to comment on opportunities together with further space for other comments. A pre-paid envelope for the return of the reply sheets was sent out with each copy.

A separate broadsheet summarized the most significant points from "Choices for the Future". A tear-off pre-paid reply questionnaire was attached containing an almost identical list of choices to those contained in the larger document for easy cross-reference of results.

In addition to the general participation exercise, three separate surveys were carried out, each using as a basis the broadsheet/tear-off reply questionnaire. In this way it was hoped to determine the views of particular sections of city-centre users. As in the initial participation exercise the views of management (through a place of work survey) and employees were sought. In addition, a household survey was carried out amongst a random sample of city residents, in order to try and obtain an unbiased response to the choices available.

The response to this exercise totalled 2000 replies, and included 30 000 comments and 45 000 references to the various choices. Examination of the responses showed that there were no particular favourite combinations of choice. On the contrary, there was considerable variety, and almost as many sets of choice preferences as there were respondents. It was, however, quite straightforward to bring together the individual choices which were most popular together with the most frequently occurring written comments.

A summary of the results of this vital stage in the process is set out in the Appendix of the Draft Proposals document. The main points to emerge were:

(i) The city centre must be made a more pleasant place. It must be made easier to move around as a pedestrian, there must be less conflict with vehicles, character must be retained and enhanced, new development must be on a scale that "fits in". Respondents want a familiar, pleasant, congenial place in which to work, shop, live and find recreation.

(ii) The city centre's character and environment is highly valued. Modern development is seen as having caused extensive damage and added little of value. Older buildings and areas must be retained and, where necessary, restored.

(iii) Further development of the city centre's commercial life should be encouraged; not by way of large-scale, or dramatic, expansion, but by allowing the gradual and varied evolution of the centre's office, industrial and shopping functions.

(iv) The city centre should increasingly be a place for leisure and recreation, and tourists should be welcomed and catered for.

(v) More people should be enabled to live within the city centre; housing provision should be an important element of the plan.

(vi) Movement needs to be reorganized particularly in favour of pedestrians (especially in Northumberland Street and around Grey's Monument). Buses should also be given priority, but there must be less vehicular movement in the centre: general and through traffic must be diverted. This should be achieved by a re-ordering of priorities.

(vii) New road construction is not welcomed as a means of diverting traffic from the heart of the city centre, with one marginal exception between Westgate Road and Gallowgate. The potential environmental effects of new road construction is a matter of concern, particularly in the more sensitive parts of the centre.

(viii) There is a need for more parking on the edge of the city centre as well as within it. A new car park in Northumberland Road is particularly favoured.

The proposals

Public reaction is now being sought on the Draft Proposals of the Plan. In most cases the proposals reflect the public choice, although it has clearly not been possible to follow that choice on every issue because inevitably the council has a duty to be realistic, which of course includes taking foreseen economic circumstances fully into account.

At this advanced stage, it is not anticipated that there will be much discontent with the vast majority of the proposals in this document, except in one or two areas. There are still a few points of difference with the County Council relating to quantities of shopping (which the Tyne & Wear Structure Plan ministerial approval did not resolve) and on certain road alignment issues.

The Draft Proposals

The document is in two main parts. Pages 10–42 set out the proposals on a topic-by-topic basis and pages 44–58 show all the significant proposals specifically on larger scale plans for each of seven areas within the city centre.

In contrast to the 1961 Plan, the preparation of the 1981 Plan commenced in a depressed economic context, a situation which could well continue for much of the period of the Plan's implementation. Private investment is not nearly as forthcoming as during the early 1970s; public investment is being held at present levels or being cut back other than for the construction of the Redheugh Bridge. There will be very little investment in new roads during the next five years, whilst the effects of the substantial investment in the Metro are yet to be fully realized.

The degree to which private investment in the city centre will change during the next few years, the likely future level of public investment, and the effects of the Metro are all factors which lead to a degree of uncertainty. This is reflected in the approach adopted in preparing the Plan and in the nature of the proposals which have eventually emerged. An approach was called for which would not only produce some flexibility in the proposals themselves, but which would stimulate investment in the city centre, particularly from the private sector. This has resulted in the absence of any targets or ceilings as far as the extent of development is concerned. This is not to say that any amount or type of development would be allowed in any area. The approach adopted is one of steering particular developments to those areas where they will bring the greatest benefit to the community at large. To this end the Plan identifies numerous development opportunities for particular uses throughout the city centre. The Draft Proposals also seek to enhance the quality of the environment of the city centre and therefore strike a balance between change and development on one hand, and on the other the retention, improvement and conservation of the best which already exists in the city's buildings and fine streets.

To plan for both new development and for conservation at a time of financial restrictions and high unemployment is by no means easy. The City Council, however, have ascertained that in spite of the recession the business world is interested in investing about £100 million in conservation and development in the city centre and about half of this investment is being actively pursued. At the same time it is of the utmost importance that this investment is channelled carefully and wisely so as to sustain and provide more employment and to keep and enhance Newcastle's architectural and historic heritage. The proposals in the Local Plan, and the objectives to which they are directed, seek to achieve this goal, as the following outline demonstrates.

Offices (Fig. 52)

A steady demand in recent years has taken up virtually all of the available modern office space. The proposals are aimed at strengthening the city's economy and creating new jobs. Primarily:

Offices

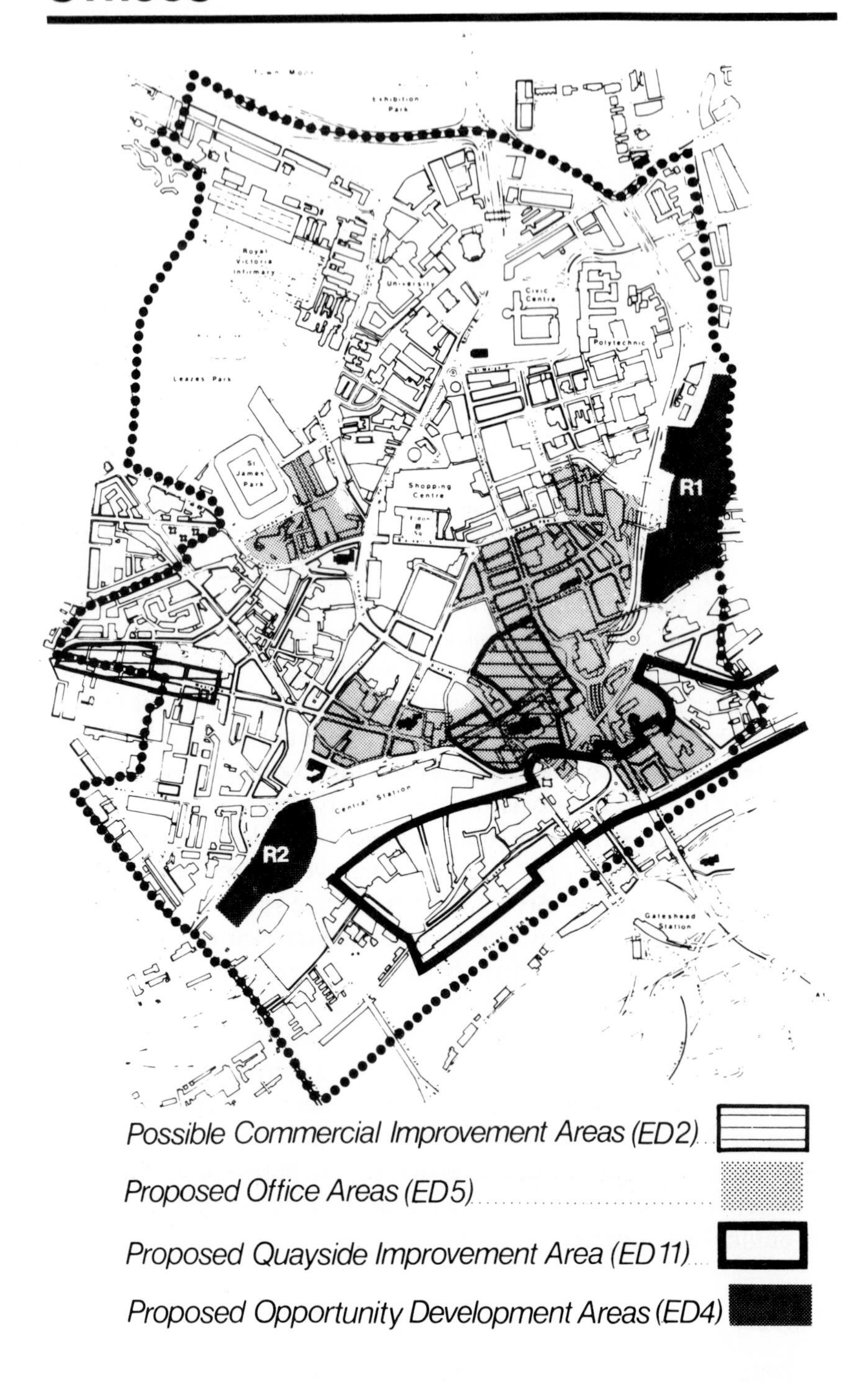

Figure 52. Proposals for office development, Draft City Centre Local Plan, Newcastle upon Tyne. (Source: Newcastle upon Tyne City Council, 1981.)

Industry

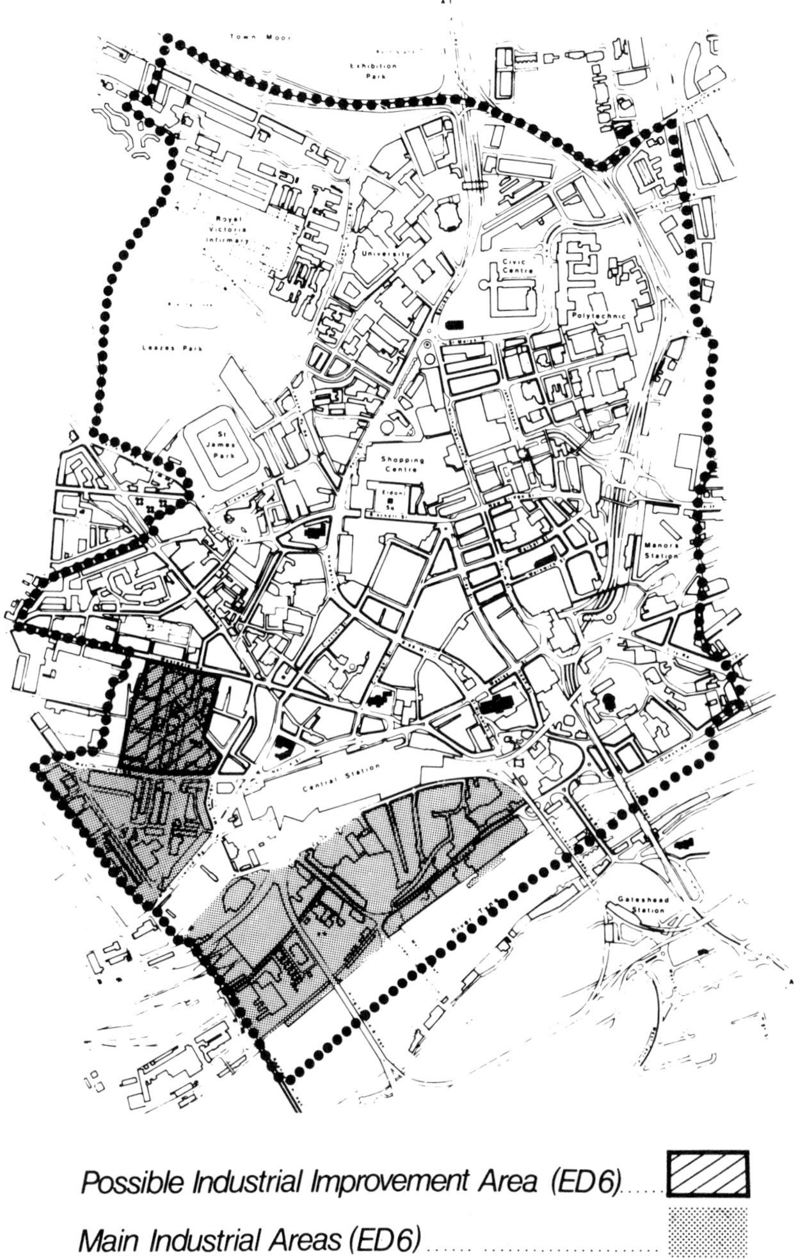

Figure 53. Proposals for industrial development, Draft City Centre Local Plan, Newcastle upon Tyne. (Source: Newcastle upon Tyne City Council, 1981.)

(i) The city centre will continue to be developed as the regional office centre.
(ii) Office development will be concentrated in two main areas: at St. James and in the present main office area in the south and east of the centre. Potential sites for up to 140 000 m^2 of new office space have been identified in these areas. Outside these areas there would be a presumption against office development.
(iii) The refurbishment of existing offices will be encouraged.
(iv) Offices will be allowed to form a part of the development proposals for the two large "opportunity development" areas on the fringe of the city centre at Manors, and west of Central Station.

Industry (Fig. 53)

Manufacturing industry and storage have declined in significance although the city centre still contains a number of large important industrial employers, such as Scottish and Newcastle Breweries. The proposals are aimed at retaining this industrial base, and encouraging small firms in such mixed-use areas as the Quayside, which will be declared an Improvement Area under the Inner Urban Areas Act 1978.

Figure 54. An internal view of the Eldon Square regional shopping centre.

Shopping

In recent years there has been a substantial increase in new shopping floor space. In particular, Eldon Square (Fig. 54) has made the city centre more attractive to shoppers and in the near future the Metro will make it more attractive still. There is now evidence of considerable pressures for further increases in shopping floor space.

A major concern is the future of the older, more southerly part of the shopping centre. The hub of shopping activity has been moving northwards, especially since the opening of Eldon Square. This has led to a decline in commercial activity in Clayton Street, Grainger Street and in other southern parts of the city centre. The proposals are therefore directed towards limiting major shopping development in the more modern northern parts of the city centre, whilst strengthening the older and more historic southern part. Primarily:

(i) Measures will be taken to consolidate Newcastle's position as the principal regional shopping centre, but there will be no major expansion of shopping floor space.

(ii) Measures will be adopted to support and improve shopping facilities within the southern part of the shopping centre including a shopping development west of the Central Station.

(iii) No large-scale shopping redevelopment will be permitted in the Haymarket area (at the extreme northern end of the city centre).

(iv) The environment of the shopping area will be further improved, including more pedestrianization.

(v) The introduction of non-retail frontages into principal shopping streets and malls will not be permitted.

Housing

The city centre provides its residents with an environment and range of facilities unique within the region, although the number of residents has been in decline throughout this century. This decline is now being reversed, however, with the construction of 250 new housing units in the former Crown Hotel and in the YWCA schemes. The proposals aim to continue this trend to increase the city-centre population. Primarily:

(i) The provision of additional housing accommodation will be encouraged. Proposals will be considered on their merits throughout the city centre.

(ii) A number of sites and areas have been identified where housing will be particularly encouraged. These include the Blackfriars and Leazes areas.

(iii) Refurbishment of existing houses will be encouraged in such areas as Framlington Place and Leazes Crescent.

Figure 55. Blackfriars medieval friary before renovation.

Figure 56. Blackfriars medieval friary after renovation.

Tourism

Tourism is one of the growth industries in the area. It is of increasing importance in Northumbria and there is no reason why Newcastle should not share in this growth. The city centre contains a great deal of potential tourist interest. This potential is only beginning to be realized by such projects as the restoration of Blackfriars, the Medieval Friary (Figs 55 and 56). Primarily:

(i) The tourist potential of the city will be promoted.
(ii) Measures will be undertaken to exploit the areas around Blackfriars and the Quayside for tourist-based activities.

Education and hospital (Fig. 57)

The northern part of the city centre is dominated by three major institutions; the University, the Polytechnic and the Royal Victoria Infirmary. Each has expanded in recent years in its own well-defined precinct within which further development and refurbishment will take place.

Character and environment (Fig. 58)

The general character and appearance of the city centre is subject to constant change. In carrying out the proposals which have been described previously, care will be taken to maintain and enhance the character of Central Newcastle, whilst at the same time allowing necessary change and development to take place. Primarily:

(i) Careful control of existing Conservation Areas will continue.
(ii) The Central Conservation Area will be extended to include the Quayside up to Broad Chare and the Westgate Road Area from Bath Lane to Rutherford Street (Fig. 58).
(iii) High standards of design will be required in all new developments in the city centre.

Movement

Newcastle is the major focal point in the transport system serving Tyne & Wear and as such the system in the city centre is subject to considerable pressures. In formulating the movement proposals the broad principle was adopted that in certain areas one form of movement would be given priority over others.

(a) Highway and traffic—main proposals

(i) A ring road (Fig. 59) will distribute traffic around the city centre with access to different central area localities by means of local access road design to prevent through movement. On the west side of the city centre the ring

Education & Hospital

Figure 57. Proposals for education and hospital development, Draft City Centre Local Plan, Newcastle upon Tyne. (Source: Newcastle upon Tyne City Council, 1981.)

Character & Environment: Conservation Areas

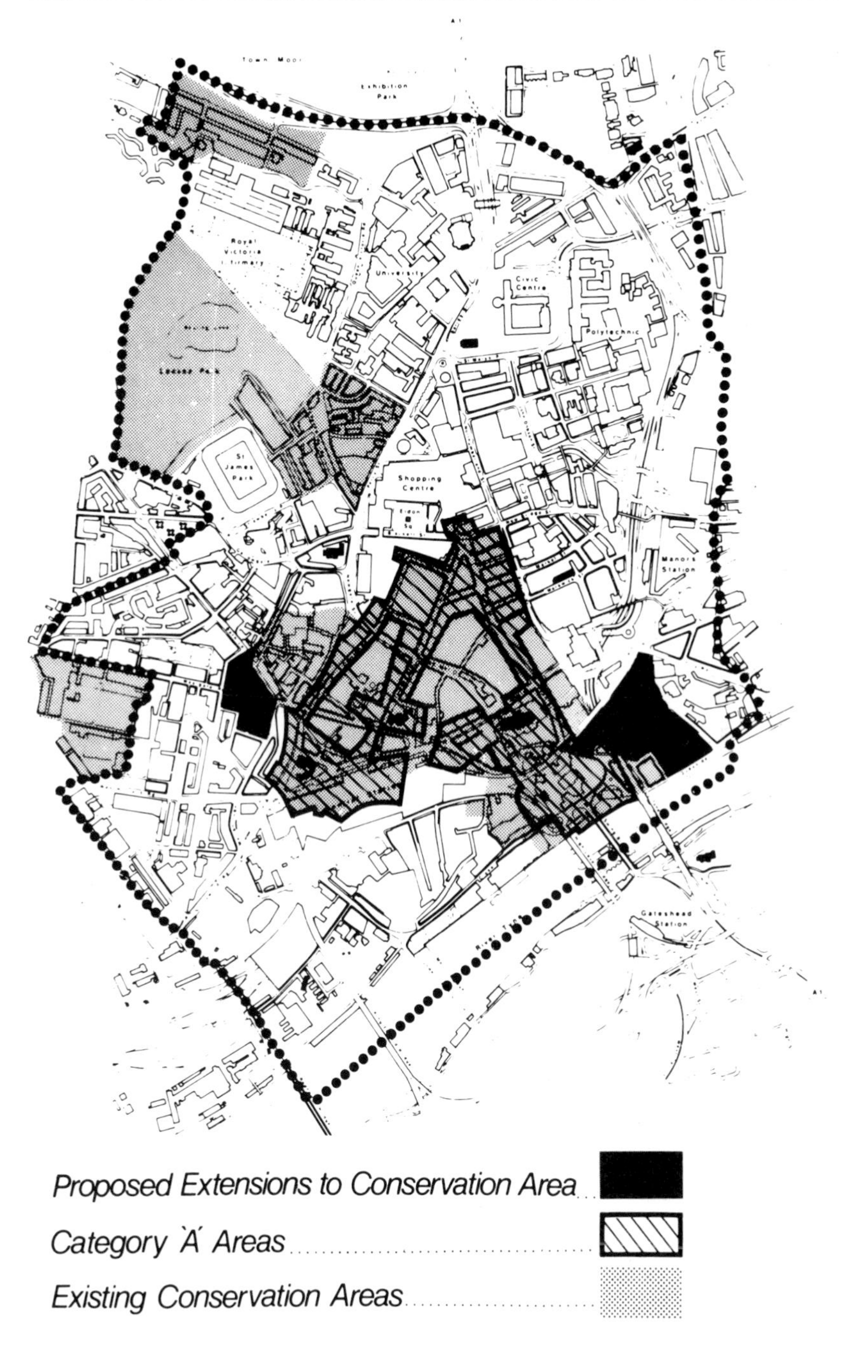

Figure 58. Proposals for the conservation area, Draft City Centre Local Plan, Newcastle upon Tyne. (Source: Newcastle upon Tyne City Council, 1981.)

Movement: (1) Proposed Ring Route

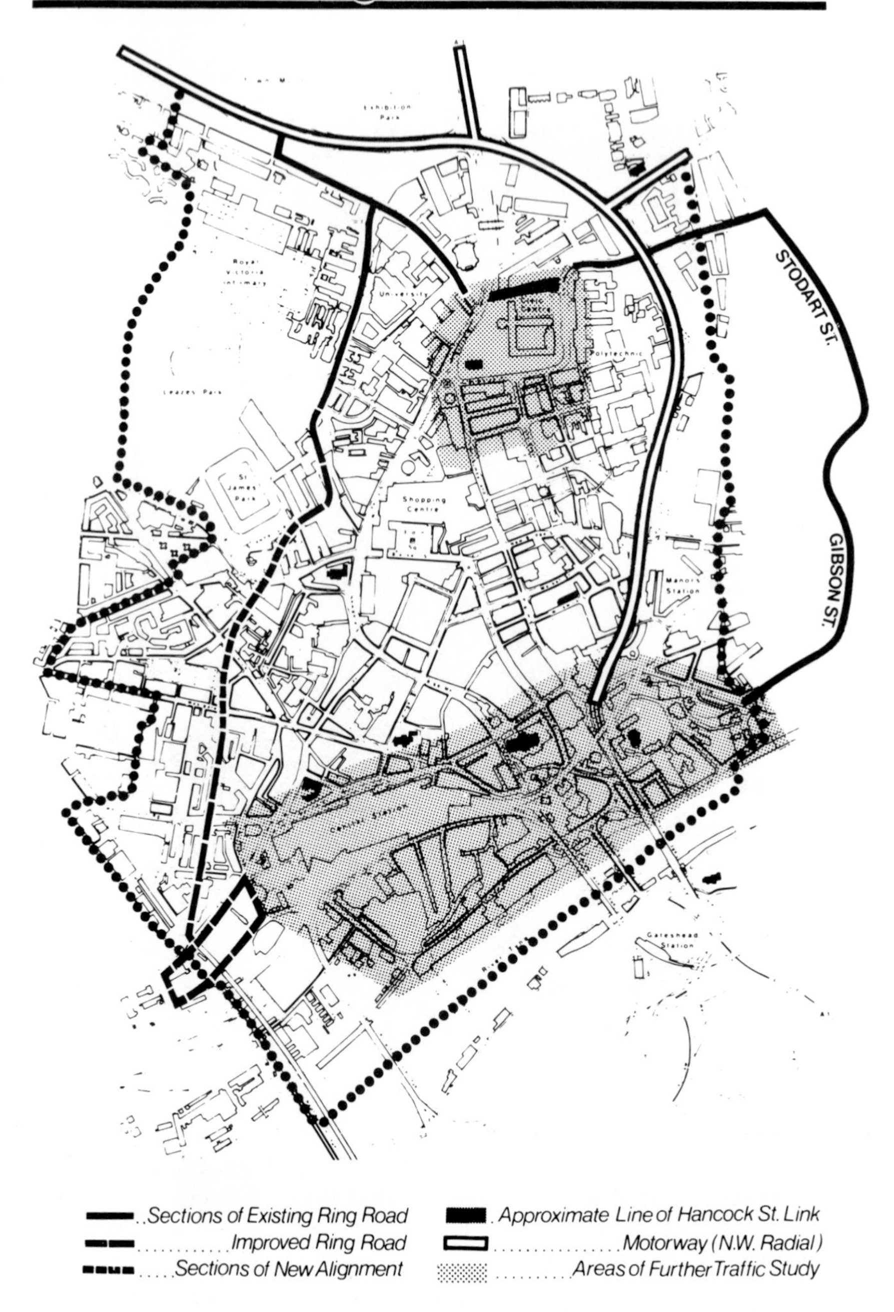

Figure 59. Proposals for the ring road, Draft City Centre Local Plan, Newcastle upon Tyne. (Source: Newcastle upon Tyne City Council, 1981.)

route would primarily use existing roads, although some new road building would be involved.

(b) Pedestrians—main proposals

(i) Further improvements for pedestrians will include the creation of a pedestrian priority area around Grey's Monument, and the removal of buses from Lower Northumberland Street.

(c) Public Transport—main proposals

(i) The introduction of the Metro will result in the re-organization of bus services, with fewer services coming into the centre.

(ii) Marlborough Crescent Bus Station will be retained.

(d) Parking—main proposals

(i) Four sites have been identified as possible multi-storey car parks.

(ii) A park and ride facility is to be provided on the site of Manors Goods Yard.

CONCLUSION

The 20 years which have elapsed since the preparation of the 1961 Plan have brought major changes to Newcastle city centre, culminating over the last five years in the completion of the Eldon Square Shopping Centre, the opening of the Metro and the renewal of the main drainage lines. This massive investment has constituted an act of faith in the future of the city centre and has produced a set of physical structures which are designed for an active life well into the next century. This fact acts as a major constraint on the scope for change in the near future, as too do the economic down turn of the late 1970s and the general shift of public attitudes in favour of conservation.

The chief tasks for the new City Centre Plan are to consolidate the progress of renewal and improvement around the major new structures and, in so doing, to incorporate certain features which were considered less important 20 years ago and to mitigate some of the less desirable side-effects of recent developments. Thus the 1981 Plan gives particular attention to the more peripheral parts of the city centre, some of which have suffered decline because of competition from the newer areas or have been affected by planning blight owing to their being scheduled for long-term redevelopment. Extra space is required for new roads and car parks, offices, manufacturing and shopping, but generally these schemes are small-scale and are designed to reinforce the local economy and physical fabric of the separate sub-areas. Greater emphasis is now being placed on the reintroduction of residential accommodation and to the improvement of areas with tourist potential.

Newcastle's central area is designed for the twenty-first century. Recent investment has reinforced its centrality within the city and the wider conurbation and region. The next few years are unlikely to see that dominance eroded, though within the city centre new investment will be more dispersed and should enhance the city centre's reputation in other directions beside shops, offices and public services. If carried through sensitively, such changes should benefit not only the local interests in the area involved but also those elsewhere in the North-East and indeed visitors from further afield. The public participation exercises have demonstrated that there exists a considerable will to see events move in the direction outlined by the Plan, but the latter's implementation depends not just on planners and the general public but on a whole complex of economic, social and political forces.

REFERENCES

Newcastle upon Tyne City Council (1961). "Central Redevelopment: First Report". Newcastle upon Tyne.

Newcastle upon Tyne City Council (1976). "Local Plan: Where Do We Go From Here?" Newcastle upon Tyne.

Newcastle upon Tyne City Council (1977). "Local Plan: Report of Findings". Newcastle upon Tyne.

Newcastle upon Tyne City Council (1978). "Local Plan: Choices for the Future". Newcastle upon Tyne.

Newcastle upon Tyne City Council (1979). "Local Plan: Choices for the Future—Public Response". Newcastle upon Tyne.

Newcastle upon Tyne City Council (1981). "Local Plan: Draft Proposals". Newcastle upon Tyne.

FIFTEEN

Conclusion

A. G. CHAMPION

The essays in this volume have focused their attention on the current trends and future prospects relating to the city centre, a small area of land compared with the extent of the whole city or urban region but one which has an importance far in excess of its spatial coverage. The city centre has traditionally held the urban region together and has at the same time reflected the strength and nature of the wider area. It is the changing character both of this symbiosis and of the surrounding region that seems likely to bring the city centre to the forefront of public concern during the next decade and that has prompted this volume as a starting point in such discussions. The relative shift in the location of economic and demographic vitality away from the major urban concentrations towards medium-sized and smaller cities can be seen as a major threat to the city centres of the former, while a parallel restructuring of space within urban regions is also tending to produce marked changes in the role of the city centre.

Arising from the preceding contributions are a number of apparent conflicts of ideas over the way in which the city centre is thought to be evolving, though at the same time there are strands of agreement on certain aspects. Several contributors have set their remarks against a backcloth of the long historical evolution of the city centre and have sought comfort from its apparent durability. Others, meanwhile, have pointed to the great problems faced by city centres and by the major urban concentrations of which they are part, as well as emphasizing the latest technological developments and economic trends which are likely to affect the scale and nature of activities choosing to compete for a central location. This concluding chapter examines the extent of agreement over the future of the city centre and explores the background to aspects over which less consensus seems to exist, aiming to provide foundation for reflection and further study.

SCALE OF INVESTMENT

There is wide agreement among the contributors that the level of new investment in city centres in the foreseeable future will be much lower than it has been over the

THE FUTURE FOR THE CITY CENTRE
ISBN 0 12 206240 X

last two decades. Since the Second World War, major developments have taken place, as bombed areas have been rebuilt and older fabric has been torn down to make way for more extensive and specialized CBD activities. Burns has outlined this pattern of rapid change, as too have the case studies of Paris and Newcastle, with the latter paving its way towards becoming "the Brasilia of the North" through its new investment in shops, offices and transport infrastructure. The city-centre plans which look forward over the next 10-15 years, by contrast, accept a relatively modest level of change, according to Holliday's review. The opportunities for major redevelopment appear to be much fewer and it seems likely that there will be much greater emphasis on small-scale schemes, on improvement and rehabilitation, and with this directed to the more peripheral parts of the city centre rather than on the more accessible points which have seen the greatest activity in recent years.

There also appears to be fairly general agreement on the immediate reasons behind this transformation in the planning environment. Most important among these are the international recession and the downturn in population growth rates which have affected the majority of advanced capitalist nations since the early 1970s. In relation to property development and retailing respectively, Lee and Thorpe have painted a gloomy picture of the level of new investment which can be expected, while Goddard and Marshall have raised questions concerning the effect of new information and communications technology on the labour requirements of most city centres. Certainly forecasts of the continuation of strong economic growth made in the 1960s have proved over-optimistic, leading towards an over supply of office and shopping floor space in relation to immediate needs. Even without such a need to reassess national economic trends, however, investment patterns in the city centre would still have been changing in the last two decades of the century because, with so much new development, the scope for further renewal has diminished. Commercial and planning interest would likely have turned to the more peripheral parts of the city centre but the economic downturn will mean slower change for these areas and will doubtless involve more varied and less massive results than have been the outcome of the past two decades.

UNDERLYING FORCES

The contributors appear to be less agreed over the longer-term prospects for the city centre and over the nature of the underlying trends affecting investment patterns and the location of activities in the whole urban system. A major question concerns whether the more modest scale of change expected between now and the year 2000 is essentially the product of long-term cycles in capital investment or relates to a set of forces which are causing a secular downturn in the traditional role of the city centre. On the one hand, Whitehand, with the experience of his studies of the evolution of settlement morphology over the centuries, can point to alternating cycles of faster and slower change in urban development and renewal akin to, and perhaps associated with, the 40- to 60-year periodicity of the economic fluctuations recognized by Kondratieff or the more frequent oscillations observed by Kuznets. A similar cyclic effect could result from changes in attitudes amongst politicians and the electorate. It certainly appears that the greater involvement of the general public in planning decisions and the growth of concern for environmental conservation since the mid-1960s has increasingly frustrated the activities of commercial interests. This could be interpreted as a relatively short-term reaction to the massive changes which have taken place recently, as well as perhaps being a form of involuntary response adjusting to the reality of economic trends. Equally, the lessons taught by the practical difficulty of implementing grandiose schemes, like that of Les Halles recounted by Bateman and Burtenshaw, may produce only a temporary check on development decisions and be forgotten in a few years time by a new generation of planners and politicians.

On the other hand, some of the chapters in this volume give a hint that current events may be essentially irreversible and that the city centre may be moving into a new era and into largely uncharted waters. For instance, in relation to public participation, it can be inferred from Angell's remarks that a more open pattern of decision making is something which is here to stay and which is perhaps only one manifestation of a new ordering of values as advanced nations move into a post-industrial society, with their people to some extent throwing off the shackles of a full-blooded capitalist ethic. Under this interpretation it is the current period and the so-called "foreseeable future" that can be considered revolutionary in character rather than the past two decades which may instead be viewed as the last fling of the former way of doing things. Reinforcing this more dramatic interpretation of current changes is Hills' observation of the 50 per cent decline in the use of public transport in the next 20 years, leading to serious doubts as to whether it has a future beyond the end of the century. In similar view, Goddard and Marshall have shown how the reorganization of big business is offering much less scope for office employment in city centres outside the exclusive club of "world cities" and suggest that the latest developments in telecommunications can only serve to exacerbate the well-established tendency for the decentralization of lower order retailing and office functions to suburban nodes within individual cities.

REACTIONS TO SLOWER CHANGE

Besides the uncertainty over the nature of long-term trends, there are also differences between contributors in their reactions to the immediate prospect of slower growth and the more limited scope for major developments in the city centre. Lee, the developers' consultant, and Thorpe, representing retailing interests, are clearly aghast at the small amount of growth that they anticipate in the use of city-centre facilities over the foreseeable future. For very obvious reasons concerning the vitality of their economic sectors, they are being forced to make painful adjustments to fit the new circumstances. The representatives of the planning profession, however, seem much less perturbed and indeed even appear to show some signs of quiet elation over these new trends. Burns and Angell give the impression that the planner's task could well be a much lighter one characterized by a general effort towards tidying up the physical condition and economic character of the city centre and perhaps not plagued so markedly by the frustrating delays which have been such a feature of the major urban renewal schemes like the Barbican and Les Halles.

It is relatively easy to identify the reasons behind this contrast in reactions but they reveal a serious problem. As far as planning attitudes are concerned, authorities in Britain and a number of other countries have for several decades been pursuing policies designed to reduce development pressures in the city centre by decentralizing activities to suburban nodes and new towns, with the underlying aims of improving the efficiency and environment of the city centre and of reducing both construction and operating costs there. Meanwhile, those involved in running the mainstays of the city centre economy believe that conservation, let alone improvement, is impossible without business and public confidence and, therefore, see further large-scale investment as a necessary prerequisite for the upgrading of the remaining rundown parts of the city centre. The thorny dilemma is well exemplified in the context of transport, for while a lower level of economic activity in the city centre would no doubt tend to reduce the traffic congestion problems surveyed by May, it would, at the same time, magnify the economic crisis which Hills has highlighted for the urban public transport system.

THE ROLE OF ALTERNATIVE FUNCTIONS

Several of the contributors seem to hold out some hope that this dilemma can be resolved by the encouragement of other activities besides shops and offices. Holliday, in concluding his review of the recent round of city-centre planning exercises, calls for a new vision of the city centre, aimed particularly at making fuller use of the areas of opportunity on the fringes of the central area. In this context, Robson and Pace attach great importance to the protection and indeed stimulation of the small craft industries and service businesses which are currently located in these more peripheral sites, taking advantage of the low rents resulting from planning blight or the imminent prospect of major redevelopment. Not only are these areas characterized by a high employment density, thereby reinforcing the role of the city centre as a job focus, but many of their activities are closely tied into the businesses in the more nodal parts of the city centre. Their presence reinforces, rather than detracts from, the vitality of the city centre, as is also recognized by Kerndal-Hansen's notion of "part-centres" comprising the craft and specialist-interest nodes in the "Ideplan" for Copenhagen. Their retention, along with the pedestrianization and improvement of the small streets which lead off from the Ströget (the main shopping street) is considered to provide a more healthy foundation for the long-term viability of Copenhagen's city centre than a further concentration of retail resources.

Above all, these more visionary views are attempting to broaden the basis of the attractiveness of the city centre and reverse the recent trends towards greater specialization. In particular, housing has steadily been squeezed out of the more central parts of cities, so it is interesting to note Hamnett's observations on the process of gentrification, involving the upgrading of residential areas within or adjacent to the city centre by the influx of middle class households, which represents something of a vote of confidence in these areas. Maitland reminds us that, in medieval times, the city centre was often the place where the more wealthy and prestigious families dwelt, taking advantage of easy access to the principal urban facilities. The potential importance of such housing lies not merely in the return to a productive and attractive use of land and property which have largely been abandoned but also in its indirect effects on the range and standard of urban amenities available locally and on the character of the area. With increased leisure time, more people are coming to appreciate the concentration of social, cultural and educational facilities which are traditionally associated with city centres. Moreover, concerted efforts to introduce additional attractions could well provide a magnet for longer-distance visitors as well as for the city's own population. Such a hope appears to underlie elements of the 1981 plan for Newcastle city centre, according to Angell's description of the proposals for introducing more housing in selected parts of its frame area and for giving the Quayside and Blackfriars special attention as tourist attractions.

DIFFERENCES BETWEEN CITIES

It would be a mistake, however, to believe that all city centres can equally take advantage of these alternative functions. Even among the fairly small number of so-called "millionaire cities" there exists a great range of circumstances, for instance between Newcastle's compact city centre providing the regional focus for not many more than one million people and those of London and Paris, which not only serve regional populations of over 10 million but also act as national capitals and international centres. According to the foregoing contributions, the latter are seen as much more resilient than the provincial centres, for though they are as much at the mercy of international economic fluctuations as other cities, they have increasingly benefited from the growth of transnational organizations and from the concentration of businesses into fewer hands. Goddard and Marshall describe in some detail the processes behind these changes, while their impacts on London and Paris are documented clearly by Foulkes and Burtenshaw/Bateman respectively. Moreover, as shown by Hamnett, it is largely the higher-level manpower needs associated with these activities that has boosted the move of residential populations back into the central area. Provincial city centres, by contrast, having already lost much of their manufacturing activity and now beginning to see their tertiary workforces declining, will be able to benefit only to a relatively minor extent from the current growth in quaternary functions.

At the risk of oversimplification, it is possible to identify a widening gap between the two extreme types of city centre and two different combinations of problems, a gap which the general growth in shops and offices over the past two decades has tended to obscure. It is essentially a difference between city centres which have too much of everything and therefore face problems of land-use competition and congestion and those which have too little of most things and face a major task in retaining their present scale of activities. It is clear from many points in the foregoing chapters that city-centre functions not only depend on remaining attractive to their surrounding populations but are also highly interrelated amongst themselves. The presence of business headquarters, the gentrification of housing, the maintenance of cultural and entertainment facilities and the attraction of tourists and other visitors all tend to mesh together to produce a magnetic force which is more than the sum of the individual parts, while conversely a loss in any one of these elements could engender a vicious circle of cumulative decline. Ironically, it appears that the type of city centre which has most need of alternative functions to compensate for its loss of vitality in shops, offices and other employment is also the type with the least potential for attracting them. Perhaps, therefore, Copenhagen, as a national capital but not a major hub of international business, represents an intermediate type of city centre which will have the fewest problems in adjusting to the circumstances of the next 20 years.

SOURCES OF UNCERTAINTY

Any attempt at foreseeing the future is fraught with uncertainties both about the way in which circumstances will change and about the manner in which people will respond to them. There are relatively few points on which the contributors to this book are largely in agreement, these being that the next two decades will afford much lower opportunities for new investment than the recent past, that greater emphasis will be put on smaller-scale schemes and on renovation rather than redevelopment and that greater efforts will be made to increase the social and cultural role of city centres. Beyond this, the consensus tends to break down, though some of the disagreements can be attributed to differences in their standpoint and interests in the city centre, particularly between the commercial developers and environmental planners, or to differences in the type of city centre on which they base their remarks, particularly between the major metropolis and the provincial centre. Among the most serious sources of uncertainty, however, are the changing energy situation, the evolution of social attitudes and patterns of behaviour, and particularly the degree of political commitment given to the city centre. In the past, a combination of civic pride and vested interests has tended to work against the decentralization process but accelerating changes in the broader organization of space may render this position increasingly untenable.

The last ten years have witnessed some quite dramatic changes in the demographic and economic circumstances of the country as a whole which could hardly have been foreseen at the beginning of the 1970s. These seem to have had a particularly strong impact on the inner areas of our largest cities. Over the past two decades, too, the social revolution that has taken place has produced a liberalization of attitudes and behaviour that surely would have astounded the youth of the early 1960s had they been able to perceive the things to come. This was a development that was fostered as much in the suburbs as in the older parts of the urban environment. We must be tempted therefore to think in terms of some major upheavals occurring in the years ahead but there remains the fundamental problem of identifying new events that might cut across those underlying processes already at work. Most portents suggest these are likely to come in what we might broadly call the communications field—through new information technologies, substantial alterations to our daily time budgets on movement, the growth in home-based working, leisure and shopping activities, and perhaps the introduction of new forms of transport. If this is true then the city centre will become the main focus of spatial concern, for it is here that there is the greatest existing concentration of all of the various types of interaction. Until these possibilities begin to unfold, however, the future for the city centre looks to be one of more modest change. The readers of this book over the next few years will be able to test the validity of this summary view and the more specific prognoses of the contributing authors.

SUBJECT INDEX

F

G

H

I

L

M

N

No. 1 *Land Use and Resources: Studies in Applied Geography. A Memorial to Sir Dudley Stamp* (1968)

No. 2 *A Geomorphological Study of Post-Glacial Uplift with Particular Reference to Arctic Canada* (1970)
J. T. ANDREWS

No. 3 *Slopes: Form and Process* (1971)
Compiled for the British Geomorphological Research Group by D. BRUNSDEN

No. 4 *Polar Geomorphology* (1972)
Compiled for the British Geomorphological Research Group by R. J. PRICE and D. E. SUDGEN

No. 5 *Social Patterns in Cities* (1973)
Compiled for the Urban Study Group by B. D. CLARK and M. B. GLEAVE

No. 6 A contribution to the International Hydrological Decade—*Fluvial Processes in Instrumented Watersheds: Studies of Small Watersheds in the British Isles* (1974)
Edited for the British Geomorphological Research Group by K. J. GREGORY and D. E. WALLING

No. 7 *Progress in Geomorphology: Papers in Honour of David L. Linton* (1974)
Compiled and edited for the British Geomorphological Research Group by E. H. BROWN and R. S. WATERS

No. 8 *Inter-Regional Migration in Tropical Africa* (1975)
I. MASSER and W. T. S. GOULD with the assistance of A. D. GODDARD

No. 9 *Agrarian Landscape Terms: A Glossary for Historical Geography* (1976)
I. H. ADAMS

No. 10 *Change in the Countryside: Essays on Rural England, 1500-1900* (1979)
Compiled and edited for the Historical Geography Research Group by H. S. A. FOX and R. A. BUTLIN

No. 11 *The Shaping of Southern England* (1980)
Edited by D. K. C. JONES

No. 12 *Social Interaction and Ethnic Segregation* (1981)
Edited by P. JACKSON and S. J. SMITH

No. 13 *The Urban Landscape: Historical Development and Management* (1981)
Edited by J. W. R. WHITEHAND

No. 14 *The Future for the City Centre* (1983)
Edited by R. L. DAVIES and A. G. CHAMPION

In Preparation
No. 15 *Redundant Spaces in Cities and Regions?* (1983)
Edited by J. ANDERSON, S. DUNCAN and R. HUDSON